TOURO COLLEGE LIBRARY
Kings Hwy

WITHDRAWN

mylabschool™

Where the classroom comes to life!

From watching actual classroom video footage of teachers and students interacting to building standards-based lessons and web-based portfolios . . . from a robust resource library of the "What Every Teacher Should Know About" series to complete instruction on writing an effective research paper . . . **MyLabSchool** brings together an amazing collection of resources for future teachers. This website gives you a wealth of videos, print and simulated cases, career advice, and much more.

Use **MyLabSchool** with this Allyn and Bacon Education text, and you will have everything you need to succeed in your course. Assignment IDs have also been incorporated into many Allyn and Bacon Education texts to link to the online material in **MyLabSchool** . . . connecting the teachers of tomorrow to the information they need today.

PEARSON

VISIT www.mylabschool.com to learn more about this invaluable resource and Take a Tour!

Here's what you'll find in mylabschool™

Where the classroom comes to life!

VideoLab ▶

Access hundreds of video clips of actual classroom situations from a variety of grade levels and school settings. These 3- to 5-minute closed-captioned video clips illustrate real teacher–student interaction, and are organized both topically *and* by discipline. Students can test their knowledge of classroom concepts with integrated observation questions.

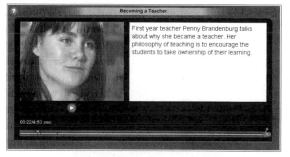

◀ Lesson & Portfolio Builder

This feature enables students to create, maintain, update, and share online portfolios and standards-based lesson plans. The Lesson Planner walks students, step-by-step, through the process of creating a complete lesson plan, including verifiable objectives, assessments, and related state standards. Upon completion, the lesson plan can be printed, saved, e-mailed, or uploaded to a website.

Here's what you'll find in (mylabschool™

Where the classroom comes to life!

Simulations ▶

This area of MyLabSchool contains interactive tools designed to better prepare future teachers to provide an appropriate education to students with special needs. To achieve this goal, the IRIS (IDEA and Research for Inclusive Settings) Center at Vanderbilt University has created course enhancement materials. These resources include online interactive modules, case study units, information briefs, student activities, an online dictionary, and a searchable directory of disability-related web sites.

◀ Resource Library

MyLabSchool includes a collection of PDF files on crucial and timely topics within education. Each topic is applicable to any education class, and these documents are ideal resources to prepare students for the challenges they will face in the classroom. This resource can be used to reinforce a central topic of the course, or to enhance coverage of a topic you need to explore in more depth.

Research Navigator ▶

This comprehensive research tool gives users access to four exclusive databases of authoritative and reliable source material. It offers a comprehensive, step-by-step walk-through of the research process. In addition, students can view sample research papers and consult guidelines on how to prepare endnotes and bibliographies. The latest release also features a new bibliography-maker program—AutoCite.

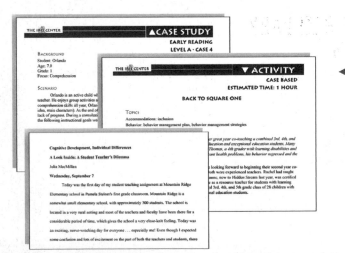

◀ Case Archive

This collection of print and simulated cases can be easily accessed by topic and subject area, and can be integrated into your course. The cases are drawn from Allyn & Bacon's best-selling books, and represent the complete range of disciplines and student ages. It's an ideal way to consider and react to real classroom scenarios. The possibilities for using these high-quality cases within the course are endless.

Understanding Reading Problems

Assessment and Instruction

SEVENTH EDITION

Jean Wallace Gillet

FLUVANNA COUNTY (VA) PUBLIC SCHOOLS

Charles Temple

HOBART AND WILLIAM SMITH COLLEGES

Alan Crawford

CALIFORNIA STATE UNIVERSITY - LOS ANGELES

TOURO COLLEGE LIBRARY
Kings Hwy

PEARSON

Boston ■ New York ■ San Francisco
Mexico City ■ Montreal ■ Toronto ■ London ■ Madrid ■ Munich ■ Paris
Hong Kong ■ Singapore ■ Tokyo ■ Cape Town ■ Sydney

Executive Editor: *Aurora Martínez Ramos*
Editorial Assistant: *Lynda Giles*
Executive Marketing Manager: *Krista Clark*
Production Editor: *Janet Domingo*
Editorial Production Service: *Publishers' Design and Production Services, Inc.*
Composition Buyer: *Linda Cox*
Manufacturing Buyer: *Linda Morris*
Electronic Composition: *Publishers' Design and Production Services, Inc.*
Interior Design: *Publishers' Design and Production Services, Inc.*
Cover Administrator: *Kristina Mose-Libon*

For related titles and support materials, visit our online catalog at www.ablongman.com.

Copyright © 2008, 2004, 2000 Pearson Education, Inc.

All rights reserved. No part of the material protected by this copyright notice may be reproduced or utilized in any form or by any means, electronic or mechanical, including photocopying, recording, or by any information storage and retrieval system, without written permission from the copyright owner.

To obtain permission(s) to use material from this work, please submit a written request to Allyn and Bacon, Permissions Department, 75 Arlington Street, Boston, MA 02116 or fax your request to 617-848-7320.

Between the time website information is gathered and then published, it is not unusual for some sites to have closed. Also, the transcription of URLs can result in typographical errors. The publisher would appreciate notification where these errors occur so that they may be corrected in subsequent editions.

Library of Congress Cataloging-in-Publication Data

Gillet, Jean Wallace.
    Understanding reading problems : assessment and instruction / Jean Wallace
Gillet, Charles Temple, Alan Crawford.—7th ed.
        p.   cm.
    Includes bibliographical references and index.
    ISBN-13: 978-0-205-52028-2 (alk. paper)
    ISBN-10: 0-205-52028-6 (alk. paper)
    1. Reading--Ability testing. 2. Reading—Remedial teaching.   I. Temple, Charles A.,
1947–   II. Crawford, Alan N.   III. Title.
    LB1050.46.G55 2008
    372.48--dc21

                                                                    2007019128

Printed in the United States of America

10 9 8 7 6 5 4 3 2 1 RRD-VA 11 10 09 08 07

11/14/07

Contents

Preface

Teaching is more exciting and demanding today than ever before. At the federal, state, and local levels, increased demand for accountability and student achievement require today's classroom teachers and literacy specialists to be able to

- Monitor and document the instructional progress, strengths, and needs of all students
- Select, administer, and interpret diagnostic measures in reading and reading-related areas
- Plan, implement, and evaluate the effectiveness of corrective and remedial instruction
- Use a wide variety of instructional methods, materials, and strategies to teach literacy, and
- Prevent literacy problems before they develop.

Teachers need tools, strategies, and well-informed diagnostic judgment to monitor students' literacy development and implement corrective instruction when appropriate. They must be able to use continuous developmental assessment devices, teach literacy using real literature and informational text with a wide variety of teaching methods, integrate reading and writing across all subject areas, and help every student become an effective, strategic reader who meets or exceeds required benchmarks. The assessment and instructional means to do so are the heart of this edition, as they have been since the first edition appeared some 25 years ago.

The concepts and principles that guided the development of the first six editions, and that made this book a leader in its field, have been strengthened and expanded in this, the seventh edition.

- Each chapter features authentic vignettes and case studies of real teachers and learners, with clear, vivid writing that engages readers.

- Every topic and reference has been scrutinized and the most current research and practices have been cited.
- Recent legislation affecting all classrooms, students, and teachers is discussed and interpreted.
- Revised and expanded coverage of teaching reading and writing for English language learners, including legal and statutory requirements, demographics, and No Child Left Behind legislation, helps teachers meet the literacy needs of these students.
- New and expanded coverage of literacy issues and students with special educational needs and disabilities helps every classroom teacher be informed and ready to teach every child.
- Greatly expanded treatment of the reading needs of students beyond beginning reading and the primary grades helps teachers be ready to teach for literacy success in grades four through twelve.
- Expanded coverage of topics such as portfolio assessment, emergent literacy, spelling and writing development, phonemic awareness, guided reading, Lexiles, adaptive instruction for students with special needs, tutoring programs, and assessment for students with limited English proficiency helps teachers meet the many challenges of today's diverse classrooms.

The seventh edition examines both traditional and contemporary means of assessing literacy strengths and needs, as well as developmental and corrective instruction for students in kindergarten through high school, combining the best of time-tested methods with cutting-edge strategies for diagnosing and teaching. Preventing reading problems, as well as diagnosing and correcting those already occurring, is emphasized throughout the book.

Chapter 1 presents a surprising evidence-based argument for the importance of literacy in our lives, and explains the four important "moments" of literacy assessment: assessment for screening and placement, diagnostic assessment, monitoring assessment, and outcomes-based assessment. It previews the major types of informal and formal assessments discussed in subsequent chapters, surveys the most important aspects of reading ability, and lays out a scheme of typical reading development from emergent to mature reading.

Chapter 2 describes the functional reading levels most often referred to when discussing student achievement, and lays the foundation for the informal, periodic assessments classroom teachers routinely use. The selection, administration, scoring, and interpretation of informal reading inventories are detailed using actual case data. Supplemental assessments, including word recognition, decoding, and reading strategies, are discussed.

Chapter 3 details the ongoing monitoring and assessment devices classroom teachers use to monitor and document student progress, including running records, systematic observation of reading behaviors, and the assessment of text difficulty with guided reading levels, grade-equivalent readability formulas, Lexiles, and cloze procedures. Expanded coverage of student portfolios in authentic assessment is included in this chapter, with sections on types and purposes of portfolios, organizing a portfolio program, conducting conferences, and evaluating portfolios.

Chapter 4 is new to this edition, and is devoted to the assessment of spelling and writing development. The developmental nature of learning to spell, predictable spelling stages and strategies, and assessment devices that help place students on a developmental continuum are discussed. Monitoring and documenting progress in writing using sampling procedures, skills checklists, Six Traits writing evaluation, and writing rubrics are detailed with lively examples of student writing.

Chapter 5 deals with the nature and uses of formal assessments, including fundamental concepts of measurement, characteristics of norm-referenced and criterion-referenced tests, benchmarks and rubrics, and federal- and state-mandated standards and assessments.

Chapter 6 offers a comprehensive look at emergent literacy development, including aspects of language development, phonological awareness, print awareness, and book and print concepts. It lays out detailed assessment techniques for emergent readers, and includes a discussion of evidence-based emergent literacy assessment. Teaching strategies to foster emergent literacy are keyed to assessment findings.

Chapter 7 gives detailed explanations of methods for the assessment and teaching of phonics and word recognition, reading fluency, vocabulary, and reading comprehension. Meeting students' identified needs with effective instruction in comprehension, word recognition and analysis, fluency, and vocabulary is emphasized.

Chapter 8 addresses the needs of older readers, those in grades four through high school, in reading, writing, and study skills. This chapter, written with the help of our colleagues Dr. Samuel Mathews and Dr. Josephine Peyton Young, focuses on strategies for learning from text and writing to learn. It also addresses motivational issues that often involve older students with a history of educational underachievement.

Chapter 9 focuses on assessment and teaching of reading and writing with students who are English language learners, including updates on legal and statutory requirements and demographics. Increased and updated attention to teaching English language learners has been provided with Sheltered Instruction Observation Protocol (SIOP) activities, the interaction of regulations affecting English language learners with No Child Left Behind, Reading First, the revised Individuals with Disabilities Education Act, and recent research on meeting the literacy needs of these students.

Chapter 10 deals with philosophical, legal, and instructional issues related to the assessment and instruction of students with special educational needs and disabilities. Recent changes in relevant legislation are discussed and ways of identifying and assessing students with special needs are outlined. The responsibilities of regular education and special education teachers are discussed. The chapter includes an updated review of research on dyslexia.

We would like to thank the reviewers of the seventh edition: Idriss Abdoulaye, Florida Memorial University; Deborah E. Bordelon, Xavier University of Louisiana; Michele C. Gerent, St. Petersburg College; Bonnie Hoewing, University of Northern Iowa; Rita E. Meadows, University of South Florida; Heather Ruetschlin, University of Maryland—College Park; and Lucille A. Smassanow, SUNY New Paltz.

As in previous editions, we express our gratitude to all of the many friends, colleagues, students, and users of this book who have, over the years, guided our thinking, challenged our biases, and opened our eyes. We are the teachers we are, and this book is what it is, because of you.

Jean Gillet
Charles Temple
Alan Crawford

About the Authors

Jean Gillet has been a classroom teacher, staff development specialist, university educator, and reading specialist. Her professional interests include the diagnosis and correction of reading difficulties, children's developmental spelling, and children's writing. She has published extensively on these topics, including contributing to classroom instructional materials on writing and spelling. She is coauthor of several textbooks for teachers on language arts, reading, writing, and spelling. She holds a master's degree in reading from Oakland University, Rochester, Michigan, and a doctorate from the University of Virginia. She is an elementary reading specialist in central Virginia.

Charles Temple stays busy teaching education courses at Hobart and William Smith Colleges in Geneva, New York; and writing books for children. Dr. Temple studied with the late Edmund Henderson at the University of Virginia, where he explored reading instruction, reading disabilities, invented spelling, and what was to become emergent literacy with many others who have gone on to do good work in the literacy field. He has written books on emergent literacy, invented spelling, writing instruction, language arts, diagnosis and remediation of reading disabilities, and children's literature. He is a director of Critical Thinking International, Inc., (www.criticathinkinginternational.org) a non-profit corporation that develops materials and fields mid-career professionals for teacher training projects around the world. Temple has most recently offered literacy workshops in Haiti, El Salvador, Argentina, Romania, and the Republic of Georgia.

Alan Crawford is Emeritus Professor of Education at California State University, Los Angeles. He is Past President of the California Reading Association and has done extensive teaching, consulting, and writing on teaching reading in the elementary school, especially for English language learners. Alan has written curriculum for teaching reading in Spanish and serves on the Editorial Review Board of Lectura y Vida. He served as IRA's representative to UNESCO for many years, and was a Senior Literacy Specialist at UNESCO in Paris during International Literacy Year (1989–90). He is a director of Critical Thinking International. He frequently presents workshops on a volunteer basis for international development projects in Latin America, Europe, Asia, and Africa.

Reading and Its Assessment

Chapter Outline

I magine a world in which all children entered kindergarten with exactly the same preparation for reading. They all had listened to someone read to them for the same thousands of hours and gained the same familiarity with books; had amassed the same number of words in their vocabularies; and had lived with families who supported their learning in the same ways and to the same degree, and had the same expectations of success in school. Imagine that all children came from the same cultural background, too, and all the significant folk in their lives spoke the same language and used that language the same way to express the same ideas. Imagine the children carried out every task with the same ability and the same amount of energy, and every child finished every learning task at exactly the same time. As the years went by, these children learned exactly the same way from teachers who taught the same lessons with the same success. The children learned to read the same number of words, were equally interested in the same topics, had the same background knowledge that enabled them to understand the same texts, and read all the same books at the same rate.

What a nightmare! One thing you can say about such a scenario, though, is that you wouldn't be reading this book about assessing children's literacy and differentiating instruction. Here in the real world, children are delightfully different in all the ways that make us humans interesting to each other, even though these differences complicate the work of teachers. Because children and older students differ in all of the ways just mentioned and then some, the job of assessment is to help the teacher figure out as closely as possible what aspects of literacy the students have developed and to what degree—so that we can build on students' strengths to make them successful readers.

Framing the Issues

In terms of the language they bring to school, their fluency in reading, the amount of reading they do, and the ability to use reading to understand, children in the United States differ more than you may realize—and in the following sections we show how much. Our point here is not to suggest that our goal is to make all children the same. And we are aware that putting a strong emphasis on reading and writing standard English runs the risk of stigmatizing those who fail to do these things well (Stuckey, 1990). But there is a lot of evidence that the better people read, the better off they are.

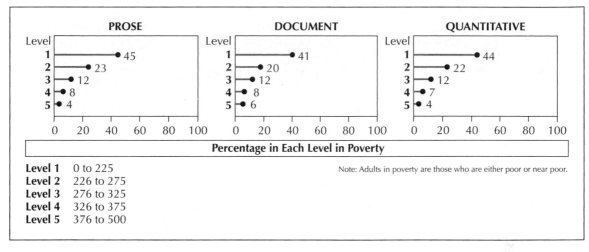

FIGURE 1.1 *Percentages of Adults in Poverty, by Literacy Level*

Note: Adults in poverty are those who are either poor or near poor.

Source: U.S. Department of Education. National Center for Education Statistics, National Adult Literacy Survey, 1992.

The National Adult Literacy Assessment (NALS, 1992) showed rather dramatically that the average adult's likelihood of having a job rose in close step with that person's reading ability (see Figure 1.1). So did the person's income (see Figure 1.2).

Keith Stanovich (1992) demonstrated that children and adults who read more were "smarter" than those who didn't. By "smarter," he meant that they had bigger vocabularies and more knowledge of the world.

UNESCO (2006), the United Nations Educational, Scientific, and Cultural Organization, has found that in society after society, people who can read are healthier and less prone to violence than those who cannot.

In an amazing study done in rural Uzbekistan in the 1930s when adult education was just bringing literacy and learning to traditionally illiterate peasants, the Russian psychologist, A. R. Luria (1976), found that those adults who had recently learned to read were better able than their illiterate counterparts to reason logically, ask questions about things they didn't know about, and even reflect on their emotions. Being able to read, in other words, affected people's consciousness.

Hayes and Ahrens (1988) found that just about anything written down—even children's books—were a far richer source of vocabulary than everyday speech or adult television shows (see Figure 1.3).

Wells (1985) demonstrated that written language exposes us to a whole different vocabulary from speech, so people who do not read are effectively shut out of many conversations about the business of daily life.

It is hard to avoid the conclusion that we are doing children and older students a great favor by teaching them to read well—and seriously fail them when we do not.

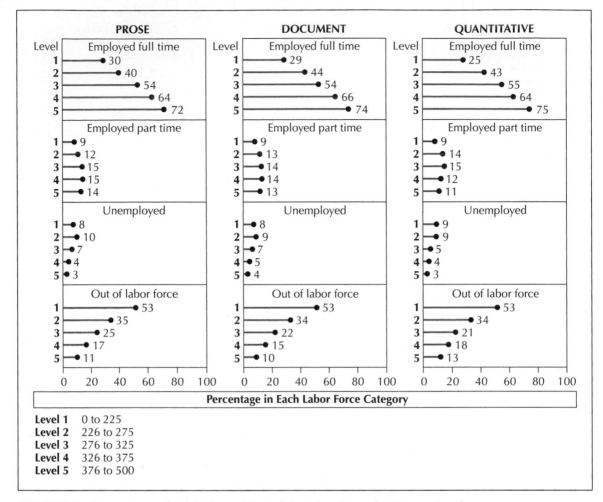

FIGURE 1.2 *Percentages of Adults In and Out of the Labor Force, by Literacy Level*

Source: U.S. Department of Education, National Center for Education Statistics, National Adult Literacy Survey, 1992.

The task of teaching reading is easier in some cases than in others, though. Consider the differences in children's development of aspects of reading.

Hart and Risley's 1995 study showed enormous differences in the language exposure of preschool children as young as 4 who came from different socioeconomic groups. Children from English-speaking professional families had three times as many words addressed to them as children from English-speaking families receiving welfare (see Figure 1.4).

The result, as Beck et al. (2002) reported, is that some children in first grade have at least twice as many words in their vocabularies as other children.

	Rank of Median Word	Rare Words per 1,000
I. Printed texts		
Abstracts of scientific articles	4,389	128.0
Newspapers	1,690	68.3
Popular magazines	1,399	65.7
Adult books	1,058	52.7
Comic books	867	53.5
Children's books	627	30.9
Preschool books	578	16.3
II. Television texts		
Popular prime-time adult shows	490	22.7
Popular prime-time children's shows	543	20.2
Cartoon shows	598	30.8
Mr. Rogers and Sesame Street	413	2.0
III. Adult speech		
Expert witness testimony	1,008	28.4
College graduates, friends, spouses	496	17.3

FIGURE 1.3 *Selected Statistics for Major Sources of Spoken and Written Language*
Source: *Adapted from Hayes and Ahrens (1988).*

Why does vocabulary matter? Knowing word meanings is a major part of verbal intelligence because knowing words is a measure of how much a student has already learned. But knowing words also makes future learning more likely because words serve us as receptors for experience: We tend to notice what we already have names for (Brown, 1955).

Children differ tremendously in the amount of reading they do, as well. Wilson, Anderson, and Fielding (1988) found that the 20 percent of fifth-grade children who

	Professional Families	Working Class Families	Families Receiving Public Assistance
Words per hour	3,000	1,400	750
Total words in first 4 years	50,000,000	30,000,000	15,000,000

FIGURE 1.4 *Language Exposure of Preschool Children*
Source: From Hart and Risley, 1995

read the most read 50 times as much as the 20 percent who read the least (see Figure 1.5). The bottom line is that far too many of our students don't read as well as we would like them to.

According to the National Assessment of Educational Progress (2005), one out of every four fourth graders could not read at a *basic level*: That is, they could not "demonstrate an understanding of the overall meaning of what they read." Reading at a basic level meant that the fourth graders could "make relatively obvious connections between the text and their own experiences and extend the ideas in the text by making simple inferences." When black and Hispanic students were singled out, three out of five could not read at this level. A *proficient* level of performance on the NAEP reading test meant "that students should be able to extend the ideas in the text by making inferences, drawing conclusions, and making connections to their own experiences. The connection between the text and what the student infers should be clear." Two out of five students tested could read at this level; and when black and Hispanic students were singled out, only one in eight could perform at the level of proficiency. (For a sample question from the NAEP, see Figure 1.6.) The results are essentially the same at the eighth-grade level.

And they matter. In previous generations, U.S. schools were tacitly expected to reproduce a working class, a professional class, and an elite class (Anyon, 1981). The in-

Percentile rank	Minutes of book reading per day	Words read in books per year
98	65.0	4,358,000
90	21.1	1,823,000
80	14.2	1,146,000
70	9.6	622,000
60	6.5	432,000
50	4.6	282,000
40	3.2	200,000
30	1.3	106,000
20	0.7	21,000
10	0.1	8,000
2	0.0	0

FIGURE 1.5   *Differences in Amounts of Independent Reading by 5th Graders*
Source: Anderson, Wilson, and Fielding, 1988

DR. SHANNON LUCID: SPACE PIONEER

by Vicki Oransky Wittenstein

When Shannon Lucid was growing up in Bethany, Oklahoma, during the 1950s, she dreamed of exploring outer space. She loved pioneer stories about America's West, and felt she had been born too late.

But then she read about rocket inventor Robert Goddard. She realized that she had not been born too late to be a space explorer!

And explore space she did. On September 26, 1996, after a month's delay, Dr. Lucid returned to Earth after spending more than six months on the Russian space station Mir.

Dr. Lucid was the second American astronaut to live aboard Mir as part of a program to study how long-term travel in space affects the human body. The results will help the National Aeronautics and Space Administration (NASA) develop an international space station. . .

Source: From "Dr. Shannon Lucid: Space Pioneer" by Vicki Oransky Wittenstein from *Highlights for Children*, January 1998. Copyright © 1998 by Highlights for Children Inc., Columbus, Ohio.

. . .

According to the passage, what was the purpose of the space station *Mir* program?

A. To learn how the body reacts to long-term travel in space

B. To observe how people from different cultures live together

C. To see what the seasons look like from outer space

D. To take pictures of the Earth and of water currents

65% of the fourth graders answered this question correctly

FIGURE 1.6 *Sample Question from the NAEP*

dustrial jobs held by the majority of the workers—and agricultural work before that—required low levels of literacy. But in the past two decades the United States has lost huge numbers of such jobs. The modern workplace requires employees who can read, write, think, solve problems, and work in teams (see Figure 1.7). The reading profile of U.S. students that emerges from the National Assessment of Educational Progress seems well-adapted to the industrial era of the 1950s, but woefully ill-suited to the constantly changing, information-oriented job market of the time we live in.

Our job as reading teachers is not to prepare students for any particular job, but rather to help them develop the communicative and intellectual skills they will need to have a satisfactory range of life choices. A good many of our students will not read as well as they need to in order to enjoy those choices. We will need to work with students at all levels to determine what skills they need, and we must teach in such a way as to develop those skills.

Employers say they are impressed by job candidates who have excellent communication skills, good grooming habits, and relevant work experience. . .

Top 10 Qualities Employers Seek

1. Communication skills (verbal and written)
2. Honesty/integrity
3. Teamwork skills (works well with others)
4. Interpersonal skills (relates well to others)
5. Motivation/initiative
6. Strong work ethic
7. Analytical skills
8. Flexibility/adaptability
9. Computer skills
10. Organizational skills

JobWeb.com—Career development and job-search advice for new college graduates.

FIGURE 1.7 *What Employers Want*

Source: Copyright © National Association of Colleges and Employers
62 Highland Avenue Bethlehem, PA 18017-9085
Phone: 610/868-1421 or 800/544-5272 Fax: 610/868-0208

Reading Assessment

Assessment means gathering, analyzing, and interpreting information to tell how well a student reads. Assessment covers everything from informal observations of a student's reading to the use of commercial tests. Assessment practices include

- Deciding what we need to know about a child's or group of children's reading.
- Deciding what measures will tell us what we want to know.
- Gathering information.
- Interpreting the information.
- Making decisions on what to do next, based on the new information.

There are different purposes for assessment and different audiences for the information that assessment brings to light:

1. **We assess to guide our instruction.** We may assess to
    - **Determine students' reading levels** (independent, instructional, and frustration) so we can place students in materials at the right level.

- **Locate children's strengths and areas of need** to aim our instruction. Children need encouragement in all aspects of literacy development, and if there are a few or several aspects in which they are not progressing adequately, we need to locate those so we can offer specially tailored help. For example, a child may have learned many sight words, but have low reading fluency. We need to monitor her reading so we can identify the need to work on her fluency.
- **Identify children's literacy strategies** so we can strengthen them. For example, we know that good readers preview texts and set purposes for reading to help them understand better. Does each child know how to do this?

2. **We assess to monitor the success of instructional approaches.** Approaches vary in their success with individual children, or with whole classrooms of children. We assess to

- **Find out if a teaching approach or set of materials is working for a child.** For example, to build reading fluency, teachers may use "buddy reading" or a computer program. But does the child know how to take advantage of these activities? Or in teaching word study, the teacher wants each child to study words that are right at his level of development of word knowledge. Is this the case? In guided reading, we want children to read some texts that are moderately challenging, and some texts that are easier. Is this the case for each child?
- **Find out what strategies seem best suited to whole groups of students.** Research shows that schools that are most effective in helping all children learn to read and write are those in which teachers monitor how well instruction is working, and use this information as they work with other teachers to find ways to improve instruction (Cunningham & Allington, 2006; Taylor, 1999). Teachers may monitor a host of factors, from classroom routines and management strategies, to teaching methods, to materials, to ways of working with instructional aides and parent volunteers, to ways of assessing children.

3. **We assess to give feedback to children and their parents.** Findings from assessment should be communicated to children and their parents, so both can work toward the children's success. We assess to

- **Show children what they are doing well and what they can do better.** We communicate information in a way that helps children understand and purposefully reinforce those strategies they are using successfully, and that can point the way toward improvements.
- **Help the children set goals for better performance**, and to monitor their progress toward meeting those goals.
- **Help parents understand how children are performing in learning to read**, and what parents can do to help.

4. **We assess to make decisions on the placement of children in special instructional services.** All children in the United States are entitled by law to special education services as they need them, and they are also entitled to special support to learn the

English language, if necessary. Parents may request that their children be screened for such services, but teachers may also identify students who need more support than what is likely to be available to them in the regular classroom. In either case, special screening is called for, including specialized tests that are normally administered by school psychologists. But the teacher's own observational records and assessment results play a useful role in these decisions.

5. **We assess to make sure all students are meeting state standards for learning.** The federal No Child Left Behind Act that passed in 2002 mandated that every child in the United States be tested in reading from grade 3 through 8. The tests are developed by the individual states. Because the tests have considerable consequences, many teachers are using more frequent assessments given throughout the year that show their students' progress toward meeting the standards on which their state tests are based.

6. **We assess ourselves as teachers or as teachers-to-be,** in order to make sure our professional knowledge is up to date and that our practices are serving our students as best they can. We assess our professional knowledge, both in order to keep ourselves up to date and to meet teaching licensing requirements.

Different Assessments for Different Phases of Instruction

Teachers use different kinds of assessments for different purposes at different points in the year. Schools with reading programs funded under Federal legislation as "Reading First" schools (http://www.ed.gov/programs/readingfirst) require four different types of assessment at four points during the year and many other schools follow suit. The four are *screening assessments*, *diagnostic assessments*, *monitoring assessments*, and *outcomes-based assessments.*

Screening assessments. Before instruction begins at the beginning of the year, teachers may administer screening measures to determine which children are at risk for reading difficulty and may need more support during the year. The screening instruments they use are as economical as possible because they may be given to an entire class or an entire grade. So they typically examine only a few key aspects of literacy, just enough to identify the children who need extra attention.

Diagnostic assessments. Another kind of assessment is used to identify more precisely a student's needs, so that the teacher can develop a teaching plan that is right for that child. If children have been identified by the screening tests as needing special help, the diagnostic instruments take up where the screening instruments left off. They tell not just that the child needs to know more letters of the alphabet but which ones; not just that she is a struggling reader, but that she is weak in comprehension, especially in making inferences. Individual diagnostic instruments may test specific skills, like a test of phonemic segmentation or a test of reading fluency. Others, like an Informal Reading Inventory, are more comprehensive and test many areas of reading ability.

Monitoring assessments. Monitoring assessments, sometimes called *formative assessments,* are done to see if a child's instruction is "on-track." They range from informal observations to formal probes.

Monitoring assessments may be done at regular intervals—every month or every quarter for most students, but more often for students who seem to have more difficulty learning. It is advisable that monitoring assessments be designed with the end-of-year assessments in mind. Because of No Child Left Behind, nearly all children in U.S. public schools are now tested at the end of their third through their eighth years. Given the impact of end-of-year state tests in reading, it is advisable that monitoring assessments be designed with end-of-year assessments in mind, to make sure all students are learning what they will be expected to know.

Outcomes-Based Assessments. Outcomes-based assessments are also referred to as grade-level reading *standards-based assessments,* because the desired outcomes of a year's teaching are reflected in each state's learning standards. Standards-based assessments are used to test the skills that are named on the state's standards for learning in literacy. In most states, those skills include phonemic awareness, phonics, fluency, vocabulary, and comprehension, since these areas were named for emphasis in the No Child Left Behind Act.

Approaches to Assessment

Below we will look further at these and other kinds of assessment approaches that are used to measure and investigate children's reading and writing abilities.

Norm-Referenced Tests. Standardized or norm-referenced tests of reading compare children's performance with that of large numbers of other students. For example, tests such as the Stanford Achievement Test and the California Achievement Test report children's reading performance in comparison to other students at their grade level. The tests are given under rigorously controlled conditions, so the results will be comparable. Norm-referenced tests are typically used, along with other information, to inform decisions about placing a child for special reading services. But these tests traditionally have lacked an obvious connection with any school curriculum, so it is difficult to tell what aspect of a school's instruction has contributed or failed to contribute to the children's performance.

Standards-Based Tests. Standards-based tests have come about in recent years as individual states have set standards for achievement in reading and other subject areas at each grade level, as they have been required to do by the federal No Child Left Behind law (http://www.ed.gov/admins/lead/account/saa.html#peerreview). Standards vary from state to state, but in most states they are specific enough to guide teaching. In California, for example, first graders are expected to meet English Language Content standards, of which the following is a small sample (see Figure 1.8).

Reading

1.0 Word Analysis, Fluency, and Systematic Vocabulary Development

Students understand the basic features of reading. They select letter patterns and know how to translate them into spoken language by using phonics, syllabication, and word parts. They apply this knowledge to achieve fluent oral and silent reading.

Concepts About Print

1.1   Match oral words to printed words.
1.2   Identify the title and author of a reading selection.
1.3   Identify letters, words, and sentences.

Phonemic Awareness

1.4   Distinguish initial, medial, and final sounds in single-syllable words.
1.5   Distinguish long- and short-vowel sounds in orally stated single-syllable words (e.g., *bit/bite*).
1.6   Create and state a series of rhyming words, including consonant blends.
1.7   Add, delete, or change target sounds to change words (e.g., change *cow* to *how; pan* to *an*).
1.8   Blend two to four phonemes into recognizable words (e.g., /c/ /a/ /t/ = cat; /f/ /l/ /a/ /t/ = flat).
1.9   Segment single-syllable words into their components (e.g., /c/ /a/ /t/ = cat; /s/ /p/ /l/ /a/ /t/ = splat; /r/ /i/ /ch/ = rich). . . .

FIGURE 1.8   *English Language Content Standards*

Source: http://www.cde.ca.gov/be/st/ss/enggrade1.asp

Standards-based tests are meant to assess each student's performance on the standards set by the states. Students may be promoted to another grade or held back, depending on their performance, and schools may suffer sanctions if they do not make "adequate yearly progress." Standards-based tests are sometimes called *high-stakes testing* since a child's performance on such a test can determine whether she is promoted to the next grade, and the performance of many children can decide if a school is achieving or underachieving.

Informal Reading Inventories.   Informal Reading Inventories (Betts, 1946), or IRIs, are comprehensive measures of students' reading abilities. IRIs, which are treated in detail in Chapter 2, are administered to individual children to examine their word recognition, fluency, comprehension, and overall reading levels. They are called "informal" because in contrast to standardized reading tests, IRIs have usually not been normed by elaborate field testing with large numbers of children. Rather, they are created from samples of grade-level texts, usually written by the test authors and matched to grade levels according to readability formulas. In addition to written passages, IRIs consist of lists of words and text passages of graduated levels of difficulty—and the passages and word lists are usually from early first grade or "pre-primer" through grade 8 or higher.

Teachers may create their own IRIs, but many good ones are commercially available, including the *Qualitative Reading Inventory* (Leslie & Caldwell, 2005) and the *Classroom Reading Inventory* (Silvaroli & Wheelock, 2000). *The Developmental Literacy Inventory*, written by your present authors (Temple, Crawford, & Gillet, 2008, in press), combines an Informal Reading Inventory with assessments of emergent literacy.

Running Records. Developed by Marie Clay (1993) to support her Reading Recovery program, running records are teacher-made assessment devices administered to individual students to monitor their fluency, word recognition accuracy, and reading levels. Running records are partially based on the Reading Miscue Inventory, but are simpler to administer. Running records are usually carried out with younger readers in the first two grades, with whom they may be used every month or more frequently, both for diagnostic testing and for monitoring. The running record allows the teacher to observe

- The student's word-reading error rate.
- The student's self-correction rate.
- The kinds of "miscues" (incorrect word identifications) that the student makes: visual, structural, or meaning-based.
- Other behaviors, such as the direction in which the student reads, the number of repetitions of words, and so on.

We will say more about running records in Chapter 2 of this book.

Authentic Assessment. Sheila Valencia and her colleagues (Valencia, Hiebert, & Afflerbach, 1993) popularized the idea of the "authentic assessment" of literacy. Authentic assessment addresses the problem that most assessment has students carry out contrived tasks that are not always representative of what they do in purposeful reading and writing. Contrived tasks may not yield the full picture that includes what students have achieved, and also how they think about literacy, their interests and motivations, preferences, strategies, likes and dislikes. Authentic assessment thus involves both *informal* and *structured observations* (sometimes called *kidwatching*) and *work-sampling*, including *portfolios*. Authentic assessment also includes the use of *rubrics*.

Kidwatching. *Kidwatching* is a term coined by influential literacy educator, Yetta Goodman (Goodman, 1985; Owocki & Goodman, 2002) to refer to a host of observations, ranging from observations quickly captured on sticky notes, to home visits, to more formal assessments.

Kidwatching is informed. That is, teachers learn more from observing children in the daily life of the classroom if they know a good deal about language and literacy processes, as well as how children talk, read, think, investigate, and interact with each other and the world.

Kidwatching is nonjudgmental. Teachers record events or pieces of language as they occurr, without filtering them through judgments. Planning what to do on the basis of the collected evidence will happen later, preferably after many different kinds of information have been collected.

Kidwatching uses diverse sources of information. Goodman (2006, n.p.) writes: "Kid-watchers use a variety of tools to document their observations, including informal conversations, formal interviews, check sheets, observation forms, field notes, port-folios, and home visits." Using many sources of information, including not only the teacher's observations but the child's and the family's points of view, as well as more formal assessments, allows teachers to make small adjustments—and some-times larger ones—to instruction and classroom procedures.

Portfolios.   Another type of authentic assessments, portfolios are collections of chil-dren's works. They may be maintained by the teacher as a way of keeping a diverse col-lection of artifacts related to a child's progress in learning to read and write. But usually they are maintained in collaboration with each child. The teacher (and the child) should decide in advance the sorts of items that should be kept in the portfolio. These might include

- Lists of books read.
- A reading journal.
- Repeated reading score sheets.
- Written works chosen as indicative of the child's best work and range of work during a particular time period.
- A list of topics for the child's writing.
- Learning logs.
- Running records.

Periodically—at least once a month or once each marking period—the teacher schedules a *conference* or *interview* with the child. Ahead of the conversation, both the child and the teacher should look through the portfolio to find signs of progress and areas that need work. During their conversation, the child describes what he has learned during this period and sets goals for improvement during the next period. The teacher may ask questions to find out what things the child likes and doesn't like to read, what strategies he is using in reading, and aspects of the reading instruction that might be changed for his benefit. The teacher makes suggestions to help the child learn.

Rubrics.   According to Adrade (2002):

A rubric is a scoring tool that lists the criteria for a piece of work, or "what counts" (for example, purpose, organization, details, voice, and mechanics are often what count in a piece of writing); it also articulates gradations of quality for each criterion, from excellent to poor.

Rubrics have the advantage of allowing teachers to observe and evaluate an authentic performance, such as a child's oral reading or a piece of writing written for a real purpose other than testing. They also have the advantage of teaching. Especially when they are shared with a student before he or she carries out a task, the rubrics tell the child how to do a task well.

Rubrics may be already designed by educational experts. Rubrics may also be developed by teachers, or even by the students themselves. When students participate in designing a rubric, they may become more strategic in reading—that is, they have a better idea how they should try to perform.

It helps to think of a rubric like a chart. Each row names an important aspect of performance on a task, and in the boxes under each column are descriptions that range from unsatisfactory to satisfactory to excellent performance on that factor.

The Process of Learning to Read at Different Stages

The reading stages that follow are not written on stone tablets; they are, for us, a convenient way to organize our thinking about reading and our discussions about children. The stages into which we divide the process of learning to read are as follows:

- **Emergent Literacy**. Children in this stage are discovering basic concepts about print and the language that print represents, and they are learning to associate pleasure with reading, books, and being read to. Usually, these children are found in preschool, kindergarten, and first grade.
- **Beginning Reading**. Children in this stage know enough, at least on a tacit or nonverbal level, about reading and print to begin to learn individual words, or acquire a sight vocabulary, from their encounters with them. These children are often first graders, but both younger and older students may be beginning readers.
- **Building Fluency**. Children who are building fluency, typically in grades 2 and 3, can recognize many words automatically and are reading passages that are several sentences long without too much stumbling over words. They are comprehending what they read, for the most part, so their reading has become fairly rapid and accurate and their oral reading is fairly expressive. Children at this stage are no longer beginners, but they are not yet fluent independent readers. At this stage, the amount of reading that children do and their degree of success with it have a tremendous impact on their progress to the next stage.
- **Reading to Learn and for Pleasure**. Children in this stage, usually from grade 3 on up, may be reading chapter books for pleasure and homework assignments for learning. By this stage, good readers are pulling dramatically farther ahead of strug-

gling readers in their ease of reading, the amount of time they spend reading outside of school, and the number of pages they read each week.

- **Mature Reading**. Mature readers are those who read and compare many sources of information on a topic. They can read "against the grain" of a text and use the reading experience as a way of generating original ideas of their own. They can also recognize and appreciate an author's style and technique. Although many readers do these things in the lower grades, this kind of adult-like reading is more common in middle school and above; high school or college students who don't have these advanced reading skills have an increasingly difficult time.

Of course, individual students will go through stages of reading at different rates, but if they vary too much from the norm, difficulties can occur. As you can see from these descriptions, in each stage students develop new reading abilities, and new challenges are placed on those abilities by the curriculum.

Emergent Literacy

The stage that once was called *reading readiness* or *prereading* is now known as *emergent literacy* (Teale & Sulzby, 1986). *Emergent literacy* refers to a process that represents the child's growing discoveries about print: that writing corresponds to spoken words; that the print, not the pictures, tells the story; that print is composed of a certain set of letters arranged just so on a page; and that those letters stand for spoken words in a certain way.

As Neuman and Dickinson put it:

Emergent literacy refers to the developmental precursors of formal reading that have their origins early in the life of a child. This conceptualization departs from an older perspective on reading-acquisition that sees the process of learning to read as beginning with formal school-based instruction in reading or with reading-readiness skills taught in kindergarten. (2000, p. 12)

We should note that some use the term *emergent literacy* in a much more expansive way. Patrick Groff (n.d.), for instance, claims that *emergent literacy* carries within it the assumption that reading ability develops without being taught (a position he vigorously opposes), and he warns his followers to be suspicious of anyone who uses the term.

But the term *emergent literacy* was introduced by researchers with very different intentions. When Hermine Sinclair, Charles Read, Emilia Ferreiro, Marie Clay, Bill Teale, Elizabeth Sulzby, Shirley Brice Heath, and Jana Mason began to instruct our field about emergent literacy more than 20 years ago, they were showing us that many literacy-related concepts can be developed early in childhood and without direct teaching. But because that was true, they worried that teachers would take it for granted that all children had these concepts and would not teach the children who lacked them the important things they needed to know (see the discussion of "Print Orientation Concepts" in

Chapter 6). Understanding emergent literacy puts teachers in a position to support children's literacy in concert with the ways they learn and also to help fill in gaps in children's store of literacy-related concepts.

Emergent literacy is fascinating for adults to observe, and many of the things young children say and do with writing, spelling, reading, and books are delightful and amusing. But for children, moving toward literacy is serious business. Children who successfully explore concepts about print during this period lay down a foundation that helps them to profit from reading and writing instruction later on.

Children who do not acquire foundational concepts about print will very likely struggle with beginning reading and subsequently fall farther and farther behind their peers unless extraordinary steps are taken to help them. Connie Juel (1988) has shown that nearly 90 percent of the first graders who were behind their peers in reading were still in the bottom group four years later—but by then, the distance between them and the average readers was immense. This occurred in spite of the usual range of special intervention services that were available to assist them.

For this reason, intensive early intervention programs such as Reading Recovery (Clay, 1985; Pinnell, 1989), Success for All (Slavin et al., 1991), Book Buddies (Johnston, Invernizzi, & Juel, 1998), and Early Steps (Morris, 1993) are widely used with children in the early grades.

Beginning Reading

Children reach the stage of beginning reading when they learn to recognize words appearing in different contexts. For example, a child who recognizes the word *Coca-Cola* only when it appears on the soft drink bottle but not when it appears in a newspaper ad is recognizing the word as a meaningful symbol but not as a word. When the same child suddenly realizes that *Coca-Cola* is the same word when it appears on signs, newspaper coupons, and Mom's shopping list, then the child has acquired it as a sight word, a word that is immediately recognizable without analysis. This stage marks the beginning of true reading, but it comes only after much prior learning. As we saw in the discussion of emergent literacy, before children can begin to acquire a sight vocabulary, or a corpus of words that they recognize immediately at sight, they must

- Be able to pay attention to spoken language and its parts.
- Understand something about the way reading is done.
- Know a good deal about the nature of print.

An additional challenge in the period of beginning reading is to learn to recognize words and attend to their meaning at the same time. If all we do is teach children to recognize words, we will give them a distorted idea of what reading is, for reading is much more than identifying the words on a page. On the other hand, we can't get around the fact that children must learn to recognize words with increasing accuracy and automaticity if they are to progress in reading.

Building Fluency

Children in the fluency-building stage of development have moved beyond the highly predictable books that beginners enjoy. These post-beginners enjoy what are often called *easy readers*. Examples of these books are Arnold Lobel's *Frog and Toad* stories (*Days with Frog and Toad, Frog and Toad Are Friends,* and so forth), James Marshall's *Fox* books (*Fox on Wheels, Fox in Love, Fox at School,* and so forth), Cynthia Rylant's *Henry and Mudge* books, Else Holmelund Minarik's *Little Bear* books, and many of Dr. Seuss's books.

Easy readers often consist of either a single story or three or four short, catchy episodes per title, in books of about 40 to 60 pages each. They feature relatively short words that are often repeated, with one to three sentences on each page accompanied by supportive pictures. The Bank Street *Ready-to-Read* series, Scholastic's *Hello Reader!* series, Random House *Step into Reading* books, and Harper Trophy's *I Can Read* books are typical. Since they are widely available in inexpensive paperback versions, every first-, second-, and third-grade classroom should have a good supply of these books. Any school librarian will be able to advise on their selection.

Children in the fluency-building stage can also enjoy picture-story books, especially if the books have been read to them once or twice already. Books such as Mercer Mayer's *Just Me and My Dad* or Normal Bridwell's *Clifford the Big Red Dog* contain vocabulary that is challenging to some children, so the children should be familiar with them before trying to read them on their own.

If children haven't learned to recognize many words automatically by early second grade, they will not fully experience the spurt in reading rate and fluency that we associate with this period. The gap between these lagging readers and their classmates will be growing. Unfortunately, they often begin to feel like failures, and that attitude itself may compound the problem. We must keep working to build these children's abilities to recognize words, and we'll want to provide lots of easy books so that they can practice reading. We can't neglect reading to them, either. They need to keep up their intake of written language for the information, vocabulary, and text structure that it yields. Otherwise, their future hurdles will loom even higher.

Reading to Learn and for Pleasure

The stage of reading to learn and for pleasure may begin in late second grade or early third grade and last from then on, though most students will diversify their reading with what we call *mature reading* by the time they reach middle school or even sooner. Children at this stage are reading to get somewhere. The operations of reading have become mostly automatic now, and their full attention can be focused on reading for meaning. Reading has truly become the vehicle for learning. After students have built fluency in their reading, they enter a long period in which their reading ability is put to use, when we hope that they will read a great deal, because they find reading both an enjoyable pastime and a source of information that they wouldn't get otherwise.

At this point, reading becomes its own best teacher. Students who have the habit of reading are consuming dozens of books, thousands of pages, and hundreds of thousands of words a year. This reading practice equips them with an expanded vocabulary, familiarity with varied sentence structures, a broad knowledge of the forms of written language, and acquaintance with most of the topics they are likely to come across in print. Until recently, few would have considered any of these to be components of reading ability, but now we realize that these achievements, all of them gained through practice in reading, probably make as much difference to a person's ability to read as any of the traditional skills of reading do.

Good readers are gaining a wealth of information about the world and a wealth of vocabulary. This knowledge and this vocabulary are what readers comprehend with: As the schema theory of comprehension predicts, we need to know a little bit about the topic before we can learn something new about it. Readers who read a lot are going to know a little bit about a lot more topics and will be better readers because of it (Hirsch, 1987).

After second grade, students are expected to use their reading to learn content. Learning from reading raises a new set of problems. How are questions posed in texts? How are they answered? How are arguments set up in texts? How are they resolved? For those who up to now have thought of reading as pronouncing words aloud or following a story line, these new tasks are real challenges. How will children learn to meet them? Clearly, many children will not learn how to learn from text without guided practice. That is, teachers need to show them how to do it.

When we speak of comprehension in reading, the literary critic Louise Rosenblatt (1978) suggests that we should make a distinction between what readers do with fiction and what they do with nonfiction. There is a difference between reading in which we gain information, such as reading a history text or a bus schedule, and reading for more indirect enlightenment and vicarious pleasure, such as reading a novel. She calls the first kind *efferent reading*; the second kind, she calls *aesthetic reading*.

In the moments when we are reading aesthetically, Rosenblatt believes, we are summoning up our own experiences and fantasies in response to the words in a book. The meaning of the text resides in just this event: It is a real-time experience of orchestrated thinking and reverie, jointly created by the text and our minds.

Rosenblatt's position is referred to as *reader response criticism*, and it raises interesting questions about the ways in which we should understand and teach reading comprehension. If a good part of the meaning of a text comes from the reader, not just from the book, then teaching reading for meaning means thinking about texts and bringing associations from personal experiences to the reading. It means that we should consider readers to be authorities on their own understanding. It means that we cannot ever fully measure reading comprehension. It also means that the potential for human misunderstanding is very great because the meaning of anything resides ultimately in what each individual makes of it. In fact, sharing books and discussing our responses to them turn out to be some of the best ways we have of building a community of understanding, or an *interpretive community*, as David Bleich (1975) has called it.

Mature Reading

This last developmental reading stage is hard to quantify in terms of grade levels, for as the grades increase, the span of reading levels in any classroom widens geometrically. The best readers in an elementary school are probably mature readers while only in fourth or fifth grade, whereas the poorest readers in those grades are likely beginning readers. The same is true for middle schoolers and high school students; the best readers in middle or high school typically can read college texts and adult best-sellers comfortably. They are mature readers, regardless of their grade. Likewise, millions of adults are not and never will be mature readers, largely because they don't read enough to ever get very good at it.

Mature readers have arrived, through instruction and years of sustained practice, at the apex of reading development; they can read almost anything they choose to, comfortably and successfully. That is not to say that they won't ever struggle with reading; one could find college textbooks, toy assembly directions, or government documents to challenge the reading abilities of even the best adult readers. But most of what they want to read will be accessible. Because they don't struggle with it, mature readers generally read a great deal; they are the ones at the top end of the scale who read 4 or 5 million words a year (Anderson, Wilson, & Fielding, 1985).

Mature reading includes what is sometimes called *critical reading*, or mentally arguing with texts. It also includes *aesthetic reading*, reading for an appreciation of the craft of good writing. Let's look at each of these in turn.

Critical Reading.   Some years ago, parent watchdog groups asked the U.S. government to place restrictions on the amount of violence and commercialism in children's television programming. The government backed away, in effect giving an old response: caveat emptor ("Let the buyer beware"). Since the "buyers" in this case were young children, the government's response raised the question: Should we teach our children to be critical of what they hear and read so that they can defend themselves against the manipulation of those who want their money or their loyalty for cynical purposes? Many educators believe that we should; therefore, the term *critical reading* is heard more and more these days. *Critical reading* means arguing with books or authors, in particular analyzing books for hidden biases or subtle suggestions that one group is superior to another. Box 1.1 contains an example of critical reading, in which a group of 7- and 8-year-olds discuss gender bias in fairy tales.

Aesthetic Reading.   Another dimension of mature reading is aesthetic reading, savoring the artistry (or examining the shortcomings) of well-crafted or slapdash prose. An illustration of aesthetic reading is found in David Bleich's (1975) approach to reader response. Bleich first asks his students to retell a work that they have all read, and he notes the variety in what students choose to include in their summaries. Then he asks students to name the most important parts of a work, and again he notes the effect of each reader's individual experiences and tastes in making such seemingly straightforward judgments because there is invariably much variety in what readers choose. Next, he

BOX 1.1   *An Example of Critical Reading*

A mixed group of second- and third-graders are discussing the story *Beauty and the Beast*.

"Suppose," says the teacher, "Beauty had been a boy in this story, and the Beast had been a girl."

A howl goes up from the class.

Alice looks troubled. "But then Beauty, the boy, would be *younger* than Beast, the girl . . ."

"So? Why would that matter? Besides, they don't tell you how old they are," says Alexander.

"But then, I mean, it's not right for a girl to ask a boy to go to the prom or something . . ." Alice still looks troubled.

"I've heard—this is what my Mom says—there's not a law against it or anything, but it's not right for a girl to ask a boy to marry her. This is what my Mom says. I don't know if it's true," says Charlotte.

"So why should that matter?" says Julian. "But I have another problem. The boys in the story are always the worse ones. I mean, the boys in the fairy tales just run up to a girl they don't even know and say 'Will you marry me?' "

"I know," adds Sarah. "I wish they'd say, 'Why no! How can I marry you? I don't even know you. I don't know what your *attitude is!*' "

"Boys in the fairy tales want to marry somebody they don't know anything about. I mean, they might not even *change their underwear!*" says Charlotte.

Allison takes a different tack. "I'm going to be a person who's the exact opposite of Beauty. Pretend there's fire in here. You go up to that person and he says, 'So! Why'd you ask me? You help 'em!'; But Beauty . . . You wouldn't have to tell her anything. She'd just go!"

"What does that have to do with how boys are and girls are?" asks the teacher.

"Well, I'm not saying boys are *always* selfish . . ." Allison doesn't want to go further.

"What bugs me is that in the fairy tales, the guys are always doing things outside, and the girls are just basking around in their beautiful dresses," says Joanne. Several children nod.

Source: Charles Temple. "Suppose *Beauty* Had Been Ugly? Reading Against the Grain of Gender Bias in Children's Literature." *Language Arts* (March 1993). Used by permission.

asks students to comment on the most important devices in the work; he hears the students commenting on such things as voice, characterization, description, plot, and irony long before he has introduced the technical terms for these things.

A kind of aesthetic reading that teachers and students sometimes do, often without realizing it as such, is to connect reading and writing. For example, some time after they have read and discussed *Maniac Magee* by Jerry Spinelli, a teacher asks a fifth-grade class to reread the first chapter and lays out this challenge: Find all the tricks you can that the author used to make the story of Maniac Magee seem like a legend. The students work in groups and come up with the jump-rope rhyme, the way the author introduced characters as if they were already famous, and the way the author mentioned several exaggerated versions of Maniac's background. After discussing those, the teacher then invites the students to use some of these devices in writing original legends of their own.

Now that we have described these two aspects of mature reading, it should be clear that these kinds of reading need not wait until high school or college. Indeed, the example of critical reading in Box 1.1 came from mixed group of second and third graders. Children just as young are capable of making aesthetic responses to written works. We chose to call these activities *mature reading* only because they strike us as the most mature kinds of reading we do, even though in many cases we begin doing them at an early age.

The practices of mature reading, that is, critical reading and aesthetic reading, can be applied to any sort of text. Of course, as students grow in their reading maturity, they will seek out more challenging books. Our question is not so much what they read at this point but how much they think about what they read.

Few students will be referred to a remedial reading teacher for failing to read or write in the ways that we have just described. We have included this discussion, though, because it is important for reading teachers to know where reading development is headed. The ultimate goal is not just that students understand what somebody else has written, but that they know where they stand on the author's claims or be able to find an interesting interpretation of the work and be able to state their positions clearly. Aspects of these goals, of course, might be included in our instruction at any level.

Assessing Readers at Different Stages

What Do We Need to Know from Assessing Emergent Readers?

There are a number of things we need to assess and monitor with respect to what emergent readers are learning about literacy.

Emergent readers are usually preschool, kindergarten, and first-grade children, who are developing concepts about language and print and knowledge of the alphabetic writing system that form the foundation on which later reading is built. Children develop all these at different rates and to different extents; but giving children special, finely-tuned intervention early on can help many of them avoid reading failure and make progress as readers and writers. Assessment of children's early literacy is essential.

So what do we need to know? Effective early literacy assessments focus on the following:

- **Concepts about print and awareness of what books are and what they are for**. The more developed holistic sense children have of what literacy is about, the better they will be able to focus their attention to the details they must understand in order to read. Without an orienting sense of what literacy is and what books are for, early literacy instruction may be confusing for some children.

- **Awareness of sounds in language.** Writing represents spoken language, and in English, writing represents language at the level of words, onsets and rimes, and phonemes, as we discuss in Chapter 3. The problem is that in speech, children can use language without thinking about it; but when they learn to read and write, children must be conscious of words, rimes, and phonemes. Those things must be real for young learners because young learners will need to think hard about the relations between spoken units of spoken language and units of print.
- **Knowledge of the alphabet.** Children must know many letters of the alphabet in order to begin to develop the ability to read. Knowledge of the alphabet is an indicator of the amount of print exposure they have had. The more letters they know, the more print they are likely to have seen. But knowing letters is also important in itself. The more letters they know, the more successfully they can explore how print and speech go together. There is a difference between letter identification and letter retrieval. Because some disabled readers have difficulty naming letters quickly (Katzir & Pare-Blagoev, 2006), some assessments of early literacy include a timed letter identification task.
- **Knowledge of some words**. Virtually all children in the United States are exposed to print before they begin formal reading instruction. Many of them learn to identify some words: their own names, names of fast-food restaurants, words from favorite book titles. The number of words they can identify while still prereaders is a sign of emergent literacy.
- **Listening comprehension.** Children need to have receptive language developed to the degree that they can follow books read aloud to them by the teacher and also comprehend texts themselves when they become readers. Some, but not all, emergent literacy assessment instruments include measures of listening comprehension.
- **Knowledge of letter-to-sound correspondences (phonics).** Children need to develop ideas about the relations between letters and sounds in order to learn to read. As the discussion of invented spelling in Chapter 4 will make clear, most children don't wait to be taught, but with even a little encouragement will begin to speculate actively on what those relationships are. Children's understanding of letter-to-sound correspondences can be assessed beginning in kindergarten and continuing through first grade. (Phonics knowledge will continue to be assessed in beginning readers and in older struggling readers.)

Contemporary assessment of early literacy, then, tracks the development of concepts about print, awareness of sounds, awareness of letters, knowledge of words, and (sometimes) listening comprehension. Note that we do not concern ourselves so much with children's ability to recognize colors or shapes, or to repeat numbers back, or to distinguish a ringing bell from a chirping bird. Although some educators do concern themselves with general indicators like these of children's readiness to learn, when we are assessing early literacy it is best to focus on literacy-related factors because they have been shown to predict more reliably children's future success as readers than the more general measures of learning readiness have (see Snow et al., 1998). Also, teachers need to assess and monitor children's emergent literacy repeatedly during the school year, and the children must be assessed one at a time. Note, too, that most of the factors listed above should be assessed—it won't do to focus on only one. In practice, though, concepts about print tend to develop before the other factors do, so you may stop assessing those concepts after children have shown that they have them, and keep focusing on the other factors.

Measures of Emergent Literacy   Teacher-made measures of emergent literacy can be fashioned after the Early Reading Screening Inventory (Morris, 2000) and the Print Concepts Assessment (after Clay, 1993), both of which are presented in Chapter 4. The Early Reading Screening Inventory, as the name implies, has been widely used to identify young readers in early first grade who will need additional help to learn to read. Other emergent literacy assessment programs are in use around the United States, some of them promoted by individual states. The PALS, the Phonological Awareness Literacy Survey (http://pals.virginia.edu/), is provided to school districts in Virginia and is widely used elsewhere as both a screening and a monitoring tool. The Illinois Snapshot of Early Literacy is promoted by that state as a screening tool. The Texas Education Agency developed the Texas Primary Reading Inventory (http://www.tpri.org/About/), with versions for kindergarten through third grade. It can be administered as a screening, diagnosis, and monitoring tool. At the University of Oregon, the Dynamic Indicators of Basic Early Literacy Skills (DIBELS) was developed with a federal grant and is available to teachers for free online. DIBELS can be used as a screening, diagnosis, and monitoring tool. It begins with a preschool version that assesses initial sounds or "onset fluency." At kindergarten are added tests of phonemic segmentation fluency, letter-naming fluency, and nonsense-word reading fluency, and these continue through first grade, where an oral reading fluency measure is also added, and continues through third grade. These are called *fluency* tests because each child's response is timed, and the speed of the child's responses is noted in addition to accuracy (see http://dibels.uoregon.edu/measures.php).

What Do We Need to Know about Beginning Readers and Beyond?

Beginning readers are those who are starting to read words in connected text. Just as it is important to know that they have their emergent literacy concepts and abilities in place, it is also critical to know if each child is making progress in all aspects of beginning reading. These aspects include word recognition—including having a *sight vocabulary* stored in memory, *decoding skills* so that a child can read a word he didn't know before, and the ability to *use context* to help identify words. Reading *fluency*—accuracy, rate, and intonation—needs to develop apace as well. *Vocabulary* should be growing by thousands of words each year, and they will need to learn vocabulary from reading. *Comprehension* is the ultimate goal of reading, and we want to know how this ability is growing, too. Comprehension is a complex of many factors that include having and using *world knowledge, getting main ideas, making inferences,* having *metacognition* or *cognitive monitoring*— (that is, knowing if the text is making sense), and following the *patterns* of different kinds of fictional and informational texts to construct meaning. We also care about their *attitudes toward reading,* and what kind of text and how much of it they read. But one measure that combines all of these factors is their reading levels (see Chapter 2).

Word Recognition. Word recognition has several aspects to it:

- **Sight vocabulary.** These are the words a reader has stored in memory that can be recognized instantly. Sight words are learned from reading. Words that may initially be decoded or figured out from context become sight words after repeated exposures. Students' sight vocabulary can be effectively measured using an Informal Reading Inventory.
- **Decoding ability**. Young readers frequently encounter words they do not have stored in memory. One way they can read them—and the National Reading Panel and the No Child Left Behind legislation have chosen this as the most important way—is to **decode** the word, or work out its identity by matching its letters and its sounds, using **phonics knowledge.** Children differ in their ability to decode, and a task of assessment is to measure their ability to do it. Decoding ability can be inferred from a readers' performance on an Informal Reading Inventory, especially if words are presented in the flashed and untimed presentation (see Chapter 2).

  Some tests, including DIBELS and the Woodcock-Johnson-III Basic Reading Battery, assess phonics knowledge by testing children's reading of nonsense words, like *Vaj, Kol, Nak,* and the like. The advantage to having children read nonsense words is that we are assured they have never seen them before, so the words must be read by pure decoding. The disadvantage is that, since they are nonsense words, the children can't use the normal self-correction skills that come from arriving at a word they know in their speech. Another disadvantage is that some of the nonsense words do not conform to English orthography. For example, DIBELS uses *doj, ol,* and *huf,* even though there are no single-syllable words in English that are spelled that way.

  Another test of phonics knowledge is done by means of children's spelling. The assessment inventory built into Kathy Ganske's *Word Journeys* (2002) has children spell challenging words, and then gives teachers advice on (1) analyzing spelling errors to assign the children to probable levels of invented spelling and (2) pinpointing the aspect of phonics knowledge that the children need to learn.
- **Identifying words from context**. When unrecognized words occur in meaningful texts, readers have two other ways besides decoding to figure out what they are. One is the syntax of the sentence. For example, if we read "Give me the _____," we can be pretty sure that whatever fills that blank is a noun or something that can function like a noun. But suppose the text said, "It was midnight. The safe cracker

had opened the safe and taken the money. Just as he reached the door, the lights went on and a voice said, 'Stop. Now turn around slowly. Give me the _____.' " Now we would probably guess that the missing word was not only a noun, but *money*, because the meaning of the text limits our choices to that word. Both of these examples go under the name of *using context to support word identification*.

Assessing Vocabulary.   Vocabulary development is recognized more and more as a critical variable in learning to read. But how do we know how many words a child knows? As we will see in Chapter 4, it depends on what we mean by *know*. Does she have a vague idea what the word means? Can she understand the word when she reads it or hears it, but not use it? Does she know all of the meanings of it? These questions show what a complicated thing it is to assess vocabulary. Vocabulary has often been assessed as a part of an Informal Reading Inventory and other reading tests. But with the advent of No Child Left Behind and Reading First, teachers are being called upon to assess vocabulary proficiency more systematically.

When states specify that teachers use scientifically-based tests of vocabulary—that is, tests with proven validity and reliability—the choices are rather limited. A group commissioned by the U.S. Department of Education to approve assessment instruments for use in federally funded programs yielded a very limited list of approved instruments for assessing vocabulary at the points of screening, diagnosing, monitoring, and outcomes-based assessment. More will be said about assessing vocabulary in Chapter 7.

Assessing Comprehension.   Reading comprehension, or understanding what is read, consists of several abilities. Students' *prior knowledge* (sometimes called *world knowledge*) is needed to contextualize the new information they gain from the text. And students need to *read actively*, using their prior knowledge and clues from the text to set purposes and raise questions to answer while reading. They need the ability to *find main ideas* and *supporting details* and *recall* them later. They also need to be able to make *inferences* to construct meanings when ideas are not explicitly stated. They need to be able to *follow the patterns of different kinds of texts*, both *fictional and informational*, as guides to constructing meaning. And they need to keep building their inventory of *vocabulary*. They must do all this while *reading aloud and silently*.

That is a lot for a teacher to assess! In practice, when teachers want to observe this many factors, they often rely upon an Informal Reading Inventory (see Chapter 2) because those are some of the most comprehensive measures.

Measuring Attitudes and Interest.   It has long been noted, and was recently very eloquently affirmed by Allington (2005), that children learn to read by reading. As we note in Chapter 5, children differ enormously in the amount of reading they do, and as Stanovich (1992) has pointed out, those who read more benefit enormously, in increased vocabulary, increased world knowledge, better spelling, and even greater measured intelligence. Somewhere between reading ability and the amount of reading that actually gets done is the will to read, a positive attitude toward reading, a deep interest in books and reading. Where that motivation and interest is lacking, we have a problem. Teachers would do well to assess students' attitudes toward reading,

Surveys can look into children's general attitude toward reading. *The Elementary Reading Attitude Survey* (McKenna & Kear, 1990) is one widely used instrument that will reveal how students are feeling about reading and reading instruction in general.

Assessing Spelling Knowledge. Children's knowledge of spelling develops in two ways. One way is the level of words they can spell. For instance, we would expect a second-grade child to be able to spell *train, queer,* and *float,* but not *conceive* or *profitable,* while a sixth grader should be able to spell the harder words. Another way their spelling develops is that they work their way through stages of spelling knowledge, and each stage is a way of thinking about the ways written words are structured. In Chapter 4 of this book, we will show ways of assessing children's spelling development quantitatively (that is, to determine their grade-level equivalent of spelling) and qualitatively (that is, to examine their errors to infer the kinds of judgments they are making about the ways English words are spelled).

Differentiated Instruction

Differentiated instruction begins with good assessment. *Screening assessment* indicates which students are where they are expected to be, which are above grade level, and which need additional support. *Diagnostic assessment* indicates how strong each student is in different aspects of reading and writing development. Based on diagnostic assessment, students will have different kinds of instruction designed for them. They will be placed in different levels of books for guided reading. They will be given different groups of words for word study, and possibly placed in different points in the sequence of phonics instruction. The teacher will construct focused lessons on aspects of comprehension—on setting purposes for reading, summarizing, visualizing, making inferences, understanding vocabulary from context, learning new information, and interpreting the text. The students will be placed in different levels of text for fluency practice. They will be placed at their instructional level of spelling words to learn, even if that falls a year above or below their grade placement level. The assessment picture will be rounded out by other information gained from interviews with the students to determine the topics they are interested in, the kind of reading they most prefer, and the conditions they need to help them learn.

Once a course of instruction has been established for students, they will be given *monitoring assessments*. Unlike the daily observations, these may be more formalized and done on a schedule. The results may be shared with other teachers or with the reading specialist, and will serve as an occasion to decide whether the present plan of instruction should be followed or if different strategies should be tried to improve each student's learning. In addition, though, the teacher will practice Kidwatching by making a habit of asking a small number of children every day how they are working, what exactly they are doing when they read and write, what they appear to be interested in, what kinds of tasks they are succeeding in, when they work best, and when they get off task—in sum, how the teacher can help each one be successful in this class.

Late in the year will come the outcomes-based assessments, which are based on the state learning standards for each grade level. This is a serious accountability event. While the daily informal assessment and the periodic monitoring assessments will be focused on children's development as readers, writers, and learners in general, these monitoring assessments will also have one eye on these outcomes-based assessments.

Summary

After imagining what schools would be like if all young readers were the same, we offer a list of ways that literacy matters in people's lives: It makes people more employable and gives them access to higher income, better health, bigger vocabularies, and a different sort of consciousness.

We then catalog some of the reasons why we assess readers—to find appropriate levels for teaching, to find skills that are in greater or lesser supply, to decide if a course of instruction is having success, to place a child in special services. Then we survey the approaches to assessment that are available: Informal Reading Inventories, running records, curriculum-based assessments, observations, portfolios, rubrics, and, of course, standardized assessments.

It helps to look at literacy in different stages. In this book we consider the phases of reading to be *emergent literacy, beginning reading, building fluency, reading for pleasure/reading to learn,* and *mature reading.* We briefly point to the means of assessing reading in these different phases, topics that are expanded on in later chapters.

(mylabschool™
Where the classroom comes to life!

MyLabSchool is a collection of online tools for your success in this course, your licensure exams, and your teaching career. Visit www.mylabschool.com to access the following:

- Online Study Guide
- Video cases from real classrooms
- Help with your research papers using Research Navigator
- Career Center with resources for:
    - Praxis exams and licensure preparation
    - Professional portfolio development
    - Job search and interview techniques
    - Lesson planning

References

Allington, R. (2005). *What really matters for struggling readers*. Boston: Allyn & Bacon.

Anyon, J. (1981). Social class and school knowledge. *Curriculum Inquiry*, 11(1), 3–42.

Bear, D., Invernizzi, M., Templeton, S., & Johnston, F. (2000). *Words their way: word study for phonics, vocabulary, and spelling instruction* (2nd ed.). Upper Saddle River, NJ: Merrill.

Beck, I. L., McKeown, M. G., & Kucan, L. (2002). *Bringing words to life*. New York: Guilford.

Betts, A. E. (1946). *Foundations of reading instruction, with emphasis on differentiated guidance*. Chicago: American Book.

Bleich, D. (1975). *Readings and feelings: An introduction to subjective criticism*. Champaign, IL: National Council of Teachers of English.

Brown, R. (1955). *Words and things*. Garden City, New York: Basic Books.

Clay, M. M. (1986). *The early detection of reading difficulties*. Portsmouth, NH: Heinemann.

Clay, M. M. (1993). *An observational survey of early literacy achievement*. Portsmouth, NH: Heinemann.

Cunningham, P., and Allington, R. (2006). *Classrooms that work: They can all read and write* (4th ed.). Boston: Allyn & Bacon.

Deno, S. L. (1985). Curriculum-based measurement: The emerging alternative. *Exceptional Children, 52*, 219–232.

Ganske, K. (2003). *Word journeys*. New York: Guilford.

Goodman, Y. M. (1985). *Kidwatching: Observing children in the classroom*. Newark, DE: International Reading Association/National Council of Teachers of English.

Goodman, Y. M. (2006). *Kidwatching*. Retrieved July 22, 2006, from http://www.reading.org/downloads/publications/books/bk558-27-Goodman_Kidwatching.pdf

Goodman, Y. M., & Burke, C. L. (1972). *Reading miscue inventory: Procedure for diagnosis and evaluation*. New York: Macmillan.

Groff. P. (n.d.). *Emergent literacy: A code word for whole language*. Strasburg, VA: National Right to Read Foundation. http://www.nrrf.org/031_emergent_literacy.html.

Hart, B., & Risley, T. (1995). *Meaningful differences in the everyday experiences of young American children*. Baltimore: Brookes Publishing.

Hayes, D. P., and M. Ahrens (1988). Vocabulary simplification for children" A special case of "motherse." *Journal of Child Language, 15*, 395-410.

Henderson, E. H. *Teaching spelling*. Boston: Houghton Mifflin.

Hirsch, E.D. (1987). *Cultural literacy*. Boston: Houghton Mifflin.

Johnston, F. R., Invernizzi, M., & Juel, C. (1998). *Book Buddies: Guidelines for volunteer tutors of emergent and early readers*. New York: Guilford.

Juel, C. (1988). Learning to read and write: A longitudinal study of fifty-four children from first through fourth grades. *Journal of Educational Psychology, 80*, 437–447.

Katzir, T., & Pare-Blagoev, J. (2006). Applying cognitive neuroscience research to education: The case of literacy. *Educational Psychologist, 41*(1), 53–74.

Leslie, L., & Caldwell, J. (2005). *Qualitative reading inventory* (4th ed.). Boston: Allyn & Bacon.

Luria, A. (1976). *Cognitive development*. Cambridge, MA: MIT Press.

McKenna, M. C., Kear, D. J., & Ellsworth, R. A. (1995). Children's attitudes toward reading: A national survey. *Reading Research Quarterly*, 30, 4, 934-956.

Morris, D. (1992). What constitutes at-risk: Screening children for first grade reading intervention. In W. Second & J. S. Damico (Eds.), Best practices in school speech-language pathology (pp. 43–51). San Antonio: Psychological Corporation.

Morris, D., Tyner, B., & Perney, J. (2000). Early Steps: Replicating the effects of a first-grade reading intervention program. *Journal of Educational Psychology*, 92, 4, 681-693.

Morris, R. D. (1993). The relationship between children's concept of word in text and phoneme awareness in learning to read: A longitudinal study. *Research in the Teaching of English, 27*, 2, 133-154.

Morris, R. D., Blanton, L., Blanton, W. E., Nowacek, J., & Perney, J. (1995). Teaching low-achieving spellers at their "instructional level." *Elementary School Journal*, 96(2), 163–177.

National Center for Educational Statistics (2005). *National Assessment of Educational Progress*. Washington, D.C.: U.S Department of Education.

Neuman, S. B., & Dickinson, D. K. (2000). *Handbook of emergent literacy*. New York: Guilford.

Owocki, G., & Goodman, Y. (2002). *Kidwatching: Documenting children's literacy development*. Portsmouth, NH: Heinemann.

Pinnell, G. S. (1989). Reading Recovery: Helping at-risk children learn to read. *Elementary School Journal*, 90, 2, 161–183.

Rasinski, T., & Padak, N. (2005). *3-Minute reading assessments: Word recognition, fluency & comprehension*. New York: Scholastic.

Rosenblatt, L. (1978). The reader, the text, and the poem. Carbondale, IL: Southern Illinois University Press.

Silvaroli, N., & Wheelock, W. (2000). *Classroom reading inventory*. Columbus, OH: Merrill.

Slavin, R. E. (1991). Synthesis of research of cooperative learning. *Educational Leadership*, 48, 5, 71–82.

Snow, C., Burns, S., & Griffin, P. (Eds.) (1998). *Preventing reading difficulties in young children*. Washington, DC: National Academy Press.

Stuckey, J. E. (1990). *The violence of literacy*. Portsmouth, NH: Boynton/Cook.

Taylor, B., Person, P. D., Clark, K.F., & Walpole, S. (1999). *Beating the odds in teaching all children to read*. Ann Arbor, MI: Center for the Improvement of Early Reading Achievement. http://www.ciera.org/

Taylor, B. M., & Pearson, P. D. (2005). Using study groups and reading assessment data to improve reading instruction within a school. In S. Paris & S. A. Stahl (Eds.), *Children's reading comprehension and assessment* (pp. 237–255). Mahwah, NJ: Erlbaum.

Teale, W., & Sulzby, E. (1986). *Emergent literacy*. Norwood, NJ: Ablex.

Temple, C., Crawford, A., & Gillet, J. (2007, in press). *Developmental literacy inventory: Reading and spelling from emergent to mature levels*. Boston: Allyn & Bacon.

UNESCO (2006). Education for all. http://www.unesco.org/education.

U. S. Department of Education. (2002). Guidance for the Reading First program. Washington, D.C.: U.S. Department of Education, Office of Elementary and Secondary Education. http://www.ed.gov/programs/readingfirst/guidance.doc.

Valencia, S., Hiebert, E., & Afflerbach, P. (1993). *Authentic reading assessment: Practices and possibilities*. Newark, DE: International Reading Association.

Wells, G. (1985). *The meaning makers*. Portsmouth, NH: Heinemann.

Wilson, P. T., Anderson, R. C., & Fielding, L. G. Children's book-reading habits: A new criterion for literacy. *Book Research Quarterly 2*, 3, 72–84.

Informal, Periodic Assessments

Chapter Outline

J ane Cooke is a literacy specialist in a Reading First school. All students in elementary grades except kindergarten are assessed at the beginning and end of the school year with an Informal Reading Inventory that is individually administered and reveals the students' functional reading levels, strengths, and instructional needs. Before the opening of school, Jane conducts staff training so that all classroom teachers know how to administer, score, and interpret the Informal Reading Inventory used by her school division. She also participates in assessment to ensure all students are assessed in a timely manner. She meets with teachers individually and in teams to help them plan ongoing instruction during the assessment periods, interpret results, and group students for instruction. She coordinates the sharing of materials so that teachers have all necessary materials at hand when they are needed and assists teachers who lack experience in classroom assessment. She compiles and disaggregates results and compiles reports fulfilling Reading First, local, and state reporting requirements. These are all important parts of her responsibilities as a professional literacy specialist.

In this chapter, we examine the kinds of periodic, in-depth assessments teachers typically administer in their classrooms at the beginning and end of the year to show growth or at various times during the year to diagnose areas of difficulty. These assessments are informal in nature; they are not norm-referenced, but rather are referenced to typical fiction and nonfiction text at successive grade levels. Their purpose is to document reading strengths and weaknesses as well as the difficulty level of text a reader can read comfortably and effectively. The purposes of informal periodic assessments are to inform students, parents, and teachers and to drive instruction.

In this chapter, we discuss reading levels and their meaning in everyday teaching, assessing reading with Informal Reading Inventories, and qualitative assessment of reading strategies, reading miscues, and decoding.

Levels of Reading Ability

After school has been in session for two weeks, teachers at Cunningham School begin their fall assessments. In the next two weeks, an "assessment window" provided by the state, they will administer the required early literacy assessments to prereaders and emergent readers, administer an Informal Reading Inventory to all students who are able to read, give developmental spelling inventories, and collect baseline writing samples from their students. One overall purpose of these assessments is to determine what each reader's reading level is early in the year. This will be compared to similar assessments conducted near the end of the year to show each student's progress. Parents and even students themselves are curious to know what their reading levels are. But what does the term *reading level* really mean?

Usually the statements and questions we hear about reading levels assume that a reader has one single reading level, but this is an oversimplification. Most readers who have progressed beyond beginning reading have three reading levels. Each level is appropriate for reading different kinds of texts for different purposes. Each has important instructional implications.

The Independent Level

At the independent level, students can read *easily,* without help. Comprehension is generally excellent, and silent reading is rapid because almost all the words are recognized and understood at sight. Students rarely have to stop reading to analyze an unfamiliar word. Oral reading is generally fluent. Occasional *miscues,* or divergences from the written text, rarely interfere with comprehension. Independent-level reading is easy and typically enjoyable for readers, and most readers self-select material at their independent level. Independent-level reading is not hard work; it is recreational.

In the classroom, we want students to read at their independent levels for enjoyment and practice. Anything they have to read and understand on their own, such as tests, homework, and centers, should ideally be at students' independent levels. Harder material will make it difficult for them to complete this reading without help.

Beginning readers, regardless of their age, may not have an independent reading level. That is, they may not be competent enough readers to find any level of material easy for them. Readers who are beyond the beginning reading stage typically have an independent level a grade or two below their present grade placement.

The Instructional Level

At the instructional level, the material is not easy but is still *comfortable.* Students are comfortably challenged and will benefit most from instruction. When we refer to a student's reading level, we mean his *instructional* reading level. Students whose instructional level is the same as their present grade placement are considered to be reading "at grade level" and to be progressing satisfactorily.

At the instructional level, comprehension is good, but help may be needed to understand some concepts or vocabulary. Silent reading is rapid enough to allow for good comprehension, though somewhat slower than at the independent level.

Some word analysis is usually necessary, but most words are recognized on sight; when an unfamiliar word must be decoded, the reader can usually do this successfully within a few seconds. Oral reading is fairly smooth and accurate, and miscues usually make sense in the context and do not cause a loss of meaning. For example, a student reading aloud at her instructional level may read *grandfather* as *grandpa* or *did not* as *didn't.* Occasional miscues that interrupt the flow of meaning do occur, but they are rare enough that the reader can maintain adequate to good comprehension.

The instructional level is the highest, or most difficult, level of text a reader can read comfortably and comprehend satisfactorily. This is the level most appropriate for instruction. Textbooks, basal readers, instructions, and anything else a student reads with instruction or help available should be at his instructional level. Students self-select material at their instructional level if their interest in the subject is high.

The Frustration Level

At the frustration level, the material is *too difficult* for successful reading. Comprehension is poor, with major ideas missed, forgotten, or misunderstood. Both oral reading and silent reading are typically slow and labored, with frequent stops to analyze unknown words. Attempts to figure out unfamiliar words are often unsuccessful. Oral reading miscues are frequent and serious, causing the reader to lose the sense of what was read. This level is named because it is frustrating for students to attempt to read such material for sustained periods of time, and their efforts often fail. This level is to be avoided in instruction.

We want students reading at the instructional level in materials for direct instruction such as trade books, language arts or reading basals, subject-area textbooks, study guides, workbooks, skills activities, and worksheets that are read in class where the teacher can provide help and guidance. But to do so, we must determine what material represents the frustration level. This means that we must have students attempt to read difficult material. Unless we explore the limits of students' reading ability, we will not know how far they can go. We have to see what strategies students can use when pushed and what strategies continue to serve well. After the frustration level has been determined, readers should not be assigned to read material that difficult.

Figure 2.1 shows the characteristics of each level and some typical kinds of reading a student might do at each level.

The Listening Level

Although it is not a reading level, there is one more level of text difficulty that is important because it relates to a student's reading abilities: the listening level. This is the most difficult text material that a student can understand when she listens to it. The listening level provides an estimate of the student's immediate potential for reading improvement.

Most readers who are still developing their reading skills can listen to and understand text read aloud to them that they cannot yet read for themselves. This is most apparent with emergent and beginning readers, who can understand many books by listening to them but might not yet be able to read anything independently. As students are exposed to text by being read to and their ability to read grows, the gap between what they can understand by listening and what they can read independently begins to close. By the time they become fluent, mature readers, there will be little difference; that is, they can understand as well by reading as by listening. But for students who have not

	Characteristics	*Typical Reading*
Independent Level: Easy	Excellent comprehension Excellent accuracy in word recognition Few words need analysis Rapid, smooth rate Very few errors of any kind	All pleasure reading All self-selected reading for information Homework, tests, seatwork, learning centers, and all other assigned work to be done alone
Instructional Level: Comfortable	Good comprehension Good accuracy in word recognition Fairly rapid rate Some word analysis needed	School textbooks and basal readers Guided classroom reading assignments Study guides and other work done with guidance Forms and applications
Frustration Level: Too hard	Poor comprehension Slow, stumbling rate Much word analysis necessary	No assigned material Reading for diagnostic purposes only

FIGURE 2.1   *Functional Reading Levels*

yet completed their development as readers, the listening level is usually higher than the instructional reading level. The listening level gives us an indication of how much their reading may be expected to advance at this point in time. We will return to consideration of the listening level later in this chapter, when we interpret Informal Reading Inventory findings.

The Usefulness of Reading Levels

Because of the tremendous variety of reading materials used in almost every classroom today, it is more important than ever to know what difficulty of texts students can read comfortably and successfully. This allows us to help students select books they can read with good comprehension and enables us to provide the support they need to learn from required texts that might be overly difficult. When we match, or *target*, readers with texts that they can read with a high degree of comprehension, students "report confidence, capability, and control when reading. [T]argeted readers choose to read, and thus read more and read better. Targeted reading is self-reinforcing, pleasurable, and productive. Poorly targeted reading can be discouraging or worse; it can produce frustrated students who do not choose to read or like to read" (Stenner, 1999, p. 2).

ASSESSMENT   *Today's climate of increased accountability requires even greater emphasis on monitoring and documenting student progress and achievement. Reading levels provide students, parents, teachers, and administrators information on where students stand in relation to the reading demands expected of them.*

Informal Reading Inventories

An Informal Reading Inventory, often called an IRI, consists of reading passages corresponding in difficulty to materials at grade levels from primer through high school and questions for each passage that are intended to test readers' comprehension after reading. Passages are arranged in order of difficulty from easiest (primer and primary grades) to hardest (usually ninth grade or beyond). There are usually at least two relatively equivalent passages at each grade level. IRIs usually also contain a Word Recognition Inventory, lists of individual words arranged in levels like those of the reading passages. In addition, many commercial IRIs have supplementary tests such as phonics inventories, cloze tests, and spelling inventories.

Figure 2.2 and Figure 2.3 show a student page and corresponding examiner's pages from a commercial IRI.

Many language arts series provide an IRI to be used diagnostically and for placement within that series. Language arts series IRI passages are selected from that series. Commercial IRIs are stand-alone assessments; they are not related to any particular set of materials. Commercial IRI passages are either selected from different sources or are specially written for the test. Passages are typically 50 to 250 words long. An IRI consists of a student's copy of the reading passages and an examiner's copy of the instrument. The examiner's copy contains the reading passages and the corresponding comprehension questions with their correct answers.

To assess oral and silent reading separately, an IRI should have two or more different passages at each grade level. The passages should be from different texts but comparable in difficulty. The grade levels that are represented should range from preprimer or primer through at least sixth-grade text, preferably higher; text typical of middle and high school reading is very useful.

Like all assessment devices, IRIs have both advantages and disadvantages. They offer the teacher a complete set of materials ready to reproduce and use. Multiple forms at each grade level allow assessment of oral and silent reading and retesting later with new material. IRIs are not difficult to administer, score, or interpret with a little practice. They are readily adaptable to use in the classroom since they can be administered a little at a time over a period of days if necessary and do not require strict administration procedures like formal tests. They are cost-effective and widely available.

They may have shortcomings, however. When an IRI from a language arts series is made up of passages from that series, students may have previously read some of the

---

Great Shellfish Bay

One of the most beautiful bodies of water in the United States is the Chesapeake Bay. A bay is a part of a sea or lake that cuts into a coastline. The name *Chesapeake* came from a Native American word that means "Great Shellfish Bay." The Chesapeake Bay also has inlets that go into the shore. An inlet is a narrow opening in a coastline. An inlet is smaller than a bay. The state of Maryland surrounds part of Chesapeake Bay. The other state that borders the Chesapeake Bay is Virginia. The Chesapeake Bay plays an important part in the history of both of these states. For example, the first capital of Maryland was St. Mary's City, and the first capital of Virginia was Jamestown. Both settlements were built on inlets from the Chesapeake Bay.

The Chesapeake Bay is rich in crabs, oysters, clams, and other shellfish. About two hundred different kinds of fish live in the bay as well. Because of this abundance of seafood, many families in the Chesapeake Bay area earn their living harvesting the sea. The people who fish the bay are called watermen. These men and women gather different kinds of seafood in different seasons.

The watermen are also known for their contribution to American history. During the Revolutionary War, they helped the French fleet, guiding their ships around the complicated waterways of the bay. With this help, American and French forces were able to trap the British army.

Watermen who catch crabs are called "crabbers." Crabbers fish for crabs in the summer using crab pots. A crab pot isn't really a pot at all—it is a large wire cage with several sections. Crabs can swim into the pot, but they cannot swim out of it. To harvest crabs, a crabber pulls the crab pot into the fishing boat, empties the pot, and sorts the catch by size and type. Then the crabber takes the catch to market.

FIGURE 2.2 *Commercial IRI Pupil Page*

Source: Gillet, Jean Wallace, Temple, Charles, & Crawford, Alan (2007). *Developmental Literacy Inventory*. Boston: Allyn & Bacon.

stories. Their comprehension scores on those passages may then be falsely inflated. Sometimes those passages are "reserved," meaning that teachers are told not to teach those stories, but students might have read them in another school or on their own.

Commercial IRIs have passages that are specially written to conform to readability levels or passages selected from other sources, but the quality of such passages can vary widely. For example, very short passages limit the number of ideas available to the reader and the number of questions. If an IRI carries on the same story from passage to

Social Studies Sixth-Grade Level: Great Shellfish Bay

Introduction: *Now you're going to read a passage about a large bay in the eastern part of the United States. You will find out how it got its name. Read carefully because I will ask you questions about it after you finish.*

Record the time at the beginning: _____.

Great Shellfish Bay

One of the most beautiful bodies of water in the United States is the Chesapeake Bay. A bay is a part of a sea or lake that cuts into a coastline. The name *Chesapeake* came from a Native American word that means "Great Shellfish Bay." The Chesapeake Bay also has inlets that go into the shore. An inlet is a narrow opening in a coastline. An inlet is smaller than a bay. The state of Maryland surrounds part of Chesapeake Bay. The other state that borders the Chesapeake Bay is Virginia. The Chesapeake Bay plays an important part in the history of both of these states. For example, the first capital of Maryland was St. Mary's City, and the first capital of Virginia was Jamestown. Both settlements were built on inlets from the Chesapeake Bay.

The Chesapeake Bay is rich in crabs, oysters, clams, and other shellfish. About two hundred different kinds of fish live in the bay as well. Because of this abundance of seafood, many families in the Chesapeake Bay area earn their living harvesting the sea. The people who fish the bay are called watermen. These men and women gather different kinds of seafood in different seasons.

The watermen are also known for their contribution to American history. During the Revolutionary War, they helped the French fleet, guiding their ships around the complicated waterways of the bay. With this help, American and French forces were able to trap the British army.

Watermen who catch crabs are called "crabbers." Crabbers fish for crabs in the summer using crab pots. A crab pot isn't really a pot at all—it is a large wire cage with several sections. Crabs can swim into the pot, but they cannot swim out of it. To harvest crabs, a crabber pulls the crab pot

FIGURE 2.3   *Commercial IRI Examiner's Pages*

Source: Gillet, Jean Wallace, Temple, Charles, & Crawford, Alan, (2007). *Developmental Literacy Inventory.* Boston: Allyn & Bacon.

into the fishing boat, empties the pot, and sorts the catch by size and type. Then the crabber takes the catch to market.

Record the time at the end: _____.

326 words

Flesch-Kincaid 5.7, Dale-Chall 6.4, Fry 6

Questions

1. According to this passage, how did Chesapeake Bay get its name? (from a Native American word for "Great Shellfish Bay") **Recall**

2. According to this passage, how are inlets and bays similar? How are they different? [must answer both parts correctly] (similar: both are parts of the sea or a lake that cut into the shore; different: inlets are usually smaller than bays) **Recall**

3. In the sentence, "Because of this abundance, many families earn their living from the sea," what does *abundance* mean? (richness; lots and lots of something, in this case fish and seafood) **Vocabulary**

4. According to this passage, how did watermen help win the Revolutionary War? (guided the French fleet to defeat the British) **Recall**

5. According to this passage, how does a crabber use a crab pot? (the pot is a cage that he puts in the water; the crab swims in but can't swim out; the crabber pulls the pot back into the boat and takes out the crabs) **Recall**

6. Why is the Chesapeake Bay a good place to make a living from the sea? (because many kinds of fish and shellfish live there; because the fish and shellfish are so abundant) **Inference**

7. Why might Chesapeake Bay watermen be interested in keeping the bay free of pollution? (to protect the fishing; to protect their livelihood; so they could keep making a living from the sea) **Inference**

8. Why do you think watermen catch different kinds of shellfish at different times during the year? (some things may not be ready to catch, or large enough, at certain times of the year; they need to catch different kinds of shellfish so they don't catch too many of one kind) **Inference**

Words in passage: 326   Errors in Oral Reading Accuracy: _____
                          Correct Comprehension Responses: _____

(Continued)

FIGURE 2.3   *Continued*

SCORING GUIDE FOR ORAL READING AND COMPREHENSION

(Circle the Boxes That Correspond to the Student's Scores)

	Oral Reading Accuracy	Reading Comprehension	Listening Capacity
Independent level:	13 or fewer errors	7–8 correct responses	
Instructional level:	14–33 errors	6–7 correct responses	6–7 correct responses
Frustration level:	34 or more errors	5 or fewer correct responses	

Comprehension Scores, by Type

	Recall questions	Inference questions	Vocabulary questions
Student's correct answers			
Total possible correct answers	4	3	1

Reading Rate Scoring Guide for Sixth Grade (Mid-year)

	Below average reading rate (150 wpm or less)	Average reading rate (175 wpm)	Above average reading rate (200 wpm or more)
Reading rates for this passage	More than 130 seconds? Enter the time below:	Around 110 seconds? Enter the time below:	Less than 98 seconds? Enter the time below:

Number of seconds
the student takes to
read the passage

FIGURE 2.3   *Continued*

passage, it is difficult to omit the lower levels or move from a higher to a lower level during assessment. A passage may be taken from the middle of a story with no introduction provided to help the reader understand what came before. Some IRIs use factual recall questions almost exclusively without adequately sampling other aspects of comprehension. If you have to choose a commercial IRI to use, the following section will help you evaluate their most important aspects.

Selecting a Commercial Informal Reading Inventory

To choose the best IRI for your use, examine and compare several, then select the one you believe has the most strengths and will serve your diagnostic needs best. The following aspects are important in choosing an IRI:

- Literary quality of reading passages
- Clarity and relevance of questions
- Balance of explicit and implicit question types, requiring a variety of comprehension skills
- Convenient format
- Complete instructions, including examples
- A balance of both narrative and expository passages, ideally featuring use of both types at each level
- A way to assess readers' prior knowledge of topics before passages are read

Quality of Passages.   The heart of an IRI is the reading passages. When you are evaluating an IRI, read some passages. Are they generally interesting? Look for consistently interesting, clearly written, straightforward passages with natural-sounding dialogue, colorful descriptions, and topics that a wide range of students can recognize and understand. Are sequences and cause-and-effect relationships presented clearly? Are the words and ideas in the passages appropriate for the grade levels and ages for which they are intended?

Passages should stand alone; that is, they should not sound like paragraphs taken from the middle of a story, with preceding material omitted. This is an important consideration in language arts series IRIs since a reading passage may be only part of a longer story.

Types of Text.   Some commercial IRIs are made up mostly or entirely of fiction passages. However, students must read both fiction and nonfiction texts effectively. A good IRI will have a balance of both narrative (fiction) and expository (nonfiction) material at each level.

It is not unusual to see a preponderance of fiction passages at the primary levels and a preponderance of nonfiction at the upper levels. It is not enough for an IRI to include both types of text, but have only fiction selections at some levels while including nonfiction at other levels. A good IRI will have both fiction and nonfiction passages, equivalent in difficulty and length, at each level.

Quality of Questions.   *To get good answers, we must ask good questions.* The questions that we ask are our primary way of assessing comprehension. (Retelling, or spontaneously recalling what was read, is another way that will be described later.) If the IRI questions that we ask are confusing, picky, or limited in the thinking skills they require, we will not get an accurate picture of the reader's comprehension.

Good questions should be clear and simple, follow the organization of the passage, tap the most important information conveyed, require a variety of comprehension skills, and be answerable only by reading the passage, not by general knowledge, prior experience, or illustrations.

Poor IRI questions can be answered before the reader reads the passage, so they do not assess reading comprehension but rather general knowledge. For example, in a fifth-grade passage about trash disposal, one IRI asks, "Name one product that can be recycled." Many children can answer this question from general knowledge or personal experience, without reading the passage. A better question would be, "What is something that can be recycled *that was mentioned in this passage?*" In one primer-level passage, a commercial IRI asks, "What is a sidewalk?" Most children could answer this without reading the passage.

Good questions should require extended rather than one-word answers, should call on both convergent and divergent thinking, and should not be answerable by yes or no without explanation or elaboration. They should not be repetitious.

As the sidewalk example above shows, vocabulary questions are often poorly worded. They should feature passage-based contexts for the words; for example, "In the sentence *Jim put the package on the bar,* what did *bar* mean?" is a better question than "What does *bar* mean in this story?" or, worse, "What is a *bar?*" Vocabulary questions should require readers to use context to figure out the meaning of a word or phrase. The most common meaning of a word may not make the best question. The meaning of the word or phrase must be indicated by the surrounding context.

IRI comprehension questions should not call for the reader's personal opinion or experience or for answers that cannot be evaluated objectively. The following are examples of such poor questions, which do not require reading comprehension.

"Would you like to have a dog like Sandy?"
"What is something you are afraid of?"
"What do you think might happen in the next part of the story?"

There is nothing wrong with questions like these *in instruction,* but they are not appropriate testing questions because they do not require comprehension of the reading passage to answer.

Format and Instructions.   To assess oral and silent reading comprehension separately, the IRI you use should have at least three different passages of equivalent length and difficulty for each level. Most commercial IRIs have three to six equivalent forms, allowing you to use alternate passages for retesting or for assessing listening comprehension.

Are the different forms and grade levels clearly labeled and easy to locate? Are pupil pages coded in some way so that the grade level of the passage is not apparent to the student? Is a record or summary sheet provided to help you summarize your findings? Are the directions for administering the IRI clear and concise? Are there directions for interpreting findings? Are there examples of students' responses for you to study and practice interpreting?

Commercial IRIs include the following:

Applegate, M. D., Quinn, K. B., & Applegate, A. J. (2004). *The critical reading inventory.* Upper Saddle River, NJ: Pearson/Merrill/Prentice Hall.

Burns, P. C., & Roe B. D. (2006). *Informal reading inventory* (7th ed.). Boston: Houghton Mifflin.

Cooter, R. B., Jr., Flynt. E. S., & Cooter, K. (2007). *Cooter/Flynt/Cooter comprehensive reading inventory.* Upper Saddle River, NJ: Pearson/Merrill/Prentice Hall.

Ekwall. E., & Shanker J. L. (2000). *Ekwall-Shanker reading inventory* (4th ed.). Boston: Allyn & Bacon.

Gillet, J.W., Temple, C., & Crawford, A. (2007). *Developmental Literacy Inventory.* Boston: Allyn & Bacon.

Johns, J. L. (2005). *Basic reading inventory* (9th ed.). Dubuque, IA: Kendall/Hunt.

Leslie, L., & Caldwell, J. (2005). *Qualitative reading inventory-4.* Boston: Pearson/Allyn & Bacon.

Silvaroli, N. J., & Wheelock, W. H. (2003). *Classroom reading inventory* (10th ed.). New York: McGraw-Hill.

Stieglitz, E. L. (2002). *Stieglitz informal reading inventory* (3rd ed.). Boston: Allyn & Bacon.

Woods, M. L., & Clark, K. J. (2003). *Analytical reading inventory* (7th ed.). Upper Saddle River, NJ: Pearson/Merrill/Prentice Hall.

Administering an Informal Reading Inventory

Giving an IRI generally takes 30 to 50 minutes, but how long it takes depends on how well the student reads, how many passages are read, and how many parts of the IRI are used. It does not all have to be done in one sitting. If you are giving an IRI during regular instruction time, break up the testing into a number of short sittings, with the student reading one or two passages at a time and finishing the IRI over a period of several days. This allows you to give an individual test without taking too much time away from other students or activities. You will need a student copy of the passages, an examiner's copy for recording each student's responses, pencils, and a stopwatch for timing the reading.

Where to Start

One of the first questions IRI users ask is, "Where should I begin testing?" It would not be economical to begin at the lowest level and proceed upward until the frustration level was reached. Where to begin depends in part on your assessment purpose. If you are testing to see whether material at a particular level of difficulty would be comfortable reading, begin there. If the reader is successful, you may proceed to higher levels or stop. If the reader is unsuccessful, you should drop down to a lower level.

Many experts advocate giving the word recognition test, leveled lists of single words, as a way of determining where to start. Administration procedures for the word lists are included in the section entitled "Assessing Recognition of Words in Isolation." In essence, the word lists are given first, and the examiner begins giving the reading passages at the level where the reader began to miss more than 90 percent of the words on the list.

This is a very common procedure, and the most common use for the graded word lists. However, it often happens that students can recognize words with accuracy but cannot comprehend text at the same level of difficulty. When this happens, we end up starting the IRI considerably above the reader's real instructional level. For that reason, some teachers don't give the word recognition inventory until after they have assessed oral reading, reading comprehension, and listening comprehension. There are good reasons for either method.

Starting with Word Lists.   Let's say that you have been taught to use the graded word lists as the initial assessment. You may start with the easiest level, preprimer or primer, or a level one or two grades below the reader's present grade, and proceed to successive lists until the student begins to miss many of the words. (This is a very general statement, but the specific guidelines are contained in a subsequent section.) You then begin administering passages at the highest level where the reader scored 90 percent or higher, representing the independent level. But what if the student recognized individual words well, but had poor comprehension of passages at the same level? You will have to drop down to lower level passages until you find the student's instructional level. You will read more about the specifics of word list administration in a section to follow.

Starting with Passages.   Another way to begin is to start with reading passages you think will be easy, move up or down as needed, and administer the word lists later. Let's say that a new child has just been enrolled in your third-grade class. Records from his previous school can take some time to arrive; even with them, you wish to form your own judgment of his instructional level, so he can be appropriately placed immediately. So your first, most general question might be, "Is he instructional at grade level?" You begin the IRI with a third-grade passage. His oral reading is fairly fluent and largely correct, with some miscues that mostly make sense. He answers seven of nine comprehension questions correctly. He also reads another third-grade passage silently within a reasonable length of time, and again answers most of the questions accurately. You decide that third-grade material is comfortable for him, a good instructional level. Your first diagnostic question has been answered. You can, for the time being, stop giving the IRI and place him temporarily in a group that is reading material at grade level.

However, you still don't know several things: Is his instructional level significantly above grade level? What is his approximate listening level? Later, perhaps in the next week or so, you will want to continue IRI testing with this student, determining his independent level by administering passages below his instructional level, his frustration level by continuing to give successively harder passages until the frustration level is reached, and his listening level by reading successively harder passages to him until he can no longer answer questions about what he has listened to. These procedures are detailed in the sections to follow.

Your assessment purpose might not be to determine whether a reader is instructional at grade level, but more generally to determine just where his instructional level is. Let's return to our example of the new student in your class. Perhaps your first diagnostic question is not, "Is he instructional at third grade?" but rather, "What is this child's instructional level?" You can start with third-grade passages, or you can begin lower. Let's say that you begin with a second-grade passage. His oral reading is rapid, expressive, and accurate, and his comprehension excellent; he answers correctly all questions and occasionally supplies details not called for in the answers. Second grade seems like his independent level, doesn't it? You'll proceed upward then; you could skip the second-grade silent passage for the moment and go on to third grade, or you could even skip third and go to fourth if you thought his reading was that strong.

But let's change the scenario a bit. When he reads the second-grade passage he struggles with it, reading fairly slowly with numerous miscues, many of which don't make any sense. In this case, of course, you will want to move down, to first-grade passages and lower if necessary, until you determine a level that is comfortable and successful for him. With an IRI, you can move in either direction with ease, or even skip a level and come back to it later if necessary.

Where to Stop

Once you've started, by either method described above, your next question is bound to be, "When should I stop testing?" Most IRIs feature a scoring key after each passage that allows you to determine whether the passage represented the reader's independent, instructional, or frustration level without having to compute any percentages.

For example, look again at Figure 2.3, "Great Shellfish Bay." After the comprehension questions, you'll see a box that tells you how many miscues may be made for this 326-word passage to fall within each reading level; in this case, up to 13 miscues represent an independent level, from 14 to 33 miscues represent the instructional level, and 34 or more miscues represent the frustration level.

Next to the boxes for recording the number of miscues, you'll see another box into which you enter the number of comprehension questions the reader answered correctly, regardless of their type. In this example, answering 8 questions correctly indicates the independent level, 6 or 7 correct answers indicate the instructional level, and 5 or fewer correct answers indicate the frustration level.

If the IRI you're using does not contain such a feature, you will have to quickly figure the percentage of accuracy for the comprehension questions on the spot. When the reader's comprehension score reaches about 50 percent, the frustration level has been reached. (We discuss scoring procedures in more detail in a section to follow.)

When the quality of the reading shows that the grade level just read was clearly at the frustration level, you should stop the reading portion of the testing. If you are not sure whether the reader can go any further, another level may be given then or in another sitting. When the reader's frustration level has been reached, the listening comprehension portion of the assessment begins. This procedure is detailed in the section "Assessing Listening Comprehension" later in this chapter.

Step-by-Step Administration

In this section we go back over the general procedures we describe above and fill in the details.

1. Give the Word Recognition Inventory first in order to find out where to begin, or begin at a level at which you think the student will be able to read easily. (If you overestimated, you can drop back to lower levels.) This practice is discussed in the section "Assessing Recognition of Words in Isolation" later in this chapter.
2. At each level, give the oral reading passage first. Show the student where to begin reading and where to stop and say, "Please read this passage out loud to me. When you are finished, I will ask you some questions about what you have read."
3. Follow along on your copy and carefully mark down the miscues, or divergences, from the text. Later they will be analyzed to provide information about the reader's use of word analysis, syntax, and meaning during oral reading. Marking of miscues is discussed in the section "Marking Oral Reading Miscues" later in this chapter.
4. When the oral reading is completed, remove or cover the passage and ask the comprehension questions. Jot down key words or phrases from the student's answers. Within reason, you can probe for more information or ask a student to explain or justify an answer.
5. Give the silent reading passage for the same level. Show the student where to begin and stop reading. Remove or cover the passage when the reader is finished. Then ask the comprehension questions for that passage as above.
6. If the student answered 50 percent or more of the comprehension questions correctly or is within the instructional-level criteria for the test you're using, proceed to the next level. In general, it's best to test both oral and silent reading at each level, but not always. If oral reading comprehension scores are low but silent reading comprehension is still above 50 percent, discontinue the oral reading but continue silent reading at higher levels until these scores also drop below 50 percent and remain there. If the student shows poor silent comprehension but oral comprehension scores are still above 50 percent, discontinue the silent reading but continue the oral reading. Discontinue the reading portion of the IRI when both oral and silent reading comprehension falls to the frustration level. If you're not sure, give one more level.

Reinspection and Comprehension

Most often, a reader's comprehension of IRI passages is assessed by asking comprehension questions and by expecting *unaided recall;* that is, answering without looking back to the passage. Most IRI directions tell you to cover or remove the passage after reading so the student can't look back at it. But there are drawbacks to this approach:

- When *reinspection* (looking back to the passage) is not allowed, both recall and comprehension are being tested. Readers might comprehend but fail to recall information, causing us to underestimate their comprehension.
- Readers may fail to include information in a response because, to the reader, it appeared obvious, redundant, or secondary to other information. Reinspection tends to encourage more complete answers.
- Recall without reinspection is more a test-taking skill than an everyday reading strategy. In classroom reading, students usually discuss material and answer questions with the material before them rather than with books closed. In real, everyday reading, we are typically able to look back at, or reread portions of, material we did not understand.

When we do not allow readers to reinspect an IRI passage when they answer questions, we place an unreasonably heavy burden on the process of recall and short-term memory (Gipe, 2006; Rubenstein, Kender, & Mace, 1988). But most IRI directions clearly state that students should not look back, except when specifically asked to do so in a question assessing their locational skills (for example, "Find and read me the sentence that tells you the goldfish was happy.").

Therefore, we must face the question of whether we are testing reading comprehension, which surely involves memory but involves other factors as well, or whether we are instead testing the reader's short-term memory.

One of our reasons for using an IRI is to assess students' reading in as natural a way as possible, but disallowing reinspection appears to run counter to what people really do when they read. You can incorporate reinspection fairly easily into standard IRI administration by directing the reader to locate some specific information in the passage after the retelling and questioning.

Some commercial IRIs have reinspection or "look-back" items included in the comprehension questions, but many do not. In this case, it is a simple procedure to direct the reader to "Look back and find the place where it says that . . ." or the like, noting whether the reader is able to scan for the desired information or must begin reading all over again and whether the information can be located. One reinspection item per reading passage is probably enough. If the IRI you're using doesn't have such items, you may want to add one to each passage, adjusting the scoring criteria to accommodate an additional item.

Retelling and Comprehension

Another issue involves the use of questions alone, rather than allowing students to *retell*, or recall in their own words, what they remember from passages. By asking questions, we shape students' comprehension; questions provide clues to what we believe is important for readers to remember and include in their answers. Because of this, an effective way to learn more about students' comprehension is to ask them to retell what they read and either record what each student tells you or use a checklist of all of the information in a passage, allowing the student to use her own words in recalling these items. Retelling should be done *before* asking any comprehension questions.

Some commercial IRIs include retelling in their comprehension assessment. Figure 2.4 shows an examiner's page from one that does. You will see that both a checklist for retelling and a set of questions is included for each passage. Students are asked to retell the passage without prompting or probes before questions are asked. Even when a retelling checklist is included, not all teachers use them. They add considerably to administration time and are not included in scoring.

In retellings, readers are not expected to recall verbatim, and few do. The examiner decides if the retelling matches the information in the passage. Information that is recalled may be checked off on the list, or items may be numbered in the order in which the reader recalled them. The second method helps the examiner to determine if the reader recalled information in roughly the same order as it occurred in the passage or if the retelling was not sequentially ordered. Information that is included in a retelling but is not in the passage may be noted as well.

Retellings are not scored, but they are evaluated subjectively based on the quantity, completeness, and accuracy of the most important information or ideas in the passage. Although these judgments may contribute to our diagnosis and implications for instruction, they are typically not included in determining overall reading levels.

An important qualification to this statement, however, is that the widely used Developmental Reading Assessment (DRA2) (Beaver, 2006) features retelling as a key component of determining the reader's performance level. After the student reads the passage and before questions are asked, the student is directed to "tell in your own words what happened in the story starting at the very beginning." The examiner's copy lists the characters, setting, and story events. The teacher checks off whether characters, important details, and vocabulary or special phrases from the passage, setting, ending, and story events were included in the recall and if story events were recalled in sequence or out of sequence.

If the initial retelling is complete, the teacher may move to another passage or stop. If the retelling is incomplete, the teacher gives a general prompt by saying, "Tell me more." If the student adds information about the previously omitted elements of the story, no further questioning is done. But if the retelling is still incomplete, the teacher asks specific questions to elicit omitted information, such as "Who had to stop? Why did the police officer tell the bus to stop? Where did Mother Duck and her babies go?"

This instrument assesses comprehension both by retelling and by responding to questions, which makes it unique among IRIs. At any grade level, a student's performance may be rated as 4/Proficient, 3/Basic Understanding, 2/Partial Understanding, or 1/Minimal Understanding. A score of 4 or 3 is required for the student to be instructional at that level. A score of 4 is achieved when the student's retelling is spontaneous and is accomplished with only one general prompt or one comprehension question. A score of 3 is achieved when the student's retelling is done with the use of more than one general prompt or one question. A score of 2 is achieved when the retelling is done with prompts

Level: Two

Retelling Scoring Sheet for "Whales and Fish"

Main Idea

_____ Whales
_____ and fish both live
_____ in the water
_____ but they are different
_____ in many ways.

Details

_____ Whales are large
_____ animals.
_____ They must come
_____ to the top
_____ of the water
_____ to get air.
_____ Whales breathe
_____ in air
_____ through a hole
_____ in the top
_____ of their heads.
_____ At the same time,
_____ they blow out
_____ old air.
_____ Fish take in air
_____ from the water.
_____ Mother whales give birth
_____ to live whales.
_____ The baby whale comes
_____ to the top
_____ of the water
_____ right away
_____ for air.
_____ The baby drinks milk
_____ from its mother
_____ for about a year.
_____ Most mother fish lay eggs.
_____ The babies are born
_____ when the eggs hatch.
_____ Right after they are born,
_____ the baby fish must find their own food.

Main Idea

_____ Whales
_____ and fish are alike
_____ in some ways too.

Details

_____ Whales
_____ and fish have flippers
_____ on their sides.
_____ They have fins
_____ on their tails.
_____ Flippers
_____ and fins help whales
_____ and fish swim.
_____ Fins move
_____ and push the water away.

49 Ideas

Number of ideas recalled _____

Other ideas recalled, including inferences:

Questions for "Whales and Fish"

1. What is this passage mainly about?
   Implicit: how whales and fish are alike and different

2. According to the passage, how are whales and fish different?
   Explicit: whales breathe air and fish take in air from the water; whales give birth to live babies and fish lay eggs; baby whales get food from their mother, and baby fish have to get it for themselves

FIGURE 2.4 *Commercial IRI Retelling Scoring Sheet*

Source: From Leslie, Lauren and JoAnne Caldwell. *Qualitative Reading Inventory 4.* Published by Allyn and Bacon, Boston, MA. Copyright © 2006 by Pearson Education. Reprinted by permission of the publisher.

and/or questions that elicit some, but not all, of the additional correct information, while a score of 1 is achieved when the student provides little correct information even when prompts and questions are used (Beaver, 2006; Seattle Public Schools, 2006).

Marking Oral Reading Miscues

While the student is reading aloud, you will mark all of the oral divergences from the text, or miscues, on your copy of the passage. These important reading behaviors are considered in two ways; they are *counted* to determine the reader's degree of oral reading accuracy and *analyzed* to determine what word attack strategies the reader used during the oral reading.

Miscues include

- *Substitutions* of real or nonsense words.
- *Insertions* of extra words.
- *Omissions* of whole words or phrases.
- *Self-corrections* occurring immediately or later during the reading.
- *Words provided* by the examiner.
- *Reversals* of word order.

Very long *pauses* and *repetitions* of words or phrases may also be marked but are not counted as errors.

Box 2.1 contains a simple coding system that will allow you to record all miscues accurately. Most commercial and reading series IRIs will have a suggested system for marking miscues; these are usually very similar. There may be small differences; for example, some systems show self-corrections marked with a check: some with the letters SC and a line showing which part of the word, phrase, or sentence was corrected: and some with a C in a circle. All these marks mean the same thing. Small differences are unimportant, but it is important to be able to read what another examiner has marked. It's best if everyone uses the same system, but if everyone using IRIs in your school or team doesn't use the same marks, be sure you are familiar with the variations.

Figure 2.5 shows a sample passage with miscues marked.

Assessing Listening Comprehension

When the student can answer correctly only about half of the questions for a passage, functional reading has broken down. One very important aspect remains to be tested, however: the student's listening comprehension. As we discussed earlier in this chapter, the listening level, the highest level of text a reader can comprehend when listening to someone read aloud, provides a rough estimate of a student's potential for reading improvement. It helps us to form reasonable expectations for growth in reading.

When reading comprehension scores indicate that the reader has become frustrated (scores 50 percent or less), read one of the next level passages aloud to the student and then ask the comprehension questions. Before you read, say something like,

BOX 2.1

A System for Marking Oral Reading Miscues

1. *Substitution of a word or phrase:* the student's word written over a word in text

   dog
   The doll fell from the shelf.

2. *Insertion of a word not in text:* a word written in over a caret or small arrow

   down
   The doll fell ^ from the shelf.

3. *Omission of a word or phrase:* the omitted element circled

   The ⟨big⟩ dog ran away.

4. *A word given by the examiner:* parentheses placed around that word

   The climbers were assisted by ⟨Sherpa⟩ tribesmen.

5. *Miscue spontaneously corrected by the reader:* check mark next to original coding

   doll ✓
   The big dog ran away.

   or © next to original coding

   doll ©
   The big dog ran away.

   or sc with line showing corrected element

   doll sc
   The big ⟨dog ran away.⟩

6. *Reversal of order of words:* proofreader's symbol of inversion used

   "Let's go," ⟨shouted⟩ Sally.

7. *Repetition of word or phrase:* wavy line under repeated element

   The climbers were assisted . . .
   ‿‿‿‿‿

8. *Pauses longer than normal:* slashes for pauses, one per second

   The / / controversial theory . . .

"You've worked hard and the last passage was difficult. This time I want you to listen carefully while I read out loud. Afterward I'll ask you questions as I did before." Read normally, not too slowly or with exaggerated expression. If the student gets more than half of the questions correct, read a passage from the next level in the same way. Proceed until you reach a level at which the student gets 50 percent or fewer of the questions correct, then stop.

Assessing Recognition of Words in Isolation

A component of an IRI that is used to assess recognition of words in isolation (words in lists, not in context) is the *Word Recognition Inventory (WRI)*. This instrument consists of

---

Narrative First-Grade Level: Jack's Dinner

Introduction: *Sometimes it's hard to stop what you are doing when you are called to dinner. Read to find out what happened when Jack was busy at dinner time. I will ask you questions about the passage after you finish reading.*

Record the time at the beginning: _____.

Jack's Dinner

"Come to dinner," said Jack's Mother. [Mom]

Jack didn't want to come.

He was busy. [building]

He was bending wire. He was pounding nails. He was mixing [making] paint. He was making a toy.

"I don't care if you're busy. Come now." Mother sounded cross. [cr...cruel]

"Just one more minute," said Jack. He kept bending wire. He kept pounding nails. He kept mixing paint.

"Now, Jack," said Mother. "Your dinner will be cold." [get]

Jack came to dinner.

He showed Mother his toy truck.

"That's so cool!" said Mother. "I didn't know you could make a toy truck."

Record the time at the end: _____.

FIGURE 2.5 *Sample IRI Passage with Miscues*

Source: Gillet, J., Temple, C., & Crawford, A. *Developmental Literacy Inventory.* Published by Allyn and Bacon, Boston, MA. Copyright © by Pearson Education. Reprinted by permission of the publisher.

graded lists of individual words, usually primer level through grade 6, typically included in commercial IRIs.

The WRI is used to assess sight recognition and some aspects of phonic and structural analysis. Since the words appear in isolation, the WRI is not used to assess how students recognize words in context or to assess comprehension in any way.

As was mentioned previously, a secondary purpose of the WRI is to help determine where to begin administering the reading passages of the IRI. For this purpose, the WRI is given before the IRI, and the examiner begins having the student read story passages at the grade level where he first began to miss some words. When it is used only to provide information about the student's word recognition, the WRI can be given after the rest of the IRI.

The WRI consists of graded word lists for the student to read and a corresponding set of examiner's pages for the teacher to mark and score. Figure 2.6 shows two levels of word lists from a commercial WRI. The student's copy contains only the individual words, arranged in lists. On the examiner's copy, each word is followed by two blanks for filling in what the reader said when errors occurred.

Typically, each word in succession is shown to the student for a very brief exposure of less than one second; the word is uncovered for a longer look if it is not identified

3rd	Flashed	Untimed
station		
ought		
idea		
coach		
type		
damp		
elbow		
mystery		
yourselves		
midnight		
motorcycle		
insect		
study		
easier		
headache		
match		
quit		
alive		
moment		
range		
Total Errors:		

0–2 errors = Independent Level

3–6 errors = Instructional Level

7 + errors = Frustration Level

FIGURE 2.6 *Word Recognition Inventory, Examiner's Page*

Source: Gillet, J., Temple, C., & Crawford, A. *Developmental Literacy Inventory.* Published by Allyn and Bacon, Boston, MA. Copyright © by Pearson Education. Reprinted by permission of the publisher.

immediately. There are several similar ways to reveal each word for only a brief expo-sure. One is to use a file card to cover each word, drawing the card down the list to briefly reveal each word as the student reads down the list; another is to use two file cards, moving one to briefly uncover the word, then covering it again with the other card; a third is to use a card with a small rectangular window cut in it and slide the card down the list so that each successive word appears briefly in the window. Most teach-ers find that with a bit of practice, one or another of these methods is most comfortable for them. How the words are shown is less important than whether each word is re-vealed briefly yet completely and whether the administration is smooth and fluent. This might take a little practice.

Words that the reader recognizes immediately and accurately are checked off on the examiner's copy; words that are incorrectly identified or sounded out are noted in the blanks following each word. Some commercial IRIs have only one column of blanks, but most have two; those that have two blanks after each word are providing spaces for the examiner to note if the word was recognized automatically or had to be decoded by the reader. Percentages of accuracy are derived for each list of words by counting the er-rors made.

Deriving percentages is really academic since we are not interested in setting a functional reading level from reading word lists but rather in analyzing the student's word recognition strategies and assessing how well the student recognizes words auto-matically. Scores for each list may be entered on the IRI record sheet.

To summarize, the steps in administering an IRI are shown in Box 2.2.

Scoring an Informal Reading Inventory

Scoring procedures for an IRI are fairly simple. Word recognition in isolation, oral reading accuracy, and comprehension are scored by percentages, which help the teacher determine the student's independent, instructional, and frustration reading levels.

Because IRIs are often used to determine a student's independent and instructional levels, the criteria for setting these levels are very important. IRIs have been widely used since the 1940s, when Betts (1941, 1957) and others popularized their use, and the criteria for setting levels were derived largely from clinical experience. For many years, the minimum instructional-level criteria attributed to Betts—95 percent oral reading ac-curacy and 75 percent comprehension—were widely accepted.

Today some authorities still use the Betts criteria, although 70 percent comprehen-sion is most often used. However, the long-standing oral reading accuracy criteria have been challenged as too stringent. Ninety percent is widely accepted as the lower end of the instructional range for oral reading accuracy (Johns & Magliari, 1989) and for tak-ing a running record to determine whether a student is reading instructional-level ma-terial (Clay, 2000).

Oral Reading Accuracy

For each oral passage that was read, score the oral reading accuracy by counting the uncorrected miscues, which are shown in Box 2.1.

The issue of whether to count miscues that the reader corrected is an important one. Many clinicians do not count self-corrected miscues because self-correction shows that the reader is monitoring whether the passage makes sense. But some count all miscues, corrected or not, and some commercial IRIs instruct users to do so. In informal assessment there are some issues on which practitioners disagree. You should discuss these issues with experienced IRI users and with your colleagues and use your best judgment as a teacher.

While you are learning to give and score an IRI, it is helpful to tape-record the oral reading so that you can replay it and be sure you caught all the miscues. It might also help you to make a check or tally mark at the end of each line of print, one for each uncorrected miscue in that line. It makes counting up easier.

To obtain a reader's total accuracy score, you must know not only how many miscues occurred, but also how many words are in the whole passage. In other words, what percentage of the total words does each individual word contribute?

BOX 2.2

Steps in Administering an Informal Reading Inventory

1. Begin the assessment one or two grade levels below the student's present grade or basal level or at a level you think will be easy for the student. Remember, you can move back as well as forward in the IRI if the reading is still too difficult.
2. Administer the first oral reading passage. Mark the miscues during the oral reading. You may tape-record the oral reading for greater accuracy if it does not distract or annoy the reader. Record the retelling. Ask the comprehension questions and record the gist of the answers.
3. Administer the silent reading passage at the same level. Ask the comprehension questions and record the gist of the answers.
4. If the student was not reading comfortably and successfully at this level, move back to a lower level and administer the oral and silent reading passages as before. Then continue to move forward in the IRI, skipping the level that you already administered when you come to it.
5. If the student was reading comfortably at the level on which you began testing, continue to move forward in the IRI, giving oral and silent passages as above, until the comprehension scores drop to 50 percent or less.
6. When you have located the frustration level, read one of the next-level passages aloud to the student and ask the comprehension questions as before. Continue assessing listening with one passage per level until the listening comprehension score drops below 50 percent. Then stop the IRI.

Most commercial IRIs do the math for you, providing a box or chart showing how many miscues represent the independent, instructional, and frustration levels for that passage. As we mentioned in the previous section on administration, if you look back at Figure 2.3, you will see a box at the end of the passage indicating how many miscues may be made for the passage to fall within each reading level; in this case, up to 13 miscues represents an independent level, from 14 to 33 miscues represents the instructional level, and 34 or more miscues, the frustration level. (These scores do not reflect whether the miscues made sense within the passage; that issue is discussed in a later section entitled "Qualitative Analysis of Oral Reading Miscues." This discussion refers only to the total accuracy of the oral reading.)

If you are using an IRI that provides you only the total number of words in the passage, you will have to calculate the oral reading accuracy score.

Let's use the marked oral reading passage in Figure 2.5, "Jack's Dinner," as an example. This passage contains 93 words. The reader made five uncorrected miscues.

To calculate oral reading accuracy:

1. Determine the number of words that were read correctly by subtracting the number of miscues from the number of words in the passage.
2. Divide the number of words in the passage into the number of words correct.
3. Multiply the resulting decimal number by 100 to get the total accuracy score. Round off to the nearest whole number.

By making 5 uncorrected miscues in a passage of 93 words, the reader read with 95 percent accuracy.

1. $93 - 5 = 88$
2. $88/93$
3. $.95 \times 100 = 95\%$

As you score each oral reading passage, write the percentage of accuracy on the examiner's copy of the passage. The oral reading accuracy scores will contribute to your determination of the student's independent, instructional, and frustration levels.

The most widely accepted criteria for oral reading accuracy are these:

Independent level: 97 percent or higher
Instructional level: 90–96 percent
Frustration level: below 90 percent

If these criteria seem high, remember that sentence context provides a powerful word recognition aid. In sentences, words are constrained by their grammatical usage and meaning. An unknown word in a sentence does not appear there arbitrarily, as it might in a list, but because it fits grammatically and semantically. The number of alternatives for any individual word in context is therefore small. When a student misses more than about 1 in 10 running words, comprehension will be affected.

Reading and Listening Comprehension

Score the silent and oral reading comprehension questions separately for each passage and determine the percentage of questions answered correctly. Do the same for any passages you used for listening comprehension. These passages are all scored in the same way.

If the IRI that you are using does not have a box for checking off the number of correct answers and the corresponding level, you will have to determine the percent of correct answers, as you would if you were grading a test or quiz. To determine how much each question counts, divide the number of questions into 100. The answer represents the percentage each question counts. Multiply this number by the number of correct answers to obtain the comprehension score for each passage.

Jot the score for each passage on the examiner's copy of that passage. Repeat the same procedure for all passages that were read to the student. The comprehension scores will contribute to your determination of the reader's independent, instructional, frustration, and listening levels.

The most widely accepted criteria for reading and listening comprehension scores are these:

> Independent level: 90 percent or higher
> Instructional level: 70–89 percent
> Frustration level: below 70 percent

In our discussion of administering IRIs, you were told to continue testing until a score of 50 percent or lower was attained. By doing so, you can be sure that the frustration level has been reached.

Scoring the Word Recognition Inventory

The WRI is easy to give and score. When a word is correctly identified during the brief exposure, it is checked off in the column labeled *Automatic* (or whatever the designation is on your IRI for the brief exposure of each word) on the examiner's sheet; if an error is made, the error is written on the blank instead of a check. Then the word is uncovered for a longer exposure, and the student's second attempts are written in the column labeled *Decoded* (or whatever the designation is on your IRI for the longer, or untimed, exposure of the word). If the reader corrects the error after looking at the word again, a check may be placed in that blank.

Each column is scored separately for each level. Some WRIs like the one shown in Figure 2.6 show you how to derive an independent, instructional, or frustration level from these scores. If not, you will derive a percentage score for each column, as though you were grading a quiz.

The most widely accepted criteria for word recognition in isolation are these:

> Independent level: 90 percent or higher
> Instructional level: 70–89 percent
> Frustration level: below 70 percent

Student _____ Age _____ Grade _____
Date tested _____ Tested by _____

Level	WORD RECOGNITION INVENTORY		ORAL READING		COMPREHENSION		
	Automatic	Decoded	Total Accuracy	Total Acceptability	Oral Reading	Silent Reading	Listening
P							
1st							
2nd							
3rd							
4th							
5th							
6th							
7th							
8th							
9th							

READING LEVELS

Independent   _____

Instructional   _____

Frustration   _____

Listening   _____

Retelling   _____

_____

Strengths: _____

_____

Needs: _____

Prior Knowledge: _____

Recommendations: _____
_____
_____
_____
_____
_____

FIGURE 2.7   *Informal Reading Inventory Record Sheet*

These levels are most useful when the WRI is used to show where to begin the reading passages. You will not determine a functional reading level from reading word lists alone, but you will use this information in analyzing the student's word recognition strategies and assessing how well the student recognizes words automatically.

Keeping Track of Scores

After you have derived scores for word recognition in isolation, oral reading accuracy, oral and silent reading comprehension, and listening comprehension, enter the scores on a record sheet, which can be stapled to the front of the examiner's copy of the student's IRI. Having all the pertinent scores and observational notes you made during the testing on one sheet aids in interpreting the student's performance. (Interpreting IRI results is discussed in the next section.)

A model score record sheet is shown in Figure 2.7. On this sheet are spaces for recording all scores from the IRI and WRI, notes, observations, and information about the student such as age and grade.

The necessary scores for determining the functional reading and listening levels from an IRI are summarized in Table 2.1. If the IRI that you prefer to use specifies somewhat different score criteria, use those given in the IRI instructions.

Interpreting an Informal Reading Inventory

As with all assessment procedures, IRI scores are not an end in themselves. They should be interpreted and then applied in instructional planning. To do so, the student's functional reading levels must be determined, and patterns of strength and need must be noted and addressed.

Establishing Reading and Listening Levels

The scores that are derived from the oral reading and comprehension measures are used to determine overall levels. Scores for both oral reading accuracy and comprehension should meet the criteria for the instructional level to be sure that the reader will be comfortable at that level.

TABLE 2.1   *Criterion Scores for Establishing Reading and Listening Levels with an IRI*

	Oral Reading	Comprehension
Independent Level	97%	90%
Instructional Level	90%	70%
Frustration Level	below 90%	below 70%
Listening Level	—	70%

Figure 2.8 and Figure 2.9 show examples of oral reading and comprehension scores for a second grader and a sixth grader. Let's consider what the scores tell us about each student's reading levels.

The child whose scores are shown in Figure 2.8 reads easily at the primer (P) level with accurate word recognition and excellent comprehension. All scores are at the independent level.

At the first-grade level, her oral reading accuracy is still good, although she made more miscues, and comprehension is good in both oral and silent reading. An oral reading accuracy score of 94 percent and comprehension scores of 75 percent and 80 percent are within the instructional level. First-grade material represents a good instructional level for this youngster. In second-grade material, both word recognition and comprehension break down. Second-grade material represents her frustration level.

The listening comprehension score of 80 percent at third grade shows that this second grader can listen to and understand material at a third-grade level of difficulty, while the listening score of 60 percent at fourth grade shows that this level of material is presently too hard for her to understand adequately even when she hears it. The 80 percent score at third grade also represents this youngster's *potential* reading level; that is, she has the vocabulary and verbal concepts to understand material appropriate for third graders when she hears it. This is a positive sign; she has considerable potential for improving her reading. However, she presently is able to read only first-grade material.

In Figure 2.9, the student's scores at second grade are within the independent level. (Since independent-level scores were obtained at second grade, first-grade and primer levels were not assessed.) His scores at both third and fourth grades fall within the instructional range, so we can say that fourth-grade material represents his highest instructional level; his instructional reading level actually includes both third- and fourth-grade material.

Since all fifth-grade scores are in the frustration range, we conclude that fifth-grade material is too difficult for this student to read, but the 90 percent listening comprehension score at sixth grade shows he can understand material at his present grade level

| Grade | Oral Reading | Comprehension | | Listening |
		Oral	Silent	
P	97	100	100	—
1	94	75	80	—
2	88	60	50	—
3	—	—	—	80
4	—	—	—	60

FIGURE 2.8   *Sample IRI Scores for a Second Grader (in Percentages)*

Grade	Oral Reading	Comprehension		Listening
		Oral	Silent	
2	99	100	90	—
3	94	85	80	—
4	91	70	70	—
5	86	50	55	—
6	—	—	—	90

FIGURE 2.9   *Sample IRI Scores for a Sixth Grader (in Percentages)*

when he hears it. This sixth grader's listening comprehension score shows that he has the ability to read at grade level, although he is presently instructional at a fourth-grade level.

The process of deriving percentages of correct responses and using these scores to determine reading levels is called *quantitative analysis.* It is useful, but it is incomplete because it lacks the essential element of in-depth analysis of the student's responses. To determine what the reader knows and where help is needed, we must determine the strategies underlying the correct and incorrect responses. From this perspective, *how many* correct responses the student made is less important than *which* responses were right and *why.* This assessment is termed *qualitative analysis* because it focuses on the quality of responses and the strategies that the reader demonstrated.

Quantitative analysis helps us determine the levels of difficulty of text the reader can deal with successfully. Qualitative analysis helps us determine what the student has mastered and what skills and processes are lacking. Both analyses are needed to develop a prescriptive program for a reader.

Qualitative Analysis of Oral Reading Miscues

The context in which a word occurs is a powerful aid to word recognition, but context is provided only by connected text. When we make a transcript of the oral reading of IRI passages, we can analyze word recognition within the real act of reading. Therefore, accurate marking and analysis of miscues are important.

Even very fluent readers make occasional miscues, especially when the material is unfamiliar. Some miscues change the meaning of the sentence or passage very little; others change the author's meaning significantly and can interfere with the reader's comprehension.

By examining and evaluating a reader's miscues, we can better understand what the reader is doing while reading. We can see more than just whether the reading is highly accurate. We can see, through the miscues themselves, whether the reader is using context and sense-making strategies to actively construct meaning. Students who generally make acceptable, or qualitatively "good," miscues need a different kind of word-attack instruction to help them read more accurately than those whose miscues generally don't make sense.

Comparing Miscues.   Let's say two readers read the following three sentences aloud:

> The day was warm and sunny. Tom and Mandy packed a lunch. They brought ham sandwiches, chips and pickles.

One student reads:

> "The day was *hot* and sunny. Tom and Mandy packed *their* lunch. They brought ham sandwiches, chips and *peaches.*"

The other student reads:

> "The day was warm and *sandy.* Tom and Mandy *picked* a lunch. They brought ham sandwiches, chips and *pirckles.*"

Each reader made three uncorrected miscues. Their overall accuracy scores for this paragraph would be the same, but the first reader's miscues more nearly preserved the meaning of the paragraph, while the second reader's miscues made less sense and probably interfered more with her comprehension.

Hot and *warm,* when discussing weather, are closer in meaning than *sunny* and *sandy.* It makes better sense, and is more like the meaning of the text sentence, to say the day was *hot and sunny* than *warm and sandy.* Although it isn't grammatically correct, "packed *their* lunch" is closer to the original meaning of the sentence than "*picked* a lunch." *Peaches* aren't much like *pickles,* but they are at least both foods that might be found in a picnic lunch; *pirckles* is a nonsense word, even though it looks and sounds more like *pickles* than *peaches* does. Although both readers made three miscues, the first reader's miscues were qualitatively better, in the sense of preserving the intended meaning, than the second reader's.

Scoring Miscue Acceptability.   When considering the quality of miscues, we reread the passage as the reader read it, with all the miscues just as we marked them, and decide whether each miscue significantly changes the meaning of the passage or sentence in which it occurs. We do not look only at the individual word, but at the miscue within the phrase, sentence, or passage context. Circle, highlight, or write MC for Meaning Change over miscues that significantly change the meaning of the context. If we were marking the sentences read in the foregoing examples, we would mark only the first reader's *peaches* as a meaning-change miscue, and all three of the second reader's miscues as meaning changes, as shown in Figure 2.10.

What Makes a Miscue Acceptable?   At this point, you might wonder how much a miscue must change meaning to be considered significant. It can be argued that any change in the author's words, no matter how small, changes the author's meaning. But

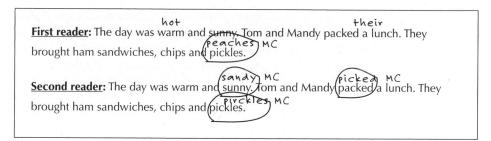

FIGURE 2.10 *Two Readers' Meaning-Changing Miscues*

we are not concerned here with tiny or subtle meaning changes. Instead of asking ourselves, "Does this miscue change the meaning?" we ask, "Does this miscue change the meaning *significantly?* Is this a *big* meaning change?"

Whether the meaning is changed a lot, a little, or hardly at all depends on the miscue *and its surrounding context.* That's why miscues must be considered in their context, not taken out of context, placed in a list, and evaluated, as some IRI instructions say. We try not to split hairs, in terms of meaning, but rather to be aware of big changes in meaning. A word, phrase, or sentence can make good sense even when it is grammatically incorrect, so we avoid making hard-and-fast rules such as "changes in parts of speech always result in meaning change."

With experience, we've found that there isn't much ambiguity about most miscues; it's clear either that little or no meaning was lost or that the miscue changed the meaning a great deal, and the ones we have to puzzle over are rare. With these, we usually read someone else what the sentence was supposed to say and what the reader said and ask whether they think the miscue was significant.

Dialects and Miscues.   An important issue in miscue analysis is the role of nonstandard English dialects in oral reading accuracy. As we have seen, counting all the miscues and deriving an accuracy score do not take into account whether the reader's errors make sense. Nor does this process take into account whether the reader is translating standard English text into her own familiar, albeit nonstandard, oral dialect.

For example, let's say the sentence reads like this:

Rose said, "This is my mother."

The reader, a dialect speaker, reads this:

Rose say, "This my mother."

Quantitatively, the reader has made two uncorrected miscues: the omission of *is* and the substitution of *say* for *said.* Qualitatively, the oral reading does not correspond exactly to the written words, but it does represent an accurate translation into a widely used nonstandard dialect, with no loss of meaning. In most dialects it is grammar, not meaning, that differs from the written text (McWhorter, 2000).

It is important not to confuse dialect miscues with true word recognition errors because doing so results in underestimating the word recognition abilities of many dialect speakers. Likewise, it is not helpful to assume that all miscues produced by dialect speakers will be acceptable and not provide the help they may need to develop greater accuracy and automaticity in word recognition. By listening closely to the informal speech of your dialect-speaking students, you will gain enough familiarity with its conventions to recognize true dialect miscues, which are generally acceptable, from those that interfere with comprehension.

When you are marking a dialect speaker's oral reading, it's best to mark what the reader says, then rescore the passage for acceptability. If they are dialect usages, most of the miscues will be insignificant.

What about Names?   Names are especially tricky for readers. Often, students stumble over names in a passage even when they read harder words correctly. We generally don't count names as miscues more than once in a passage, provided that the reader calls the character by the same wrong name each time. That is, if *Phillip* is read as *Phil,* or even as *Pillip* throughout a passage, we count it only the first time. If *Phillip* were read as *Phil* a few times, then changed to *Flip,* we'd count each change once.

Some people count name miscues as a separate error each time; this seems excessively strict. Others count it if the name seems to change the gender (calling *Phillip Phyllis,* for example). Check the instructions for administering your IRI and follow what the authors recommend if it makes sense to you.

Formal Miscue Analysis.   A useful device for analyzing a reader's miscues in great detail is the Reading Miscue Inventory (RMI) (Goodman, Watson, & Burke, 2005). Miscues are analyzed according to graphic and phonological features, syntactic function and grammatical acceptability, correction or dialect involvement, and the degree to which the original meaning was preserved.

Although it is time-consuming, the RMI makes the evaluation of miscues more objective and less subject to examiner opinion than informal miscue analysis. It takes account of the oral reading and comprehension of a whole story or complete passage rather than only a text portion as in an IRI and can include analysis of the reader's comprehension of the passage as well as accuracy of the reading. It can be used independent of an IRI or as a miscue analysis training device.

Another helpful resource is Sandra Wilde's *Miscue Analysis Made Easy* (2000). Wilde's detailed case study approach and extensive use of examples provide excellent training in the use of miscue analysis. Also helpful is Wilde's discussion of *retrospective miscue analysis* (Goodman & Marek, 1996), an instructional technique in which readers listen to their tape-recorded readings and discuss with a teacher the strategies they used, or might have used, to figure out unfamiliar words that resulted in miscues. By reflecting on their efforts, readers can become more self-aware and strategic. Another source for information about retrospective miscue analysis is Rita Moore and Carol Gilles's *Reading Conversations: Retrospective Miscue Analysis with Struggling Readers, Grades 4–12* (2005).

Analyzing Reading Comprehension

By looking at oral and silent comprehension scores across several grade levels, we can determine if the reader's comprehension during either oral or silent reading is particularly weak or strong, and whether such patterns are age-appropriate. We can also look at responses to the different types of comprehension questions within or across grade levels to see whether the student has particular strengths or weaknesses in the comprehension skills required by the questions.

If readers consistently demonstrate better comprehension after oral reading and lower comprehension scores after reading silently, we can conclude that they need to hear themselves say the words aloud to understand what they are reading. Such readers translate, or *recode*, print into speech and derive meaning from the spoken words. This is typical of many beginning readers, especially those whose early reading instruction has been primarily oral.

When they read silently, they sometimes lose their places because their voices help "anchor" them in the print. It is not surprising when they show consistently better oral than silent comprehension. However, when an older student reads this way, we are concerned. Fluent silent reading for meaning is needed to keep up with the amount of reading that is required in upper grades.

Readers beyond the beginning stage can read faster silently than orally. Oral reading speed is limited by how clearly we can speak; about 200 words per minute is very rapid speech, and even fluent oral readers do not read aloud that fast. However, fluent silent reading may vary from 200 to 400 or more words per minute depending on the difficulty and familiarity of the material and the reader's purpose. Fluent adult readers read challenging material silently at about 250 words per minute (Perfetti, 1985), and they read easy interesting material for pleasure even faster, up to 600 words per minute. By the end of second grade, fluent readers read at about 90 words per minute, and rates increase by about 20 words per minute each year until sixth grade, when fluent readers read at about 180 words per minute (McCormick, 2003). The reading demands of the upper grades require that students shift from oral reading to fluent silent reading for meaning.

Somewhere between second and fourth grade, most readers begin this shift toward more silent reading and characteristically show better silent comprehension. This is developmentally appropriate; it certainly does not indicate that these older students show an oral reading weakness or that they should begin a lot of remedial oral reading. On the contrary, in the upper grades oral reading should be deemphasized while silent reading is emphasized.

Comprehension Skill Patterns

Some readers have consistent difficulty with a particular kind of comprehension question. For example, one might have little difficulty with questions requiring direct recall of explicitly stated information but have much more difficulty with inferences, main ideas, or vocabulary items. If we go back to the comprehension questions following the reading passages and consider each kind of question, we can see whether there was a particular type of question with which a student had consistent difficulty. Figure 2.11 shows the major types of questions that usually appear in IRIs.

By systematically looking across grade levels we can see what, if any, pattern emerges. Was there a type of question that repeatedly gave the student difficulty at different levels or one that the student consistently answered correctly? Looking for individual patterns in comprehension responses allows us to design appropriate comprehension activities for students according to their individual needs.

However, we must be certain that the questions really tap the comprehension skills that they say they do. IRI questions are notoriously hard to classify. Even experienced teachers attempting to classify comprehension questions by type often classified questions quite differently from the authors of a particular IRI (Gipe, 2006).

Unquestioning acceptance of IRI question categories, or of all IRI questions as good questions, is unwise. Comprehension patterns can often be discerned, however, and helpful teaching strategies devised from these judgments, if teachers continually use critical judgment. Don't take either the quality of questions or the way the author clas-

---

Literal Comprehension (Answers to questions explicitly stated in passage)

Topic:	What event was this story about?
	What was this passage mostly about?
Main Idea:	What was the most important thing the author said about dogs?
	What was the most important information in this passage?
Important Detail:	What kind of animal was Nitwit?
	What did Bob do when he got home?
Sequence:	What happened after Jill heard the window break?
	Where did the children go first?
Characterization:	What did Ms. Willis do that showed she was angry?
	How did Bruce act when he saw Jamie again?
Re-Inspection:	Find the sentence that describes Ben's new bike and read it to me.
	Find the place in the story where the children began to argue and read it out loud.

Interpretation and Judgment (Answers to questions not explicitly stated in passage)

Inference:	Why do you think Jim spoke roughly to the dog?
	What makes you believe Cathy might enjoy flying?
Vocabulary:	What did Rita mean when she said "I'm simply green"?
	What is a "chopper" in this story?
Prediction:	What could happen if the delivery boy loses the package?
	If Shana runs away, where might she go?

FIGURE 2.11   *Sample Comprehension Questions*

sified them on faith. Read the passages and each of the questions, and consider carefully whether you think the questions are appropriately labeled by type. Then, if you discern a consistent pattern in a student's response to particular question types, you have a working hypothesis about the student's needs.

Begin instruction based on your hypothesis that a student needs practice in particular areas, but continue to evaluate on the basis of how the student responds to that instruction. Only further teaching will reveal whether your working hypotheses were accurate.

Patterns in Listening Comprehension

If students achieve 70 percent or better on the comprehension questions after listening to a passage read aloud by the examiner, we assume that they can understand similar concepts and vocabulary when they hear it, although they cannot read that level of material for themselves. We refer to the highest grade level at which the student had 70 percent or better as the student's *listening comprehension level.* This level is important because it helps us to determine what we can expect this student to achieve; thus, the listening level makes it possible to set reasonable instructional goals.

As we discussed earlier in this chapter, most students who are not fluent, mature readers can listen to someone else reading aloud and understand material that they cannot yet read successfully. Most of them, especially the younger ones, are still learning and developing as readers while they have been competent listeners and language users for a lot longer. Therefore, their listening levels are somewhat above their instructional reading levels, which is predictable, for it shows that they are not yet able to read as well as they can think.

Some youngsters will have instructional reading and listening comprehension levels that are the same. Material too difficult for them to read is also too difficult for them to understand on an auditory basis. This is fine. What it shows is that they are reading just as well as they can and that at this present time, there is not much room for improvement. These students are reading right at their potential, using all their ability to read as well as they can. They need support and further instruction, but if they are poor readers, they will probably make steady but not spectacular gains in reading. The listening comprehension level represents a sort of overall goal in reading improvement.

The listening comprehension level is dynamic, not fixed. As children grow older and have more experiences, they can understand more difficult material because they have gained knowledge and experiences to which new information and experiences can be related. The average 7-year-old can listen to and understand stories that are appropriate for second or third graders and understand them, but ninth-grade material would be too difficult conceptually. By the time the child is 12 or 13, however, ninth-grade materials might well be comprehensible because vocabulary, store of concepts, and experiences have grown in those intervening years. The listening level represents an estimate of *present* functioning. Establishing a student's listening level once and using it as an ongoing standard, however, is no more appropriate than expecting last year's instructional level to be the same next year.

Here are three examples, all second graders:

Jenny

Jenny's listening comprehension level is late second grade. Since she is in second grade, we infer that her verbal intelligence is roughly average for her age and that she has the necessary concepts and vocabulary to learn to read second-grade material successfully, although presently, she has a first-grade instructional level. Although her instructional level is low, she can improve her reading with appropriate instruction and support.

Matt

Matt has a listening comprehension level of sixth grade. He has the concepts and vocabulary to listen to and understand very advanced material, and he is obviously very bright. In spite of his potential, he is achieving at grade level and has an instructional level of late second grade. Therefore, his achievement is average for his grade, although he has the potential for higher achievement. The finding that Matt is not performing at his full potential is not necessarily negative. If he is comfortable, motivated, and interested, there is no need for concern. If he appears to be apathetic, bored, or frustrated, then he certainly needs greater intellectual challenge.

Sandy

Sandy has an instructional level of first grade, and his listening level is also first grade. Although Sandy's achievement is below grade level, it is in line with his present potential. Sandy might be a slow learner or of below-average verbal intelligence; he might have learned to read later than others, or he might have a limited background of experience with print. At any rate, his performance and potential appear to be in line at the present. Sandy needs much support and instruction, and as he becomes a more proficient reader, his listening level will increase. This in turn will make further reading improvement possible.

Analyzing Word Recognition in Isolation

As we discussed in earlier sections, the Word Recognition Inventory, consisting of graded lists of words, is used to assess students' automatic recognition of words at each level, as well as some aspects of word analysis and decoding. Since words appear in isolation rather than in context, the student's use of context and word meaning as a cue to recognition is not assessed with this device. The WRI is administered by showing each word for a very brief exposure, using either a file card or a card with a window cut in it, to briefly reveal each word. Words that are not recognized immediately or that are misidentified are shown for a longer, untimed exposure.

The student's immediate sight word recognition is assessed by the Automatic, or timed exposure, portion of the instrument. A large sight vocabulary forms the basis of fluent, effective reading. A reader who has a good sight vocabulary of common, frequently occurring words will usually score around 90 percent or better on automatic recognition of words, at least at the lower grade levels. At any grade level, scores much below 70 percent indicate that the student probably does not recognize enough of the words to read fluently and effectively at that level of difficulty.

The responses in the Decoded, or untimed, columns give us information about the phonic and word analysis strategies that a student can use when he does not recognize a word immediately. Students who typically correct an initial error when decoding the word show us that though their sight recognition is weak, their decoding skills are solid. Students who make unsuccessful attempts to decode unrecognized words but who typically preserve the initial consonant or blend sounds in their attempts show us that they have a grasp of initial sounds but may be weak in decoding middle or final sounds. By looking for patterns in both correct and incorrect responses, we can begin to determine what word attack skills need to be reviewed or taught.

Supplementing Informal Assessments

A number of other assessment procedures and devices may be used periodically to supplement informal measures and explore particular areas of students' reading in detail. These include procedures that help us to obtain information about how readers attempt to construct meaning from text and tests of word recognition and decoding.

Helping Students to Become Strategic Readers

We know that effective readers are actively involved in the process of comprehending what they read. They use strategies such as previewing the text, creating predictions about the content, self-questioning, summarizing at various points in the story, and continually monitoring their own understanding as they read (Eilers & Pinkley, 2006). Effective readers do not simply take in meanings found in text; they actively construct meaning for themselves by interacting with the text, reviewing what is already known, and integrating new information with prior information (Pressley et al., 2001; Schmitt, 2001; Yopp & Yopp, 2004).

Metacomprehension Strategies. *Metacomprehension* refers to readers' awareness of their own comprehension during reading and their ability to self-monitor comprehension. "Researchers agree that awareness *and* monitoring of one's comprehension processes are critically important aspects of skilled reading," wrote Mokhtari and Reichard (2002). Metacomprehension is of tremendous importance when the text being read is nonfiction. "Because expository text is so central to educational practice (especially in science and social studies instruction), the ability of students to monitor their own understanding of these texts seems very important" (Wiley, Griffin, & Thiede, 2005).

When readers activate what they already know and integrate new information in ways that make sense to them, and when they select and use appropriate strategies to help them understand and remember what they read, they are becoming strategic readers. When readers fail to use prior information or lack sufficient prior information to make sense of new information, when they overrely on word attack skills at the expense of context, or when they fail to monitor their own understanding, they are not making progress toward becoming strategic readers. They may need a program of instruction that teaches them how and when to use effective strategies as they read.

Schmitt (1990) developed the Metacomprehension Strategy Index (MSI), a 25-item multiple-choice questionnaire that teachers can use to evaluate students' awareness of reading strategies in middle elementary grades and beyond. The MSI measures awareness of predicting and verifying, previewing, purpose setting, self-questioning, drawing from background knowledge, and applying "fix-up" strategies (p. 455). Students respond to items by indicating what would be good strategies to use before, during, and after reading. This is an example item (p. 459):

Before I begin reading, it's a good idea to:

a. Think of what I already know about the things I see in the pictures.
b. See how many pages are in the story.
c. Choose the best part of the story to read again.
d. Read the story aloud to someone.

After scoring students' questionnaires, you can determine which strategies students are aware of and which strategies students need to learn and practice using. Mokhtari and Reichard (2002) developed a similar self-reporting instrument, the Metacognitive Awareness of Reading Strategies Inventory (MARSI) for students in sixth through twelfth grades whose instructional reading level is at least fifth grade. Students agree or disagree with statements like, "I think about what I know to help me understand what I'm reading," "I try to get back on track when I lose concentration," "I adjust my reading speed according to what I'm reading," and "I decide what to read closely and what to ignore." (p. 253) Mokhtari and Reichard identified three strategy subscales or factors: Global Reading Strategies ("I have a purpose in mind when I read"), Problem-Solving ("When text becomes difficult, I begin to pay closer attention to what I'm reading"), and Support Reading Strategies ("I ask myself questions I like to have answered in the text").

Since both these devices are self-report instruments, students might say they use particular strategies but in reality fail to use them; "awareness of strategies does not guarantee that students actually use them" (Mokhtari & Reichard, 2002, p. 249). Both instruments appear to provide useful information about students' strategic awareness when combined with other diagnostic information.

Think-Aloud Strategies. Thinking aloud during reading can help students' comprehension (Cunningham & Allington, 2003; Lloyd, 2004). Readers' verbal self-reports about their thinking processes during reading, called *think-alouds,* can be used to obtain information about how readers construct meaning from text (Laing & Kamhi, 2002; Oster, 2001; Wade, 1990).

During a think-aloud procedure, a reader reads portions of a passage, one or a few sentences at a time. After each portion is read, the reader is asked to tell what the passage is about, what is happening in the passage, or what clues the reader is using to understand the passage. Nondirective probes such as "Tell me more about that" or "Why do you think so?" are used to extend the reader's responses.

The procedure may be tape-recorded and the record analyzed to determine whether the reader generates tentative hypotheses about the topic, uses information from the text to support hypotheses, relates information in the text to prior knowledge, integrates new with old information, and deals with conflicts between new and old information. Strategic behaviors such as rereading and indications of anxiety or uncertainty are noted by the examiner.

Box 2.3 shows the procedure for administering and interpreting a think-aloud.

Word Recognition and Phonics Tests

Decoding ability is often assessed by asking readers to decode nonsense words such as *dap, rike, faught, blunch,* and so forth. The validity of such measures is questionable since such assessments are probably the only time children are ever expected to read nonsense words. Many children are confused by such a task and attempt to read nonsense words as real words, believing that their teachers would never ask them to read something that makes no sense.

An alternative to nonsense word decoding assessments is the Names Test (Cunningham, 1990), a list of first and last names of fictitious students. Each name is "fully decodable given commonly taught vowel rules and/or analogy approaches to decoding" (p. 125).

A student is asked to pretend to be a teacher reading a class list of names as if she were taking attendance, a familiar task to most students. A name is counted correct if all syllables are pronounced correctly, regardless of where the student places the stress or accent (for example, YO-lan-da or Yo-LAN-da). Errors are noted phonetically and analyzed to reveal what phonic patterns the student needs to review or learn. The Names Test is shown in Figure 2.12.

Some commercial tests that are intended to assess mastery of phonics skills and decoding are available. Usually, they consist of letters and letter groups to identify and sound out, real words and *pseudo-words* (nonsense words like *mif, drake,* or *faught*) to sound out using common phonic generalizations, and letters-plus-word-stems (like *p - in* or *s - ate*) to combine, or blend, into pronounceable words.

Some commercial IRIs include separate phonics inventories. Some assess phonics knowledge by decoding nonsense words, while others assess the early phonemic awareness of emergent and beginning readers. For example, the Stieglitz Informal

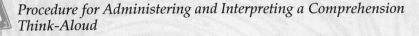

BOX 2.3   *Procedure for Administering and Interpreting a Comprehension Think-Aloud*

I. PREPARING THE TEXT

Choose a short passage (expository or narrative) written to meet the following criteria:

A. The text should be from 80 to 200 words in length, depending on the reader's age and reading ability.

B. The text should be new to the reader, but on a topic that is familiar. (Determine whether the reader has relevant background knowledge by means of an interview or questionnaire administered at a session prior to this assessment.)

C. The text should be at the reader's instructional level, which can be determined by use of an informal reading inventory. Passages at this level are most likely to be somewhat challenging while not overwhelming readers with word identification problems.

D. The topic sentence should appear last, and the passage should be untitled. Altering the text in this way will elicit information about the reader's strategies for making sense of the passage and inferring the topic.

E. The text should be divided into segments of one to four sentences each.

II. ADMINISTERING THE THINK-ALOUD PROCEDURE

A. Tell the reader that he or she will be reading a story in short segments of one or more sentences.

B. Tell the reader that after reading each section, he or she will be asked to tell what the story is about.

C. Have the student read a segment aloud. After each segment is read, ask the reader to tell what is happening, followed by nondirective probe questions as necessary. The questions should encourage the reader to generate hypotheses (what do you think this is about?) and to describe what he or she based the hypotheses on (what clues in the story helped you?).

D. Continue the procedure until the entire passage is read. Then ask the reader to retell the entire passage in his or her own words. (The reader may reread the story first.)

E. The examiner might also ask the reader to find the most important sentence(s) in the passage.

F. The session should be tape-recorded and transcribed. The examiner should also record observations of the child's behaviors.

III. ANALYZING RESULTS

Ask the following questions when analyzing the transcript:

A. Does the reader generate hypotheses?

B. Does he/she support hypotheses with information from the passage?

C. What information from the text does the reader use?

BOX 2.3   *(Continued)*

    D. Does he or she relate material in the text to background knowledge or previous experience?

    E. Does the reader integrate new information with the schema he or she has already activated?

    F. What does the reader do if there is information that conflicts with the schema he or she has generated?

    G. At what point does the reader recognize what the story is about?

    H. How does the reader deal with unfamiliar words?

    I. What kinds of integration strategies does the reader use (e.g., visualization)?

    J. How confident is the reader of his or her hypotheses?

    K. What other observations can be made about the reader's behavior, strategies, etc.?

Source: Wade, S. (1990, March) "Using Think Alouds to Assess Comprehension" from *The Reading Teacher,* March, *43*(7), 345. Reprinted with permission of the International Reading Association.

Reading Inventory (Stieglitz, 2002) includes a test of phonemic awareness with these four subtests:

a. **Rhyming Words,** in which the student listens to pairs of words and tells if they rhyme or not; for example, "Do *fun* and *sun* rhyme?"

b. **Blending Speech Sounds into Words,** in which the student listens to the examiner say words by pronouncing each phoneme separately, and tells what the word is; for example, "If I say *s-o,* what word am I saying?"

c. **Isolating Speech Sounds,** in which the student listens to a word and pronounces a single phoneme from it; for example, "What is the sound at the beginning of this word? *jar*"

d. **Complete Segmentation of Phonemes,** in which the student listens to a word and pronounces each of its phonemes separately; for example, "What sounds do you hear in the word *five?*"

Tests like these may be useful for screening purposes since they are fairly quick to administer and do not require analyzing the student's WRI responses. But this analysis helps teachers to develop the diagnostic skills and judgment they need to fully explore students' abilities. Commercial decoding tests are adequate for screening purposes but should not replace careful study of what a child can do.

The Names Test

Jay Conway	Wendy Swain
Tim Cornell	Glen Spencer
Chuck Hoke	Fred Sherwood
Yolanda Clark	Flo Thornton
Kimberly Blake	Dee Skidmore
Roberta Slade	Grace Brewster
Homer Preston	Ned Westmoreland
Gus Quincy	Ron Smitherman
Cindy Sampson	Troy Whitlock
Chester Wright	Vance Middleton
Ginger Yale	Zane Anderson
Patrick Tweed	Bernard Pendergraph
Stanley Shaw	

Preparing the Instrument

1. Type or print legibly the 25 names on a sheet of paper or card stock. Make sure the print size is appropriate for the age or grade level of the students being tested.
2. For students who might perceive reading an entire list of names as being too formidable, type or print the names on index cards, so they can be read individually.
3. Prepare a protocol (scoring) sheet. Do this by typing the list of names in a column and following each name with a blank line to be used for recording a student's responses.

Administering the Names Test

1. Administer the Names Test individually. Select a quiet, distraction-free location.
2. Explain to the student that she or he is to pretend to be a teacher who must read a list of names of students in the class. Direct the student to read the names as if taking attendance.
3. Have the student read the entire list. Inform the student that you will not be able to help with difficult names and encourage him or her to "make a guess if you are not sure." This way you will have sufficient responses for analysis.
4. Write a check on the protocol sheet for each name read correctly. Write phonetic spellings for names that are mispronounced.

Scoring and Interpreting the Names Test

1. Count a word correct if all syllables are pronounced correctly regardless of where the student places the accent. For example, either Yó/lan/da or Yo/lan´/da would be acceptable.
2. For words where the vowel pronunciation depends on which syllables the consonant is placed with, count them correct for either pronunciation. For example, either Ho/mer or Hom/er would be acceptable.
3. Count the number of names read correctly and analyze those mispronounced, looking for patterns indicative of decoding strengths and weaknesses.

FIGURE 2.12 *The Names Test*

Source: Cunningham, P. M. (1990, October). "The Names Test: A quick assessment of decoding ability" from *The Reading Teacher* 44(2), 124–129. Reprinted with permission of the International Reading Association.

Summary

This chapter discusses the assessment of student performance based on informed teacher judgment. Assessments designed for instruction include teacher-made tests and procedures, observations, interviews, informal diagnostic procedures, and so forth.

Informal diagnostic procedures make possible *qualitative* analysis of reading behaviors as well as use of *quantitative* scores. They are useful in determining a reader's *independent, instructional,* and *frustration* reading levels and reading strength and needs.

An *Informal Reading Inventory (IRI)* is individually administered for these purposes. IRIs consist of text passages for oral and silent reading at consecutive grade levels from primer through high school and corresponding comprehension questions. During oral reading, *miscues,* or divergences from the text, are recorded, counted to determine a reader's oral reading fluency, and analyzed to reveal word recognition strategies and use of context. Responses to comprehension questions are used to determine reading levels and reveal comprehension skills and strategies. *Retellings* may be used in addition to questions. When the frustration reading level is reached, subsequent passages may be read aloud to the reader to determine his *listening comprehension* level, an indicator of potential for reading improvement.

An informal *Word Recognition Inventory (WRI)* consisting of graded lists of individual words may be used to assess sight vocabulary and decoding skills out of context. Sight recognition is assessed by exposing individual words for a very brief moment, and phonic and structural analysis skills are assessed by reexamining missed words in an untimed exposure.

Think-alouds, or students' verbal self-reports of their thinking during reading, may be used to assess students' use of strategies and attempts to construct meaning from text. *Supplementary phonics tests* may be used to further study the reader's decoding skills.

MyLabSchool is a collection of online tools for your success in this course, your licensure exams, and your teaching career. Visit www.mylabschool.com to access the following:

- Online Study Guide
- Video cases from real classrooms
- Help with your research papers using Research Navigator
- Career Center with resources for:
    - Praxis exams and licensure preparation
    - Professional portfolio development
    - Job search and interview techniques
    - Lesson planning

References

Beaver, J. (2006). *Developmental reading assessment 2.* Boston: Pearson Learning Group.

Betts, E. A. (1941, June). Reading problems at the intermediate grade level. *Elementary School Journal, 40,* 737–746.

Betts, E. A. (1957). *Foundations of reading instruction.* New York: American Book.

Clay, M. (2000). *Running records for classroom teachers.* Portsmouth, NH: Heinemann.

Cunningham, P. (1990). The names test: A quick assessment of decoding ability. *The Reading Teacher, 44*(2), 124–129.

Cunningham, P., & Allington, R. (2003). *Classrooms that work: They can all read and write.* Boston: Allyn & Bacon.

Eilers, L. H., & Pinkley, C. (2006). Metacognitive strategies help students to comprehend all text. *Reading Improvement, 43*(1), 13–30.

Gipe, J. P. (2006). *Multiple paths to literacy assessment and differentiated instruction for diverse learners, K-12* (6th ed.). Upper Saddle River, NJ: Pearson.

Goodman, Y. M., & Marek, A. M. (1996). *Retrospective miscue analysis: Revaluing readers and reading.* Katonah, NY: Owen.

Goodman, Y. M., Watson, D. J., & Burke, C. L. (2005). *Reading miscue inventory* (2nd ed.). Katonah, NY: Owen.

Johns, J. L., & Magliari, A. M. (1989). Informal reading inventories: Are the Betts criteria the best criteria? *Reading Improvement, 26*(2), 124–132.

Laing, S. P., & Kamhi, A. G. (2002). The use of think-aloud protocols to compare inferencing abilities in average and below-average readers. *Journal of Learning Disabilities, 35*(5), 436–448.

Leslie, L., & Caldwell, J. (2006). *Qualitative reading inventory-4.* Boston: Pearson/Allyn & Bacon.

Lloyd, S. L. (2004). Using comprehension strategies as a springboard for student talk: After teacher modeling of read-aloud and guided reading strategies, student-driven conversations "take off" with questioning in literature circles. *Journal of Adolescent and Adult Literacy, 48*(2), 114–124.

McCormick, S. (2003). *Instructing students who have literacy problems.* Upper Saddle River, NJ: Pearson.

McWhorter, J. (2000). *Spreading the word: Dialect and language in America.* Portsmouth, NH: Heinemann.

Mokhtari, K., & Reichard, C. A. (2002). Assessing students' metacognitive awareness of reading strategies. *Journal of Educational Psychology, 94*(2), 249–259.

Moore, R. A., & Gilles, C. (2005). *Reading conversations: Retrospective miscue analysis with struggling readers, grades 4–12.* Portsmouth, NH: Heinemann.

Oster, L. (2001). Using the think-aloud for reading instruction. *The Reading Teacher, 55*(1), 64–69.

Perfetti, C. A. (1985). *Reading ability.* New York: Oxford University Press.

Pressley, M. R., Wharton-McDonald, R., Allington, R., Block, C. C., Morrow, L., Tracey, D., et al. (2001). A study of effective first-grade literacy instruction. *Scientific Studies of Reading, 5,* 35–58.

Rubenstein, H., Kender, J. P., & Mace, F. C. (1988). Do tests penalize readers for short term memory? *Journal of Reading, 32*(1), 4–10.

Schmitt, M. C. (1990). A questionnaire to measure children's awareness of strategic reading processes. *The Reading Teacher, 43*(7), 454–461.

Schmitt, M. C. (2001). The development of children's strategic processing in reading recovery. *Reading Psychology, 22*(2), 129–151.

Seattle Public Schools. (2006). *Developmental Reading Assessment, grades K-3: Guide to administering and scoring the DRA.* Seattle: Seattle Public Schools.

Stenner, J. (1999). *Matching students to text: The targeted reader.* New York: Scholastic Center for Literacy and Learning.

Stieglitz, E. (2002). *The Stieglitz Informal Reading Inventory: Assessing reading behaviors from emergent to advanced levels* (3rd ed.). Boston: Allyn & Bacon.

Wade, S. E. (1990). Using think alouds to assess comprehension. *The Reading Teacher, 43*(7), 442–453.

Wilde, S. (2000). *Miscue analysis made easy: Building on student strengths.* Portsmouth, NH: Heinemann.

Wiley, J., Griffin, T. D., & Thiede, K. W. (2005). Putting the comprehension in metacomprehension. *Journal of General Psychology, 134*(4), 408–421.

Yopp, R. R., & Yopp, H. K. (2004). Preview-predict-confirm: Think aloud about the language and content of informational text. *The Reading Teacher 58*(1), 79–83.

Ongoing Assessments

Chapter Outline

*C*arly Adams, a fourth-grade teacher, keeps an assessment folder for each student in her class. Each student's folder contains different kinds of assessment information collected over the course of the year. It is early October, and Carly is preparing for a conference with Ben's parents. During the conference, she will explain how Ben's growth and progress have been assessed this fall and will answer his parents' questions about assessment results and implications. At various points during the coming year, Carly will add new assessment information and will be able to show Ben's parents how his progress has been documented. At another formal conference in the spring, she will share end-of-year assessment results including his achievement of state-mandated goals for all students in his grade statewide.

A review of Ben's various assessments will help Carly to be fully informed for the conference. Also, it allows us a chance to peer over her shoulder, so to speak, and consider the kinds of literacy-related assessments that are typically used with students, both formal and informal, periodic and ongoing.

First, Carly scans a sheet that contains all of Ben's standardized achievement test scores. On the reading section of the test given at the end of third grade, Ben's scores fell in the 30th percentile, with subtest scores ranging from the 16th to the 41st percentile. Carly looks at this sheet first, but it is not the most important; in fact, she considers these standardized test scores to be among the *least* informative to her in teaching Ben. However, she reviews them because she knows that standardized test data have great importance to her principal, as well as to Ben's parents.

These results indicate that Ben is functioning significantly below average in reading in comparison to others of his age and grade in the norm group and in the local group being tested at the same time; in fact, they show that Ben performed as well or better than only about 30 percent of other third graders taking the test, while about 70 percent performed better than Ben. His performance was also below the *mean,* or average, score which was at about the 50th percentile. In addition, Ben failed to meet state-required standards in reading and writing at the end of third grade.

Carly next turns to other informal assessments she gave Ben during the first weeks of this year. These include

- *Running records,* or annotated copies of material Ben has read aloud, with miscues and other reading behaviors noted.
- An *Informal Reading Inventory* given at the beginning of the year, showing Ben's oral and silent reading rates, oral reading accuracy, types of miscues that occurred, and comprehension after oral and silent reading of passages at successive grade levels.

- *Observation records,* or notes Carly took while she observed Ben working in a variety of learning situations.
- *Cloze procedures,* or reading passages with words systematically deleted and replaced by blanks to be filled in by the reader.
- *Spelling records* showing patterns and high-utility words Ben has mastered and the dates they were successfully tested.
- *A list of books read* so far this year.
- *A writing progress inventory,* showing Ben's progress in using various forms and voices in writing.
- *A portfolio* that Ben has just begun, containing work samples he chose that show what he is learning and work he is proud of.

Carly Adams's choice of assessments demonstrates her philosophy of reading and teaching. Her use of different measures and samples of reading and reading-related behaviors shows her belief that reading is not a single operation, nor is reading the same each time it occurs, but changes according to the material being read and the reader's purposes. In Carly's use of multiple sources, information from one source builds on, or is contrasted by, information from other data sources. The result is a multidimensional picture of the student's reading performance in a variety of situations and with different kinds of materials: an authentic, dynamic portrait of a reader.

Similarly, we can infer that Carly holds an *interactive view* of the reading process; that is, she believes that reading is a complex process involving the coordination of a variety of skills, processes, and operations occurring in concert with one another. This is in direct contrast to the dated, but still widely held, *summative view,* that reading is the result of mastery of a set of skills that can be learned and practiced in isolation from each other, but sum up to effective reading when each has been mastered.

We can illustrate this summative view of reading by comparing it to learning to swim. One could be taught each separate operation in swimming and practice each operation in isolation. For example, one could learn the arm movements necessary to do the front crawl and practice them while standing on the side of the pool, then lying prone on a bench, and finally while standing in shallow water. One could then be taught and practice turning the head to the side and breathing in, then turning the head down and blowing out, again first on the side of the pool, then standing or crouching in water, and so forth. But *at no point* would one be swimming. Even more important, one could master each and every separate skill, demonstrate mastery of each on the side of the pool and while standing or crouching in the water, and then *fail to swim* when trying to put the skills together in one operation.

Anyone who swims can attest that swimming is more than the sum of its separate skills. So it is with reading. Carly Adams knows that reading is not just the sum of all its parts, but the result of the *interaction* of all the necessary operations, in concert with each other, combined with what the reader knows and brings to the reading, his or her motivation and purposes for the reading, and the complexity of the text being read, in authentic (not test-like) reading situations. So when preparing an assessment picture of a reader, she prefers to use a variety of behavior samples in real reading acts, combined with her informed observations of the reader in authentic learning situations, to strengthen and support the instructional decisions she makes. And she makes sure that the data she collects are gathered at regular, frequent intervals so that an accurate record of the reader's progress is developed. Without the ongoing assessments that Carly provides, the picture of Ben's achievement would be one-sided and unnecessarily grim.

The administration, scoring, and interpretation of IRIs was described in the preceding chapter. In this chapter, we will discuss some kinds of informal, ongoing assessments, including student portfolios, that will help you compile a complete picture of students' literacy achievement.

Running Records

Running records of students' oral reading are one of the most widely used ongoing assessments teachers use. Running records are transcripts of reading material that is at a comfortable level of difficulty (the *instructional level*), with the reader's oral reading errors or *miscues*, correction attempts, comments about the text, and other reading behaviors marked using a standardized system of marks (Clay, 1993, 2000, 2005). Taking a running record is very much like marking an oral reading selection in an IRI, described in Chapter 2. Running records are made periodically to show the reader's mastery of successively difficult texts, types of miscues made, strategies used in figuring out unfamiliar words, and comprehension (Fountas & Pinnell, 1996). Many teachers find running records helpful in documenting a reader's progress at systematic intervals because they are taken during authentic reading tasks without interrupting the flow of a lesson. Dated copies of running records in a reader's assessment file provide concrete documentation of her progress.

Running Records to Document Progress

Running records were first used in conjunction with Reading Recovery, an early intervention program designed by Marie Clay (1993, 2005; Shanahan & Barr, 1995; Swartz & Klein, 2002). Clay devised running records as a way of keeping track of a reader's use of key *strategies* and growth toward higher levels of difficulty of text on a daily basis. A Reading Recovery teacher takes a running record of the reader's second reading of a new book, done the day after the child has read the new book independently for the first time. Since a new book is introduced daily in a Reading Recovery lesson, running records are taken daily to document the child's progress.

In the years since Reading Recovery's introduction, running records have become widely used in other remedial and tutorial programs and during everyday group instruction. For example, during a guided reading lesson the teacher takes a running record of one student reading yesterday's new book while the others listen; in this way, each child in the group is assessed about once a week. Other teachers prefer to take a running record every few weeks; for older students, this generally provides sufficient information about reading progress without becoming burdensome for the teacher.

In our own classrooms, we take running records weekly for remedial students who are reading short, easy materials; and monthly or less often for developmental readers who are reading longer texts such as chapter books and novels. Figure 3.1 shows an example of a running record.

Running Records and Text Difficulty

Another important use of running records is to determine whether readers are self-selecting materials that are too easy, too difficult, or just right. Ideally, students self-select a lot of what they read. Self-selection helps children to read more and develop literary tastes and preferences, but it may also mean that what they read is not challenging enough to spur their development.

It's understandable why students would select easy books: Reading them is usually very enjoyable because the reader doesn't have to work very hard at it. Consider your own and other adults' self-selected pleasure reading materials. If you are like most adults, you would rather read popular best-selling fiction and nonfiction than the "good-for-you" novels that your English teachers assigned you.

Children are no different. Leave it entirely up to them, and they'll generally choose the easy, the familiar, and the popular over material that might make them think, wonder, or struggle the least bit. But texts that are a stretch for us help us to become better readers, thinkers, and communicators. Issues related to text difficulty will be discussed further in the section "Monitoring Types and Difficulty of Texts Read" in this chapter.

Teachers can use running records to check whether what students are choosing is very easy for them. If students are reading material orally for the first time (i.e., "reading it cold") at close to 100 percent accuracy with few miscues, then the material represents their *independent level.* You may recall from Chapter 2 that the independent level represents reading that is easy. Some reading at the independent level is good for you, but a steady diet of it will not help you to grow as a reader.

If students are reading at around 90 percent or greater accuracy, making a few miscues that either make sense or are spontaneously corrected, then the material represents their *instructional level.* Recall that the instructional level represents material that is comfortably challenging. This is ideal for growth in reading. It is easy enough to be read without a struggle but not so easy that it can be done with the mind on automatic pilot.

If students are reading at much below 90 percent accuracy and their miscues generally don't make sense, or if they can't correct their miscues or don't try to correct, then we deduce that the material is at the *frustration level.* Reading at this level is unpleasant and discouraging; little is learned from the reading, but negative attitudes about reading might quickly develop. You might want to review the descriptions of these functional reading levels at the beginning of Chapter 2.

2 "I'm sorry," said the dog. "I don't know how to get

home."

1 "Are you lost?" asked a kind elephant.

"Yes, we are," said the goldfish.

"Then I will take you home," said the elephant.

"This is very kind of you," said the dog.

1 "It is fun to go places and see things," said the

elephant. "But it is good to go home, too."

"Yes, it is," said the dog.

Before long the dog and her goldfish were home.

"That was so much fun," said the goldfish.

"Where will we go now?"

1 "Now we will sit at home by the fire," said the

dog. "That is what I want to do."

"Anything to keep you happy," said the goldfish.

"You are very kind," said the dog.

Scoring for Oral Reading:

# of Errors	0	1	2	3	4	5	6	7+
%	100	99	98	97	97	96	95	

Independent   Instructional   Frustration
                                             Go to next lower level

FIGURE 3.1 *A Running Record*

ASSESSMENT

In a traditional or formal approach to assessment, "tests rule." That is, tests are used to measure the product or outcome of instruction and to compare students to others. While test results have their uses in comparing groups of students to others, they are of relatively little use in helping teachers make informed decisions about instruction and individual students. Often, careful observation of students is necessary to document what individuals are attempting, achieving, and struggling with.

Observations of Reading Behaviors and Strategies

Classroom-centered observations help teachers make instructional decisions and help parents and students better understand student achievement. In this model the teacher, rather than the test, is the tool. The informed teacher is ideally placed to observe and collect information about students continuously, unobtrusively, and interactively, and to make sense of classroom events (McCormick, 2003; Owocki & Goodman, 2002). But observation doesn't just happen; it must be planned and carried out systematically and accurately, or valuable opportunities to learn about students will be lost. In the following sections you will learn about various ways to carry out effective student observations.

Observing Readers

The classroom teacher is in the best possible position to observe and record students' daily interactions with text. These observations can be very helpful in communicating to parents, completing report cards and progress reports, talking with students about their progress, and meeting instructional needs.

The lists that follow show many of the behaviors, both positive and negative, that we observe in our work with students. You can add other behaviors you observe.

Physical Behaviors

- Points to words accurately during reading (for beginners).
- Frequently loses place during silent or oral reading.
- Reads quickly; appears not to look carefully at print; skips large portions of text; typically tries to finish before anyone else.
- Appears to be very absorbed in reading for pleasure; is not distracted by environmental activity during reading.
- Does not read during sustained reading; leafs through text, draws, puts head down, looks out the window, annoys others, etc.
- Vision appears uncomfortable during reading; squints, turns head to the side, closes one eye, holds text closer or farther away from eyes than normal.

Cognitive Behaviors

- Predicts easily about material to be read, or rarely offers a prediction.
- Recalls directly stated information easily or with difficulty.
- Demonstrates understanding of cause-and-effect relationships or little understanding.
- Produces inferences, conclusions, applications easily, with difficulty, or rarely.
- Offers personal opinions and/or experiences related to the reading.
- Uses background knowledge or prior information to understand text.
- Responds critically to aspects of plot, characters, author's style, illustrations.
- Draws comparisons between this material and other texts.
- Expresses enjoyment of an activity or text or pride in success.

Reading Strategies Observed

- Uses one or more strategies spontaneously before seeking assistance or rarely attempts a strategy before seeking help.
- Uses only one strategy exclusively (this is usually decoding or sounding out or, less often, contextual guessing).
- Tries another strategy when the first attempt isn't successful.
- Uses context or sense making and decoding together.
- Reruns or rereads to get past a difficult part or to self-check.
- Indicates with words or gestures when reading doesn't sound right or doesn't make sense ("What?" "Huh?" "Wait a minute," a puzzled look, etc.).
- Attempts self-correction, whether successful or not.
- Effectively uses text aids like headings, bold print, charts, maps, tables, and summaries.

Recording Observations

One way to keep track of your observations while ensuring that you observe each student systematically is to make copies of an observation record sheet marked with a square for each student like the one in Figure 3.2. The squares should be large enough to accommodate a sticky note. Each square is labeled with a student's name. Observations are noted on the sticky notes that are then attached to the student's square. As additional observations are made, the notes are stacked one atop the other. Many observations can be kept on one sheet, and there is no need to transfer your comments to another sheet. A drawback of this system is that sticky notes may fall off.

Another way to record observations is to write them directly on a calendar page with a student's name in each weekday square; the month is already printed on it, and dates are jotted in each student's square as they occur, as shown in Figure 3.3. Or you can make a number of blank sheets with the squares ruled. Notes are made directly on the sheet, with the date marked. This system eliminates having to recopy notes from one place onto the sheet, but space for comments is limited.

A third system involves making notes on index cards that may be carried in a pocket or on a clipboard, as in Figure 3.4. Index cards allow room for numerous or extended comments, but the notes have to be transferred to another sheet for permanence.

Blair	Brianna	Vincent	Luke
Jan. 12 – Made two self-corrections during reading.			
Raquel	Lauren	Carla	Richard
Antoine	Kevin	Carlos	Marisa
		Jan. 16 – Volunteered to read first today!	
Scott	Terri	Sherita	Denzel
Jan. 9 – Helped Huang check spelling during writing.			
Anthony	Jamahl	Huang	Paula
			Jan. 10 – Used a dictionary for first time, self-initiated.

FIGURE 3.2 *Observation Record Sheet with Sticky Notes*

A fourth system involves keeping a separate observation sheet for each student like the one shown in Figure 3.5. This system is convenient for monitoring a few students, such as members of a remedial group or mainstreamed students with special needs. Sheets may be kept in daily work folders, in a binder, or on a clipboard. This system is cumbersome for large groups but allows plenty of room for each observation and eliminates recopying.

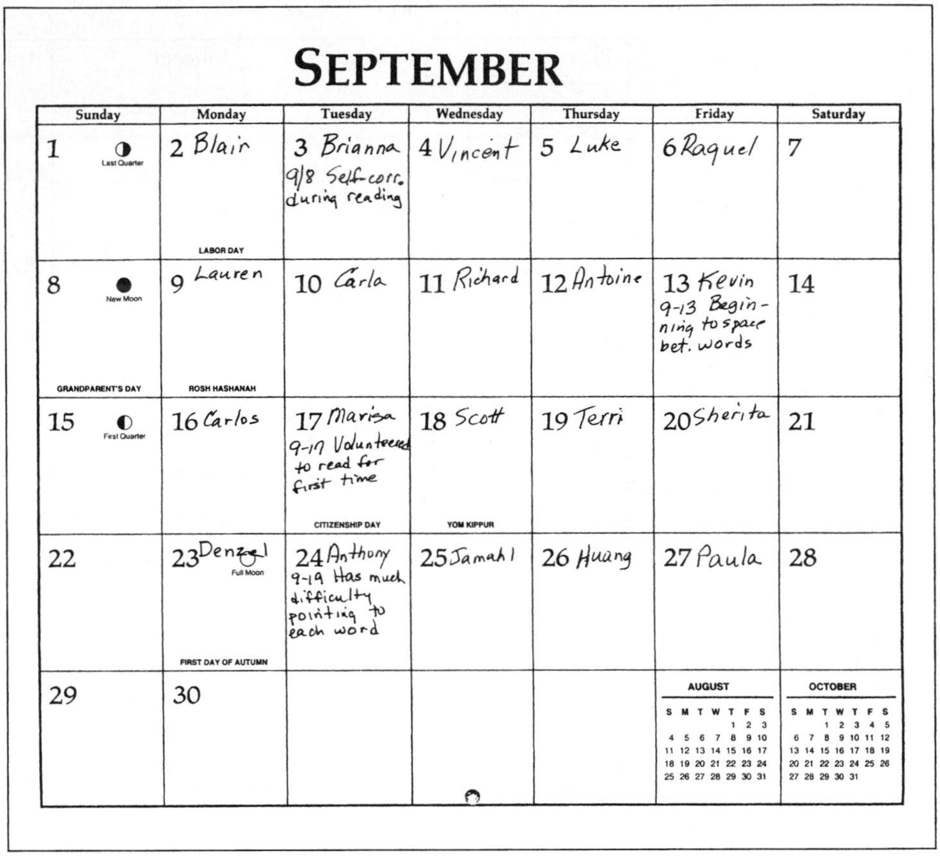

FIGURE 3.3 *Observations on Calendar Page*

Whatever system you choose to record your observations, you must be careful of several issues: using objective language, observing every student, and including observation time in your plans.

1. *Use Objective Language.* Record what occurred in factual terms, rather than your interpretation of the behavior. Write *what* the behavior is, or *how often* or *in what circumstances* the behavior occurs. For example, "Richard repeatedly pulled the book away from his reading partner" tells what occurred; "Richard has trouble sharing a book with a partner" is unspecific and judgmental. "Joanne looks out the window for most of the sustained reading period" is factual; "Joanne wastes her reading time" is judgmental. Record what the student said or did, not what he or she *is*. Avoid sweeping generalizations such as "Justin hates to read," "Nakia works well in groups," or "Timmy is uncooperative."

Lauren Wells

9-12 Lauren points accurately to each one-syllable word
but gets "off" on multi-syll. words

9-17 Lauren struggled w/pointing as she read "hippopotamus" —
wants to make it two words - but got it right after
3 tries!

9-26 Pointing is more accurate — self-corrects errors
as they occur.

Patrick Logan

9-8 Doesn't attend closely to print — takes a quick look
and guesses wildly.

9-17 Tried self-correction w/o reminder for the first time!

9-24 Self-correcting, or attempting to, about half the time,
usually successful.

FIGURE 3.4 *Observation Index Cards*

2. *Observe Every Student.* You might sometimes observe certain students more often than others, especially if they are having particular difficulty or showing a growth spurt, but in general you should make sure you observe every child before starting another round of observations. The record-keeping systems shown in Figures 3.2 and 3.3, in which all notes are kept on one sheet with labeled squares, help you to keep track of which students you have observed recently. An empty square indicates that you need to observe that individual.

Student: Denzel Miller   **Grade:** 1

Date	Observed Behavior
9/6	Denzel uses random letters to write. Letter formation shaky, no spaces. Could not read what he had written to me.
9/17	Denzel still uses random letters if he writes alone, but with encouragement he used a few beginning sounds today: M (mom), B (basketball)
9/26	Beginning sounds are appearing w/more regularity; random letters are beginning to drop out
10/13	Observed Denzel sounding out beginning sounds to himself as he wrote today! First time w/o being reminded!

FIGURE 3.5   *Individual Student Observation Sheet*

If we don't pay attention to this, we might unwittingly observe some students many more times than others. There are many reasons for this, some better than others. Students who are having great difficulty, are discipline problems, or are just more engaging or likeable than others tend to be observed more often. Whatever the reason, it is unfair to observe some students often and others infrequently.

3. *Plan Observation Time.* Plan systematically for student observations. Whether it's daily, once a week, or every other week, block off such time in your schedule. If you don't, observation can get pushed aside by the daily demands of teaching. If you look at your last observation notes and find that it's been longer than a few weeks since you kept any observation records, you'll know that you need to carve out some time on a more regular basis.

Monitoring Types and Difficulty of Texts Read

Another important record to keep is what texts students are reading, what types or genres are preferred, and how difficult the texts are. These are most important in programs in which students are self-selecting at least a portion of what they read, as they should be. But required or teacher-selected material should also be documented.

One way to do this is to keep a running list in each child's work folder or in a binder that shows the materials being read, their genres, and some indication of their difficulty. Another way is for students to keep such a list individually, and share it with you in periodic conferences. Older students can easily keep their own records; they should record the title and author, the type of material (joke book, short story collection, historical or contemporary fiction, biography, science, etc.), and their self-assessment of its difficulty for them (easy to read, pretty hard book, over 100 pages long, etc.). For longer works that take more than a day or so to finish, the starting and ending dates may be recorded.

Such lists show you at a glance how much and what kind of reading the child is doing. If a student appears to be reading one kind of material exclusively, consider encouraging him to try another author, topic or genre. If only very easy books are attempted, introduce the student to a little more challenging material; for the one who always chooses too-difficult, discouraging texts, guidance in selecting more manageable books is needed. The one who takes months to read a single book needs to be led to shorter works or material at a lower readability level, or needs to increase her time spent reading.

These records can also be very effective in demonstrating to parents just what their children are capable of and interested in. This can help them provide appropriate materials for reading at home. Also, most students enjoy getting a panoramic look at what they are reading, and gain satisfaction in watching their lists grow and change. Such information can help students become more reflective and self-evaluative. You will read more about helping students become self-evaluative in the sections to follow about portfolios.

There are several ways to informally determine the difficulty level of different materials. These include using the book's guided reading level, the readability level, lexiles, and cloze procedures. Each of these methods is discussed in the sections to follow.

Guided Reading Levels

One way of determining text difficulty is to refer to the guided reading level for a book. *Guided reading* (Fountas & Pinnell 1996, 1999, 2001) is a literature-based approach in which books of many types and genres are grouped in general categories of difficulty. Factors such as length, print size and layout, vocabulary and concepts, language structures used, text structures, genre, predictability and supportive patterns within the text, and illustration support (Fountas & Pinnell, 1996, p. 114) are used to assign books to levels that are identified by the letters A through Z, corresponding roughly to kindergarten through sixth grade.

Fountas and Pinnell refer to this as developing a *text gradient,* which they describe in this way: "A gradient of text reflects a defined continuum of characteristics related to the level of support and challenge the reader is offered. . . . A gradient of text is not a precise sequence of texts through which all children pass. Books are leveled in approximate groups from which teachers choose particular books for individuals or reading groups" (1996, p. 113).

Guided reading levels A through C represent books that are very easy to read. They typically focus on one idea or have one very simple story line; have one or two lines or sentences per page; feature large, well-spaced print; and have very high illustration support; that is, there is a direct correspondence between the picture and the words on each page. Patterns, repetition, and topics familiar to young children (playing, getting dressed, bedtime, etc.) make these texts very supportive for the youngest readers.

Levels C through I roughly correspond to first-grade material. Story lines become gradually more complex, with more words and longer sentences used. Vocabulary becomes progressively more challenging, and inflectional endings such as -*ed* and -*ing* are common. A full range of punctuation is used, including quotation marks, question marks, commas, and exclamation marks. By Level G, most pages have four to eight lines of print, and sentences are longer. Stories have multiple events and characters, new vocabulary is introduced, and the words rather than the illustrations carry the story line.

Levels I through M roughly correspond to second-grade material. There is considerable overlap between typical second-grade and third-grade reading, and Levels M through P roughly correspond to third-grade reading. At these levels texts are longer, with more sentences per page and unusual or challenging vocabulary appearing. Genres include realistic fiction, informational nonfiction, folktales, and fantasy. Some books at these levels are beginning chapter books that allow readers to read longer selections and sustain interest and comprehension through longer texts. Stories have multiple characters and episodes, there may be fewer illustrations, and more abstract concepts and themes are present.

Levels P through Z represent typical material for fourth through sixth grades. As readers progress to higher levels, they find the texts becoming gradually longer, more complex, more challenging to read and understand, and much less dependent on illustrations. By Level P, many books no longer have illustrations at all. Literary language, figurative language, literary devices like flashbacks, and dialogue become more challenging, topics are more specialized, themes and ideas are more mature.

Figure 3.6 shows the typical text gradient of guided reading levels by grade level.

Many publishers of trade books for classroom and library use now list the guided reading level for many of their titles in their catalogs. Fountas and Pinnell also list hundreds of titles by level in their books on guided reading: *Guided Reading: Good First Teaching for All Students* (1996), *Matching Books to Readers: Using Leveled Books in Guided Reading, Grades K–3* (1999), and *Guiding Readers and Writers Grades 3–6: Teaching Comprehension, Genre, and Content Literacy* (2001). Finally, many teachers level their own books, following guidelines suggested by Fountas and Pinnell (1996) for establishing grade level and reader expectations.

Readability Estimates

Teachers can also use the publisher's estimate of the text's readability, often shown on the back or front cover. Readability estimates are determined by using arithmetic readability formulas, and are expressed as decimal numbers showing the estimated grade level of difficulty in years and months. A reading level, or RL, of 4.0, for example, is read

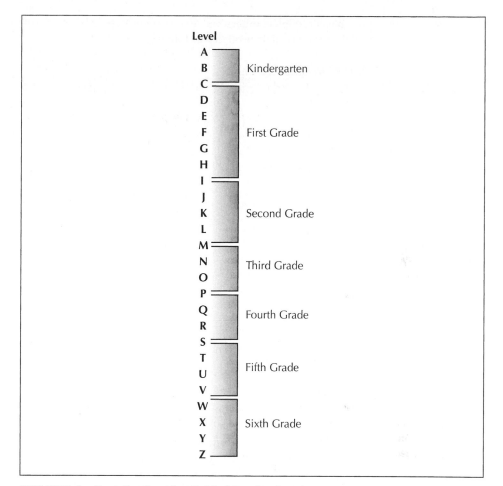

FIGURE 3.6 *Text Gradient for Guided Reading Levels*

Source: Adapted from Fountas and Pinnell (1996, 1999, 2001).

as fourth grade, no months, or the beginning of fourth grade; a reading level of 4.5, as the fourth grade plus five months, or about mid-fourth grade. Above sixth grade, readability levels may simply be expressed as MS, or middle school, HS, or high school, or YA, or young adult (usually middle to older teens). Conversely, materials for beginning readers may be marked P, or primer, or Beginning Reader, or the like.

Difficulty of text is considered to be a function of word and sentence length, rather than of the information conveyed. The assumption behind readability formulas is that easy-to-read texts have short words and many short sentences, while harder-to-read texts have many longer words and fewer, longer sentences. Many school media specialists have simple computer programs that compute the readability level of texts using several comparable formulas when three 100-word samples are typed in. It is also possible, although cumbersome, to compute these levels by hand using readability formula charts. A widely used device follows:

The Fry Readability Chart

1. Select three 100-word samples, one each from the beginning, the middle, and the end of the passage or book. Count proper nouns, dates (1776), numerals (5,380), number words (5th), acronyms (NATO), and symbols (+, &) as single words. Mark the text after the 100th word.
2. Count the **number of sentences** in each 100-word sample, estimating to the nearest tenth of a sentence in the case of an incomplete sentence at the end of a passage. Average these three numbers by adding them and dividing by 3.
3. Count the total **number of syllables** in each 100-word passage. Do so by reading the words *aloud*; there is a vowel sound in each syllable of a word. Do not be misled by how a word looks; *idle* is short but has two syllables, but *through* is long and has only one. For dates, acronyms, symbols, and the like, count each *character* as a syllable; 1918 has four, GNP has three, and = has one. Average the number of syllables by adding and then dividing by 3 as above.
4. Plot on the graph shown in Figure 3.7 the location of the average number of syllables and the average number of sentences. Most will occur near the heavy curved line on the graph. The perpendicular lines show the approximate grade-level areas. If the syllable and sentence averages fall outside or at the extremes of a grade-level band, check your arithmetic for error and if necessary recalculate using three new samples.

Lexiles

Another determiner of the difficulty or readability of texts is a measure called a *lexile.* A lexile is a number assigned to a text that indicates the difficulty of the text based on sentence length and word frequency. The lexile system was developed in the late 1980s using sophisticated statistical procedures that measure the average length and complexity of sentences and the familiarity, or frequency of occurrence, of each word (Chall & Dale, 1995). Instead of yielding a grade-level equivalent, lexile measures yield a number on a scale from 200 to 1700. A lexile of 200 corresponds to the simplest primer-level materials, while a lexile of 1700 represents the most challenging technical text one might encounter in graduate school. Figure 3.8 shows how lexile levels correspond to grade-level equivalents.

An additional feature of lexile measurement is that lexiles also represent a student's reading comprehension level. Thus, both a book and a reader have a lexile. The same scores are used to measure the difficulty of texts and the reading ability of readers, which allows teachers to closely match readers with texts they can read comfortably and successfully. This practice of matching students to texts based on lexile measures is referred to as *targeting:* that is, matching readers with books that are appropriately challenging, that match readers' interests and reading purposes, and that readers have a high probability of being able to read with good comprehension and enjoyment (Stenner,

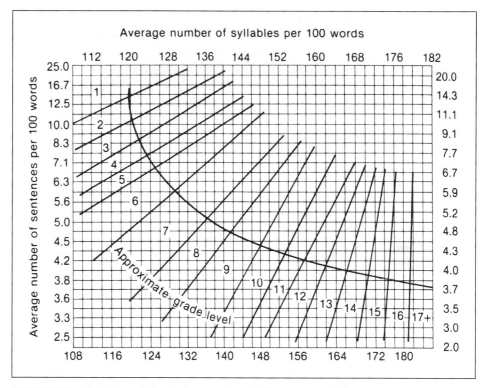

FIGURE 3.7 *Fry's Graph for Estimating Readability—Extended*

Source: Fry, Edward, "Fry's Graph for Estimating Readability," *Elementary Reading Instruction,* The McGraw-Hill Companies, 1977. Reproduced with permission of The McGraw-Hill Companies.

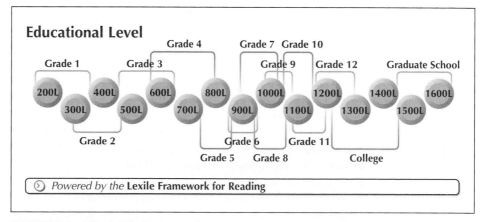

FIGURE 3.8 *The Lexile Framework*

Source: Reprinted from Scholastic Reading Counts! website by written permission of Scholastic, Inc.

2001). When students read material at or near their lexile level, we can expect them to read with about 75 percent comprehension. If they read materials that are 250 or more lexiles below their level, their comprehension increases to about 90 percent or better. But if they read materials that are about 250 lexiles above their current level, comprehension drops to about 50 percent. Thus, by knowing both a reader's lexile and that of various books, we can aim readers toward materials they can read successfully, comfortably, and confidently (Stenner & Wright, 2002).

Like other readability measures, the lexile measure uses sentence length as one of the two criteria for difficulty. Intuitively, we know that longer sentences are harder to read; this may have to do with both sentence complexity and the demands longer sentences place on the reader's short-term memory. But while classic readability formulas also measure average word length, the lexile measure uses the frequency of occurrence of words in print as an indicator of how common or familiar the words are likely to be to readers.

Since a lexile is also a measure of reading ability, a reader also has a lexile. "In the Lexile Framework, reading ability is measured by determining what Lexile passage readability a person can read with 75 percent success" (Stenner & Wright, 2002, p. 11). Students read passages of text at successively higher lexile levels to read and answer comprehension questions or to complete sentences about the passage. The lexile level of material at which the reader performs at 75 percent correct is the reader's present lexile level. While the lexile level of a text is static, the reader's lexile level is dynamic; with progress, the reader will be able to read more challenging materials and move up the lexile scale.

Many consider lexiles a better way of representing both a reader's instructional level and the difficulty of material than grade equivalents. Grade equivalents are hard to interpret. What does it mean if we say that a reader is presently reading at, say, a fourth-grade level? If the reader is a fourth grader, the interpretation is that the reader is doing fine. But if the reader is in a higher grade, the interpretation is negative; here's an older student who is able to read like someone only in the fourth grade. Many older students are embarrassed, even angered, by grade-level equivalents. They resist our efforts to get them to read materials at their instructional level because they feel they are too old for such books, even if the topic is interesting and the difficulty level is appropriate.

In contrast, lexiles sound more objective. Instead of comparing the reader's performance to other students, the performance is measured in terms of a scale of text difficulty that is independent of grade-level expectations. We can tell a parent, "Your child is reading at a lexile level of 600. To read successfully at the next grade level, he needs to increase his lexile level to about 700. He should be reading at least three hours a week at home in order to make this progress. Here are some books at about a 600 lexile level that he could read comfortably and successfully." We can tell a student, "Since the beginning of the year you have increased your lexile level from 800 to 870. This shows that you're making steady progress in reading. Choosing books with lexiles between 860 and the low 900s will help you continue to improve. These books might have been too hard for you a few months ago, but you're ready for them now." We can give parents suggested reading lists corresponding to students' lexile levels, thus giving parents much-needed help in providing books for home reading.

A reader's lexile measure can be determined in several ways. A number of commercial tests including the Scholastic Reading Inventory; Stanford 9 Achievement Test, Metropolitan Achievement Test 8, and various state tests such as the North Carolina End of Grade Test have been linked to the lexile framework and yield lexile levels as well as other forms of scores. Informally, we can determine a student's approximate lexile level by having the student read a page or two from several books with known lexile levels. If the reading proceeds smoothly and with good comprehension, we infer that the student reads at least at that lexile level. If the reading is not fluent or the reader does not comprehend the text easily, we try a lower-lexile text. Usually two or three samples will give us an approximate lexile level. If the student chooses a book at a comfortable lexile level and reads it with enjoyment and good comprehension, we have confirmation of our estimate. The key to this procedure is to know the lexile level of various books. Presently tens of thousands of books now have lexile measures that are available to teachers. Many publishers of trade books provide the lexile for individual titles in their catalogs.

Cloze Procedures

A cloze procedure is another way of matching readers and texts. First developed in the early 1950s as an instructional alternative to readability formulas (Taylor, 1953), a cloze procedure shows how well students can read a particular text or selection by having them supply words that are systematically deleted from the text. The result is an estimate of whether an individual, group, or class is likely to find the material too easy, comfortable, or too hard. Teachers have used cloze procedures for decades to select materials and plan instruction because cloze assessment is authentic, requiring readers to read and make sense of real text, and because passages are easy to devise and score. They are often used when teachers are evaluating textbooks, supplemental materials, or classroom magazines for purchase, or forming groups for differential instruction. Figure 3.9 shows part of a cloze passage developed for a reading class.

Constructing a Cloze Passage

1. Choose a text selection of about 275 to 300 words that students have not read.
2. Leave the first sentence intact (or the first two sentences, if the first sentence is very short). Randomly select one of the first five words in the next sentence and delete every fifth word thereafter, replacing it with a blank. Make each blank the same size. If a word to be deleted is a proper noun, skip it and delete the next word.
3. Continue in this fashion until you have 50 blanks. Finish the sentence in which the 50th deletion occurs and include one more intact sentence. Make a separate answer sheet or have students write answers directly on the passage.

Administering a Cloze Passage

1. Show students how to complete a cloze passage, using example sentences or short paragraphs. Encourage them to use what they already know as well as language in

Cliff swallows live throughout much of the western part of North America. Their nests __1__ made of mud and __2__ fastened to the sides __3__ cliffs. They like to __4__ in colonies, often with __5__ or even thousands of __6__ packed rather closely together—__7__ cities of mud houses.

__8__ that live together in __9__ usually have developed special __10__ of communicating and special __11__ of living that give __12__ a good chance to __13__ .

ANSWERS:

1. are	2. usually	3. of	4. live	5. hundreds
6. nests	7. little	8. Animals	9. groups	10. ways
11. ways	12. them	13. survive		

FIGURE 3.9   *Portion of a Cloze Passage*

the passage to try to figure out the *exact word* that belongs in each blank. Some classes or groups may need extended practice before doing the "real thing."

2. Explain that no one will get every word correct, and that getting about half of the words right is a good score. If they don't know this in advance, students can get very anxious and some might give up in frustration.

3. Allow as much time as needed to complete the passage individually without rushing. This is not a timed exercise.

Scoring and Interpreting a Cloze

1. Count as correct every *exact* word from the text, even if it is misspelled. Don't count synonyms, even if they make sense. Doing so will affect the score criteria, which were developed using exact replacements only. Also, students will argue endlessly about what is "close enough."

2. Multiply the total number of correct replacements by 2 to determine each student's score on the 50-item passage.

3. Create three lists:
   - Students whose score was *above 60 percent correct.* The material is at or close to their *independent* reading level. They can probably use this material without guidance or support.
   - Students whose score was *between 40 and 60 percent correct.* The material probably represents their *instructional* reading level. They can read it most effectively if they are given support and guidance such as visual organizers, study guides, or directed discussion.
   - Students whose score was *below 40 percent correct.* The material is likely at their *frustration* level and is too difficult for them to read. More suitable material should

be found for them. If they are required to read that material, they will need extensive support and guidance such as listening to the material read aloud and direct experience with the topic.

Student Portfolios

A *portfolio* is a collection of materials that demonstrate how each student is progressing in learning content, mastering operations, broadening and refining tastes and interests, and moving toward more mature or complex developmental stages. Portfolios represent *authentic assessment,* or analyzing how students demonstrate learning by performing meaningful, purposeful real-life tasks (Ediger, 2003; McCormick, 2003).

Students and teachers systematically collect representative samples of work over time and reflect on what the samples show about the students' achievement, goals, and capabilities. Portfolios can be used with any grade level and subject to showcase achievement, document progress over time, demonstrate effort, and foster students' decision making, self-evaluation, and reflection (Cohen, 2006; Gipe, 2003; Jasmine, 1992; McMahan & Gifford, 2001).

Showcasing Achievement

One purpose of portfolios is to showcase one's best work. Students might choose work that they believe represents the pinnacle of their achievement in one or more curricular areas. The emphasis is on products, rather than processes. For example, a student may select his best spelling papers, perfect math tests, or best pieces of writing. Another way students can think about their best work is to consider work that they feel particularly proud of. This might not necessarily have received the highest grades but might represent results they are especially pleased with. For example, in selecting work for a math portfolio, a sixth grader included several pages of algebra problems that were not all solved correctly. She explained that she was proud that her teacher had included her in an advanced group that was studying beginning algebra. Although it was not easy for her, she was proud of being selected for advanced work.

Documenting Progress

Another purpose of portfolios is to show progress in a particular subject area, skill, or process. For this purpose, students choose work samples that show increasing complexity, mastery, or difficulty (McMahan & Gifford, 2001). For example, a student might select first drafts of original stories at monthly intervals, dated spelling tests showing mastery of increasingly difficult patterns, or math worksheets moving from simple to complex computations. Such examples are particularly useful for communicating with students and parents about students' developmental progress.

Demonstrating Effort

Another useful purpose is to demonstrate areas or processes in which the student might not excel but is putting forth considerable effort. For example, reluctant writers might feel discouraged about the amount of writing they can produce but they might be surprised to see that over time their written pieces are growing longer and more readable. Likewise, a writer might choose to include a composition that represents a great deal of work, even though the final product was not outstanding. Or a student who rarely persists long enough to finish a project might be encouraged to select work that demonstrates persistence and completion.

Fostering Self-Evaluation and Reflection

Another important function of portfolios is to help students develop the objectivity to step back from their own work, reflect on its quality and importance to them, and evaluate their own strengths and abilities (Galley, 2000). When students do this, they move toward becoming independent learners, able to rely on their own judgments rather than being bound by what teachers or peers think of their work. This is particularly valuable for adolescents, who can be devastated by peers' harsh judgments. Self-evaluation helps students to value their own instincts and judgments and retain self-respect when others don't value their work. Self-evaluation helps students to feel ownership of and responsibility for their work (Hansen, 1994, 1996; Jervis, 1996; Temple, Ogle, Crawford, & Freppon, 2005).

Kinds of Portfolios

Before you can determine what will go into students' portfolios, you must decide the purpose for keeping them. The content of a portfolio depends on

- The intended audience.
- The purpose for developing a portfolio.

A simple *collection portfolio* contains a wide variety of work because its purpose is to form a pool of materials. From it, certain pieces or samples may be drawn for other purposes, such as to create another kind of portfolio, demonstrate growth in different areas, or familiarize students with the fundamentals of portfolio collection. Its audience is the teacher and student. This kind of portfolio is sometimes referred to as a work folder or drop file and is widely used in many classrooms, even where teachers don't think they are using portfolios.

A *showcase* or *display portfolio* contains examples of the student's best work, chosen specifically to show growth and achievement in a particular subject area in which the student excels, such as math, art, or writing. Its purpose is to display the depth and breadth of the student's talents. The audience is the student, teacher, parents, and others whom the student wants to impress, such as college admissions officers, competition judges, or leaders of selective programs. Showcase portfolios are fairly common in high schools and in programs for gifted and talented students.

The *progress* or *assessment portfolio* is the kind most teachers think of when they think of student portfolios. This portfolio contains examples of the student's best work and work that shows marked growth, as does the showcase. However, it also contains selected work in progress, work that represents significant effort even if the product is not extraordinary, and copies of relevant assessment devices. These may include chapter and unit tests, standardized achievement tests, interest and attitude inventories, developmental checklists, lists of achievement benchmarks, lists of books read, running records of oral reading, videotapes and/or audiotapes, students' goal statements and written self-evaluations, teachers' evaluations and anecdotal records, notes on student-teacher portfolio conferences, and parent comment sheets. The purpose of an assessment or progress portfolio is to demonstrate progress, achievement, and effort. Its audience is the student, teacher, and parents.

What Goes into a Portfolio?

Here is a list of possible inclusions in a reading-writing portfolio. Some items listed may not be available or are not used in your classroom or school; some items you consider important may not be listed. Adapt it to fit your purposes and students.

- *Baseline or Beginning Samples.* These are the students' earliest samples of work in any area, such as reading journal entries, running records, audiotapes of oral reading, and first writings. These are collected to establish a baseline with which to compare later work.
- *Reading Journal Entries.* Reading journals, also known as *reading response logs* and *literature logs*, are notebooks that students use to record their responses to what they are currently reading. Simple summaries should give way to more thoughtful responses such as character studies, opinions about the characters' actions, and so forth. Reading journal entries can be collected quarterly, monthly, or at other intervals to show growth in critical thinking and types of literature selected.
- *Learning Log Entries.* Like reading journals, learning logs are often used to have students respond in writing to topics in science, math, and social studies. For example, students may write their thoughts or opinions about subject-area topics like pollution, rain forest preservation, or the dangers of smoking; describe the steps to be followed in solving a math problem; or summarize the new information they learned from a reading assignment, discussion, or demonstration. Periodic sampling from the learning log helps develop a picture of the student's growth in thinking, writing clarity, and subject-matter knowledge.
- *Writing Samples.* A common component of elementary portfolios is the sampling of students' writing at periodic intervals. Earlier writings can be contrasted with

TOURO COLLEGE LIBRARY

later efforts to show growth in any or all of the writing areas: use of prewriting strategies, development of early and later drafts, use of strategies to clarify and extend content, sentence formation, standard English usage and grammar, spelling, punctuation, and so forth. In addition to selecting pieces from different times of the year, students should be guided to select pieces written for different purposes and audiences: original stories, retellings of familiar stories, nonfiction or expository writing, persuasive pieces, letters, poetry, and so forth. At least twice a year, they should choose pieces that illustrate the steps in the writing process, from prewriting through successive revised drafts to editing, polishing, and sharing of the completed piece. In doing so, students and parents can observe the process of composing as well as the final product, the various ways writing is used in everyday life, and their growth in many areas.

- *Records of Oral Reading.* Many teachers use periodic running records to determine the accuracy and fluency of students' oral reading and their use of decoding, syntax, and context strategies to identify unfamiliar words as they progress to more challenging reading levels. Teachers use a system of conventional marks to record what a reader says while reading a portion of text aloud at a comfortable level of difficulty. Audiotapes of the student reading aloud at timely intervals may also be included, as they graphically demonstrate to the student and parents how the student's oral reading fluency and accuracy are progressing.

- *Lists of Books Read.* Each student should keep a list of books read in and out of school, noting the title, author, number of pages read, genre, and beginning and ending dates. At intervals such as quarterly or at the end of a grading period, students can evaluate their reading habits in a number of ways. They can graph the number of books read each month or quarter, or the amount of time they spend reading. They can evaluate whether they are developing balance in their reading habits by selecting various genres or authors and set appropriate goals for the next period. Lists of books read help students, parents, and teachers see what and how much students are reading and whether they are developing wide reading habits.

- *Text Samples with Written Responses.* Periodically, students can choose a current or recently completed book and photocopy a page or two to illustrate the types and difficulty of text they are reading. This makes a good accompaniment to the list of books read, which might not convey much to parents if the books are unfamiliar to them. Students should include a written rationale for their choices, a response to an open-ended question about the text, a summary or critique of the book up to that point, or other written commentary.

- *Audiotapes of Oral Presentations.* Audiotapes are useful for capturing students' story retellings, oral reports, and book talks as well as oral readings. They are an excellent way of documenting students' growth in oral language use, fluency, vocabulary development, and sentence structure.

- *Video.* Video is invaluable in offering students a chance to observe and evaluate their reading, speaking and listening skills. It also offers parents and others a unique opportunity to see students in classroom situations they would otherwise miss as well as providing a way to include three-dimensional projects in portfolios that otherwise could not be included. Video can be used to record drama activities such as improvisations, reader's theater, skits and plays, presentation of projects and research, book talks and read-aloud activities, poetry readings, dramatic choral readings, debates, panel discussions, and so forth.

- *Photographs.* Although they are less compelling than video, photographs are simpler and less expensive to use while still offering a way to capture students' projects, plays, and other strictly visual work. Photographs can be useful in documenting learning activities like plays, skits, artwork, science projects, animal care, and constructions.

- *Conference and Student Self-Evaluation Records.* These include forms used to document when the student and teacher met to discuss the portfolio and students' written reflections on their progress and achievements. These inclusions document students' ability to reflect on their strengths, make decisions, set goals, and work toward achieving them.

- *Assessments.* These may include results of standardized tests, classroom tests, Informal Reading Inventories, interest inventories, anecdotal records, skills or benchmark checklists, and so forth. These document student achievement and progress that may be mandated by the school or district and are more informative to teachers and parents than to students. Some teachers prefer to keep assessments in private folders that are separate from students' daily work, shared with parents at conferences, and transferred with portfolios to the next grade at the end of the year.

These inclusions are summarized in Box 3.1.

Organizing a Portfolio Program

Most teachers already have some system of keeping track of students' work, such as work folders into which students keep current work to collect and send home, a drop file in which graded student work is kept for displays and parent conferences, or even a bulletin board of excellent work.

The first thing you will need to decide is how comprehensive your portfolios should be. What subject areas or skills do you want to document in this way? If you have never used portfolios before, it may be best to keep things simple at first. You might decide to choose one particular area, such as reading, writing, or math, and include only materials related to that area at first. Whether you choose to include one subject area, several, or all areas, avoid trying to do too much at once. If students are new to the portfolio process, it is easier to start simply and add complexity later than to have to cut back or streamline later.

At the beginning, you will need to organize storage materials and communicate what you are doing to students and their families (Cohen, 2006). You should also inform your administrator that you are trying a new way of documenting student progress that will supplement your classroom grades, standardized test scores, and other numerical data.

BOX 3.1

Possible Inclusions in Reading-Writing Portfolios

Baseline or entry writing samples, running records, reading inventories, other assessments

Interest inventories

Lists of books read

Book reports or reviews

Book summaries

Reading response journal entries

Running records of oral reading

Literature logs

Character studies

Personal journal entries

Original creative writing: stories, poetry, plays, etc.

Successive drafts of work showing the writing process

Subject area reports and projects

Photographs, audiotapes, and/or videotapes of student work

Teacher-student conference records

Student self-evaluations and goal statements

Parent review and comment forms

Records of extracurricular achievements

First, each student needs a sturdy folder. Many teachers use cardboard folders with pockets or expanding file folders that can hold a lot. Regular open-sided file folders can't hold very much, and papers begin to spill out. Also, they are not useful for storing non-paper materials, such as artwork, audiotapes of oral reading, and so forth. Students can decorate or otherwise make their folders unique.

Next, find an accessible place for portfolio storage. Plastic milk crate boxes, plastic storage tubs, or even a cut-down cardboard box can house the folders, as long as it is easily accessible to students. File cabinets can be dangerous as they can tip over if students lean on an open drawer while looking for their folders.

In classrooms where teachers have job charts or rotating duties, a new job may be added: portfolio helper, who makes sure the portfolios are neatly stored in alphabetical order at the end of the day. For students who may not have mastered alphabetical order, each student can be assigned a number and folders arranged in order. Checking folder order daily reinforces alphabetical and numerical ordering, and each student will get this practice in turn.

Next, prepare a letter to parents explaining that students will collect much of their work in a special folder to document what they are doing and how they are progressing. Explain that students will be asked to share the responsibility for choosing what work goes into their portfolios, and that such choices require students to consider what may be their best work, their most challenging work, work of which they are most proud, and so forth. Invite parents to view the collected work at conferences, at open houses, and during visits to the classroom. Figures 3.10 and 3.11 are sample parent letters for primary and middle grades.

Next, explain to students what they will be doing. If possible, have another teacher who already uses portfolios come to your room, perhaps with a few of her students, to show what portfolios look like and why students keep them. Or borrow a few portfolios from another classroom—with students' permission—to demonstrate. Explain that many professionals, such as artists, photographers, actors, and models, compile portfolios that visually represent their experience and achievements and that the students' portfolios will likewise show their talents and progress. Pass out the empty portfolios for personalization, show how they are to be stored, and perhaps ask students to find one or more current pieces of work to be included.

All work should be dated. Dating all work helps students see their progress across time, as well as how long a particular project took. Many teachers use rubber stamps for this purpose. Office-type date stamps work well and look very official. Some use different stamps to indicate the stage of some written work: "1st Draft," "Revised," "To Be Edited," and "Completed" are useful categories, with space for the student to write in the date.

Finally, an overall plan for reviewing portfolios, selecting work, and reflecting on it should be developed. Work may be reviewed and selected monthly, quarterly, or at the end of each report card period, depending on the grade level, subject area, type of work being done, and other defining characteristics of the class. For example, young students might benefit from more frequent reviews; important work that takes a long time to complete, like research reports, projects, and ambitious writing efforts, need fairly long intervals between reviews; and students with low self-esteem may need frequent reviews to feel successful.

Let's say, for example, that you decide to have your third-grade class select work in reading and writing on a monthly basis. You have reviewed the list of possible inclusions found in the previous section and posted a list of the things students will be selecting to include. You have sent a letter home informing parents, introduced your class to the concept and purpose of portfolios, had students personalize folders, and taught them how portfolios are to be stored, ordered, and retrieved.

The first entries in portfolios will be the baseline samples referred to in the previous section. In each area, have students collect their first pieces of work: for example, their initial writing samples, reading journal entries, reading response log entries, and first oral readings on tape. (If students use composition books for reading response logs and learning logs, as most do, they will include dated photocopies of their first entries.) In the first weeks you will add each student's first running records, Informal Reading Inventory, interest inventory, skills checklist, and so forth.

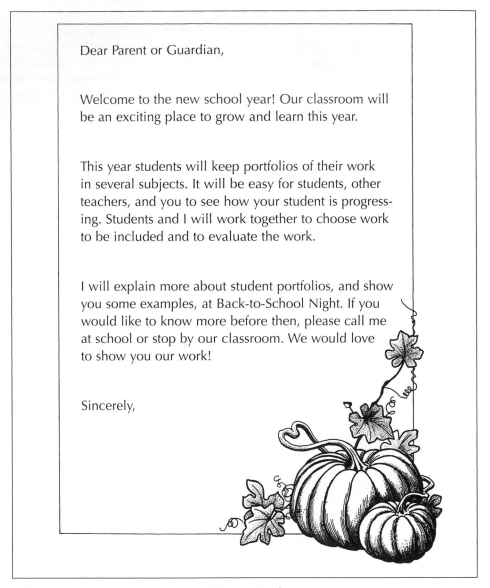

Dear Parent or Guardian,

Welcome to the new school year! Our classroom will be an exciting place to grow and learn this year.

This year students will keep portfolios of their work in several subjects. It will be easy for students, other teachers, and you to see how your student is progressing. Students and I will work together to choose work to be included and to evaluate the work.

I will explain more about student portfolios, and show you some examples, at Back-to-School Night. If you would like to know more before then, please call me at school or stop by our classroom. We would love to show you our work!

Sincerely,

FIGURE 3.10   *Sample Parent Letter, Primary Grades*

One way to organize the baseline samples is to have each student use a construction paper pocket or mini-folder, a 12 inch × 18 inch sheet of construction paper folded in half and stapled on the sides with the date or month on the front. This keeps all the baseline samples together. Another way is to separate the samples into areas (such as reading, writing, and assessments), place them in separate mini-folders, and add related samples to them later.

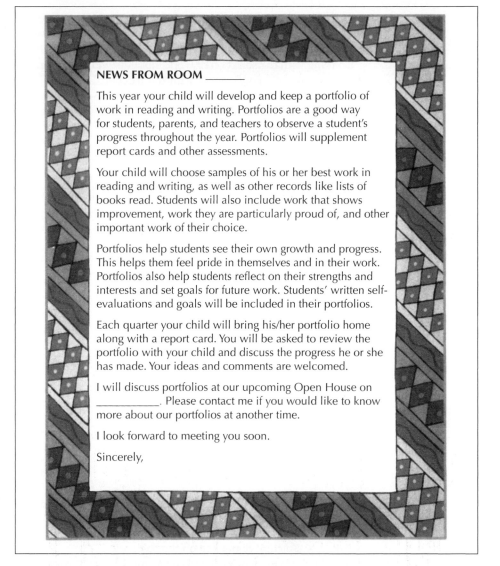

NEWS FROM ROOM _____

This year your child will develop and keep a portfolio of work in reading and writing. Portfolios are a good way for students, parents, and teachers to observe a student's progress throughout the year. Portfolios will supplement report cards and other assessments.

Your child will choose samples of his or her best work in reading and writing, as well as other records like lists of books read. Students will also include work that shows improvement, work they are particularly proud of, and other important work of their choice.

Portfolios help students see their own growth and progress. This helps them feel pride in themselves and in their work. Portfolios also help students reflect on their strengths and interests and set goals for future work. Students' written self-evaluations and goals will be included in their portfolios.

Each quarter your child will bring his/her portfolio home along with a report card. You will be asked to review the portfolio with your child and discuss the progress he or she has made. Your ideas and comments are welcomed.

I will discuss portfolios at our upcoming Open House on _____. Please contact me if you would like to know more about our portfolios at another time.

I look forward to meeting you soon.

Sincerely,

FIGURE 3.11 *Sample Parent Letter, Middle Grades*

Now, at monthly intervals, you will plan for students to review their current work, select samples to add to their portfolios, and compare earlier and later work. Using the same organizational scheme, students may collect all of that month's samples in a mini-folder of a different color, dating the front, or they may add later samples to the separate mini-folders they are keeping for each subject area. Whatever organizational scheme you use, remind students to date everything and to refrain from including items in their portfolios with the intention of organizing it later. Portfolios can quickly become chaotic! Allow time for your "organizationally challenged" students to sort and arrange their portfolios frequently.

Along with the selection of work, students will engage in self-evaluation, goal setting, and portfolio conferences with the teacher. Evaluation and conferring with students and parents are discussed in sections to follow.

Primary Grades

Primary graders' portfolios will necessarily be simpler than those of older students. A simple drop file, into which students drop all of their current work in the chosen subject, works well. At regular intervals, say, once each week, time should be set aside for students to look at everything in their folders, choose particular pieces on the basis of some general criteria, and remove other pieces. The pieces that are removed can be sent home immediately.

For example, a first-grade teacher using portfolios for the first time set aside time on Friday afternoon for portfolio review. Students were to look at everything in their folders and set aside several work samples:

- Their best writing done that week
- Something they had worked very hard on
- Something they were very proud of

Other work was put into large, sturdy envelopes to take home that afternoon. Parents were to review the work, sign the empty envelope, and return it to school on Monday. Work that was selected to include in portfolios was briefly shared and either discussed either with the whole class, a small group, or a friend or discussed with the teacher in a brief portfolio conference. Here is an example of part of a quick whole-group sharing:

Teacher: As we go around the circle, hold up one piece you chose and tell us why you chose it. Amanda, will you begin?

Amanda: I chose this story about my dog because I think it's a good story and because I drew a picture of my dog on the back.

Bruce: I chose my word study test because I got all the words right.

Middle and Upper Grades

Older students can take more responsibility for selecting work to be included, keeping some of their own records, and responding thoughtfully to their own work and effort. They can also arrive at more sophisticated judgments about how their work is changing and how they are progressing (Graves & Sunstein, 1992; Paris, 2001). If students are inexperienced in keeping portfolios, they will need a hands-on demonstration of what portfolios are, just as younger students do. Again, bringing in samples can be very helpful. At one middle school, the art teachers visit each language arts class to show their own and others' professional art portfolios. They explain how artists use portfolios to visually demonstrate their talents and invite students to draw comparisons between an artist's portfolio and a student's language arts portfolio. Students from other classes with portfolio experience can also visit classes to share their portfolios and their part in the evaluation process.

If portfolios are to follow students from one grade to the next, a selection of the previous year's portfolios can be studied. On the other hand, if portfolios are routinely returned to students at the end of the year, other teachers might have a few that they kept as samples from students who moved out of the district or for other reasons.

Teachers who are new to the portfolio process might make a note to keep one or two portfolios for this purpose, perhaps photocopying the contents at year's end so the students can keep theirs. Another way is to build a sample portfolio by photocopying exemplary pieces from a variety of students' work. Protect students' privacy by securing permission from them and by removing names from photocopied work.

Evaluating Portfolios

Portfolios are more than a way to document progress. They are also an effective way of helping students become reflective and self-evaluative. After your baseline samples have been selected, begin teaching students how to self-evaluate and set goals for themselves. After they master these processes, they will use them each time they select new material to be included in their portfolios. Students of all ages, even the youngest, can learn to evaluate their own work and set goals for themselves (Galley, 2000).

Teaching Self-Evaluation

Teach students to self-evaluate the same way you would teach any new operation: by defining what students are to do, modeling the operation for them, having them practice the operation in small groups and discuss what they did, and having them practice the operation individually. This is the basic scaffold for teaching self-evaluation in any subject area.

Let's say, for example, that you want students to practice self-evaluating their writing. You would define the criteria for evaluating a composition by listing with students the things that make writing effective; these would include the writing skills that are appropriate for your grade. With the whole group, compare a sample you made up or one from a previous year with the listed criteria and note its strengths. This whole-group modeling may be repeated with other samples until students are comfortable with it.

In another lesson, present small groups with a composition similar to the one you used for your demonstration. Have each group use the criteria chart to write an evaluation stating the strengths of the sample. (Young students can share their findings orally.) Repeat as necessary, changing the composition of each group so that students work with a variety of peers. When they are able to do this easily in small groups, they can work individually on a sample you provide. Or they can apply what they have learned in an individual evaluation of a current composition of their own. For their first time doing this individually, baseline samples are fine. Self-evaluation cards like those shown in Figure 3.12 can be used to begin the process of student self-evaluation.

Students can also learn to self-evaluate their selections of other kinds of work. After they have learned how to self-evaluate their writing samples, they can practice the same process using selections from their reading response journals and learning logs, selections of content-area work, and so forth. You might need to reteach the process for each different kind of portfolio selection, or your students might need only to review the procedure described above and develop criteria charts for good work in each area.

For example, criteria for effective literature responses might include writing the date, title, author, and copyright date; describing a character and the reasons for certain actions; explaining a conflict and its resolution; discussing the author's writing style or use of dialogue, narration, and so forth; and using correct writing mechanics. Criteria for effective learning log entries might include writing the date and subject area, writing the question or issue being responded to, using correct sentence structure and mechanics, and including drawings or diagrams to illustrate the entry. Criteria for effective research might include selecting a topic of interest to the researcher, using various sources of information, taking notes, creating an outline, organizing information, and producing an edited final draft.

Criteria charts should be developed with students and displayed for them to refer to when they are evaluating their portfolio selections. As time passes, the charts can be updated and additional criteria can be added. As students become more proficient at self-evaluation, they will begin to internalize the criteria for good work, and will have less need for charts and prompts.

Teaching Goal Setting

After students have practiced self-evaluation and are comfortable finding their own strengths, they are ready to begin setting goals by finding areas for improvement. Self-evaluation helps students see the positives and feel pride in their work. Goal setting helps them strive toward greater challenge, growth, and mastery. The criteria charts for effective work are used again, this time to find things that students need to continue practicing.

Goals should be realistic and specific. You might list some hypothetical needs, followed by examples of goal statements that are either vague or unrealistic.

Consider the example of a student who doesn't read very much. A goal for him might be to read more. "I will read more," however, is too vague, while "I will read 100 pages every day" is unrealistic. Students can brainstorm better goals for this example: "I will read for 20 minutes every night," "I will read five books this month," or "I will finish reading (title) by (date)."

You can then return to the criteria chart developed for a particular area, review how a selection may be evaluated for its strengths, and then extend the lesson by having stu-

Student Self-Evaluation Card

Name _____ Steve _____ Date _____

Think About: _____ Why did I choose _____
_____ this piece? _____

My Self-Evaluation _____ This is my best _____
poem. I used good words
and made word pictures.
I read it to my friends.
_____
_____

Student Self-Evaluation Card

Name _____ Irma _____ Date _____

Think About: _____ How does this report _____
compare to your first one? _____

My Self-Evaluation _____ I put in lots more _____
information. I used more books
and I used two encyclopedias.
My spelling was better too.
_____
_____

FIGURE 3.12 *Student Self-Evaluation Cards*

dents brainstorm how it could be improved. As a class or in small groups, have students write specific, reasonable goals as if the piece were their own. Repeat this process until students are able to confidently find strengths, then areas of need, and write one or two meaningful goals for sample selections.

Then have students write goals for improving their own selections. Have volunteers share their initial goals and invite peer feedback, so that students practice writing goals that they really can work toward. Here are some examples of specific, realistic goals:

- "I want to make my stories more interesting by using more colorful words."
- "I will use an outline to help me organize my next report."
- "My goal is to have a punctuation mark at the end of each sentence."

Remind students that working toward one or two goals at a time is enough; trying to master too many things at once can be discouraging, even overwhelming. Reviewing goals and how students are working toward them is discussed in the section entitled "Portfolio Conferences."

Teacher Evaluations

Teachers' evaluations of students' strengths and needs are a fundamental part of the portfolio process. First, these evaluations provide important information about students' abilities and progress. Second, you validate students' efforts, helping them to see their achievement and growth and guiding them to explore new areas and interests. Third, your evaluations help you evaluate and modify your instructional program; awareness of students' strengths and needs gives direction to instructional change. There are several ways you can use the portfolio process to document students' achievement, progress, and needs (Graves & Sunstein, 1992; Jervis, 1996).

One way is through *portfolio conferences.* Because the student-teacher portfolio conference is such an important part of the process, we describe in detail how to conduct these sessions in the section entitled "Portfolio Conferences." To avoid unnecessary redundancy, we will say here that your input in these conferences and your records of their content provide crucial documentation of students' progress and effort, their growth in goal setting and decision making, and your attention to individual instruction.

A second important source of teacher evaluations is *anecdotal records.* This term refers to notes teachers make while they are observing students in various classroom situations, sometimes referred to as *kidwatching* (Owocki & Goodman, 2002). Kidwatching includes two perspectives: *involved observations,* which take place while the teacher is actively working with students, and *objective observations,* which take place while students work independently. Anecdotal records are notes kept during kidwatching or shortly thereafter while the observation is fresh in the teacher's mind. They should report, rather than judge or interpret; they are intended to document what student do and say, thus forming an objective record of students' day-to-day operations.

At the beginning of this chapter we suggested several ways to keep anecdotal records systematically: using a grid with a square for each student and carrying the clipboard around the room, keeping an index card for each student and making dated entries on each card, using a calendar page with a student's name on each square and recording observations on sticky notes, and so forth. You may want to review Figures 3.2 through 3.5. We also discussed how to organize classroom observations and how to use specific, objective language in recording what you observe.

A third way of incorporating teacher evaluations into portfolios involves traditional *grading.* In a sense, report card grades and portfolios are like oil and vinegar; they share fundamental characteristics but don't mix very well. In salad dressing, oil and vinegar contribute different but compatible flavors to the salad; in student evaluation, traditional grades and portfolio documentation contribute different but compatible information to the portrait of students' progress.

Grades show where students are in comparison to others. When they are compared to their peers, we may think of this as "grading on a curve," or determining where the individual stands in comparison to a distribution with the performance of the lowest and highest students as the boundaries. When students are compared to a set of preestablished criteria, as on a criterion-referenced test or a teacher-made test for which the teacher knows what a "typical" class might do, they are being compared to a hypothetical peer group or to a set of expectations designed to fit a hypothetical group of peers. Either way, students are compared to each other. Portfolios, on the other hand, allow comparison of students to themselves, since earlier and later works by the same student are being compared. Both kinds of comparisons are valid; both communicate to students, parents, and other teachers, and both contribute to each other.

Many teachers believe that work selected to be included in a portfolio should not be graded since the portfolio is intended in large part to be a celebration of the student's unique abilities, achievements, and progress. Instead of assigning a letter grade, such work might be evaluated in narrative form, with comments attached to the work. Since the portfolio is designed to hold only a sampling of a student's work, other similar work can be graded and sent home to parents.

Comments attached to portfolio work samples may vary in length, but should be concise and positive, noting specifically what the student did well and, as necessary, indicating areas for possible further practice. Such evaluations should be done after students have self-evaluated the sample, to avoid influencing what students think of their own work. The student "owns" the portfolio, so comments should be addressed to the student by name and should be written on cards or notes attached to the work, not directly on the work itself.

In the beginning, you may find that writing a comment for each selected sample is time-consuming, but with practice you will find that it takes less time to write more meaningful, less general comments. For one thing, not every work sample needs to be accompanied by a teacher comment. Often students' self-evaluations, plus comments you make about the sample in a conference with the student, are sufficient. Also, a few minutes is not too long for you to spend commenting on work that may have taken the student days, even weeks, to complete. As a general rule, the longer it took the student to complete the work, the more time its evaluation deserves. Samples that were quickly completed, like a worksheet, spelling quiz, or Math Minute, can be evaluated quite quickly: for example, "Look how many more problems you completed this time, Liz!" or "Alex, this sample shows me how hard you've worked on spelling vowel sounds," are sufficient for short assignments. Figure 3.13 shows some sample narrative comments that are more substantive.

Parent Evaluations

Parents' input into their children's portfolios is valuable for several reasons. First, their comments show that they are aware of at least some of the things their children do in the classroom.

Jan. 20

Juanita,
    Your different drafts show how hard you've worked on this piece. You showed you could find and add more information in each draft.

12-12

Steven,
    Your birthday poem really made me smile! I could almost hear the noisy party! You used strong adjectives and verbs to make it lively.

FIGURE 3.13 *Sample Teacher Evaluation Comments*

Second, parents' comments show whether they understand some of the fundamentals of today's instruction, like the importance of home reading, children's use of invented spelling, and the stages of the writing cycle. Parents' comments can show you where you need to make an explanatory phone call, invite parents in to observe or talk informally, send samples home more often, plan a parent education event, or other efforts to better inform parents.

Third, parents' comments can give you valuable insight into variables in the children's lives outside of school that may bear on their interests, difficulties, areas of strength, behavior, and motivation. Your awareness of home influences in the child's life helps you teach the whole child.

Fourth, parents' comments can be very validating and encouraging to the student. Parents welcome opportunities to observe their children's progress and development. Portfolios offer the perfect opportunity to inform and involve them. Parents can gain a clearer understanding of their children's strengths and weaknesses from seeing sequential work samples than from test scores or grades. Parents also appreciate that teachers see their children as unique individuals, too. And parents become active participants in their children's education, even if they cannot participate in traditional parent activities like classroom volunteering or parent-teacher organizations.

One way parents can contribute to the evaluation process is by completing a *parent response form* to be returned to school with the portfolio or selected samples after review at home. Figure 3.14 shows two samples of this kind of form. They should be kept short and simple, but allow room for parents to write their comments.

Parents should be invited to review their children's portfolios regularly, whether during a scheduled conference, an open house, a classroom event, or a drop-in visit. Questions and concerns can be addressed in conferences or on the phone. You will read more about portfolio conferences with parents in the next section.

Portfolio Conferences

Students' evaluation and goal setting culminate in portfolio conferences. When teachers and students confer, they become collaborators in the evaluation process. When students confer with peers about portfolio selections, they give and receive encouragement on their efforts and achievements and gain awareness of their strengths. When students and teachers confer with parents, they can help parents gain a comprehensive view of the student's work and abilities and a better understanding of their child's development.

Teacher-Student Conferences

Formal teacher-student conferences often occur in the later part of the quarter or report card period. However, informal conferences may occur much more often at your discretion. Conferences vary in length depending on the student's age, the portfolio contents, and other factors; however, 10 minutes or so for most elementary students is a fair

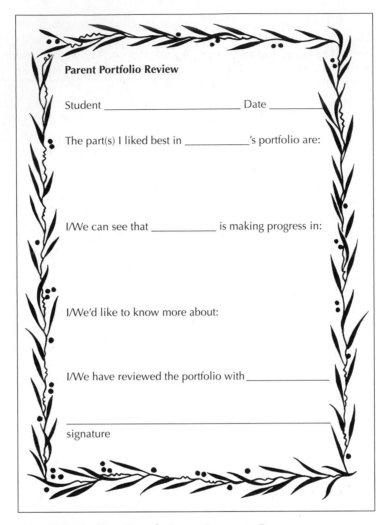

Parent Portfolio Review

Student _____ Date _____

The part(s) I liked best in _____'s portfolio are:

I/We can see that _____ is making progress in:

I/We'd like to know more about:

I/We have reviewed the portfolio with_____

_____
signature

FIGURE 3.14   *Two Sample Parent Response Forms*

estimate. Conferences with middle and high school students may take longer, unless the conference is limited to discussing one sample or goal. Some teachers post lists showing which students will have their conferences that day, and hold conferences while students are working independently or in small groups. Students should review their portfolios prior to the conference so they can discuss their progress and goals.

Teacher-student conferences typically have three main parts:

1. *The teacher compliments* the student on some aspect of the portfolio, such as organization, selection of samples, thoughtful self-evaluations, and so forth. The conference should begin on a positive note.

Parent Response Form

Student _____ Date _____

Student comments: I chose this work because . . .

It shows my progress because . . .

Parent comments: I/We think that this work shows . . .

Parent questions:

Parent(s) signature _____

FIGURE 3.14 *(continued)*

2. *The student recognizes areas of growth* shown by selected samples and discusses his reading and writing progress with the teacher. This may include discussion of how previous goals have been met or worked toward.
3. *The student sets goals* for the next interval, with the teacher's help if necessary.

You can see why students need time to review their portfolios before conferences and to know what they should look for. If you need to draw a student out during a conference, you can use questions like these:

- How does your portfolio show what you are learning?
- How can you tell from your work that you are growing as a reader (writer, etc.)?
- What can you do well in writing?
- What might your portfolio tell about you to a person who didn't know you?
- What kinds of things do you like to read (write) about?
- What does this piece tell about you as a reader (writer)?
- How have you worked toward the goal(s) you set for yourself last time?

These open-ended questions are intended to get the student thinking and talking about the work. The student should talk more about the work than the teacher does. Avoid dominating the conference or cross-examining the student.

Students should review their previous goals and reflect on how they are meeting them. This will help them set goals for the next interval. Some students may need help in setting realistic or attainable goals. Some whose goals were ambitious or long-range may continue working toward them. Not every student will have attained the previous goals or set new ones, but it is important for each one to reflect on her progress toward attaining them. It may be helpful for the student to write what her most recent goal was and how she has attained it.

Portfolio conference records should reflect the dates of student-teacher conferences, areas discussed, goal setting, and other relevant comments. Figure 3.15 shows a cumulative portfolio conference record on which the teacher has listed the dates, topics, and goals of Kendra's conferences with her. Figure 3.16 shows an individual conference form completed after one conference with Carrie.

Peer Conferences

Peer conferences are for sharing selected work, explaining choices and goals, and getting helpful feedback from others. Like other examples of cooperative learning, peer conferences can be beneficial for both parties; the owner of the portfolio gets to show off some of his best work and accomplishments, and the portfolio partner gets to see what others are including in their portfolios and offer encouragement.

Students need to be taught, however, how to make these conferences positive and helpful. Demonstrate with one student how to listen attentively, make positive comments about specific aspects of the work, and ask thoughtful questions. Then let students practice conferring with a partner and evaluate what they did in groups before you have students schedule peer conferences. Students could create a class list of Peer Conference Do's and Don'ts to which they could refer as they work together. Figure 3.17 shows a sample partner review form.

Parent Conferences

Portfolios can be invaluable in helping you to explain to parents what their children are working on, where their academic strengths lie, what skills and processes they need to develop, and how they are progressing. Portfolios give parents a "bird's-eye view" of

Date	Selection	Observations	Goals
Student __Kendra__		Teacher __Mrs. Gillet__	
9-16	"My Dog"	Baseline story– 3 sents. Took 25 mins.	Fluency
10-11	"Puppies"	First attempt at expository. Knows a lot! 9 sentences	encourage her to write about what she knows
11-20	"Barry"	Response to reading *The Bravest Dog Ever.* She loved the story! Wrote 1 ½ pp.	continue topic-related reading

FIGURE 3.15 *Cumulative Conference Form*

their children's work that report cards, test scores, and other evaluative information cannot provide.

When you confer with parents, begin by highlighting the student's strengths and using portfolio samples to show how far the student has progressed to date. It is much easier for parents to understand their child's needs after they have heard you acknowledge the child's strengths. Portfolio samples can be used to show areas that students need to practice and to interpret test scores, report card grades, and so forth. Goal statements and conference records document students' active role in learning.

Parents' comments and concerns should be noted on the teacher's copy of the parent-teacher conference form you use to document such conferences; if your school does not already have such a form, you can adapt the one shown in Figure 3.18.

Student-Teacher Portfolio Conference

Student _____ Carrie M. _____ Date __ 11-12 __

Student Comments/Evaluation:

"... my best story so far."
(what makes it good?)
    it's long
    I've been working a long time
       on it
    I just like it

Student Goals:

finish it
publish it

Teacher Comments/Evaluation

Carrie spoke w/great enthusiasm
about this piece; shows real pride.
Her comments show awareness of
her <u>effort</u>. Goals vague — doesn't
yet have clear idea of what's next.

Student signature _____

Teacher signature _____

FIGURE 3.16 *Individual Conference Form*

Portfolio Partner Review

Name _____ Date of review _____

I reviewed _____'s work sample.

I think this sample shows that _____ can . . .

I think _____ did these things well in this sample:

I think _____ learned . . .

And I learned . . .

Signature _____

FIGURE 3.17 *Portfolio Partner Review Form*

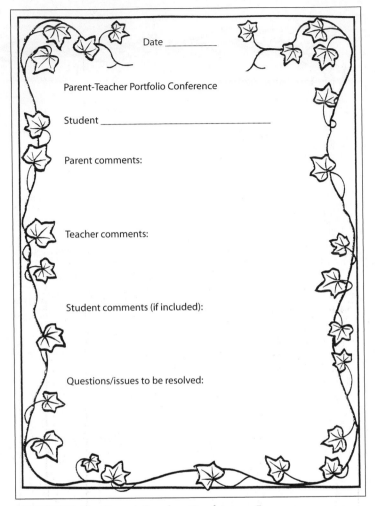

FIGURE 3.18 *Parent-Teacher Conference Form*

Summary

This chapter describes a variety of assessments that a teacher might make on an ongoing basis throughout the year. These assessments and observations can add to other, more in-depth or formal measures to compile a complete picture of a student's literacy development and achievement.

Running records are transcripts of text read aloud by a student with the reader's miscues, correction at-tempts, comments and other reading behaviors marked. Running records may be collected periodically to show the reader's progress in mastering progres-sively more difficult text, word recognition and word analysis strategies, and comprehension. They are also used to show how well a reader is handling self-se-lected materials and whether such materials are chal-lenging enough to promote reading growth.

Observations of reading behaviors and strategies can be informative in planning instruction and in communicating about students' progress with students themselves, their parents, and other teachers. Physical and cognitive behaviors, social interactions during reading, and reading strategies that may be observed during reading are listed in the chapter. Several methods of recording observations are illustrated, including using a sheet of labeled squares, a calendar page, index cards, and individual student observation sheets. Maintaining objectivity, using objective language to describe behaviors, systematic planning for observations, and observing each student regularly are discussed.

Types and difficulty of texts can be recorded on individual reading lists. There are several ways to determine the difficulty of texts. *Guided reading levels* are levels of difficulty, identified by the letters A through Z, assigned to books by placing them along a *gradient of difficulty* ranging from the simplest materials for beginners to books at about a sixth-grade level. Many publishers list the guided reading levels for books they sell, and teachers can also level books themselves by referring to leveling criteria and guidelines suggested by the developers of the guided reading levels. *Readability formulas* are another way to estimate the difficulty of texts, yielding a grade-equivalent reading level based on sentence and word length. Charts and procedures for using two popular readability formulas are included in the chapter. *Lexiles* are another measure of text difficulty. Lexile levels, ranging from 200 to 1700, are based on sentence length and complexity and word frequency. Lexiles are also used to represent students' reading comprehension levels. Thus, both a book and a reader have a lexile level. This allows teachers to match readers with texts they can read comfortably and successfully, a procedure called *targeting. Cloze procedures*, or selections of text with words systematically deleted, can also be used to determine whether a particular text represents a reader's or a group's independent, instructional, or frustration reading levels, rather than yielding a grade-equivalent score. This is another way of targeting readers and texts. Procedures for creating and using cloze procedures are included.

Authentic assessment refers to assessment of students' demonstrated learning by performing meaningful, real-life tasks for real purposes. *Portfolios* provide a means of collecting materials that demonstrate how a student is progressing in learning content, mastering operations, and/or showing developmental progress or growth. Portfolios are typically used to *showcase achievement, document progress, demonstrate effort,* and *foster self-evaluation and reflection.* Beginning a portfolio program requires teachers to determine in what subject areas or skills such documentation is desired; prepare basic materials for storage; and communicate purposes and procedures to students, parents, and administrators. Primary-grade students often use a simple drop file system, periodically choosing work to keep and taking the rest home. Older students can select work for inclusion on the basis of a variety of criteria and engage in self-evaluation as well as *teacher-student* and *peer portfolio conferences.* A variety of kinds of materials are suggested for inclusion in reading-writing portfolios.

Teaching students to self-evaluate is important in the portfolio assessment process. Students confer with teachers, peers, and parents to share their observations about the own progress, strengths, and goals for further learning.

mylabschool
Where the classroom comes to life!

MyLabSchool is a collection of online tools for your success in this course, your licensure exams, and your teaching career. Visit www.mylabschool.com to access the following:

- Online Study Guide
- Video cases from real classrooms
- Help with your research papers using Research Navigator
- Career Center with resources for:
  - Praxis exams and licensure preparation
  - Professional portfolio development
  - Job search and interview techniques
  - Lesson planning

References

Chall, J., & Dale, E. (1995). *Readability revisited: The new Dale-Chall readability formula.* Cambridge, MA: Brookline Books.

Clay, M. M. (1993). *Reading Recovery: A guidebook for teachers in training.* Portsmouth, NH: Heinemann.

Clay, M. M. (2000). *Running records for classroom teachers.* Portsmouth, NH: Heinemann.

Clay, M. M. (2005). *An observation survey of early literacy achievement* (2nd ed.). Portsmouth, NH: Heinemann.

Cohen, L. (2006, April). The power of portfolios. *Early Childhood Today.*

Ediger, M. (2003). Data driven decision making. *College Student Journal, 37*(1), 9–15.

Fountas, I. C., & Pinnell, G. S. (1996). *Guided reading: Good first reaching for all children.* Portsmouth, NH: Heinemann.

Fountas, I. C., & Pinnell, G. S. (1999). *Matching books to readers: Using leveled books in guided reading, grades K–3.* Portsmouth, NH: Heinemann.

Fountas, I. C., & Pinnell, G. S. (2001). *Guiding readers and writers grades 3–6: Teaching comprehension, genre, and content literacy.* Portsmouth, NH: Heinemann.

Galley, S. (2000). Portfolio as mirror: Student and teacher learning reflected through the standards. *Language Arts, 78*(2), 121.

Gipe, J. P. (2003). *Multiple paths to literacy: Assessment and differentiated instruction for diverse learners, K–12* (6th ed.). Upper Saddle River, NJ: Pearson/Merrill/Prentice Hall.

Graves, D., & Sunstein, B. (Eds.). (1992). *Portfolio portraits.* Portsmouth, NH: Heinemann.

Hansen, J. (1994). Literacy portfolios: Windows on potential. In S. Valencia, E. Hiebert, & P. Afflerbach (Eds.), *Authentic reading assessment: Practices and possibilities.* Newark, DE: International Reading Association.

Hansen, J. (1996). *Doing what counts: Learners become better evaluators.* Portsmouth, NH: Heinemann.

Jasmine, J. (1992). *Portfolio assessment for your whole language classroom.* Huntington Beach, CA: Teacher Created Materials.

Jervis, K. (1996). *Eyes on the child: Three portfolio stories.* New York: Teachers College Press.

McCormick, S. (2003). *Instructing students who have literacy problems.* Upper Saddle River, NJ: Pearson.

McMahan, G. A., & Gifford, A. P. (2001). Portfolio: Achieving your personal best. *Delta Kappa Gamma Bulletin, 68*(1), 36–41.

Owocki, G., & Goodman, Y. (2002). *Kidwatching: Documenting children's literacy development.* Portsmouth, NH: Heinemann.

Paris, S. (2001). Classroom applications of research on self-regulated learning. *Educational Psychologist, 36*(2), 89.

Shanahan, T., & Barr, B. (1995). Reading Recovery: An independent evaluation of the effects of an early instructional intervention for at-risk learners. *Reading Research Quarterly, 30,* 958–995.

Stenner, A. J. (2001, January). The Lexile framework: A common metric for matching readers and text. *California School Library Association Journal, 25,* 41–42.

Stenner, A. J., & Wright, B. D. (2002, February). *Readability, reading ability, and comprehension.* Paper presented to the Association of Test Publishers, San Diego.

Swartz, S. L., & Klein, A. F. (2002). *Research in Reading Recovery: Vol. 2.* Portsmouth, NH: Heinemann.

Taylor, W. (1953, Fall). Cloze procedure: A new tool for measuring readability. *Journalism Quarterly, 30,* 415–433.

Temple, C., Ogle, D., Crawford, A., & Freppon, P. (2005). *All Children Read: Teaching for Literacy in Today's Diverse Classrooms.* Boston: Allyn & Bacon.

Chapter 4

Assessing Spelling and Writing

Chapter Outline

*R*eading, writing, and spelling are interrelated processes that support and enhance each other. Readers apply what they know about spelling to recognize unfamiliar words, and what they know about writing to construct meaning from someone else's written language. Writers apply what they know about language and speech sounds to spell, what they know about spelling and vocabulary to select just the right words to express their meanings, and what they know about written language to put their messages into written language.

Problems in reading, writing, or spelling affect the other processes. Gentry (2006) points out that too often we look only at children's reading or at their writing/spelling, but not at both; "If we don't look at both, we are destined to make mistakes . . . to be blind to the obvious" (p. 43). Assessing and monitoring students' progress in spelling and writing as well as their reading is essential to developing a comprehensive picture of their literacy.

Monitoring Spelling Progress and Problems

Learning to read words requires the operation of *recognition;* learning to spell them requires the more difficult, but related, operation of *production.* Thus, children's ability to read words usually outstrips their ability to spell them; this generally holds true for adults as well. (You can probably read any number of words that you might have difficulty spelling correctly. However, it's unlikely that you could spell a word you couldn't read.)

For beginning readers, spelling attempts can be windows that reveal the child's growing phonemic segmentation ability. Phonemic segmentation, or phonemic awareness, is a key component of early literacy. It means the ability to break a spoken word into its component phonemes, or speech sounds, and to hold these sounds in memory while searching for a letter or letter combination to represent them in writing. Young children's phonemic segmentation ability may be assessed by having them try to write unfamiliar words or whole sentences and then looking at how many phonemes they represent accurately or acceptably. A dictation test is part of the Diagnostic Survey for Reading Recovery (Clay, 1993), in which children are asked to write as much of a standard sentence as they can; there are five different sentences, each consisting of 37 phonemes. Children who can represent at least half of the sounds in one of these sentences are considered to be well on their way to developing phonemic segmentation ability. Figure 4.1 shows a first grader's performance on a sentence dictation task in September and in April.

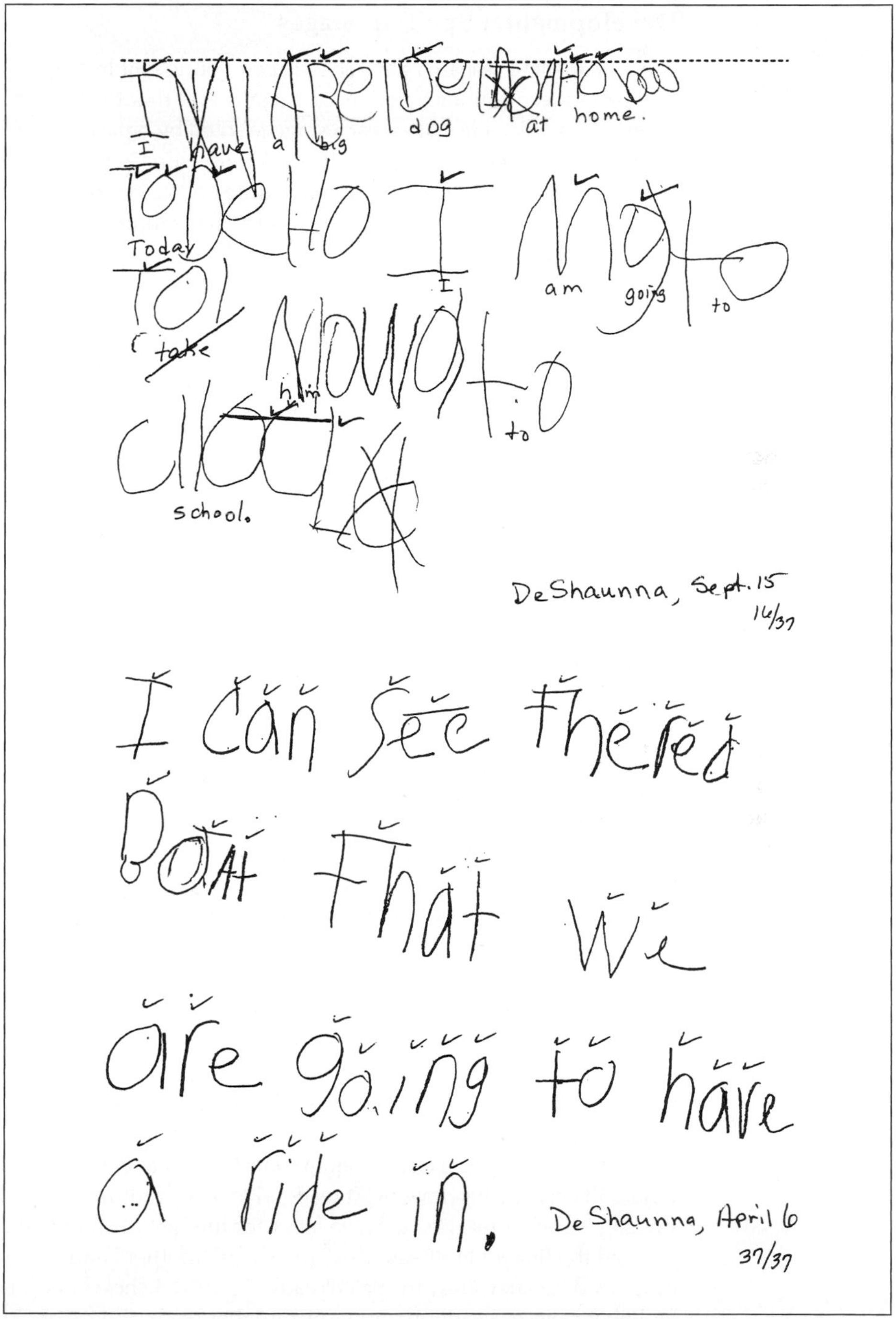

FIGURE 4.1 *Sentence Dictation Test*

Developmental Spelling Stages

Years of spelling research have shown that young children apply systematic strategies to relate speech sounds to letters and words and that these strategies develop in a sequence of predictable stages, each stage marked by typical misspellings (Ganske, 2000; Gentry, 1997, 2006; Henderson, 1990; Henderson & Beers, 1980; Read, 1971, 1975; Templeton & Bear, 1992). As children mature and gain more experience with print, their temporary spellings approximate correct spellings more and more closely. These developmental stages are described below.

Nonalphabetic Stage.   The precursor to writing, this stage is represented by writing that contains no letters or letter-like forms, but is typically made up of lines of squiggles that look like writing to the child. The writing is definitely communicative; the writer can "read" it to you, although the message is usually different each time it is read. The intent is to communicate, but the writer has not discovered that writing is made up of letters and that the message is the same each time it is read. Nonalphabetic writing doesn't last very long, but it is an important prewriting stage, similar to babbling in learning to talk. Figure 4.2 shows an example of nonalphabetic writing by Leslie, then 2 years old. The letter-like forms at the top and bottom are attempts to write her name. The body of the writing is a letter to her grandmother.

Prephonemic Stage.   Children have enough experience with print to know that it is made up of letters and that it conveys a message, but they do not yet understand that letters represent speech sounds. At this stage letters are used randomly, representing a message only the writer can read. Numerals and other characters are sometimes included. Prephonemic writing is usually written in horizontal lines but without spacing.

Figure 4.3 shows a sample of prephonemic spelling by Phillip, then in kindergarten. Phillip drew an elaborate picture of flowers, birds, and butterflies and wrote four lines of random letters beneath it. When asked to read his writing Phillip talked about the picture without reference to the writing.

Semiphonemic, or Partial Alphabetic, Stage.   As children are taught the alphabet, they begin to recognize that letters have sounds associated with them. They begin to try out this concept by representing one or more sounds, usually the initial and sometimes the final sound, with letters that have that sound. Whole words may be represented with one or two letters. Spaces between the units intended for words may appear late in this stage.

Figure 4.4 shows a classic semiphonemic/partial alphabetic piece written by a first grader to describe his drawing; it reads, "I love my mother. Me and my mother. Me and my dog." The writer used a single letter for the first sound in all but two of the words; he used the first and last sounds to represent "mother" and the entire word "dog," the only word he knew how to spell already. Figure 4.5 shows another first grader's partial alphabetic piece, a caption for her picture that reads, "Ideas of Quilts."

FIGURE 4.2 *Nonalphabetic Writing by a 2-Year-Old*

Letter-Name Stage. As children move into beginning reading, they learn more and more about the ways in which letters represent sounds in written words, and they use this information both to decode in reading and to encode, or spell, in writing. First, inventions become more word-like, with more consonant sounds represented, as in LFNT for *elephant*. Then vowels begin to appear; first the long vowels since they "say their names," as in EGL for *eagle* or BOLN for *bowling*. Finally, short vowels appear; they are usually misspelled because children try to use the *name* of the letter to approximate its sound, which works with long vowels and most consonants, but rarely works with short vowels. Typical letter-name spellings are HIT for *hot* and BAT for *bent*.

FIGURE 4.3   *Prephonemic Spelling by a Kindergartner: "Flowers"*

FIGURE 4.4   *Partial Alphabetic Spelling, First Grader: "I love my mother"*

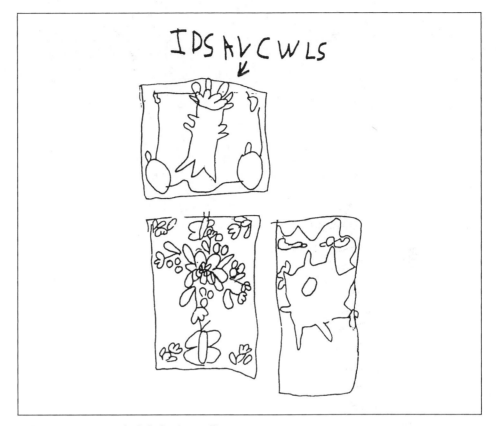

FIGURE 4.5 *Partial Alphabetic Spelling*

Source: Reprinted with permission from *Teaching Kids to Spell* by J. Richard Gentry. Copyright © 1993 by J. Richard Gentry and Jean Wallace Gillet. Published by Heinemann, a division of Reed Elsevier, Inc., Portsmouth, NH. All rights reserved.

Figure 4.6 shows a typical letter-name speller's piece. Spellings such as LUS for *loose,* WOK for *woke,* DILR for *dollar,* and FID for *found* are exemplary of spelling at this developmental stage. Billy's use of I for the vowel sounds in *dollar* and *found* are especially intriguing; they represent the use of the letter name I, which sounds like "ah-ee" if you say it slowly, for the short *o* sound in *dollar* and the *ow* sound in *found.* Similarly he used the letter name U, "yoo," for the *oo* sounds in *loose* and *tooth* that a more mature speller would represent with *oo.*

Figure 4.7 shows another first-grade letter-name speller's work. Leslie's spellings are quite complete, with all syllables represented. Long vowel sounds are represented by the vowel letter's name, as in VARE for *very,* RANBO for *Rainbow,* and NIS for *nice.* Reduced vowel sounds in unaccented syllables, sometimes referred to as *schwa* sounds, and vowel digraph sounds are not represented but collapsed into the consonant sound, as in BRN for *born,* TIGR for *Tiger,* and SANFLAWR for *Sunflower.* Irregular vowel

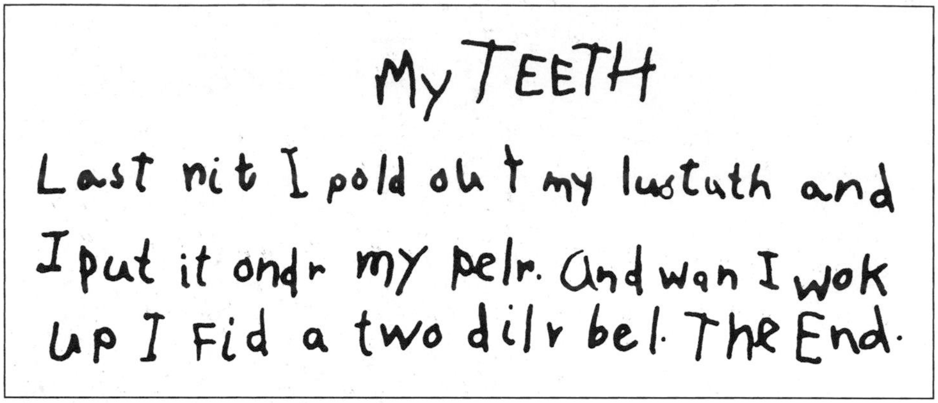

FIGURE 4.6   *Letter-Name Spelling, First Grader: "My Teeth"*

substitutions for short vowel sounds show up in WAN for *when*, GAT for *got*, and SAN for *Sun* in *Sunflower*. A few high-utility learned words are present in *is, we, was, not, he, she,* and *loved*.

Within-Word Pattern Stage.   This stage encompasses strategies of growing sophistication and is typical of many second and third graders. As their reading abilities grow and they experience more decoding and spelling instruction, children gradually move away from the primarily phonemic, or sound-based, spelling on which they previously

FIGURE 4.7   *Letter-Name Spelling, First Grader: "Guinea Pigs"*

relied. "Rather than relying on letter-by-letter and sound-by-sound processing, learners at this stage are able to chunk parts of words and process them in a more automatic fashion" (Ganske, 2000). They begin to develop strategies for spelling whole syllables and word parts, silent letter patterns, and entire words, as well as developing a visual memory for hundreds of words. They now learn words by patterns, as most spelling programs advocate, and can generate many words based on learning common patterns like CVC/*get,* CVCe/*cake,* CVVC/*hear,* and so forth.

Spellers at this stage are deeply involved with pattern mastery. As a result, their once-logical letter-name spellings, like RAN for *rain* and FITN for *fighting,* no longer look right. Learning word families and rules for dividing words into syllables allows writers to spell many words correctly and to produce very readable spelling errors. Within-word errors often result from overusing or misusing spelling rules, particularly those governing the spelling of long vowels. Within-word spellers often use the right strategy in the wrong word. Homophones, with their different spellings of identical-sounding words like *tale/tail* and *threw/through,* are particularly troublesome. Examples of within-word errors are WEAKE for *weak,* OWNLEY for *only,* HERT for *hurt,* and WRIGHT for *write.* Letter reversal errors like GRILS for *girls* are also common at this stage, and, if not corrected, they can become habitual problems.

Figure 4.8 shows another first grader's spelling representing within-word patterns. Josiah's directions for making a vest are very readable. He has used "the right spelling in the wrong word" in several cases. MEATIUM for *medium,* EATHER for *either,* and NEADLES for *needles* show his overuse of the *ea* pattern for long *e* sounds. MATEERIAL for *material* shows another long *e* strategy, again a correct strategy but not for this word. BUTTENS for *buttons* shows a typical representation of the reduced vowel sound in an unaccented syllable. SOING for *sewing* is a typical homophone-related error. Josiah's spelling is advanced for a first grader and is typical of many second- and third-grade spellers.

Syllable Juncture Stage. This stage is seen by some as an extension of the within-word stage. Certainly it encompasses many similar features and confusions. Syllable juncture spellers are usually proficient readers who read many genres of texts and write at least fairly comfortably for different purposes. Spellers at this stage are usually in the intermediate grades, from fourth to sixth or beyond.

Syllable juncture spellers usually have mastered the patterns necessary to spell most single-syllable words correctly and are concerned now with the rules and patterns for spelling multisyllable words. They must apply what they know about spelling patterns across syllable boundaries, which can cause new confusions. Doubling errors at syllable boundaries, like SILLENT for *silent* and BAGAGE for *baggage,* are common. Spellers who can spell single-syllable base words correctly now wrestle with rules about consonant doubling, dropping of silent *e,* and adding of affixes. As a result, errors like HOPEING for *hoping,* DRAGED for *dragged,* REALY for *really,* MISPELL for *misspell,* and STANDDING for *standing* often occur.

Syllable juncture spellers also struggle with issues involving stressed and unstressed syllables, especially vowel sounds in unstressed syllables. In stressed syllables,

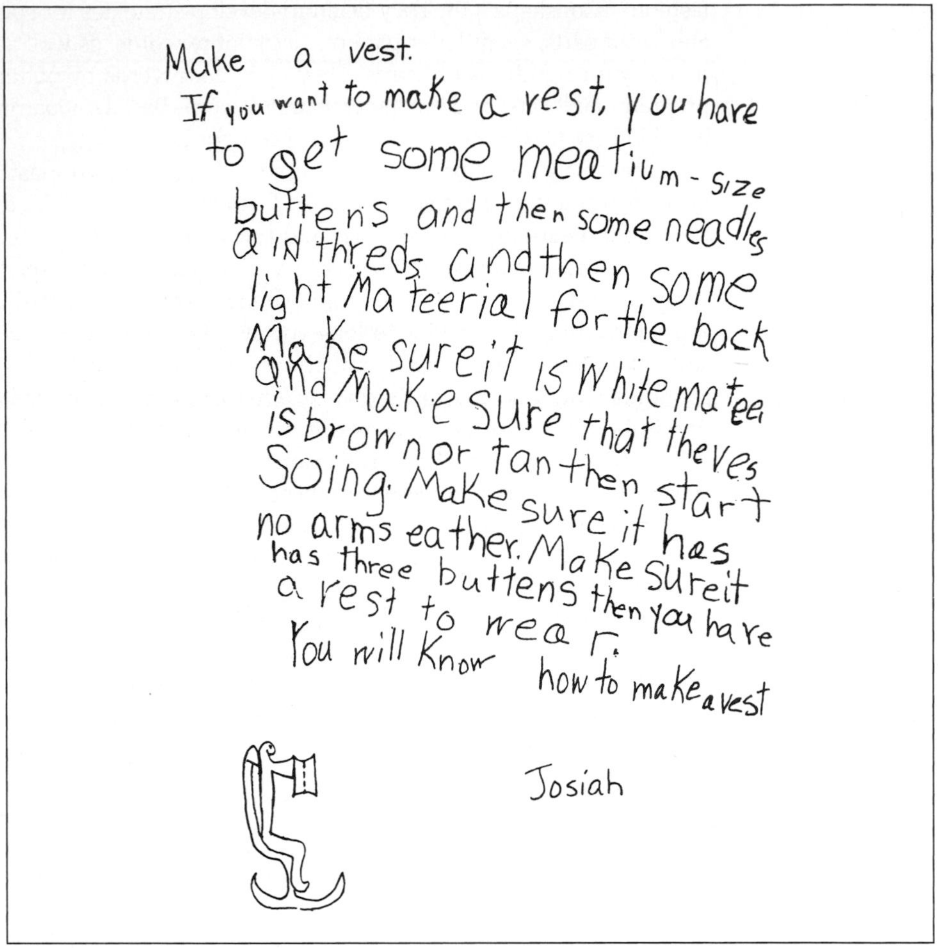

Make a vest.
If you want to make a vest, you have to get some meatium-size buttens and then some neadles and threds and then some light Mateerial for the back Make sure it is White matee and Make sure that the ves is brown or tan then start Soing. Make sure it has no arms eather. Make sure it has three buttens then you have a rest to wear. You will Know how to make a vest

Josiah

FIGURE 4.8 *Within-Word Spelling, First Grader: "Make a Vest"*

the vowel sound is usually fairly obvious. However, in unstressed syllables the reduced vowel sound, which is called a *schwa*, sounds like "uh." This reduced vowel sound can be spelled with any of the five vowel letters as in *again, agent, pencil, complete,* and *focus* or with vowel combinations like in *numerous* (Ganske, 2000, p. 20). A wide variety of unstressed-syllable errors can occur, such as APPAL for *apple,* PENCEL for *pencil,* SQUIRILL for *squirrel,* TRAMPUL for *trample,* and REGULER for *regular.* Learning how to add affixes to base words and how to deal with unstressed syllables are the big challenges of this stage.

Derivational Constancy Stage.　In this final stage of spelling development, typical of adolescence and adulthood, spellers grapple with spelling unusual or infrequently occurring words and their related forms, or *derivations.* Negotiating this final developmental stage requires that spellers develop a sense of how words are related by meaning and by their historical, or *etymological,* roots so that spelling patterns can be preserved across these *derived forms.* For example, derivational stage spellers may confuse *-tion* and *-sion,* as in CONSTITUSION for *constitution,* but they are unlikely to spell this affix as it sounds, as a syllable juncture speller would with CONSTITUSHUN. Common derivational errors are confusing *-ily* and *-aly, -tion* and *-sion,* and so forth, and failing to preserve the *derivational constancy* of related words like *sign/signal* and *decide/decision,* which can include changes in pronunciation while maintaining the spelling pattern.

Success at this stage requires that spellers develop a keen visual memory for words and a sound understanding of the meaning units, or *morphemes,* that many words contain, rather than relying on how words sound. For example, the common misspelling CONFRENCE is attributable to not relating it to its base word, *confer;* likewise, HASEN occurs when the speller forgets that the base is *haste,* and CRITTASIZE and CRITUSIZE occur when the speller forgets the base, *critic.* Studying the common Greek and Latin bases that many words contain and studying all the related or derived forms of a single base word (*critic, critical, criticize, criticism, critique*) are most helpful to spellers at this advanced stage.

Documenting Spelling Progress

With the stages of spelling development in mind, it is useful to monitor and document students' progress by periodically having them attempt to spell a group of unfamiliar words. This provides information about how they handle different common spelling features like vowel patterns, blends and digraphs, prefixes and suffixes, consonant doubling, derivational forms, and so forth. A list of words containing targeted spelling features that is used for assessment is referred to as a *spelling features list.* In the sections that follow, we describe how to use a Word Knowledge Inventory we have developed and several other spelling inventories.

The Monster Test

Richard Gentry's "Monster Test" (Gentry, 2006; Gentry & Gillet, 1993) is an example of a features test that utilizes a list of only 10 words that are spelled in typically different ways by spellers at different stages of development. This is a very quick and informative device that yields excellent information about the child's spelling stage and is useful for tracking developmental changes across the school year without a big investment in testing and interpretation time. In several of his publications including those cited above, Gentry has listed in table form typical misspellings for each word at the different developmental stages. This is a quick and easy-to-interpret device that can be used by teachers without much experience in interpreting developmental spelling strategies.

The Gentry Spelling Grade-Level Test

Richard Gentry, a spelling series senior author and spelling authority, has developed a graded list of spelling words that allows teachers and parents to determine a student's "spelling grade level" without analyzing the student's errors or stage of spelling development (Gentry, 1997) . The test consists of eight lists of 20 words each for grades 1 through 8. Words selected are those that students in a particular grade often misspelled at the beginning of that grade but typically spelled correctly by the end of that grade. A student who spells 50 percent or more of the words on a particular list is said to be spelling comfortably at that grade level. This is a quick screening device that can be useful in placing students in a commercial spelling series and in determining if further spelling analysis is indicated. The Gentry Spelling Grade Level Test is shown in Figure 4.9.

Developmental Spelling Analysis

A commercial spelling assessment procedure comprised of feature lists is Ganske's Developmental Spelling Analysis (DSA) (Ganske, 1999, 2000). The DSA inventory is made up of two lists of 25 words each for each developmental stage from Letter Name to Derivational Constancy (prephonemic and semiphonemic spellings are not assessed). The two lists for each stage are alternate forms that contain different words, each having the same target feature. A 20-item Screening Inventory is given to determine each speller's present stage of development, so that the appropriate stage list can be administered.

After the student's initial placement in a stage based on the screening inventory, one of the two lists for his given stage is administered and the list is scored for completely correct spellings as well as for correct spelling of the target feature in each word, even if the entire word is not spelled correctly. For each stage list of 25 words, a *stage score* is derived based on the number of completely correct words. A stage score of 12 to 21 correct spellings indicates that the student is at that stage of spelling development. At that stage, the student understands enough about the features presented to benefit from instruction, but does not have a complete grasp of those features. At that stage of development, instruction is "within the learner's zone of proximal development" (Ganske, 2000, p. 36) and will likely be most beneficial.

Knowing the student's present developmental stage is one piece of the puzzle. Knowing what specific features of that stage each student has mastered or has yet to master is the other important piece. Each student's spelling strengths and weaknesses are determined by analyzing how the student handled each of the five features characteristic of that developmental stage. Of the 25 words on each list, there are 5 words that contain each specific feature. Each word containing that feature is examined to see if the particular feature is spelled correctly, even if errors occurred in other parts of the word, and a point is given for each correct target feature. A score of 4 or 5 correct on any feature is a sign that the student has mastered that feature; a score of 3 or fewer indicates that the student has not mastered that feature and needs instruction there. While the stage score tells the teacher what developmental stage a student presently

GRADE ONE

1. all	8. on	15. you
2. me	9. the	16. see
3. do	10. and	17. is
4. come	11. one	18. ten
5. play	12. be	19. was
6. at	13. like	20. no
7. yes	14. am	

GRADE TWO

1. jump	8. fine	15. hope
2. apple	9. off	16. much
3. five	10. bell	17. seven
4. other	11. say	18. egg
5. that	12. part	19. sometime
6. more	13. like	20. wall
7. house	14. brown	

GRADE THREE

1. spring	8. placed	15. airplane
2. helps	9. below	16. learn
3. farmer	10. walked	17. those
4. people	11. also	18. cream
5. bones	12. often	19. eight
6. saved	13. wrong	20. carry
7. roof	14. things	

GRADE FOUR

1. worry	8. blame	15. wrote
2. twenty	9. wreck	16. iron
3. you're	10. November	17. fifth
4. dozen	11. loud	18. tomorrow
5. thumb	12. wasn't	19. writing
6. carried	13. finish	20. frozen
7. surprise	14. middle	

(continued)

FIGURE 4.9 *The Gentry Spelling Grade Level Placement Test*

GRADE FIVE

1. neighbor	8. hungry	15. library
2. parties	9. subject	16. yawn
3. rotten	10. claim	17. midnight
4. worst	11. unknown	18. steady
5. laid	12. American	19. prepare
6. manners	13. officer	20. village
7. parents	14. prove	

GRADE SIX

1. jewel	8. depot	15. hymn
2. thief	9. ruin	16. lettuce
3. avenue	10. yield	17. burden
4. arrangement	11. seize	18. canvas
5. theme	12. difference	19. grocery
6. system	13. interview	20. lawyer
7. written	14. zero	

GRADE SEVEN

1. possession	8. agriculture	15. straighten
2. yacht	9. scientist	16. establish
3. thorough	10. anchor	17. laboratory
4. gymnasium	11. announce	18. cashier
5. interrupt	12. revenue	19. wrath
6. athletic	13. patient	20. intelligent
7. secretary	14. pressure	

GRADE EIGHT

1. fierce	8. appropriateness	15. restaurant
2. analyze	9. cheetah	16. alliteration
3. committee	10. schedule	17. grievance
4. predominant	11. autobiographical	18. vengeance
5. pursue	12. executive	19. guarantee
6. chemically	13. coincidence	20. columnist
7. financial	14. seniority	

FIGURE 4.9   *(Continued)*

Source: Reprinted with permission from *My Kid Can't Spell* by J. Richard Gentry. Copyright © 1997 by J. Richard Gentry. Published by Heinemann, a division of Reed Elsevier, Inc., Portsmouth, NH. All rights reserved.

occupies and facilitates creating instructional groups, feature scoring allows the teacher to pinpoint what word features the student has mastered and which need to be taught and practiced.

For each of the four developmental stages, five spelling features are analyzed. They are as follows (Ganske, 2000):

Letter-Name Stage

- Initial and final single consonants
- Initial consonant blends and digraphs
- Short vowels
- Affricate sounds (sounds of /j/, /ch/, "soft" sound of /g/, and sound of /tr/ and /dr/ blends)
- Final consonant blends and digraphs

Within-Word Stage

- Long vowels (vowel-consonant-silent *e*)
- R-controlled vowels
- Other common long vowels (such as *ai, ay, ee, oa, igh, i*-consonant-consonant)
- Complex consonants (three-consonant blends, *ck, kn, dge, qu*)
- Abstract vowels (vowel diphthongs such as *oi, oy, ou, ew*; vowel pairs *oo, au, aw*)

Syllable Juncture Stage

- Doubling and *e*-drop with *-ed* and *-ing* (*baking, tapped*)
- Other doubling at the syllable juncture (*silent, cabbage, rabbit, habit*)
- Long vowel patterns in stressed syllables (*tulip, patient, complain*)
- R-controlled vowels in stressed syllables (*disturb, sheriff*)
- Unstressed syllable vowel patterns (*person, sugar, legal, governor*)

Derivational Constancy Stage

- Silent and sounded consonants (*hasten, muscle, condemn, exhibit*)
- Consonant changes (*office/official, explode/explosion*)
- Vowel changes (*define/definition, relate/relative, produce/production*)
- Latin-derived suffixes (*-able, -ible, -ant, -ance, -ent, -ence, -ary, -ery, -ity*)
- Assimilated prefixes (*in-, im-, ir-, il-, com-, con-, dis-, sub-, re-, bi-, tri-*)

Ganske's DSA is a system for periodic ongoing assessment that yields a wealth of specific information about each individual's strengths and weaknesses in spelling and word knowledge. It does, however, require considerable time and experience to interpret, and it yields information that is more detailed than some teachers want or need. Unlike spelling basal placement tests, students are not placed at grade levels, but rather placed in a developmental sequence at which instruction is most likely to be helpful to them. Students can be grouped for differential instruction and weekly word lists tailored to their specific strengths and weaknesses. Ganske's book *Word Journeys* (2000) contains a wealth of specific teaching strategies, word lists, and student examples that support instruction based on this assessment. Another resource for instruction is Bear, Invernizzi, Templeton, and Johnston's *Words Their Way: Word Study for Phonics, Vocabulary, and Spelling Instruction* (1996).

Monitoring Writing Progress

Assessing students' writing and providing ongoing feedback are critical in encouraging young writers' progress. However, it is important to remember these points about writing assessment:

- Not everything should be assessed or evaluated. Most of children's writing should be for the purpose of communication, not evaluation.
- Assessment should teach; that is, children should learn about writing from the assessment of their work.
- Criteria for assessment should be clear and explicit.
- Children should be involved in the assessment of their writing.
- Assessment should show strengths and progress as well as needed improvement. (Temple, Ogle, Crawford, & Freppon, 2007)

As with spelling, many teachers find it useful to monitor and document students' progress in composition and the use of writing strategies across the year. One way to do so is to collect dated writing samples for comparison across time; another is to compile a checklist of writing features and strategies that students might reasonably be expected to gain facility with across time.

Writing Samples

Collecting dated writing samples is easy, and you can either set aside time for everyone to write a piece to be collected or select and photocopy a piece from each student's writing folder or portfolio at intervals. When you set aside time for everyone to write an assessment sample, you can assign a general topic or form of writing or you can allow students to choose. Letting them choose their own topics makes the writing somewhat more authentic, but asking everyone to write on the same generic topic (e.g., a lost pet, a description of an object or picture, a holiday celebration) or to produce the same form of writing (e.g., a letter, a story from the imagination, a descriptive paragraph) makes it easier to compare each writer's samples.

Some teachers resist assigning writing topics or styles even for assessment, or prefer writers to select their own pieces. In this case, reviewing each student's writing folder or portfolio at intervals and selecting pieces to compare is the course to follow. Students can share in the selection process. The samples collected are more likely to represent authentic writing in which the writer has some investment, but they should represent what the writer typically produces. The purpose of this sampling is not to showcase the student's best writing, but to show growth from one part of the year to another.

When we collect dated samples across a school year, we write comments either on a copy of the sample or on an attached comment sheet. We usually note how the student appears to be managing tasks such as selecting a topic; forming sentences and paragraphs; using the writing cycle to first develop and elaborate on ideas, then check for mechanical problems; and aspects of writing mechanics like capitalization, punctuation, and spelling. We also note things that we observed during the writing, if possible, such as difficulty finding a topic, ease and fluency of the writing, the writer's degree of independence during the writing, ability to reread the piece, and what the writer had to say about the topic or the piece.

Writing Checklists

A checklist of writing skills and strategies can also be used to show how and when students achieve certain benchmarks of writing across the school year. When used with dated samples, this provides comprehensive documentation of the student's writing progress.

Figures 4.10 and 4.11 are examples of writing progress checklists that can be adapted for a range of grades. The benchmarks are typical of students' writing at different ages, but you might have different expectations for your students that can be incorporated into your own checklists. These lists are for primary and elementary grades; middle school teachers could easily adapt the elementary standards for middle school grades.

Six Traits Writing Evaluation

The Six Traits model for writing assessment (Spandel, 2005) highlights six key aspects of writing: *ideas and content, organization, voice, word choice, sentence fluency,* and *conventions* (Temple et al., 2007).

1. *Ideas and content* means having something to say and saying it clearly to the reader. This trait includes knowing something about the topic before writing about it, having an original point of view, and providing details that engage the reader's interest.
2. *Organization* means the writing has a beginning, middle, and end. It may include supporting main ideas with details, sticking to the topic, and making clear transitions from one point to another.
3. *Voice* means using words that express ideas well, even if the writer isn't sure how to use or spell them. Writing with a well-developed voice approaches the writer's oral fluency and expressiveness. If a piece has voice, you can hear the person behind the writing.
4. *Word choice* shows the writer's meaning with precise words and specific, memorable details. The writer uses fresh ways of expressing ideas, avoiding clichés.
5. *Sentence fluency* means a reader can easily read the work aloud. There are sufficient numbers of sentences to convey the meaning, and the sentences are varied in their length and form.

	October	February	May
Composing Easily thinks of topic Can talk about topic before writing Maintains focus Expresses complete thoughts Produces at least 3 related sentences/ thought units			
Style Has a personal "voice" Uses vivid vocabulary Uses descriptive words Organization appropriate to topic and genre			
Usage Inflects plurals Inflects verbs Uses pronouns Subject-verb agreement Complete sentences, not fragments or run-ons			
Mechanics Beginning capitals Proper noun capitals, including I End punctuation Indented paragraphs Spelling checked			

FIGURE 4.10   *Writing Benchmarks for Primary Grades*

6. *Conventions* include correct spelling, capitalization, punctuation, and grammar. It also includes sentence and paragraph construction.

Writers of different ages and levels of development will be more or less advanced in their performance within each trait. Spandel and her associates have listed behavioral descriptors at four levels of development:

- *Exploring writers* are young writers who are experimenting with the whole enterprise of making meaning with graphic communication. Thus, within the trait of ideas and content, exploring writers might use pictures and scribbles to express ideas.
- *Emerging writers* are still young writers, but they have advanced to the point at which they are starting to work the features of conventional writing into their graphic productions. Thus, within the trait of ideas and content, emerging writers

	October	February	May
Composing			
Establishes topic easily			
Topic sentence			
Supporting sentences			
Concluding sentence			
Minimum of one complete paragraph			
Maintains focus			
Style			
Has a personal "voice"			
Maintains voice throughout			
Vivid vocabulary			
Uses descriptive adjectives/adverbs			
Organization appropriate to topic and genre			
Varied sentence length and style			
Usage			
Inflects plurals correctly			
Inflects verbs correctly			
Pronoun-referent agreement			
Subject-verb agreement			
Complete sentences			
Some evidence of subordinate clauses in sentences			
Vocabulary appropriate for topic, audience, and genre			
Mechanics			
Capitalization correct			
End punctuation correct			
Commas correct within sentences			
Quotation marks in dialogue			
Indented paragraphs			
High-utility words spelled correctly			
Spelling appropriate for age/grade			

FIGURE 4.11 *Writing Benchmarks for Elementary Grades*

may use pictures or both pictures and mock writing in such a way that a reader might be able to guess an approximate meaning.

■ *Developing writers,* through a mix of their own inventions and discoveries and overt teaching, can produce written messages that convey clear meaning, with the beginnings of formal organization and attention to some of the conventions of spelling and capitalization. Thus, within the trait of ideas and content, developing writers create stand-alone messages that are more readily decipherable. Their works show some attention to detail.

Ideas and Content:

Clear ideas. It makes sense. _____
The writer has narrowed the idea to a manageable topic. _____
Good information—from experience, imagination, or research. _____
Original and fresh perspective. _____
Details that capture a reader's interest. Makes ideas understandable. _____

Organization:

A snappy lead that gets the reader's attention. _____
Starts somewhere and goes somewhere. _____
The writer continually makes connections within the work. _____
Writing builds to a conclusion. _____
The writer creates a memorable resolution and conclusion. _____

Voice:

Sounds like a person wrote it. _____
Sounds like this particular writer. _____
Brings topic to life. _____
Makes the reader respond and care what happens. _____
The writer has energy and is involved. _____

Word Choice:

Words and phrases have power. _____
Word pictures are created. _____
Thought is crystal clear and precise. _____
Strong verbs and precise nouns. _____

Sentence Fluency:

Easy to read aloud. _____
Well-built sentences. _____
Varied sentence length. Some long sentences, some short. _____

Conventions:

Looks clean, edited and proofread. _____
Free of distracting errors. _____
Easy to read. _____
No errors in spelling, punctuation, grammar and usage, capitalization, and indentation. _____

FIGURE 4.12   *A Rubric for Assessing Writing: Six Traits Writing Evaluation Sheet*

Source: From Charles Temple, Donna Ogle, et al. *All Children Read: Teaching for Literacy in Today's Diverse Classrooms* (with Teach It! Booklet). Published by Allyn and Bacon, Boston, MA. Copyright © by Pearson Education. Reprinted by permission of the publisher

■ *Fluent/experienced writers* express meanings more eloquently in print and take advantage of many features of fluent writing within all six traits. Thus, within the trait of ideas and content, fluent writers create works that show advancing mastery of qualities of writing, including the ability to say things clearly and in fresh and interesting ways, honoring more and more of the conventions of writing.

Six Traits writing evaluation can guide you in evaluating and grading children's written works. But it has another, equally valuable purpose, which is to call children's attention to the things they are doing well and point the way toward improvement. One highly effective way of showing children what they are doing well and what they can do to improve is to use rubrics.

Writing Rubrics

Rubrics are detailed presentations of quality criteria. Rubrics address several aspects of writing at once, and they explain clearly what constitutes a good job. Rubrics may be constructed by the teacher or by the teacher and the students together. Rubrics should be closely connected to the qualities of writing that have been stressed in the focused lessons and any checklists that have been used to guide the students' revising and editing. Students should be fully aware of the meaning of each criterion, or aspect of quality, on the rubric before they produce the work that will be assessed.

Here are the steps for using rubrics:

1. Choose four to eight qualities of writing to assess. (Consider having the children suggest qualities of good writing.)
2. Make sure the qualities of writing you assess have been carefully explained.
3. Describe good work according to each quality. You may also describe fair and poor work.
4. Share the rubrics with the students before they write the works that will be assessed.
5. Use the rubrics often so that students learn what they mean and are able to use their criteria to guide them when they write.

A sample rubric for middle elementary grades, which was adapted from the Six Traits writing evaluation, is shown in Figure 4.12.

Summary

Spelling progress and development can be documented using a *dictated sentence task* or a *Developmental Spelling Inventory*. A sentence dictation task may be used with young children or emergent and beginning readers to show their ability to segment phonemes in spoken utterances. Developmental Spelling Inventories may be used for beginning and developmental reader/writers, to show their mastery of the successive developmental stages of spelling acquisition. The developmental spelling stages (*prephonemic, semiphonemic* or *partial alphabetic, letter-name, within-word, syllable juncture,* and *derivational constancy*) are described and illustrated. Classroom Spelling Inventories are included, with directions for administering the inventories and classifying student's misspellings by word features and the speller's developmental stage. Determining a student's developmental stage and what word features have been mastered helps teachers provide differential instruction.

Growth in writing can be documented by collecting *writing samples* for comparison over time and by using *writing checklists* and *rubrics*, included in the chapter, that show how and when each student has achieved certain *benchmarks* of writing development. Six Traits assessment includes assessment of six key aspects of writing, including *ideas and content, organization, voice, word choice, sentence fluency,* and *conventions*. A Six Traits rubric is included.

(mylabschool™
Where the classroom comes to life!

MyLabSchool is a collection of online tools for your success in this course, your licensure exams, and your teaching career. Visit www.mylabschool.com to access the following:

- Online Study Guide
- Video cases from real classrooms
- Help with your research papers using Research Navigator
- Career Center with resources for:
  - Praxis exams and licensure preparation
  - Professional portfolio development
  - Job search and interview techniques
  - Lesson planning

References

Bear, D. R., Invernizzi, M., Templeton, S., & Johnston, F. (1996). *Words their way: Word study for phonics, vocabulary, and spelling instruction.* Englewood Cliffs, NJ: Prentice-Hall.

Clay, M. M. (1993). *Reading Recovery: A guidebook for teachers in training.* Portsmouth, NH: Heinemann.

Ganske, K. (1999). The developmental spelling analysis: A measure of orthographic knowledge. *Educational Assessment, 6*(1), 41–70.

Ganske, K. (2000). *Word journeys: Assessment-guided phonics, spelling, and vocabulary instruction.* New York: Guilford Press.

Gentry, J. R. (1997). *My kid can't spell!* Portsmouth, NH: Heinemann.

Gentry, J. R. (2006). *Breaking the code: The new science of beginning reading and writing.* Portsmouth, NH: Heinemann.

Gentry, J. R., & Gillet, J. W. (1993). *Teaching kids to spell.* Portsmouth, NH: Heinemann, 1993.

Henderson, E. H. (1990). *Teaching spelling* (rev. ed.). Boston: Houghton Mifflin.

Henderson, E. H., & Beers, J. W. (Eds.). (1980). *Developmental and cognitive aspects of learning to spell: A reflection of word knowledge.* Newark, DE: International Reading Association.

Read, C. (1971). Preschool children's knowledge of English phonology. *Harvard Educational Review 41,* 1–34.

Read, C. (1975). *Children's categorization of speech sounds in English.* Urbana, IL: National Council of Teachers of English.

Spandel, V. (2005). *Creating writers through 6-trait writing assessment and instruction* (4th ed.). Boston: Allyn & Bacon.

Temple, C., Ogle, D., Crawford, A., & Freppon, P. (2007). *All children read: Teaching for literacy in today's diverse classrooms* (2nd ed.). Boston: Allyn & Bacon.

Templeton, S., & Bear, D. (Eds.). (1992). *The development of orthographic knowledge and the foundations of literacy: A memorial festschrift for Edmund Henderson.* Hillsdale, NJ: Erlbaum.

Assessment for External Audiences: Formal Measures

Chapter Outline

This chapter is devoted to formal measures of reading. Two principal types of formal measures are norm-referenced standardized tests and criterion-referenced tests. Most students encounter these formal measures in the form of group achievement tests administered during the elementary and secondary grades and in college admissions tests such as the Scholastic Aptitude Test. The results of formal assessments of reading are often used to assess school, district, or state reading programs; to identify areas of strength and weakness within a curriculum; and to compare achievement patterns of schools, districts, and states.

This chapter provides information to assist you in determining the appropriateness of formal assessments for particular uses and interpreting their results. To use and interpret test scores, teachers must be knowledgeable about characteristics of tests in general and of specific tests. Without this knowledge, interpretations can be difficult at best and inaccurate at worst.

Understanding Formal Measures

For decades, formal tests were used to quantify student achievement and to assess instructional effectiveness. They are still used for these purposes. However, in recent years criticism of the validity and authenticity of formal tests has increased. Today, most schools and school divisions are required to administer and interpret formal measures and to supplement them with a variety of informal and observational assessments. What are the major criticisms of formal tests, particularly reading tests?

First, formal reading tests do not reflect what we know about the reading process. We know that reading is a complex, constructive process in which meaning results from interaction among the reader, the text, and the context in which the reading occurs. The prior experiences, background knowledge, interests, motivation, and knowledge of the reading process are reader factors. The amount and nature of the information conveyed, organizational structures, vocabulary, grammatical complexity, writing style, and even size and clarity of type are text factors. The setting in which the reading takes place, the purpose for the reading, the locus of purpose setting (i.e., whether the purpose is set by the text, the reader, or another person), the frequency of interruptions during reading, and so forth are context factors. These factors combine to enable the reader to actively construct meaning from text.

But formal reading tests most often treat reading as a series of isolated, discrete skills. Test results show how readers perform on one separate skill after another, and these scores are generally added together to yield a global or overall reading score. This practice is a holdover from the traditional view that effective reading requires mastery of a set of discrete skills, each of which can be taught, practiced, and mastered in isolation. This model of reading has largely been replaced by the interactive, constructivist model of learning to read.

Second, formal reading tests typically do not assess reading in authentic ways. In real life, comprehension is often demonstrated by doing something with the information that is gained. But in testing reading, comprehension is usually demonstrated by answering questions about a brief passage, often in a multiple-choice format. In real life, readers often read fairly lengthy selections, including whole stories, chapters, and entire books. In testing reading, selections are usually much shorter; they may be as short as a single sentence, and are rarely longer than a single page.

In real life, reading is rarely timed, and the reader determines how quickly or slowly to read the material. In testing reading, most selections are timed, and readers who don't finish the section are penalized. Most educators agree that formal tests create artificial contexts for effective reading.

Third, formal reading tests often do not match the goals of instruction. Most are geared toward retention of a quantity of factual information, which may be thought of as product. Yet most instructional programs emphasize process as much as product. Especially in the elementary grades, we are as interested in teaching students the process of learning as we are in teaching information and are as concerned with the learning process as with the products of such learning. But formal tests do not take process into account; indeed, they can create the appearance of a lack of success.

For example, imagine a class of low-achieving, reluctant readers and writers. Their teacher hopes that their test scores will increase this year; but she is even more hopeful that the students will modify their negative attitudes about reading, spend more time reading and enjoy it more, and use writing more effectively for communication and self-awareness. As the year progresses, she documents dramatic increases in the amount of reading and writing her students are doing. Their reading habits and their comments about reading reflect increasingly positive feelings about reading and about themselves as readers. However, end-of-year standardized achievement tests show only a modest increase in average reading level. If only these scores were available, it might appear that the class had made little progress in reading improvement. In this case, the formal measures that the school division used were incompatible with the goals of instruction.

Finally, formal tests most often measure skills and operations that are easily quantified and tested. Frequently, students are required to recognize, rather than produce, correct information. For example, they might be asked to choose the best title for a paragraph from several alternatives rather than to create a good title for it, or to choose the correct spelling from several misspellings rather than to spell the word correctly. Recognition is easier than production; it is easier to do, to score, and to measure. But it is generally not what we want students to learn. We teach spelling so students can spell words correctly, not so that they can merely recognize misspellings. We teach them to recognize main ideas so that they can use the information gained by reading, not so they can choose the main idea from a list. The operations that result in increased test scores might not result in real, useful learning.

In spite of these criticisms of formal tests, their widespread use continues. Why? Communities expect their schools to do an effective job of teaching young people the information and skills necessary to live productive lives and be good citizens. When students reach high school, or leave it, lacking basic skills in reading, writing, science, and mathematics, communities are rightfully concerned. They seek to make their schools accountable in a variety of ways. Most of these ways depend on achieving test scores that show what students have mastered.

Formal tests don't test all of the things we want students to know or do, but they do show mastery over certain kinds of information and operations. They yield numerical results that are fairly easy to interpret and compare. They are more economical of time and effort than many informal measures. And because they have standardized administration procedures that everyone must follow to the letter, they ensure that all students will have the same instructions, examples, time limits, and so forth. This makes it easier to compare scores from one locality to another.

Finally, the idea that "numbers don't lie" dies hard. Numerical scores seem less subjective than other results. Many people feel more comfortable with numerical scores than with other types of test results that depend more upon examiner or teacher judgments. So many communities and legislative bodies have continued to require formal test results to ensure educational accountability.

Consequently, teachers need to understand the characteristics, purposes, and features of formal tests.

Characteristics of Tests

When we select a tool to do a job, we typically know the nature of the job, the level of skill we possess, and the tools we have available. The same is true for selecting a formal measure of reading. When that selection is made, we, or those who do the selection, should know what we want to do with the results, the level of skill or support we have in administering and interpreting the test, and the options that are available for selecting a test. Most districts have selected one test or a small group of tests that will be purchased and administered to students.

In the sections that follow, we briefly describe some fundamental concepts of testing and measurement that apply to all standardized tests, not just reading tests. These basic concepts are necessary to an understanding of such reading tests.

The quality of the tool that is selected to do a certain job directly affects the quality of the outcome. For formal tests, two qualities are critical to test performance: *reliability* and *validity*. Both are necessary for a good test, but of the two, validity is the more important.

Reliability

Reliability is a measure of how stable test scores are. It refers to the results obtained from a test, not to the test itself. Every standardized reading test you consider for use should have reported reliability estimates and should identify the methods used to determine such estimates. Reliability is expressed in numerical terms by a reliability coefficient. This decimal number between 0 and 1 shows how consistent the scores are likely to be. The closer to 1.0 the reliability coefficient is, the more reliable the scores will be.

Overall reliability can be profoundly affected by the consistency of individual subtests. Survey reading tests, generally given to large groups for screening purposes, usually have few subtests, and the reliability coefficients refer to the whole test. However, some reading achievement tests and most standardized diagnostic tests have many separate subtests, and the reliability of subtest scores can vary widely. These tests should report subtest reliabilities as well as a coefficient for the entire test, and scores on subtests of questionable reliability should be discounted. If a test that is under consideration has more than one or two subtests of low reliability, another test should be considered.

Another point about judging reliability concerns the standard error of measurement. This term does not mean there are mistakes in the test; it refers to the fact that no score is absolutely precise. The standard error of measurement is a number that indicates how much an individual's score might have varied depending on random chance factors. The standard error shows numerically how accurate any score is likely to be. A small standard error indicates high reliability.

There are three types of reliability: One is *stability,* or the consistency of test scores from one administration to another with the same group of subjects; the second is *internal consistency,* or the consistency of items within a test; and the third is *equivalence,* or consistency across different forms of the same test (Salvia & Ysseldyke, 2001).

Stability. If a group of students took a test several times, each individual's score would be somewhat different each time. If the test scores have good stability, the students' rank order would remain very similar from one testing to another. The student with the highest score the first time would have the highest, or nearly the highest, score the second time; the student with the lowest score would retain very low standing, and the order of students between highest and lowest would remain nearly unchanged. If stability is lacking, a score attained once is unrelated to the score attained another time. Obviously, such scores would have little meaning or usefulness because they would be influenced by random effects.

Stability is estimated using the *test-retest method.* The same test is given twice to the same group of subjects, and the rank order of their scores on each one is compared. Between administrations, subjects might remember a number of items and will be familiar with the format. This will tend to raise everyone's scores, but the rank order of the scores will remain much the same. The rank order of the scores, not the numerical value of the scores themselves, is what is important here.

Internal Consistency. This term refers to the degree to which items within a test are related. Internal consistency is determined by comparing subjects' performance on an entire test to their performance on two halves of the same test administered separately. However, since the more difficult items often come toward the end, it would not be a good practice to split a test at the middle. Instead, alternate items are selected: one-half with the odd-numbered items, the other half with the even-numbered items. If the scores on each half are closely related, good internal consistency has been demonstrated. If scores on the two halves are not closely related, the total test score will not be reliable, and its usefulness is questionable.

Sometimes internal consistency is estimated by the *split-half method* in which students take the two halves of a test as separate tests. The scores on each half are correlated to each other and to the entire test. Other ways of estimating internal consistency involve giving the whole test once and applying one of several mathematical formulas to the total score. The computations are beyond the scope of this discussion, but you will find detailed information in any comprehensive text on measurement methods.

Equivalence.   When alternate forms of a test are used, equivalence is important. Alternate forms that are used for pretesting and posttesting must be highly equivalent if the scores are to be useful.

The *equivalent forms method* is used to estimate this aspect of reliability. It requires the construction of two different tests, each one an equally good sampling of the content being tested. Each form must also be equivalent in difficulty and length. The two forms are administered to the same students in close succession, and the scores on the two forms are correlated. This method usually yields the most conservative estimate of reliability.

Validity

Reliability is necessary, but not sufficient, for a test to be a good one. A test can yield reliable scores but still not measure what it was intended to measure. This quality of actually measuring what was supposed to be measured is referred to as *test validity*.

There are three types of validity that are often referred to in test reviews and manuals. They are *content validity*, or the degree to which the test adequately samples the subject area or body of knowledge being tested; *criterion-related validity*, or the degree to which a test is related to other validated measures of the same ability or knowledge; and *construct validity*, or the degree to which a test measures observable behaviors that are related to traits or qualities, called constructs, that are not directly observable or measurable in themselves.

Content Validity.   In assessing content validity, we ask if the test is an adequate sample of the content area or process being tested. Content validity is particularly important in achievement tests, which are designed to show subject mastery.

A spelling achievement test for elementary students that included only very difficult, unusual words from college textbooks would lack content validity because it did not represent what elementary children study in spelling. A reading test that was made up primarily of multiple-choice questions about reading passages only a few sentences long probably would not be considered a good test of reading ability by many teachers today.

Content validity is established when test makers study school curricula and submit their tests to the scrutiny of subject-area experts. The content validity of current reading tests is a major issue. Some critics claim that many reading achievement tests lack content validity because they measure only a narrow range of real reading behaviors, artificially partition the reading process into a host of separate skills, and ask trivial questions about meaningless passages.

Criterion-Related Validity. One way of establishing validity is to relate the test to other validated measures of the same ability or knowledge. The predetermined criterion may be other test scores, grades or subject-area performance, or other observable behaviors. A test has criterion-related validity if it calls for responses that relate closely to actual performance. *Concurrent validity* and *predictive validity* are both criterion-related.

When a new test is highly correlated to an existing test with established validity, it is said to have concurrent validity. Test makers frequently report coefficients of concurrent validity. But just because two tests are closely related does not necessarily mean that either one is valid, only that they measure the same attribute.

When scores are closely related to later performance on some criterion, the test is said to have predictive validity. This aspect is critically important in aptitude tests since they purport to determine whether someone has the potential to become skilled in a particular field at a later time. If students who do well on a test of mechanical aptitude later excel in woodshop and drafting, are admitted to college engineering and technical schools, or choose careers as engineers, architects, and machinists, that test is a good predictor of mechanical aptitude. The Scholastic Aptitude Test (SAT), used to predict high school students' potential for college success, is high in predictive validity because SAT scores and subsequent college grade-point averages are closely related.

Construct Validity. Traits or qualities that are not directly observable or measurable are called constructs. Attitudes, intelligence, or aptitudes are not directly measurable and must be inferred from observable behaviors. Thus intelligence, musical or mechanical aptitude, judgment, problem solving, attitudes, and interests are all constructs.

If a test has good construct validity, it allows the students to demonstrate behaviors directly related to the construct. In a test of attitudes toward reading, for example, students should be able to show how positively or negatively they would feel about getting a book for a gift, hearing a book discussed, going to the library or bookstore, or seeing someone vandalizing a book. Construct validity is important in all tests, but it is critical in psychological tests, personality tests, and attitude or interest inventories.

Interpreting Test Results

Once a valid and reliable test is selected, administered, and scored, the results are often presented in three ways:

- Distributions of test scores
- Measures of central tendency
- Measures of dispersion

Distributions of Test Scores

A *distribution* of test scores is a visual representation of a group's performance on a given test. Two dimensions are typically used to describe the distribution of test scores. One is the score on the test itself, and the other is the number of students obtaining a particular score. You may be familiar with the *bell-shaped curve* or the *normal distribution* (see Figure 5.1). In this distribution, more students scored in the average range than at either extreme.

Not all distributions are normal. Instead of most of the scores clustering in the middle, a test might yield a distribution with many very high or very low scores. This is called a *skewed* or *asymmetrical distribution* (see Figure 5.2). The shape of the distribution of scores for a class, school, or district graphically represents the overall performance of a group or groups of students.

Compare the distribution of scores in Figure 5.1 to the two distributions in Figure 5.2. At least on the surface, the three sets of scores are distributed differently for different groups of students who completed the test. There are several possible explanations for this difference.

One is that for the asymmetrical distributions, the test might not have adequately measured the construct that was the object of instruction. The distribution that shows

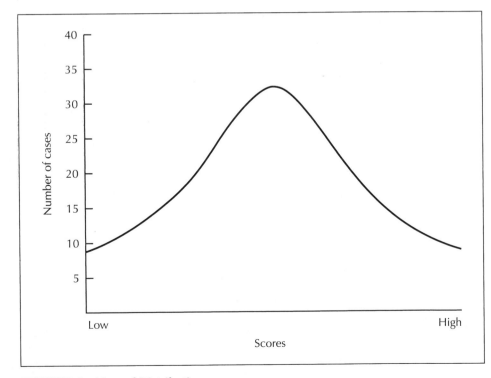

FIGURE 5.1 *Normal Distribution*

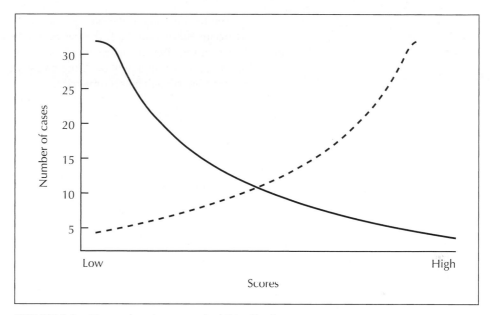

FIGURE 5.2   *Skewed or Asymmetrical Distributions*

many high scores and few low scores is indicative of a test that was probably very easy for most of those taking the test, while the opposite is true for the test illustrated by the distribution showing many low scores and few high scores.

In the latter case, the test might have been too hard for most of those who took it; in addition, variables such as disruptions during the testing, uncomfortable testing conditions, or test bias could have negatively influenced a large number of scores. For whatever the reasons, distributions that are highly skewed should be viewed with caution (Kubiszyn & Borich, 2006).

Measures of Central Tendency: Mean, Median, and Mode

Scores are most often thought of in relation to where they lie on some distribution. The most common measure of central tendency is the *mean,* or average. For example, many teachers use averages in assigning report card grades; a student who got math test scores of 67, 89, 73, 66, 92, and 80 had an average score of 78, which might be represented by a grade of C+. To get a mean score, add all the scores together and divide the sum by the number of scores.

Another measure of central tendency is the *median,* the point on a distribution at which there are equal numbers of scores above and below it. For example, if four students got scores of 14, 15, 16, and 17, the median would be 15.5, since there are two scores below 15.5 and two scores above it. In this case, the median is a point on the distribution but not an actual score, since no student obtained a score of 15.5.

The third measure of central tendency, the *mode,* represents the most frequently occurring score. If no score occurs more than once, there is no mode and the distribution is *amodal.* In general, the closer together the mean, median, and mode of a set of scores are, the more symmetrical their distribution will be. If the measures of central tendency are widely dissimilar, the distribution will be asymmetrical.

When the media report on test scores or school achievement, they most often refer to averages or mean test scores of a school or school district. It is fairly common to see mean scores for a particular school grade compared to other schools in the same division, divisions compared to each other, and divisions compared to state averages.

Measures of Dispersion: Range and Standard Deviation

Measures of dispersion of a set of scores can be expressed in two ways. The *range* of scores on a test represents the breadth of performance by a group of students. It is obtained when the lowest score is subtracted from the highest score and 1 is added to the result. A range of scores is only a gross indication of the dispersion of scores by a group of students. A more common measure of the dispersion of scores is the standard deviation (Lyman, 1998).

The *standard deviation* is an index of how scores are spread out around the mean, regardless of the shape of the distribution. In a normal distribution, most of the scores are grouped near the mean. But how many is "most"? How near is "near"? Statisticians have determined that 68 percent of the scores are arrayed around or at the mean, with smaller percentages near the extremes, as shown in Figure 5.3.

If a student's score were one standard deviation (1SD) below the mean, we would know where the score lay on the distribution; we would know that the student did as well or better than 16 percent of the norm group but that 84 percent did better. The range around the mean, from −1SD to +1SD, is considered the average range. A score of −1SD would be at the bottom of the average range.

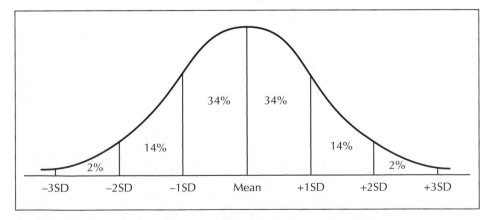

FIGURE 5.3 *Percentages of Scores within Standard Deviation (SD) Units*

The concepts of mean and standard deviation are fundamental to understanding how most scores such as those described below are reported.

Forms of Test Scores

Formal assessment scores are often reported in several different forms. While each of the forms of test scores is based on an individual student's performance, the final form of the score can vary depending upon the computations performed upon the raw score. The *raw score* shows simply how many items the student got right on the test or on each subtest. Raw scores are hard to interpret, so they are converted to more easily comparable forms. The most frequently encountered forms of test scores are grade equivalents, percentiles, stanines, Normal Curve Equivalents (NCEs), *T*-scores, and *z*-scores (Chase, 2000).

Grade-Equivalent Scores. *Grade-equivalent scores,* sometimes called *grade scores,* are frequently used in reporting reading test scores. They represent average achievement for a particular school grade. Grade scores are expressed in two-part numbers; the first number indicates the grade level, and the second number indicates the month within that grade. A grade score of 3.2, for example, means that the student correctly answered the same number of items as the average third grader in the second month of third grade.

Grade scores seem easy to understand, and many parents place great faith in them. They hope to hear that their children have achieved grade scores that are in line with the children's present grade placement; it is easy to understand scores that seem to say that your child is reading just as he "should be" for his grade. But is this what grade scores do?

Grade scores imply that there is some objective, generally accepted standard of achievement for every month of each school grade. But in reality, no such agreement exists. Such expectations are too heavily influenced by local standards, curricular goals, and learner characteristics for any one standard of achievement to exist. Grade scores imply that such objective standards exist, so they are often overinterpreted.

Percentile Scores. Percentiles are more easily understood than grade scores. Percentiles range from 1 to 99; where a score lies within this range indicates relative performance compared with the norm group. A score at the 10th percentile means the student did as well as or better than 10 percent but worse than 89 percent of the subjects in the norm group. A score at the 98th percentile means that the student did as well as or better than 98 percent of the norm group and that only 1 percent attained higher scores.

Sometimes parents misunderstand percentile scores, confusing them with the percentage of items correctly answered. Thus a parent whose child scored at the 50th percentile might think that the child had gotten only 50 percent of the items right, instead of correctly viewing the score as average.

Stanines, NCEs, T-scores, and z-scores. Other forms of scores take the distribution of scores of the norm group into account and provide comparable units across the range of scores. These standardized scores include stanines, NCEs, *T*-scores, and *z*-scores (Salvia & Ysseldyke, 2004).

Stanines are similar to percentiles. The term is derived from "standard nines," which means that the distribution had been divided into nine parts. Stanine scores range from 1 to 9; a score of 5 is the mean, and scores from just below 4 to just above 6 are considered average, with scores of 1 to 3 being below average and scores of 7 to 9 being above average.

Normal Curve Equivalents (NCEs) are derived from the average and standard deviation of a set of scores. Like percentiles, they range from 1 to 99, with a mean of 50. NCEs are widely used in the evaluation of federally funded reading and math programs. *T*-scores and *z*-scores, like NCEs and stanine scores, are based on the standard deviation. The *T*-scores range from 20 to 80, with a mean of 50. These values are computed from the standard deviations and indicate how close to the mean of the normal distribution a particular score lies. The *z*-score is based directly on the standard deviation, with a mean of 0 and a standard deviation of 1. Scores ranging from -1.0 through $+1.0$ are considered average. The range for *z*-scores is from -3.0 to $+3.0$.

Regardless of the type of test, the form of score, or the quality of the test, formal assessment of reading is only a single indication of a student's performance. Scores on norm-referenced standardized tests must be combined with other, more qualitative information to make the most valid instructional decisions.

Norm-Referenced Tests

Norm-referenced tests are developed by test publishers and administered to large numbers of students to develop *norms.* Norms represent average performances of many students in various age, grade, and demographic groups. They are used to compare the performance of students in schools to the performance of those in the norm group.

Test publishers create norm groups that include students from various geographic areas, urban and rural communities, different racial and ethnic groups, and economic groups. Many tests feature special sets of norms for local groups that may be unlike national averages—for example, urban schools, rural schools, high-achieving gifted populations, and highly affluent areas.

Norm-referenced tests serve two general purposes. Many are designed to measure achievement or past learning. These *achievement tests* vary in the scope of topics covered and the detail with which students' results are reported. Tests that assess specific knowledge and strategies associated with reading provide a range of difficulty that begins at a lower level. These tests, designed to show growth in these areas, are considered to be *diagnostic tests* (Chase, 2000).

Achievement Tests

Achievement tests are designed to measure the current level of learners' performance in a variety of areas. Many achievement tests are actually batteries of subtests representing different content or skill areas such as language arts, mathematics, science, and social studies. Tests that provide only a general performance score in each area are often called *survey tests.* Although survey tests can be helpful in pointing to areas in need of additional assessment, little detailed information can be obtained.

Achievement tests are designed to show the depth of students' knowledge and mastery of subject-area curricula. Because they are designed to assess mastery, or achievement, they are usually administered *after* the appropriate instruction has been given. Tests that are used for diagnostic purposes are often given before a program of instruction, or early on, to reveal strengths and so that instruction can be modified appropriately. The content of diagnostic and survey tests is sometimes very similar to that of achievement tests, but the purpose and timing of the testing differ.

Standardized achievement tests are probably the most common type of formal tests used in schools. Many students take a standardized achievement test of some kind yearly, often a battery covering the major curricular areas. Because subtests are usually given in separate sittings, completion of a battery can take several days or a week. Achievement tests must be given under strictly standard conditions for results to be compared across groups, so sometimes a team of school personnel administers all the tests, and sometimes the regular daily schedule is suspended so that all students can be tested simultaneously. The tests are machine-scored by the publishers, and results are sent back to the school.

Almost all achievement tests are group tests. They should be used to evaluate only groups of students, not individuals. For this reason, they are of very limited diagnostic use. They are useful only for evaluating the progress of large groups such as whole schools or all students in a grade.

To be valid, the content of achievement tests must represent typical school curricula. A math test, for example, will generally be made up of problems and calculations common to most school math programs for a particular grade. What is considered typical is decided by consulting subject-area experts, by studying widely used textbooks and materials and field-testing experimental test forms. Content validity, or how well a test represents the major aspects of the subject area, is of particular importance, but how closely the curriculum of an individual district, school, or classroom coincides with national trends is difficult to say. Achievement tests in any subject area should be carefully evaluated to see how well their content matches local curricula and materials.

Most of the widely used achievement batteries measure reading comprehension and vocabulary, English usage, science, math, and social studies. Most have forms for early elementary grades through high school, although some school districts do not begin using them until third or fourth grade. Some batteries have reading readiness tests for kindergarten and first grade.

Among the typical wide-ranging achievement batteries are the **Metropolitan Achievement Test,** the **Comprehensive Test of Basic Skills,** the **Stanford Achievement Test,** and the **California Achievement Test,** all designed for use in kindergarten through twelfth grade. The Metropolitan Achievement Test includes prereading, math, and language subtests for kindergarten; word recognition (first and second grades only), reading vocabulary, reading comprehension, language, science, math concepts and problem solving, math procedures, and social studies subtests, a norm-referenced writing test, and a diagnostic battery. The Comprehensive Test of Basic Skills includes readiness (kindergarten and first grade only), reading vocabulary, reading comprehension, spelling, language, math, social studies, science, and study skills subtests. The Stanford includes reading, language, study skills, spelling, math, science, social sciences, and listening subtests. The California Achievement Test includes reading, spelling, language, math, study skills, science, and social studies subtests.

There are also group tests of reading achievement that include only reading-related subtests. These are sometimes given at the end of each school year, usually beginning at the end of third grade. Fairly typical of this group of tests are the **Gates-MacGinitie Reading Tests,** with vocabulary and comprehension subtests and forms for kindergarten through twelfth grade, and the **Nelson-Denny Reading Test,** with vocabulary, comprehension, and reading rate subtests and forms for high school and college students and adults.

There are a few reading achievement tests for individual administration. Two examples are the **Peabody Individual Achievement Test (PIAT-R)** and the **Wide Range Achievement Test (WRAT-3).** These instruments are hybrids with characteristics of both group achievement tests and individual survey tests. Both tests are often given as diagnostic screening devices to students experiencing difficulty in either reading or math or to those with generally poor school achievement.

The PIAT-R contains reading recognition, reading comprehension, spelling, math, and general information subtests. Because it includes math as well as various reading skills and general information, the PIAT-R measures mastery of the largest part of typical elementary curricula.

The WRAT-3, often used in screening students for special education programs, is designed for ages 5 through senior adulthood. The WRAT-3 has reading, spelling, and arithmetic subtests. The reading portion of the WRAT-3 is made up entirely of lists of single words. Pronunciation within 10 seconds is the only criterion. It does not measure comprehension of either text or words, and no reading of connected text is included.

Diagnostic Tests

Diagnostic tests are norm referenced and standardized. They are administered to students who are showing signs of reading difficulties. Most diagnostic tests are individually administered. Diagnostic tests differ from achievement tests in three major ways:

1. They have a large number of subtest scores (sometimes called part scores) and a larger number of items.
2. The items are devised to measure specific skills.
3. Difficulty tends to be lower in order to provide adequate discrimination among students with reading problems.

Diagnostic tests, both the group and individual types, have numerous subtests and yield a profile of scores. Each subtest assesses a particular skill area. Developers of these tests maintain that analysis of a profile of subtest scores will reveal strengths and weaknesses in skill areas and that this analysis makes them more diagnostic than survey tests.

Diagnostic tests for group administration frequently include subtests assessing some or most of the following skills: reading comprehension, vocabulary, visual and auditory discrimination, structural analysis, numerous aspects of phonic analysis, sound blending, skimming and scanning, syllabication, sight-word recognition, and spelling. Because of the number of separate subtests, they usually have to be administered in several sittings.

An example of a group diagnostic test is the **Stanford Diagnostic Reading Test.** The Stanford, testing grades 1 through 12, includes subtests assessing auditory discrimination, auditory vocabulary, word meanings, phonic and structural analysis, and literal and inferential reading comprehension. Levels for grade 4 and beyond include reading rate, and for grade 8 and beyond include skimming/scanning/fast reading subtests. Scores are reported in grade scores, percentiles, and stanines. The test takes about two hours to administer.

There are many diagnostic reading tests for individual administration. They attempt a broad-based analysis of skills, with assessment of word recognition and decoding skills and comprehension of prose passages. An example is the **Diagnostic Assessments of Reading.** This test is comprised of six individually administered subtests assessing word analysis, oral and silent reading fluency and comprehension, spelling, and word meanings.

Some standardized diagnostic tests focus on word recognition and word analysis skills. Among these are the **Diagnostic Screening Test—Reading,** the **Diagnostic Achievement Battery,** and the **Gates-McKillop-Horowitz Reading Diagnostic Test.** The latter is probably the best known of this type of test. Designed for students with reading problems in grades 1 through 6, the Gates-McKillop-Horowitz assesses oral reading fluency of story passages without comprehension assessment, flashed and untimed recognition of whole words, recognition of nonsense words, dividing words into syllables, producing letter sounds, letter naming, sound blending, auditory discrimination, spelling, and informal writing. The test yields grade-equivalent scores and overall reading ratings of average, above average, and below average. No estimate of reading comprehension is available, and all scores depend on the student's oral reading level.

Some specialized diagnostic tests focus on oral reading ability only. The **Slosson Oral Reading Test** is one of these. The student does not read connected text; the test is made up of lists of words in isolation. It purports to furnish an instructional reading level for the student on the basis of word pronunciation alone. Because this level is derived from reading words in lists, it is largely useless.

More typical of true oral reading tests are the **Gray Oral Reading Tests** and the **Gilmore Oral Reading Test.** In these tests, comprehension results are less important to the overall scoring than oral reading accuracy and speed. The Gray Oral Reading Test is not intended as a comprehension test, but it does include comprehension questions following passages and yields a comprehension score as well as an Oral Reading Quotient that combines the oral fluency and comprehension scores. The Gilmore Oral

Reading Test yields separate oral fluency and comprehension scores. Testing is discontinued when a ceiling number of word recognition errors occur, even if comprehension continues to be adequate.

A number of individual diagnostic tests resemble Informal Reading Inventories, with silent and oral reading passages followed by comprehension questions. They differ from Informal Reading Inventories in that they are norm-referenced. The **Durrell Analysis of Reading Difficulty** and the **Diagnostic Reading Scales**—Revised are examples of these. As in a typical IRI, these tests assess sight vocabulary recognition, word analysis in isolation and in context, and silent and oral comprehension. They include graded word lists, graded story passages with comprehension questions, supplemental tests of phonics and decoding skills, and systems for determining reading levels by counting errors. Assessment of oral fluency includes counting the oral reading miscues, but no miscue analysis.

The Diagnostic Reading Scales assess comprehension with a preponderance of questions requiring short answers and literal recall; some questions are answered by yes or no. Rate of reading is measured, but does not take into account that good readers vary their rate for different reading purposes. In this test, the "instructional level" is the student's oral reading level, and the "independent level" is the student's silent reading level. This test also includes supplementary phonics subtests that assess initial and final consonant sounds, blends and digraph sounds, initial consonant substitution, auditory recognition of consonant sounds, long and short vowel sounds and variant vowels, recognition of syllables and phonograms, sound blending and auditory discrimination.

The Durrell Analysis of Reading Difficulty also assesses word recognition and word analysis, oral fluency, and silent and oral comprehension. It includes listening comprehension, identifying meanings of individual words, recognition of sounds of individual letters, blends, digraphs, phonograms and initial and final affixes, spelling, visual memory of words, and "prereading phonics abilities" including matching spoken with written sentences ("syntax matching"), identifying letter names in spoken names (such as *s* in *Esther*), and identifying and writing letters.

The **Woodcock Reading Mastery Test** is often used in special education. The Woodcock consists of six subtests: visual-auditory learning, letter identification, word identification, word attack, word comprehension, and passage comprehension. Designed for use in all grades from kindergarten through twelfth, it takes about 30 to 60 minutes to administer.

The letter identification subtest requires the student to identify letters shown in eight styles of type. The word identification subtest consists of 150 words in order of difficulty from preprimer (*the, and*) to twelfth grade (*facetious, picayune*). They are listed in isolation, and the student pronounces the words in an untimed presentation. The word attack subtest consists of 50 nonsense words to be decoded and pronounced. Items range in difficulty from *bim* to *wubfambif.* The word comprehension subtest contains 70 verbal analogies: bird—fly, fish—____. The subject reads the analogy silently and says a word to complete the set. The passage comprehension subtest consists of modified cloze items; a word is omitted from a sentence, and the subject reads the item silently, then gives a word to complete it. Early items are single sentences with a picture clue; later items contain two or three sentences and have no picture.

The Woodcock yields percentiles, grade-equivalent scores, and age-equivalent scores for each subtest and a Total Reading score representing the combined subtest scores.

Criterion-Referenced Tests

Criterion-referenced tests enable teachers to compare a student's performance to a predetermined goal or outcome rather than to the performance of others. Criterion-referenced tests provide a way of determining whether a student has met instructional goals, or *criteria* (Kubiszyn & Borich, 2000).

An asset of criterion-referenced tests is their diagnostic potential. They can indicate with precision what a student can or cannot yet do. Appropriate instructional modifications can be made, which is the major goal of any diagnostic procedure. They have greater diagnostic power than norm-referenced tests because they yield information related to specific goals rather than information relating the performance of children to one another. Also, they tend to minimize damaging competition among students, since a student's achievement is not measured in terms of someone else's achievement but rather in terms of a preset criterion. Both parents and students can then concentrate on the goals to be attained rather than on invidious comparisons among individuals or groups.

However, criterion-referenced tests might be top-heavy with objectives that are easiest to measure, such as factual material. Higher-order learning processes, such evaluation and application of knowledge, are naturally harder to assess and may be underrepresented. Also, since criteria of quality or accuracy are always arbitrary, they should be considered carefully. There is nothing magical about 80 percent, 90 percent or 100 percent accuracy. If skills are truly hierarchical, as with some math skills, then 100 percent might be necessary before the student goes on to more difficult skills. If there is no particular sequence of skills in one area, or no generally agreed-upon progression, then all quality criteria are arbitrary, and one may be just as good as another.

Goals and Objectives

Criterion-referenced testing is part of a three-part instructional model. First, the overall *instructional program goals* must be decided on and stated. These goals are usually broad statements of general educational outcomes. Examples of reading program goals might be to read different kinds of text with adequate comprehension, to appreciate different literary genres, or to recognize words fluently.

Program goals are often developed at the district or state level. Such goals rarely specify how such behaviors or attitudes will be conveyed or what specific levels of competency are required. They serve to define the general directions in which instruction will move.

Program objectives follow from instructional program goals. They define more narrowly the desired outcomes of the instruction, such as the following:

- Students will recognize and discriminate among basic speech sounds.
- Students will demonstrate effective listening skills.
- Students will identify characteristics that distinguish literary genres.

Program objectives are usually developed at the district or building level. They apply to specific educational programs, but they usually do not specify the level of proficiency desired or how such objectives will be implemented.

Instructional objectives are the specific statements of learner behavior or outcomes that are expected after a period of instruction. Instructional objectives define what specific content is taught, as in these examples:

- After completion of the Level 1 reader, students will recognize at sight all the basal words listed at the end of the book.
- After reading this story, students will formulate two inferences about the possible results of the main character's actions.
- By the end of November of kindergarten, students will name the months of the year, in order, from memory.

Instructional objectives are sometimes referred to as behavioral objectives because they describe the behaviors that learners are to demonstrate. Objectives that call for students to "appreciate" or "understand" are common, but they do not describe the behaviors to be shown. Because of this, instructional objectives often do not take into account attitudes or generally unmeasurable behaviors, instead focusing on discrete, measurable behaviors.

Good instructional objectives identify the *behavior* to be demonstrated, which is the observable learning outcome. They state the *conditions* under which the student will demonstrate the outcome: *from memory, by Friday, orally, in writing, given a list of 20 misspelled words,* and the like. These conditions are sometimes referred to as "the givens"; they are contained in objective statements such as the following:

- *Given* a list of 30 primer level basal words, the student will identify 25 words at sight.
- *Given* 20 two-digit addition problems, the student will compute all answers correctly.

Good instructional objectives also state the *criterion level* of mastery desired: the number of items correct, a percentage of accuracy, the number of consecutive times performed, the prescribed time limit (where speed of performance is required), or the essential features to be included (as in a composition or essay response).

From instructional objectives come the items that are used on criterion-referenced tests. To achieve its purpose of determining how closely a student has achieved mastery of a skill or objective, each test item must define the criterion or skill being assessed. Criterion-referenced test items are often taken directly from instructional objectives, when such tests are developed locally. When the instructional objectives have been written so that they are sufficiently clear, precise, and measurable, developing such test items is easy. For example, with an instructional objective like "After completing the Level 1 reader, students will recognize all of the basal words at sight," a criterion-referenced test item like "From the list provided, read these words with 90 percent accuracy" might follow.

As with any other kind of test, criterion-referenced test items must fairly and adequately sample the essential skills or knowledge desired. Test items must match the learning outcomes and conditions specified in the instructional objectives; this insures test validity. For example, if an instructional objective calls for students to discriminate between statements of fact and opinion in newspaper articles, then test items that require them to discriminate between statements of fact and opinion in a letter to the editor is a good match, but an item that requires them to state an opinion about the use of letters to the editor is not a good match.

When instructional programs and tests are developed locally, the tests usually match quite closely the instructional goals. So, too, do commercial skills programs that feature their own criterion-referenced tests. When tests are purchased separately from programs or when test programs are purchased but instructional programs are developed locally, a mismatch may occur between what is taught and what or how that content is tested.

When judging the objectives for a commercial criterion-referenced test or test program, keep these questions in mind:

1. Do these objectives call for appropriate learning outcomes for this subject area?
2. Do these objectives represent a balance of thinking and learning skills?
3. Are the desired outcomes realistically attainable?
4. Do these objectives fit the goals and philosophy of our schools?

Benchmarks and Rubrics

Many of today's criterion-referenced assessments refer to behavioral standards as *benchmarks*. Like behavioral objectives, benchmarks are statements of key tasks students are expected to perform or behaviors they are expected to demonstrate. Benchmarks are useful because they describe concretely what students are expected to do. Benchmarks are often used in elementary report cards and in documenting students' progress.

Some examples of benchmarks for emergent readers include the following:

- Can retell familiar stories such as "The Three Bears" after hearing them.
- Can accurately point to individual words in short memorized texts.
- Can accurately recognize at least 20 words at sight.
- Can sort pictures of common objects that have the same beginning consonant sound.

Some examples of writing benchmarks for upper elementary grades might include the following:

- The writing has a consistent central idea or topic throughout the piece.
- The writing has a clear lead and conclusion.
- Sentences are varied in length and structure throughout the piece.
- Vocabulary is precise, specific, and appropriate to the tone of the piece.
- Capitalization, punctuation, and spelling are largely correct and are appropriate to the standards of the writer's grade.

Another criterion-referenced measure is the rubric. A rubric specifies the expected performance or behavior and includes standards for demonstrating competence. Many rubrics feature a point scale that allows the performance to be rated. Rubrics are widely used to assess students' writing. For example, Figure 5.4 shows a writing assessment rubric that is based on the Virginia Standards of Learning for fifth grade.

Domain	*Rating*			
COMPOSING	*4*	*3*	*2*	*1*
Central Idea	Throughout	Consistent	Inconsistent	Weak/absent
Elaboration	Fully detailed	Adequate detail	Inconsistent detail	Little or no detail
Organization	Intact, cohesive	Consistent, few lapses	Inconsistent organization	Little or no organization
WRITTEN EXPRESSION				
Vocabulary	Vivid, precise	Consistent, clear	Bland, imprecise	Repetitive, unclear
Information	Specific	Fairly specific	General	Lacking
Voice	Clear, memorable	Recognizable	Weak or inconsistent	Lacking or inappropriate
Sentence Variety	Consistent variety	Some variety	Little variety	Monotonous
USAGE/MECHANICS				
Sentence Formation	Consistently correct	Largely correct	Inconsistent	Largely incorrect
Usage	Consistently correct	Largely correct	Inconsistent	Largely incorrect
Mechanics	Consistently correct	Largely correct	Inconsistent	Largely incorrect

FIGURE 5.4 *Sample Rubric for Evaluating Writing*

State Standards and Assessment

To ensure school accountability and establish uniform academic standards, most states have established curricular goals for the core academic areas and have developed statewide testing programs for all public schools. These tests are criterion-referenced tests, in that scores necessary to pass each test are established in advance.

Although each state's standards and assessments vary, most are similar. Curricular goals establish the basic knowledge and skills that teachers are to teach and students are to learn in each grade from kindergarten through twelfth grade. These goals are typically stated as instructional objectives—that is, they describe what the student is to do, with or without specifying the criterion. Some examples, from the Standards of Learning for Virginia Public Schools, are as follows:

- **Social Studies (Geography), grade 2:** The student will describe our nation as composed of states and locate the following on a map of the United States: Washington, DC; the states of Virginia, Maryland, West Virginia, North Carolina, Kentucky, and Tennessee; and major rivers, mountain ranges, and lakes in the United States.
- **Mathematics, grade 4:** The student will identify and represent equivalent fractions and relate fractions to decimals, using concrete objects.
- **English (Reading), grade 6:** The student will read and learn the meanings of unfamiliar words and phrases; identify word origins, derivations, and inflections; identify analogies and figurative language; use context and sentence structure to determine meaning and differentiate among multiple meanings of words; and use word-reference materials.
- **English (Reading Analysis), grade 11:** The student will read and critique a variety of poetry; analyze the poetic element of contemporary and traditional poems; identify the poetic elements and techniques that are most appealing and that make poetry enjoyable; and compare and contrast the works of contemporary and past American poets. (Board of Education, Commonwealth of Virginia, 1995/2002)

Instructional objectives for all public school students statewide are generally developed over a period of several years by committees of parents, teachers, state and local education officials, business people, and subject-area experts (historians, mathematicians, etc.). Textbooks and curricula are studied to establish what content all students should be taught. Then criterion-referenced tests are developed to measure students' mastery of required content. Versions of the tests are field-tested in selected districts across a state to determine students' current status in mastering content, as well as problems in directions, time limits, item difficulty, response sheets, and other factors. The results of field-testing are used to fine-tune the tests that will eventually be given to all students in particular grades.

States also establish minimum criteria for passing each test and develop standardized testing procedures to ensure that all students take the same test at nearly the same time under the same conditions. Allowable adaptations for special-needs students are specified, and testing may be monitored in a variety of ways to make sure that the procedures are strictly followed. As mentioned previously, standardized conditions are necessary so that results can be compared.

Because states also determine the consequences of failing to achieve at a particular level, this kind of assessment is sometimes referred to as *high-stakes testing.* The stakes, in many cases, are indeed high. In some cases, students can be retained in grade or denied high school credits or diplomas. School divisions must achieve specified pass rates by a particular year, or show a certain amount of growth toward the pass rate, in order to maintain accreditation and funding. Administrators and teachers are under tremendous pressure in some areas to maintain or raise average scores and pass rates. In order to do so, many school divisions across the country have engaged in curriculum alignment, a process by which local curricula are analyzed and modified to match the state standards. Curriculum alignment helps schools make sure they are teaching the content their states require in enough detail and depth so that students can show mastery on the tests. However, it also tends to encourage schools to delete any subject matter that is not on the statewide tests. This in turn creates rigidity in curriculum development and a focus on teaching a narrow range of knowledge, skills, and operations that teachers know will appear on the assessments (Temple, Ogle, Crawford, & Freppon, 2008).

Summary

The basic test characteristics that teachers should be familiar with are *reliability* and *validity.* Reliability refers to the consistency of test scores. Aspects of reliability are *stability,* or consistency across repeated administrations; *internal consistency,* or consistency among test items; and *equivalence,* or consistency across alternate test forms. Validity refers to how well a test measures what it was intended to measure. *Content validity* is the quality of adequately sampling the subject area or process being assessed. *Criterion-related validity* is made up of *concurrent validity,* or how closely a test is related to another test of established validity, and *predictive validity,* the degree to which test performance is related to some other established criterion. *Construct validity* refers to how well the test measures traits or constructs that are not directly observable but must be inferred from observable behavior. Intelligence is an example of a construct.

Commonly used descriptive statistics include *distributions, indices of central tendency and dispersion,* and forms of *standard scores.* A distribution is an array of scores from highest to lowest. Many standardized tests assume a *normal distribution,* a symmetrical array with most scores falling near the mean and progressively fewer scores at the extreme high and low ends. Asymmetrical distributions are referred to as *skewed.* Indices of central tendency include the *mean,* an arithmetic average; the *median,* the point in a distribution at which there are equal numbers of higher and lower scores; and the *mode,* the most frequently occurring score. Indices of dispersion describe how far apart scores are from one another. They include the *range,* or the span from highest to lowest score, and the *standard deviation,* which shows how far from the mean each score is in standard or equal increments.

Standardized reading tests usually yield several forms of test scores. *Grade scores* are two-part numbers representing a grade and month. A grade score means that the student achieved the same score as the average student in that grade. *Percentiles* are standard scores that show what percentage of the norm population scored higher or lower than the individual tested. *Stanines* are scores in which the distribution has been divided into nine equal intervals; a stanine score indicates which ninth a score fell in. *T-scores* and *z-scores* use the concepts of mean and standard deviation to show where a score lies in relation to the mean of a normal distribution.

Norm-referenced tests are based on norms, or average performances across grades, ages, and demographic groups. Norms are used to compare the performance of local students and groups to these averages. *Achievement tests* are designed to measure past learning and to assess the effectiveness of instruction. *Diagnostic tests* are designed to reveal individuals' strengths and weaknesses in particular areas.

Criterion-referenced tests are used to compare a student's performance to a predetermined goal or criterion rather than to the performance of other students. They provide a way to document whether students have met instructional goals or criteria. In developing criterion-referenced tests, broad *instructional program goals* and specific *instructional objectives* are determined. Objectives describe what students are expected to do or demonstrate and the level of accuracy required for satisfactory performance.

Benchmarks are also behavioral statements of what students must be able to do or show. They are often incorporated into report cards and student progress documentation. *Rubrics* specify in detail what features comprise satisfactory performance and often feature point scales used to rate student performance. In recent years, many states have established statewide instructional goals that describe the knowledge and skills that teachers are to teach and students are to learn at each grade from kindergarten through twelfth grade. Criterion-referenced tests are used to determine if students have met these instructional goals at an acceptable level of achievement. Such assessment is sometimes referred to as *high-stakes testing* because issues of retention, graduation, and funding are often associated with it. Many localities have conducted *curriculum alignment* in which local curricula are analyzed and modified to more closely fit state requirements. This can ensure that students are taught what they will be tested on, but can result in deleting curriculum that is not on the tests.

MyLabSchool is a collection of online tools for your success in this course, your licensure exams, and your teaching career. Visit www.mylabschool.com to access the following:

- Online Study Guide
- Video cases from real classrooms
- Help with your research papers using Research Navigator
- Career Center with resources for:
  - Praxis exams and licensure preparation
  - Professional portfolio development
  - Job search and interview techniques
  - Lesson planning

References

Board of Education. Commonwealth of Virginia. (1995/2002). *Standards of learning for Virginia public schools.* Richmond: Author.

Chase, C. I. (2000). *Contemporary assessment for educators.* New York: Longman.

Kubiszyn, T., & Borich, G. (2006). *Educational testing and measurement: Classroom application and practice* (7th ed.). New York: Wiley.

Lyman, H. B. (1998). *Test scores and what they mean* (6th ed.). Boston: Allyn & Bacon.

Salvia, J., & Ysseldyke, J. E. (2004). *Assessment* (8th ed.). Boston: Houghton Mifflin.

Temple, C., Ogle, D., Crawford, A. N., & Freppon, P. (2008). *All children readers: Teaching for literacy in today's classrooms* 2nd edition. New York: Allyn & Bacon.

Emergent and Beginning Literacy

Chapter Outline

Sarah Fellows and Howard Gao teach in a multiage kindergarten and first-grade classroom. They have 30 children between them, who range in age from 5 to almost 7 years old. Every morning before class begins the children find cards with their names written on them and place them in the "Look Who's Here Today!" pocket chart. Then the children go to the circle for Morning Message. Children take turns coming forward and choosing the printed cards with the names of the day and the month, and the numbers for the date. There are pictures of a sun, a cloud, of snow flakes, and rain that are put on the flannel board to show the weather. Sarah or Howard leads an interactive writing session, talking through a preview of the day's events and inviting a child forward to write whole words or fill in letters for some of the sounds.

Both teachers like the multiage arrangement because it helps the children whose emergent literacy is further along to read along with a more advanced peer group. Children who are still working on emergent concepts can work with peers as well. But the groups are almost constantly being formed and reformed based on the two teachers' close observation and periodic assessment of their children.

Emergent Literacy and Beginning Reading

The first five chapters of this book gave an overview of the learning-to-read process, considered the ways in which reading assessment is used for internal and external audiences, and looked in detail at both "informal" approaches to assessment, exemplified by the Informal Reading Inventory, and at "authentic" approaches (exemplified by the use of portfolios). The next four chapters will look into the special challenges of assessing and teaching each age group of students. This chapter considers emergent and beginning readers. Chapter 7 looks at developing readers, and Chapter 8 examines mature readers and adolescent readers with reading problems.

Understanding and Assessing Emergent and Beginning Literacy

Emergent literacy has the following aspects:

- Print concepts
- Letter knowledge
- The concept of word

- Phonological awareness
- Knowledge of letter-to-sound correspondences, or phonics
- Word recognition

Of course there are other important aspects of emergent literacy, such as being interested in and well disposed toward reading. Children are comprehending stories and other kinds of texts, too—especially those that are read to them. But these and other aspects of literacy are treated in later chapters.

Print Orientation Concepts

The Importance of Print Orientation Concepts.   As we saw above, the National Research Council (Snow, Burns, & Griffin, 1998, p. 5) stressed the importance of acquainting young children with "the basic purposes and mechanisms of reading." New Zealand educator Marie Clay has shown a particular genius for seeing these basic purposes and mechanisms from a child's point of view. One whole set of challenges facing a young child is knowing her way around a book. Imagine a child in a reading circle who hears instructions such as these:

> Open the book to the first page. Look at the first word. Go on to the next word. What letter does it begin with? Look at the end of the line: Don't you see that the author is asking a question? Now go on to the next page.

The teacher in this situation is assuming that the child knows how an English book is opened (it's different in Chinese); knows what a "page" is and where to find the "first" one; knows what a word is and that words in written English are arranged on a page from left to right and from top to bottom (not so in Chinese or Hebrew; and in ancient Greek, the words on the same page were alternately arranged from left to right and from right to left); knows what a letter is and that the "first letter" in a word refers to the one farthest to the left; understands marks of punctuation; and so on.

Assessing Print Orientation Concepts.   It is unwise to assume that children who are just entering school understand the mechanisms of print. There are many children in kindergarten and first grade who do not; so Clay developed the Concepts About Print Test (1979) to assess these aspects of a child's orientation to books and to written language. This test is highly recommended for kindergarten and primary-grade teachers as well as for reading clinics. It comes with one of two reusable books and is available from Heinemann Educational Books, 361 Hanover Street, Portsmouth, New Hampshire 03801-3959.

The aspects of Concepts About Print Test that are especially relevant to the present discussion of emergent literacy are

- Book orientation knowledge.
- Principles involving the directional arrangement of print on the page.
- The knowledge that print, not the picture, contains the story.

- Understanding of important reading terminology such as word, letter, beginning of the sentence, and top of the page.
- Understanding of simple punctuation marks.

The assessment of orientation concepts about written language can be carried out by using a simple illustrated children's book, one that the child being tested has not seen before. The Concepts About Print Test has two specially made books (*Sand* and *Stones*), but teachers can get much of the flavor of the procedure with a book of their own choosing. The following are some concepts that can be tested and the procedures to use with them:

1. **Knowledge of the Layout of Books.** Hand the child a book, with the spine facing the child, and say, "Show me the front of the book." Note whether the child correctly identifies the front.

2. **Knowledge That Print, Not Pictures, Is What We Read.** Open the book directly to a place where print is on one page and a picture is on the other (you should make sure beforehand that the book has such a pair of pages and have it bookmarked for easy location). Then say, "Show me where I begin reading." Observe carefully to see whether the child points to the print or the picture. If the pointing gesture is vague, say, "Where, exactly?" If the child points to the print, note whether the child points to the upper left-hand corner of the page.

3. **Directional Orientation of Print on the Page.** Stay on the same set of pages, and after the child points at some spot on the printed page, say, "Show me with your finger where I go next." Then observe whether the child sweeps his finger across the printed line from left to right or moves it in some other direction.

   Then ask, "Where do I go from there?" and observe whether the child correctly makes the return sweep to the left and drops down one line.

   Note that a correct direction pattern is like this:

   If the child indicates some other directional pattern, make a note of it.

4. **Knowledge of the Concepts of *Beginning* and *End*.** Turning now to a new page, say, "Point to the beginning of the story on this page" and then "Point to the end of the story on this page." Observe whether the child interprets both requests properly.

5. **Knowledge of the Terms *Top* and *Bottom*.** Turning to another pair of pages that have print on one page and a picture on the other, point to the middle of the printed page and say, "Show me the bottom of the page" and then "Show me the top of the page." Then point to the middle of the picture and say, "Show me the top of the picture" and then "Show me the bottom of the picture." Note whether the child responds accurately to all four requests.

6. **Knowledge of the Terms *Word* and *Letter*.** Now hand the child two blank index cards and say, "Put these cards on the page so that just one word shows between them" and then "Now move them so that two words show between them. Now move them again so that one letter shows between them" and then "Now move them so that two letters show between them." Make note of the child's response to all four requests.

7. **Knowledge of Uppercase and Lowercase Letters.** On the same page, point to a capital letter with your pencil and say, "Show me a little letter that is the same as this one." (Beforehand, make sure that there is a corresponding lowercase letter on the page.) Next point to a lowercase letter and say, "Now point to a capital letter that is the same as this one." (Again, make sure that there is one.) Repeat this procedure with other pairs of letters if the child's response seems uncertain.

8. **Knowledge of Punctuation.** Turn to a page that has a period, an exclamation point, a question mark, a comma, and a set of quotation marks. Pointing to each one in turn, ask, "What is this? What is it for?" Note whether the child answers correctly for each of the five punctuation marks.

To follow this assessment procedure efficiently, you will have to choose a book carefully and practice using the assessment questions enough times to become proficient. The procedure is easily carried out with Marie Clay's own test booklet, which is well worth the nominal cost. Alternatively, you can assess a child's concepts about print using any illustrated book that meets these criteria:

1. It should have a fairly large font size—16 points or larger.
2. It should have at least one pair of pages with print on one page and an illustration on the other.
3. It should have one page with at least three lines of print.
4. It should have one page with a single line of print.
5. It should have a page with examples of upper- and lowercase versions of at least two letters.
6. One page should have several marks of punctuation: a period, quotation marks, a question mark, and an exclamation point.

It is advisable to make up a record sheet that provides for the quick recording of information yielded by the assessment.

Alphabet Knowledge

The Importance of Alphabet Knowledge. Knowledge of letters of the alphabet has been shown to be an early predictor of later reading success (Walsh, Price, & Gillingham, 1988). Part of the reason for this, no doubt, is that those children who know more letters have had more exposure to print. But knowing letters is important in itself, for several reasons. First, even children who seemingly learn to recognize words as wholes, rather than analyzing them by their parts (see a discussion of this in the section entitled "Sight-Word Recognition" later in this chapter) need enough letter knowledge to identify at least a salient part of a word (Ehri, 1991). Second, and related to the previous point, children who voice-point (who focus visually on word units as they recite to themselves a known line of text) seem to rely on at least beginning letters to orient themselves to word units (Morris, 1993). Third, as children begin to sound out words, or begin to use their fledgling knowledge of the relations between letters and sounds to read words, they will obviously need to be able to recognize several letters. Fourth, as children begin to invent spellings for words—itself an activity that helps children learn to segment words into phonemes and also to explore the relationships between letters and sounds (Clarke, 1988)—they will need to know how to name and produce several alphabet letters. Indeed, before any direct instruction in reading is likely to be of much benefit to children, those children must be able to recognize and produce most of the letters of the alphabet (Morris, 1990).

Assessing Alphabet Knowledge.   When testing students' alphabet knowledge, we ask them to recognize all of the letters of the alphabet in both uppercase and lowercase. We also ask them to write all of the letters once each, without specifying uppercase or lowercase. The letters are always presented in a scrambled sequence so that the children cannot use serial order as a cue to identifying a letter.

For a Letter Recognition Inventory, prepare the following letters as a separate display. Prepare another copy to use as a record sheet.

d f t g n b e h l v o y m a
r c q z u p j s i x k w

D F T G N B E H L V O Y M A
R C Q Z U P J S I X K W

As you proceed from left to right across the line, point to each letter and ask the child to identify it. Enter on the record sheet only a notation of what letters were misidentified or unnamed.

Many beginning readers will have difficulty recognizing Z, Q, V, and perhaps one or two letters that they encounter out of sequence. Difficulty with b, d, p, q, and g is also common because of directional confusion.

Children who confuse letters in isolation might still read them correctly in words, though they will be more uncertain than those who do not confuse them. Children who have difficulty identifying letters other than these will need more experience with print and letters as a top priority.

The Concept of Word

The concept of word is the knowledge that spoken language comes in units of words, and that those units are represented in print by clusters of letters with spaces of either. Having the concept of word enables students to track accurately between the words as they are spoken and the words as they are represented on the page.

To assess a student's concept of word, follow this procedure designed by Morris (1998).

Teach the student to memorize the poem shown below orally, *without showing her the written version.*

My little dog Petunia
Is a very strange dog.
She bellows like a mule
But she leaps like a frog.

Once the student can say the words from memory, show her the written poem and explain that these written words say the poem just learned.

Now, read through the poem at a slow natural rate, pointing to each word with your finger as you read it. Explain that you want the student to read the poem the way you did, but one line at a time.

Ask the student to say or read the first line, pointing to each word as she says it. On the record sheet shown in Figure 6.1, enter a score of 1 under *voice-pointing* if she points

---

Concept of Word Assessment

Student: _____   Grade: _____

Teacher: _____   School: _____

Date: _____   Examiner: _____

	Line-Pointing	*Word Pointing*
My little <u>dog</u> <u>Petunia</u> 1 2	_____	_____
Is a <u>very</u> <u>strange</u> dog. 1 2	_____	_____
She <u>bellows</u> <u>like</u> a mule 1 2	_____	_____
But <u>she</u> leaps like a <u>frog</u>. 1 2	_____	_____

Word-Pointing: _____ (of 4)

Word Identification: _____ (of 8)

Total Concept of Word (Voice-Pointing plus Word Identification):

_____ (of 12)

FIGURE 6.1 *Concept of Word Assessment*

to every word in that line correctly, and a score of 0 if she incorrectly points to any word in that line. Next, ask the student to point to the word *little.* Enter a score of 1 under *word identification* if she points to it and 0 if she does not. Now ask her to point to the word *Petunia.* Enter a score of 1 under *word identification* if she points to it and 0 if she does not.

Now go to the second line and repeat the process, testing first the student's voice-pointing and then the student's word identification. Award 1 point if the student points to every word just as she says it, and a 0 if the student makes any errors. Then ask her to point to *very* and then to *strange.* Award one point for each word the student correctly points to, and a 0 for each error. Repeat these instructions for lines 3 and 4.

Phonological Awareness

Phonological awareness is the consciousness of the sounds of language. *Phonology* refers to the sound system of spoken language and is not concerned with written language. Hence phonological awareness does not include phonics because phonics deals with the relationship between alphabet letters and sounds. Phonological awareness includes the awareness of *syllables, onsets and rimes,* and *phonemes.*

- **Syllables** are the pulses of language. They are the "beats" we hear in *table* (two syllables), *heart* (one syllable), and *tricycle* (three syllables).
- **Onsets and rimes** are two parts of most single syllables: The onset is the first consonant sound, and the rime is the vowel and any consonant that follows. In *car* the onset is /k/ and the rime is /ar/; in *stop* the onset is /st/ and the rime is /op/.
- **Phonemes** are the smallest speech sounds in language. *Dog* has three phonemes: /d/, /o/, and /g/. *Fort* has four phonemes: /f/, /o/, /r/, and /t/. (Note that we conventionally represent phonemes with slashes on either side.)

Hall and Moats (1999) present the following as abilities of normally developing children in kindergarten and first grade:

At the End of Kindergarten

- *At the syllable level:* Identify single syllable words that rhyme.
- *At the onset and rime level:* Match a word with a rhyming word.
- *At the phoneme level:* Pick out words that begin with the same sound and pick an "odd word out" that doesn't begin with the same sound as the others.

Two Months into First Grade

- Given two letters (as on Scrabble chips) combine them and pronounce the word they spell (*in, on, at, it, up*)
- Given a three-phoneme word, the children can say the word that is left when the first consonant is deleted: *bat/at, sit/it, cup/up.*

By the End of First Grade

- Can pronounce two phonemes words so as to separate the phonemes: *T–oo; b—y.*
- Given longer words, can separate off the first consonant: *b–utterfly.*
- Given three isolated phonemes, can combine them to make a word: /s/ /i/ /t/ = *sit.*

Activities to Build Phonological Awareness. Activities to boost phonological awareness are recommended for kindergarten through grade 3 (National Reading Panel, 2000). They may also be recommended for older children whose reading development is considerably delayed. Activities to develop phonological awareness need not take much time during the day. Six or 7 minutes a day yields the 20 hours a year that the National Reading Panel (2000) recommends.

The Importance of Phonological Awareness. To read in any writing system, a person should be able to make accurate mappings between the spoken units of a language and the written units. A logographic writing system such as that of Chinese is made up of written characters, or *zi*, that correspond to the spoken language at the whole-word level. In a mixed logographic and syllabic writing system, such as that of Japanese, some of the units of written language (the *kanji*) correspond to whole words, and some (the *katakana* and the *hiragana*) correspond to spoken syllables. In an alphabetic writing system, such as we use in English, the units of written language (the letters) correspond to the spoken language at the level of phonemes. Phonemes are small units of sound, smaller than syllables. They are the sounds to which the letters in C-A-T correspond. Every language has phonemes, of course, but only alphabetic languages base their writing systems on them. This is a mixed blessing.

On the positive side, an alphabetic writing system gives us remarkable economy. We would need to have a million characters at the word level to write our immense vocabulary in English. We would need around 2,700 characters at the syllable level to spell that same vocabulary (Barker, 2006). But by writing our words at the phonemic level, we can make do with 26 letters.[1] But the economy of alphabetic writing systems is won at a cost because phonemes are difficult to pay conscious attention to. The fact is, we don't always hear phonemes as isolated sound units. Of the three sounds in the word *cat*, for instance, only the vowel sound between the two consonant sounds is easily identified when the sounds of the word are cut apart and played back individually on a tape recorder. The consonant sounds /k/ and /t/ cannot be recognized unless they are pronounced with a vowel sound. We know the consonant sounds are there because we can substitute different consonant sounds and change the words. Changing /c/ in *cat* to /b/ gives us *bat.* Changing the final /t/ for /p/ gives us *cap.* But as the etymology of the word consonant (sound + together) makes clear, consonants are heard only in combination with vowels or with other consonants.

---

[1] It's not an exact match at that. English has 44 distinct phonemes, and our 26 letters have to do double and triple duty to spell them all. At the same time, the alphabet contains some redundancies, such as the letter C, which sometimes sounds like S and sometimes like K.

Phonemes may be difficult for children to pay attention to unless they have had rich experience in activities that play on speech sounds, such as reciting jump rope rhymes or nursery rhymes, clapping along to Dr. Seuss, or playing Pig Latin (Bradley & Bryant, 1985). Paradoxically, it may also be hard for children—or even older people—to be fully aware of phonemes unless they have had some experience trying to sound out written words or trying to write them with invented spelling. The awareness of phonemes seems to cut both ways: It helps, and it is helped by, even children's earliest efforts at beginning to read.

Those of us who can read face another challenge as we try to attend to phonemes because our knowledge of spelling may make it difficult to focus on sounds. For instance, we may have difficulty hearing that there are two phonemes in *shoe* (/sh/ is one phoneme, and /ū/ is another) or three phonemes in thick (/th/ is one phoneme, /ĭ/ is another, and /k/ is another). Sing has three phonemes: /s/, /ĭ/, and /ng/. What may be troubling us are the *digraphs:* the single phonemes that are spelled by two letters. Less troublesome for us are the *consonant blends,* like those spelled by the first three letters in *splash* and *split.* In consonant blends, each separate phoneme is sounded. We may be confused when consonant blends are spelled in ways we don't expect. For instance, *ax* has three phonemes, /a/, /k/, and /s/, and the two consonant sounds are spelled by the single letter X.

If the facts just described are not obvious, it is surely because our awareness of spelling has made it difficult for us to attend to sounds. If we are going to help children make connections between sounds and writing—that is, to read and write—we must push beyond these difficulties and become aware of speech sounds in words.

Note, too, that being aware of phonemes is different from perceiving them. Most 5-year-old children will pick up the cat and not the bat when you ask them to, showing that they can perceive the difference between /k/ and /b/. Most will hesitate, though, if you ask them to tap their finger on the table to each of the three constituent sounds in *cat.* The difference is one of responding to the meaning of language—which young children find relatively natural—and consciously focusing on the sounds of language, or *phonological awareness,* which is much harder for children.

Phonological Awareness and the Alphabetic Principle.   Why does phonological awareness matter? A host of research has pointed to the importance of children's understanding the *alphabetic nature of the English writing system,* or the *alphabetic principle.* As we said above, written English words are spelled by letters and letter clusters that represent individual speech sounds—phonemes. As children begin to read words, they can use their awareness of the alphabetic principle to sound out words by associating letters with the sounds they spell. They can do this matching, however, only if they can break words down into their phoneme constituents. If children are not fully able—and many children are not—to perceive the sound units that make up words, they will not be able to match many letters with sounds. A child who can perceive the beginning consonant sound but not the rest of the sounds in the word *back,* for instance, will read the word as if it were spelled *bxxx.* He may thus read the word as *bike, buck,* or even *ball* or *bust* unless the context helps narrow down his choices.

Darrell Morris (1993) suggests that the sequence of learning to read words goes like this:

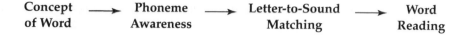

Concept of Word ⟶ **Phoneme Awareness** ⟶ **Letter-to-Sound Matching** ⟶ **Word Reading**

Other researchers, such as Stanovich (2000) and Iverson and Tunmer (1993), suggest a similar sequence (although they do not stress the concept of word).

Children can be taught to become aware of phonemes. Natural and child-friendly exercises in preschool that use nursery rhymes have been shown to be effective. With kindergarten through second-grade children, more focused sound awareness exercises have been shown to help (Blachman et al., 1995). Also, contextualized practices such as writing with invented spelling have also been shown to be worthwhile in helping children develop phonemic segmentation, word reading ability, and spelling ability (Clarke, 1988). In the following pages, we will look first at ways of assessing children's awareness of phonemes and second at ways of helping children develop awareness of them.

Assessing Phonemic Awareness by Means of Invented Spelling. One way to observe whether a first-grade child has phonemic awareness is to ask him to spell words that he does not already know. By asking the child to spell unknown words, we ask the child to rely upon his *invented spelling,* the inner capacity to forge connections between letters and sounds. Children have an amazing intuitive ability to invent spellings, and we can learn much about their word knowledge by looking at their invented productions.

A procedure for testing phonemic segmentation (after Morris, 1993), then, is to have the child spell the following list of words as you call them out. Then you can count the number of phonemes the child reasonably attempted to represent. (Guides to scoring each word are presented in parentheses.)

bite	(three phonemes: BIT = 3 points; BT = 2 points, BRRY, etc. = 1 point)
seat	(three phonemes: SET or CET = 3 points; ST, CT = 2 points)
dear	(three phonemes: DER = 3 points; DIR or DR = 2 points)
bones	(four phonemes: BONS or BONZ = 4 points; BOS or BOZ = 3 points)
mint	(four phonemes: MENT or MINT = 4 points; MET or MIT = 3 points; MT = 2 points)
rolled	(four phonemes: ROLD = 4 points; ROL or ROD = 3 points)
race	(three phonemes: RAS, RAC, or RAEC = 3 points, RC or RS = 2 points)
roar	(three phonemes: ROR or ROER = 3 points; RR = 2 points)
beast	(four phonemes: BEST = 4 points; BES or BST = 3 points; BS or BT = 2 points)
groan	(four phonemes: GRON = 4 points; GRN = 3 points; GN = 2 points)
TOTAL	35 points

Explain to the child that you are going to ask him to spell some words you know the child doesn't know how to spell. The child will have to figure out the spellings as best he can. After you call out each word (at least twice, and as many more times as the student requests), ask the student to try to spell each sound in the word. If the student says he can't, ask the student to listen to the way the word begins. What sound does it start with? Ask the student to write down a letter for that sound and letters for any other sounds he can hear. If the student is not sure how to spell a sound, ask the student to write a little dash (—).

After reading all 10 words (fewer if the test seems too arduous for a particular child), count the number of reasonable letters the child wrote for each word and compare that to the number of phonemes in the word. A child who consistently writes three or four letters that show some reasonable connection to the sounds in the word appears to be able to segment phonemes. A child who writes nothing or strings together many letters indiscriminately is not yet able to segment phonemes, and a child who writes one or two reasonable letters per word is just beginning to segment phonemes. You might calculate a score for phonemic segmentation by scoring each word according to the table at the right of each word and then comparing the total number of points the child receives to the total possible.

A Spoken Test of Phonemic Segmentation.   Invented spelling is a natural means both to assess and to practice phonemic segmentation, but it does have one drawback. To demonstrate that they can segment words into phonemes, children must also be able to match phonemes with letters, know what the letters look like, and how how to form them on paper. These latter abilities have nothing to do with segmenting phonemes. Hence, invented spelling both tests and exercises more than phonemic segmentation ability. A procedure that does not depend upon spelling and writing is an oral test of phonemic segmentation developed by Hallie Kay Yopp (Yopp, 1988). This procedure is done with one child at a time, and it takes between 5 and 10 minutes to administer. The test consists of a series of 22 one-syllable words. The child's task is to pronounce the words slowly to highlight the phonemes, after the tester shows the child how. Yopp's directions to the children work as follows:

> Today we're going to play a word game. I'm going to say a word, and I want you to break the word apart. You are going to tell me each sound of the word in order. For example, if I say *old,* you will say o-l-d. Let's try a few words together. (Yopp, 1988, p. 166)

She follows with three more demonstration words: *ride, go,* and *man.* She praises the child if the child is correct and corrects the child if she is wrong. After the trials, she reads 22 words to the child, and the child breaks the words apart one at a time as they are read. Again, the teacher gives praise or correction after each word. The words are as follows:

dog	*lay*	*keep*	*race*
fine	*zoo*	*no*	*three*
she	*job*	*wave*	*in*
grew	*ice*	*that*	*at*
red	*top*	*me*	*by*
sat	*do*		

Yopp gives the child a point for each word correctly segmented (there is no partial credit), so the scores can range from 0 to 22. When the test was given in the spring of the year to a group of 94 kindergarteners in southern California—children with a median age of 5 years, 10 months—the children got an average of nearly 12 items correct.

Yopp gives data that suggest that her task predicts children's ability to learn to sound out words more reliably than nine other phonemic segmentation tasks against which she compared it. Unfortunately, she did not compare her task against invented spelling. Mann, Tobin, and Wilson (1988), however, did find that invented spelling, when measured as a test of phonemic segmentation in kindergarten, significantly predicted reading ability in first grade.

Phoneme-to-Grapheme Correspondences (Phonics)

Because English uses an alphabetic writing system—that is, a system that represents words by matching their phonemes with letters or groups of letters—it stands to reason that children need to know what these relationships are. This conclusion has been supported by a host of studies, including Jeanne Chall's summary in the 1960s, *Learning to Read: The Great Debate;* Bond and Dykstra's *First Grade Studies* (1967); Marilyn Adams's summary from the early 1990s, *Beginning to Read;* and the National Reading Panel's more recent two reports, *Preventing Reading Difficulties in Young Children* (Snow et al., 1998) and *Teaching Children to Read* (National Reading Panel, 2000).

The National Reading Panel recommends phonics instruction in kindergarten and first grade that is explicit and systematic because research studies show such approaches to be effective. Explicit and systematic phonics instructs children to relate letters and sounds for both consonants and vowels, presents these associations in a logical sequence, and provides adequate practice for each set of associations. We recommend that phonics instruction also honor the development of children's word knowledge and be related to the reading of real text.

Stages in the Development of Word Knowledge.   There are languages in the world that have writing systems in which letters of the alphabet are closely matched with the sounds in words, with few irregularities. Finnish has such as writing system, as do Slovak and Kiswahili. Just a quick look at words like *light, photograph, weigh,* and *love* shows that English spelling is not a simple matter of each letter matching its own sound. English spelling does have a system, but the system of spelling is complex because the system of sounds is complex. We noted in Chapter 4 that, as children learn to read and spell, they proceed through stages that move from simplistic to complex understandings of the spelling structure of English. In word recognition, these stages have been described by Uta Frith (1985). According to Frith, children go through a set of stages of word recognition that she calls *logographic, transitional, alphabetic,* and *orthographic.*

Assessing Knowledge of Phonics.   There are two reliable ways to assess students' knowledge of phoneme-to-grapheme correspondences. One is by means of invented spelling. The other is by means of picture sorts, which we describe here.

Picture-Sound Identification.   Prepare a set of picture cards similar to those shown in Figure 6.2 depicting the following items or concepts:

apple	otter	gun	jar	pin	vest
ape	oats	hat	lamp	rat	wall
egg	bat	kangaroo	map	sun	zoo
eagle	dog	fan	net	tack	

Demonstrate the task.   Show the child the picture of the hat. Say, "Look. Here's a picture of a hat. Can you say the word? 'Hat.' Good. Let's see: What is the first sound we hear in 'hat'? I know. It's 'huh.' Can you hear the 'huh' sound in 'hat'? What letter spells the 'huh' sound in 'hat'? I know: It's H."

Now show the student another picture and tell the student the name of the item or concept in the picture. Ask the student to repeat the word. Correct the student if he does not say the word correctly. Make sure the student says the word.

Ask the student to say the sound the word begins with. Now ask the student to tell you what letter spells that sound.

Repeat the procedure until you have shown the student all of the consonant cards and vowel cards.

Record the student's accuracy in matching letters with sounds. Make a note to help that student learn those phoneme-to-grapheme matches that he is unsure about.

Sight-Word Recognition

Repeated exposure to written words, including some ability to sound words out by their phoneme-to-grapheme correspondences, enables a reader to acquire *sight words,* words that can be recognized instantly.

The Importance of Sight-Word Recognition.   At the stage of emergent literacy, children's ability to recognize some words is an indicator of their general exposure to print. We won't expect children to recognize very many words in later kindergarten or early first grade. Nonetheless, before children can read independently (that is, before they can make sense of text they have not dictated or heard read aloud), they must amass a number of sight words, words that they can recognize with little effort. Words that children recognize immediately are stepping stones that help them to get through text that

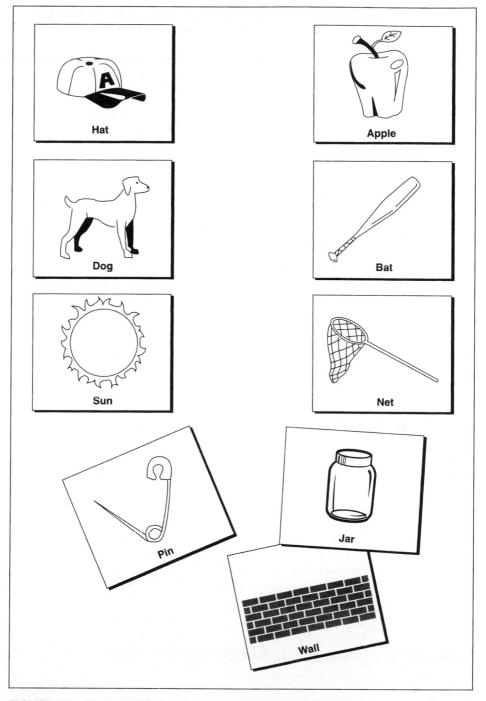

FIGURE 6.2   *Picture Cards for Picture-Sound Identification Tasks*

contains unknown words. Without sight words, reading is reduced to word-by-word decoding, and although this resembles reading in some superficial ways, it is not reading in a meaningful sense.

It is therefore important to see whether children have begun to acquire some sight words. We cannot productively ask them to identify all the words they can recognize in print, however. We must instead construct a sample list of words that they are likely to encounter in beginning reading, test them on those, and estimate from their performance what proportion of typical words they are apt to recognize as sight words in other contexts.

Assessing Sight-Word Recognition.   A useful Sight-Word Inventory has two kinds of words: *high-frequency words,* or those that often appear in print but do not necessarily follow common spelling patterns, and *decodable words,* words that follow some of the spelling patterns that children encounter in first grade.

High-Frequency Words	Decodable Words
are	*cat*
was	*hot*
you	*rob*
they	*it*
house	*up*
friend	*mop*
school	*sad*
what	*cot*
out	*net*
love	*bug*

The assessment is done with one child at a time. If you are right-handed, sit with the child on your left. Put the tag board with the word list in front of the child and a duplicated copy of the list by your right hand. (If you are left-handed, the placement is reversed.) Using two index cards, frame one word at a time to the child, asking, "What is this word?. . . How about this one?" Put a check mark on your sheet next to every word that the child recognizes. You can put an X next to any word the child does not know at sight but is able to figure out. Continue until all the words have been exposed unless the student becomes frustrated or unhappy with this experience, which might happen if the child knows only a few sight words. Use your judgment and stop if the child gets discouraged.

Teaching for Emergent and Beginning Literacy

The techniques that are used to help each youngster's literacy emerge, whether in a classroom or a clinic, should derive from two guiding principles: First, they should involve real reading and real writing in real contexts; second, they should respond to what the child knows and needs to know about reading and writing. In the following section, we suggest activities that are related to each of these assessment areas.

Reading Storybooks

By paging through and pretending to read favorite storybooks, in imitation of adults they have seen reading, children develop concepts about the form and function of written text and the kind of language that is used in print. Therefore, good instruction for emerging readers will include providing individual books on their level, with simple text, that they will enjoy. The teacher introduces the books by reading them to a child or group of children more than once and then giving them to the children and encouraging them to "read" the books to friends or parents. Opportunities for such storybook reading should be provided daily for children on all levels.

Reading Many Books, Repeatedly   Reading to children familiarizes them with books, acquaints them with characters and plots and other patterns of literature, and gradually helps them to learn the elaborated syntax and special vocabulary of written language. Best of all, it helps them come to enjoy books and feel at home with them. Reading six to eight books a day is not too many. Choose books that are simple and highly patterned at first—by either rhyming lines, repeated actions, or a strong plot.

It's fine to read the same book through more than once at a sitting. On subsequent days, reread some of the books that you read before. Repeated reading familiarizes the children with the pattern of the book. Some literary patterns are shared by many books, so if children get the pattern, they will appreciate a similar book that much more readily. This is especially true of books by the same author. Bill Martin's *Brown Bear, Brown Bear, What Do You See?* leads nicely into his *Polar Bear, Polar Bear, What Do You Hear?* Each of Cynthia Rylant's *Henry and Mudge* books prepares children for the next, as do Arnold Lobel's *Frog and Toad* series, Norman Bridwell's *Clifford* books, and James Marshall's *George and Martha* books. Folktales can do this, too, such as Ivan Bilibin's collection of Russian Folktales, many of which feature magical transformations of the hero and the exploits of the remarkable witch Baba Yaga or the many Anansi stories.

Repeatedly reading the same book serves another purpose, too: Once the children are familiar with a book, you can leave it out and invite them to "reread it" themselves or to other students. By regularly supporting and encouraging them in pretend reading, you are giving them close encounters with literature from which they will gradually learn about print.

Reading Expressively   Listen closely to a parent talking to a baby. The parent's voice makes exaggerated swoops, from high to low, from quiet to loud, from pauses to dramatic emphases. Parents' speech, sometimes called "motherese," is thought to use these exaggerated moves to attract and hold the child's attention and even show the child the significant features of speech (Stern, 1982).

Reading a book to children is like that. As we read through a story, we deliberately exaggerate the changes in our voices: from especially bright and cheerful to doleful and sad, to slow and suspenseful, to rapid and excited. We make the rhythms of language march, and we savor delightful words. By reading that way, we are showing children the dramatic contours of stories, the ebb and flow of emotions, the force and conflicts of characters, the pull of the plot, the music and cadence of rich language. Children might not sense these things unless we make them very clear and put them out there to be appreciated.

If you are new to reading aloud to children, the odds are that you will have to work on your voice to make it as expressive as it should be. Box 6.1 offers suggestions for practicing reading aloud expressively.

BOX 6.1   *Ten Pointers for Reading Aloud*

1. Read the book to yourself first to get familiar with it. You need to know whether this book is suitable for the children. If it is, you also need to think out how the characters' voices should sound, which parts have suspense, which parts are comical, and which parts are sad.
2. Arrange the children in front of you in a quiet area where they won't be distracted for the duration of the reading.
3. Preview the book for them. Show the cover and a few pictures from inside. Ask children to talk about what they see. Invite them to speculate on what might happen in the story.
4. As you read, go slowly and put animation and drama into your voice. Come up with slightly distinct voices for the characters—but don't overdo them.
5. Stop and show them the pictures. (In fact, you should practice reading books upside down so that you can show children the pictures as you read.) Allow time for the children to talk about what they notice.
6. Stop at the exciting parts and ask the children to predict what they think is going to happen.
7. After you've read on a ways, stop and ask them if it happened. Were we right about our predictions?
8. Read the book again, and invite the children to chime in on the repeated parts. Reread it another day, too. It's good for children to really get to know books.
9. Follow up. Ask them what they thought was the best (scariest, funniest, most exciting) part.
10. Leave the book out where they can look at it on their own after you've read it to them.

FIGURE 6.3 *A "Little Book"*

Little Books

Originally from Wendy Pye in New Zealand came the idea of publishing many short and colorful books on carefully graduated levels of difficulty. Now many such books are published by companies such as the Wright Group, Rigby, and Richard C. Owen, and they have strongly patterned, yet meaningful texts. Because these books are often skillfully written and their vocabularies are not limited to words with the simplest letter-to-sound correspondences, the books can be surprisingly meaningful and enjoyable.

When reading through one of these books with a child, it helps if you follow these steps:

- Determine whether the level of the book is right. After previewing the book (that is, reading several pages aloud to the child and discussing the pictures), ask the child to read the book alone. If she misreads or needs help on fewer than one word out of nine, that book is at a suitable level for instructional work.
- When you are reading a book proper, begin by previewing the book. Consider the title. Call the student's attention to the cover and discuss it. Ask for predictions of what will happen. If the child doesn't offer any, offer two alternate predictions yourself and ask, "Do you think X will happen or Y? Let's read and find out." Open the book and look at more pictures.
- Encourage the child to do as much reading as she can without your help.
- Praise lavishly but honestly. Praise specifically. Say, "I like the way you read to the end of the line and then went back and corrected the word you read wrong the first time." This calls children's attention to strategies that good readers use.

- In some books, children may begin to read by the pattern alone, plus the picture cues. Call the student's attention to individual words from time to time. Ask the student to point to the words while reading them.
- If the child's energy and enthusiasm flags, you can use these support techniques: Do echo-reading (you read a line or a page, then the child reads), or do choral-reading (you both read the text together).
- Stress meaning. Stop and discuss what is happening. Ask the student to make predictions (and make them yourself when the child won't).
- Since you are likely to be doing some form of word study in the same lesson you are reading this book, remind the student of words she has studied that appear in the text.
- Don't spend too much time sounding out. You are after fluency and success here; sounding out will come later.

Teaching Print Orientation Concepts

How do we help children to develop print orientation concepts? One solution is a big book: a giant, 3-foot-high version of a trade book. The teacher can place a big book on a chart stand, where it can be readily seen by a group of children. The teacher can have them read along as he points out features of print: where the text begins on a page, the left-to-right direction of reading, the return sweep, the spaces that demarcate words, and punctuation.

Big books were originally made by the teacher or a parent volunteer. They might be chosen to accompany a reading series of which the children have copies—that way the children can look for the features on the page in front of them that the teacher points out in the big book. Big book versions are also made up from favorite trade books. When children already know and are excited about the story line, they can more easily pay attention to the way print portrays the text, which is the point of this sort of lesson. Nowadays big book versions of children's books are now available from many sources, although many teachers still prepare their own.

Teaching the Alphabet

Many children enter kindergarten knowing most of their letters. Middle-class children are often able to point to and name all but Q, Z, J, and Y—unless, of course, their own names contain some of these letters—and write a dozen or more letters. Some children, however, enter kindergarten knowing very few letters and come to know letters in school only slowly and with difficulty (Ehri, 1989). Although it might be possible to recognize a few words by memorizing their overall appearance (focusing on the "eyes" in *look,* for example), knowing the letters is necessary for learning to read appreciable numbers of words and to write using invented spelling.

Marie Clay's work (1975) and the work of Harste et al. (1985) suggest that many children can invent their way to letter knowledge if they have models of print around them and are given early opportunities to write. However, by kindergarten, and certainly by first grade, those children who do not know most of their letters need more explicit teaching. Indeed, many studies show that children who know many letters in kindergarten are more likely to read by the end of first grade than are children who know few (Walsh et al., 1988).

How can we teach children the alphabet?

Alphabet Books

Alphabet books are arranged A to Z, usually with examples of both uppercase and lowercase letters and an illustrative picture that begins with the sound of the letter. Kate Greenaway's alphabet book, first published a century ago, is still in print, and more and more gorgeous and innovative alphabet books come out every year.

Older children in the school can make alphabet books for younger children. Or younger children can prepare alphabet books themselves, with guidance from the teacher. Either way, it is highly desirable for every preschool and kindergarten child to have a personal alphabet book.

When children take alphabet books home, send along instructions to the parent to take the time to listen to the child read the alphabet book. Remind the parent to make this an enjoyable occasion—certainly not a drill session.

Letter-Matching Games

Once the children are beginning to know some letters, you can play letter-matching games with them along the lines of the concentration game. First, make up two sets of five different lowercase letters on cards. Turn these cards face down on the table , and turn up a pair. If they are the same, you have to name them, and then you can have them. Work through all of the lowercase letters in this way. Then do the same with the uppercase letters. After children become proficient at matching lowercase letters in this way, they are ready to play with uppercase and lowercase versions of the same letters.

Sounds and Letters

As you will undoubtedly note from the foregoing discussion of concepts about print, the following procedure assumes that children are well along in their awareness of sounds in words and their notions of beginning and ends of words. For children who have reached these milestones, this procedure, from the work of the McCrackens (1987), is a worthwhile activity.

Working with first graders, they will introduce a letter, say, M:

1. They write M on the board.
2. They pronounce the letter slowly and ask the children to watch their mouths as they say it.

3. They ask the children to pronounce the letter slowly and pay attention to how it feels in their mouths.
4. They ask the children to write the letter on their individual chalk tablets, saying the letter aloud as they do so.
5. Later, they hand the children specially prepared tablets, as shown in Figure 6.4.

The teacher says the word *me* and asks the child to write the letter M in the appropriate slot in the square marked 1. Does the M come at the beginning of the word *me* or at the end? For square 2, the word is *may;* for square 3, the word is *am;* and for square 4, the word is *um.*

Teaching the Concept of Word

The concept of word, as we have seen, is the important ability to relate words in the mind with words on the page. Research by Morris (1981, 1993) has suggested that children need to develop this ability before they will advance very far in their word recognition ability because they need a concept of word to be able to focus their attention properly on word units in print. Several of the tasks that we have already introduced in this chapter as assessment devices work quite well as instructional devices, too.

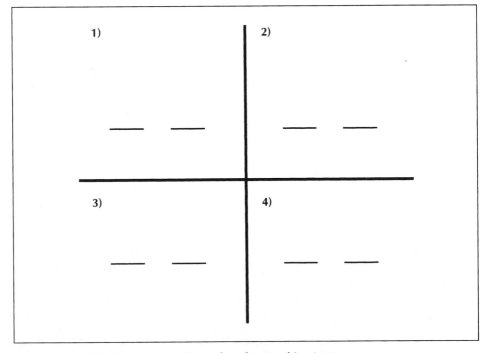

FIGURE 6.4 *The McCrackens' Procedure for Teaching Letters*

The Voice-Pointing Procedure

One way is to read text aloud—say, a big book, or a dictated chant on the chart—pointing to the print, one word at a time. Also, call attention to the word saying, "See? That word is 'fish.' See the F it begins with? That's the word 'fish.'"

When children have memorized a text, as in a little book, encourage them to point to the words as the read.

Cut-Apart Words

Have a child memorize a four- or five-word sentence or a line of poetry. Then, on a piece of tag board, write down the sentence as the child says the words. Read the words several times, pointing to them. Then cut the words apart, scramble them, and ask the child to rearrange them correctly.

If the child can rearrange them successfully, take away a word, and ask the child which word it was. If the child cannot rearrange the words successfully, make a copy of the line, leave it intact, and ask the child to rearrange the cut-apart words underneath by matching them to the words in the intact version.

Dictated Experience Accounts

An effective use of a dictated experience account goes as follows. Write a small version of text and duplicate it so that each child has two copies. Instruct the children to cut the paper so that each sentence is on its own strip of paper. Then they should cut these sentence strips into individual words. The teacher should circulate among them to identify the words they are cutting apart and encourage the children to identify them. Once the words are cut apart, the children should match the cut-apart words with the same words on the other, intact sheet, laying each word above the intact word so that it does not cover it.

Once children can do this sort of activity fairly easily, they can arrange the cut-apart words into sentences without using the intact words as a guide.

Morning Message

The morning message is a limited and more focused version of a dictated experience account. Morning message is both predictable and meaningful because the activity follows the same format every time it is used, yet it has important information. And it builds a sense of community among students and makes children feel important.

Morning message is used to open the day in many kindergarten and first-grade classrooms. The message is written on chart paper and an easel, or on a part of the chalkboard that will not be erased.

A typical message says something like this:

Today is *(day of the week)*. (The date may be included, too.) The weather today is _____. Our classroom helpers are *(students' names are written)*. Today we will _____ *(a special event is written)*. _____ (the name of a student) has a birthday today.

The teacher has the option of putting words for the day of the week, the month, and the weather on a tagboard with pieces of tape on the back for posting on the chart.

After the plan for the day is discussed with the children, the teacher and students together decide what will be written. They say each sentence more than once to fix it in memory. Then the teacher begins by writing the first few words, whereupon she invites one child at a time up to help with the writing. (See the shared writing procedure described in the section entitled "Interactive Writing.")

Morning message is a fine opportunity to teach about written language: direction of print, concept of word, capitalization, and letters and sounds. The message should be read again and again for practice once it is written and left up so that some children can revisit it.

Activities to Build Phonological Awareness.   Activities to boost phonological awareness are recommended for kindergarten through grade 3 (National Reading Panel, 2000). They may also be recommended for older children whose reading development is considerably delayed. Activities to develop phonological awareness need not take much time during the day. Six or 7 minutes a day yields the 20 hours a year that the National Reading Panel (2000) recommends.

Activities to develop phonological awareness have been shown most effective when they work with letters at the same time they call attention to sounds (Blachman et al., 1995; National Reading Panel, 2000). Perhaps this is because letters provide a visual stimulus to accompany an auditory stimulus; but in any case, associating sounds with letters will help children learn to read and spell.

Activities to boost phonological awareness can take place at several levels.

At the Syllable Level

- Children can clap the syllables in their names—"Clau-di-a," "Sha-nee-sha," "Char-lie."
- Children can raise their hands when the teacher says a word with one syllable, two syllables, three syllables.
- The teacher says, "Two syllables!" and calls on children to say words with two syllables. Then he says "One syllable!" and the children must say words of one syllable, and so on.

At the Onset and Rime Level

- Children are asked to supply rhymes to complete couplets like:

  Ding, dong, dell
  Kitty's in the _____ (well)
  Ding, dong, divver
  Kitty's in the _____ (river)
  Ding, dong, dimming pool
  Kitty's in the _____ (swimming pool)

- Children are told a target word, such as *say,* and asked to raise their hands when they hear a word that rhymes with it, as the teacher says a list of words: "*Be, bet, back, bay.*"
- The teacher says a word such as *hat.* Then she challenges the children to say a new word that begins with the sound she calls out: /s/, /b/, /f/.

At the Phoneme Level

- Sing a song that substitutes the vowel sounds:

  I like to eat, eat, eat, apples and bananas
  I like to eat, eat, eat, apples and bananas.
  I like to oot, oot, oot, ooples and bonoonoos.
  I like to oot, oot, oot, ooples and bonoonoos.
  I like to oat, oat, oat, oples and bononos.
  I like to oat, oat, oat, oples and bononos.

- Practice taking words apart into their phonemes:

  If I say *dog* /d/ /o/ /g/, you say *cat, ball, foot* the same way.

- Say a series of speech sounds and ask children to say the word they form:

  /f/ /e/ /t/ = *feet;* /s/ /o/ /p/ = *soap.*

- Using sound boxes (Elkonin, 1973), have children shove letter markers into boxes as they emphasize the phonemes while saying the words.

/b/ ↑   /e/ ↑   /t/ ↑
/p/ | /u/ | /p/ |

Exercises to Develop Phonological Awareness

For many children, the practice of writing freely and meaningfully using invented spelling provides all the exercise in developing phonemic awareness they will need.

Invented Spelling

Some kindergartners and first graders might be reluctant to write with invented spelling. It is best to begin the year by encouraging the whole group to use invented spelling in the following way. First, you should plan to have regular, at best daily, occasions for children to write and have meaningful and interesting topics for them to write about. In a pre-first-grade room, for example, the teacher read the children *Where the Wild Things Are* and *There's a Nightmare in My Closet.* After a discussion of monsters and nightmares, she passed out drawing paper and watercolors and invited the children to paint their own monster. Next the children were instructed to write the names of their monsters on the pages. Finally, they were told to write what they do to defend or protect themselves from the monster.

Had the children not had plenty of experience by now writing with invented spelling, the teacher might have kept the children in the group and asked them to think of a monster's name. Once they agreed on one, she might say, "'Long Arm Monster.' How are we going to write that? Who can think of a letter to begin it with? *Long:* luh, luh, luh." As each child thinks of a plausible letter, she can write it on the board—even if the result is LIG RM MISTR (one version of *long arm monster* in invented spelling).

Several group demonstrations of this sort might be necessary before children will begin to use invented spelling; but before long, the children will find it natural to sound out words to write them. If they ask for help, they will be more likely to ask for the spelling of a sound than for the whole word.

Exercises to Teach Phonics and Word Recognition

The goal of reading is to construct meaning from text. In order to do that, the reader must use comprehension processes, which are facilitated by fluent reading of text, which in turn is facilitated by rapid word recognition, which is facilitated by knowing letter-to-sound correspondences. In this section we focus on ways to help children learn letter-to-sound correspondences, or phonics, and also to learn to recognize words.

Kinds of Phonics Instruction

There are three general approaches to teaching phonics: synthetic phonics, analytic phonics, and phonics by analogy. Let us look at each.

One way to teach phonics is to teach children the sounds that are associated with letters or clusters of letters and how to blend sounds together to make words. This approach is called *synthetic phonics* (remember that *synthesize* means "to bring things together"; in synthetic phonics, children are bringing sounds together to make words). An example of synthetic phonics would be to teach children the sounds /p/, /a/, /n/, and /m/, and have them practice combining the sounds to make *pan, man, map,* and *nap.*

Another approach to teaching phonics is to lead children to examine the words they already know how to read for the letter-to-sound relationships they contain. This approach is called *analytic phonics* (remember that *analyze* means "to examine the parts that make up something"; and in analytic phonics, children are examining the letter-to-sound relationships that make up a word). As an example of analytic phonics, we show them the words *map* and *man,* which they can read, and point out that the letter *m* in both words makes the sound /m/.

A third approach to teaching phonics is *phonics by analogy.* Phonics by analogy is showing children that the spelling-to-sound relationships they have learned in one group of words can be used to read and spell other words. (Remember that an analogy is a comparison of one thing to another.) To practice phonics by analogy, we can have children do a word sort (discussed in the section "Word Sort") that calls their attention to the spellings of words they can already read: *man, ran,* and *pan,* for example. By studying the spellings of these words they realize that the sound /an/ is spelled *an,* and now they can read and spell *can* and *fan.*

Tying Phonics Instruction to Children's Developing Word Knowledge

Phonics instruction works best when it is keyed to children's developing word knowledge. As children develop from reading words in the logographic stage, the transitional stage, the alphabetic stage, and the orthographic stage, appropriate phonics instruction can help at each turn.

When children are first learning to read words, in the iconographic reading stage, they read them as wholes, while they may recognize the beginning or ending consonant. This is a time for language experience teaching and for shared book reading, to familiarize children with whole words. It is also a time to teach them letters and individual letter sounds (that is, synthetic phonics), using picture sorts and alphabet letter sorts (see below).

As soon as they have learned 15 to 20 letters and their sounds and have learned to recognize 30 words, they will be moving through the transitional and alphabetic stages of word recognition. You can begin to do interactive writing and pattern word sorts with them. Sound boards and word building are useful at this stage as well. All of these activities are described below.

Word Sorts

The practice of *word sorts* (Bear, Invernizzi, Templeton, & Johnson, 1996; Morris, 1982; Temple & Gillet, 1978) is a naturalistic, whole-to-part way to draw children's attention to the sound elements in words and the letter patterns that typically spell those elements. Word sorts can be used at nearly all levels of literacy development, but they are especially useful for emergent and beginning readers.

Word sorts provide students practice in identifying words, but they are meant to do more than that. They also help students to generalize patterns learned in one group of words to other words. That is, they develop *orthographic concepts* (*orthography* is another way of saying *spelling* or *letter-to-sound correspondences*). When word sorts are successful, students learn many important patterns about the ways words are put together, and these patterns help them to recognize new words.

Picture Sorts.   Before children are ready to study letter-to-sound correspondences in written words, they can use a sorting strategy to develop awareness of sounds in words. Given a collection of small cards with pictures of a pig, a pie, a duck, a penguin, a doll, a door, a pumpkin, a dog, and a paddle, children can be asked to sort together all of the pictures whose names begin like *pig* and to make a separate grouping of the pictures whose names begin like *duck*. The picture cards, like all word sort cards, should be written on stiff paper of about calling card size. See Figure 6.5.

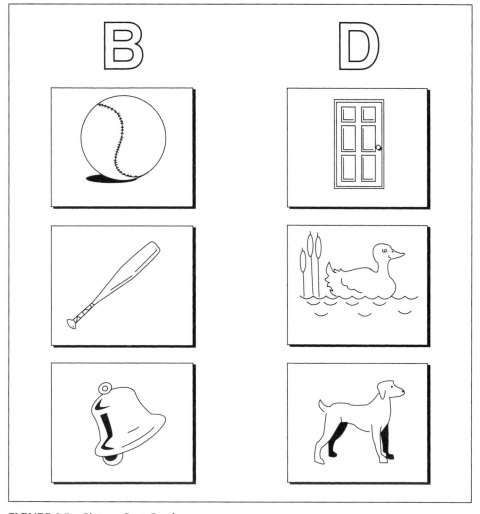

FIGURE 6.5 *Picture Sort Cards*

Picture sorts practice the categorization of sounds without relying upon reading ability. They also familiarize children with a learning strategy that can be used with written words (see below).

Beginning Consonant Sorts. Once children have become adept at picture sorts, and after they have learned to recognize many consonants and vowels, you can move on the beginning consonant sorts. Prepare two groups of 5 or 6 words that begin with the same consonant. Choose beginning consonant pairs that are visually distinct: *b* and *t,* but not *b* and *p.* To call maximum attention to the sound element, put down two picture cards of words that begin with the /b/ sound (such as a *bat*) and the /t/ sound (such as in *tip*). Then take the scrambled word cards, read one aloud, and ask the child where it goes: "Does this word begin like *bat* or like *tip?*" After you read three of the cards, ask the child to read and sort the rest of them, giving help where needed. Once children are adept with the *b* and *t* words, go on to sorting more words with different beginning consonants, still two at a time.

Phonogram Pattern Sorts. Once children can attend to beginning consonants, we can move on to one-syllable words with short vowel *phonogram patterns.* A *phonogram* is a spelling unit that consists of a vowel plus a following consonant or consonant group. For example, *at, it, ut, atch, ight,* and *oat* are phonogram patterns. Another way of putting it is that the phonogram pattern is the part that rhymes in two rhyming words, as Rebecca Trieman (1993) has pointed out.

Begin with short vowel phonogram patterns since these are far more regular and consistent than long vowel patterns. Prepare two groups of word cards with 4 or 5 words that contain different phonogram patterns, such as *at* words (*cat, fat, hat, sat*) and *ip* words (*lip, sip, rip, tip*). Scramble these words, and then place one word from each group (the guide word) face up on the table. As the child picks up each new word in the pile, she places it in the appropriate column. See Figure 6.6.

Note that the children might be able to match a word with the others in the column before they can read it. If so, you should have the child place the word in the appropriate column and then read from the guide word down the other words in the column. With encouragement, the child should now be able to read the new word. If so, the child made an important step: She is learning to read new words by attending to the beginning consonant plus the phonogram pattern.

As children become proficient at sorting pictures for beginning consonant sounds, add word cards at the bottom of each column that are spelled with the beginning sound. For instance, after sorting the pictures of the ball, the bat, and the bell, you can put a card with the written word *bee.* Point to the letter B and say, "See? This letter B makes the /b/ sound. Now you can offer word cards to put at the bottom of other picture sort columns, too."

It helps call attention to sounds if you can draw out their pronunciation when you are working with children. Some sounds are easier to draw out than others: Compare the sounds of /m/ and /k/. Thus it is best to sequence the consonant sounds you introduce to

FIGURE 6.6   *Word Cards for a Phonogram Pattern Sort*

children with the "continuant" sounds (those that can easily be drawn out) first. A sequence of sounds adapted from Johnston, Invernizzi, and Juel (1998) is as follows:

- /m/ and /s/, then /m/, /s/, and /b/, then /m/, /s/, /b/,and /r/.
- /p/ and /n/, then /p/, /n/, and /t/, then /p/, /n/, /t/, and /g/.
- /k/ (with the letter C) and /f/, then /k/, /f/, and /d/; then /k/, /f/, /d/, and /h/.
- /j/ and /l/, then /j/, /l/, and /w/.
- /v/, /y/, and /z/.
- /sh/, /s/, and /h/; then /ch/, /j/, and /h/; then /th/, /ch/, /sh/, and /wh/.

Interactive Writing.   Developed in London by Moira McKenzie, *interactive writing* (Fountas & Pinnell, 1996) works very much like taking a dictated account, except that the teacher and the children "share the pen." The procedure follows these steps:

1. The teacher and a medium-size group of students share an experience and agree on a topic. The topic may be a retelling of a story, or a poem or song, the daily news, or an idea under study.
2. The children offer a sentence about the topic. The teacher has the children repeat the sentence many times, and even count the words, to fix them firmly in their minds.
3. The teacher asks the children for the first word, then pronounces that word slowly, writing its letters.
4. The teacher now asks for the next word and invites a child up to write the whole word, or a few letters, or a single letter. The teacher fills in letters the children miss. If the child writes an incorrect letter, the teacher pastes a short strip of correction tape over it, and helps the child identify the sound and write the correct letter for it.
5. Each time a word is added, the whole text is read back by the children, with the teacher pointing to the words.

Sound Boards.   A *sound board* (Blachman, 2000) is a device for showing children how words are constructed. Cut a piece measuring 11 inches by 14 inches from a sheet of poster board, then tape three strips of a different color from the board an inch and a half deep across the long side of the board. Now make grapheme cards 1 inch by 3 inches long. Turning them long side up, write letters exactly the same size on the top half only of each card (the bottom half of the card will disappear into the pocket). Prepare cards with consonant letters on them (written with a broad tip marker in black ink) and other cards with vowel letters and vowel teams (written in red ink).

Single consonant cards should include: **b, c, d, f, g, h, j, k, l, m, n, p, qu, r, s, t, v, w,** and **z.** Digraph consonant cards (a digraph is two letters that spell a single sound) should include **ch, th, sh, wh, ck,** and **ph.**

Vowel cards should contain *a, e, i, o,* and *u.* Vowel team cards should contain **ai, ay, ey, ee, ea, ie, oo, ou, ow, oi, oy, au, aw,** and **ew.** Vowel plus consonant cards should contain **ar, er, ir, ur,** and also **al** (as in **walk, calm,** and **bald**) (after Blachman, 2000).

The top pocket is for storing learned consonants and the middle pocket is for learned vowels. The bottom pocket is for making words. A manila envelope is attached to the back of the sound board for storing grapheme cards.

To use the sound board, put a consonant such as *s* in the bottom pocket. Pronounce its sound. Then put a vowel letter *a* to the right of it and pronounce its sound. Then put a consonant letter *t* to the right of the vowel and pronounce it. Say all three sounds and then pronounce the word *sat.* Now ask the child to repeat the activity, using the same three letters. Take away the letter *s* and ask him to sound the other two letters out and pronounce the word (*at*). Then pick up a new consonant letter card such as *p* and pronounce its sound. Put the *p* to the left of *a* and *t* and ask the child to pronounce all three sounds and say the word (*pat*).

Push It Say It.   From Johnston, Invernizzi, and Juel's *Book Buddies* program (1998) comes the *Push It Say It* technique. Here you prepare word cards as follows. One set of cards should be consonants (such as *s, b, c, t, m*), and the other should be rimes or phonogram patterns (such as *at, it, op*). To carry out the activity, first demonstrate it to the child, as follows:

1. Put a consonant card and a phonogram card separately on the table in front of the child. Drawing out the consonant sound ("sssss"), push the consonant card forward.
2. Then drawing out the sound of the rime ("aaaaaat"), push the rime card forward.
3. Now pronounce the resulting word (*sat*).

Then provide the child a consonant card and a rime card and ask her to repeat what you did.

Making and Breaking Words

As an enhancement of the word study component of the Reading Recovery program™ (see below for a discussion), Iverson and Tunmer (1993) developed a procedure for "making and breaking words." The procedure is carried out with a set of plastic letters and a magnetic board (available in most toy stores) and is conducted one-on-one.

The teacher asks the child to move the letters around to construct new words that have similar spellings and sound patterns. For instance, the teacher arranges letters to make the word *and.* The teacher announces that the letters spell *and* then asks the child what the word says. If the child seems uncertain, the teacher forms the word again, using different letters, says its name, and asks the child to name the word.

As a next step, the teacher scrambles the letters and asks the child to make *and.* Again, if assembling scrambled letters proves difficult, the teacher spreads the letters apart, in the proper order, at the bottom of the magnetic board and asks the student to make the word *and* with them in the middle of the board. When the child has made the word, the teacher asks the child to name the word. If the child responds correctly, the teacher scrambles the letters and asks the child to make the word again and to name the word afterward. The teacher repeats the procedure until the child is readily able to assemble the letters and name *and.*

As a next step, the teacher puts the letter *s* in front of *and* and announces what he has just done. The teacher takes a finger and moves the *s* away and then back and says, "Do you see? If I put *s* in front of *and*, it says *sand.*" The teacher asks the child to read the word *sand,* and the child runs a finger under it. Now the teacher removes the *s* and points out that with the *s* removed, the word is now *and.* With the *s* pushed aside, the teacher asks the child to make sand. If the child correctly makes the word, the teacher asks the child to name the word he has made. Next the teacher instructs the child to make *and.* As a next step, the whole procedure is repeated, making *hand* and *band.* Now the teacher can make *sand,* then *band,* then *hand,* and *and,* asking the child to name each word as it is made. When the child can do so successfully, the teacher scrambles the letters and on the board, and puts the letters *s, b,* and *h* to one side. Now the teacher challenges the child to make *and.* If the child can do so, the child is now challenged to make *hand, sand,* and *band.* The child is asked to read each word after it is made.

Connecting Children's Literature with Phonics Instruction

An important way to connect phonics instruction with the words children read is to integrate it with children's literature. Before and while children are learning about words, letters, and sounds, they need to be surrounded with a rich language environment. The richer the language environment, the more children learn about language, both spoken and written.

Phyllis Trachtenburg has described a "whole-part-whole" sequence integrating phonics instruction with children's literature (1990, p. 649) in this way:

1. Whole: Read, comprehend, and enjoy a whole high-quality literature selection.
2. Part: Provide instruction in a high-utility phonic element by drawing from or extending the preceding literature selection.
3. Whole: Apply the new phonic skill when reading (and enjoying) another whole high-quality literature selection.

For example, the teacher reads aloud *Angus and the Cat.* Extension activities include dramatizing parts of the story or comparing the story to other dog-and-cat stories. The teacher then introduces the short /a/ sound and shows the students a printed portion of the story containing a number of short /a/ sound words, such as *cat, that, back,* and *glad.* The teacher rereads the story portion while emphasizing and underlining the target words. Students and teacher choral-read the excerpt several times, with emphasis on the target words. Students then work with a "word slotter," made of tagboard strips with a medial short *a* and movable strips with beginning and ending consonants. Students experiment with moving the initial and final letters to create new short /a/ sound words. (Students could use linking letters, letter cards, or plastic letters as well.) Students then use a "sentence slotter" to construct sentences with short /a/ sound words. (Students could use word cards for this activity as well.) Finally, a new story is presented that also features many short /a/ sound words, such as *The Cat in the Hat.* Choral and individual readings of the new book help to reinforce the use of the phonic pattern in new text.

Enhanced Writing

At the end of one lesson, ask the child to think of a sentence she wants to write the next time. Then, have the child tell you the sentence several times. If necessary, shorten it for the child to 5 or 6 words.

Ask the child to write the sentence as best she can. Accept a reasonable letter for each sound, but don't accept nonsense. As she writes, have the child put her finger between individual words.

When the child has finished writing a word, fill in letters for sounds she can't hear. Don't worry about silent letters for now. We are concerned at this stage about beginning consonants, vowels in each syllable, and ending consonants.

Later, rewrite the sentence correctly, twice, and proceed to the cut-apart words exercise.

Early Writing Workshops

Early writing workshops teach the concept of word, phonemic awareness, and the beginnings of letter-to-sound correspondences. Kindergarten is not too early to begin writing workshops with children. What do we mean by "writing workshop" at this age? A writing workshop is a time when children are encouraged to create a story or some other sort of expression on a page, confer with their teacher and their classmates as they produce it, and share the results with the class.

Naturally, kindergarten children will draw their story first. But with nudging from the teacher and support from their classmates, we should see children begin to use letters or pseudo-letters to stand for some of their ideas, especially if the writing workshop is repeated daily or at least several days a week.

We're not aiming for perfection or even partial correctness now. We know that children learn to write by getting into the game. They pick up concepts about writing by putting marks on the page, thinking about how those marks might represent ideas, and then looking with growing curiosity at the ways in which others use marks to stand for language. Little by little, the children's strategies for using marks will grow more sophisticated and will progress through something like the stages described in Chapter 1.

Demonstrating Invented Spelling: A Group Writing Workshop.   When many children know ten or more letters, are beginning to attend to sounds in words, and are ready to explore the ways letters and sounds work in words, it is time to show them how spelling works. The best way is to demonstrate the process of inventing spelling and draw the whole class into the activity.

After the children have drawn pictures, the teacher asks for a volunteer to share her picture with the class. The child comes and sits in the "author's chair," in the front of the classroom, and tells about her picture. Then the teacher asks, "If we wanted to write one thing about this picture what would it be?" The child says, "My dog is nice."

The teacher repeats the sentence several times and asks the other children to repeat it. The teacher wants the sentence firmly in everyone's mind for what comes next.

Now the teacher says, "Suppose we wanted to write 'My dog is nice.' What word do we want to write first?"

"My dog," someone says.

"Let's say, 'My.' " says the teacher. "We want to write 'my.' " (The teacher is exaggerating the pronunciation.)

"What sound do we hear in 'my'? Watch my lips as I say it."

"Mmmmm," someone says.

"Mmmmmm," repeats the teacher. "Does anyone know what letter makes the sound 'Mmmmmm'?"

"M?"

"M!" says the teacher and writes the M on the board, describing the writing motions as she goes.

"Does anyone hear another sound in 'My'?" asks the teacher.

The children look at her blankly, so she goes on to the word *dog.*

If someone had heard the vowel sound in *my* and later offered a letter for it, chances are that letter would have been I, not Y. The teacher would have accepted the I. She knows that children aren't learning individual spellings at this stage; they are just learning that letters represent sounds. On the other hand, she would not accept A or U or T. Those letters bear no logical relationship to the sound of I. Since this logic is what she's aiming for, to accept random letters in a demonstration like this would just confuse children.

The teacher might repeat these group demonstrations several times a week. At first, she is showing children that it is acceptable to try to invent spellings, and she is encouraging them to do it themselves. As the demonstrations proceed, she is showing children sound-to-letter relationships, modeling the logic of alphabetic writing.

Early Writing Workshop: Individual Children.   The writing workshop is offered daily or at least several days a week. At first, the children will draw and will share their drawings with the class, telling the story as they do. The teacher or a parent volunteer might also ask the child to dictate a sentence about the picture, which the teacher can write across the bottom or on the back. The child can take the picture home and reread the sentence with a family member.

Once children know some letters, the teacher might open one or two sessions each week with a group dictation demonstration (see above) and then invite children to write about their own drawings.

If the group demonstration has done its job, children need only be encouraged to write one thing about their picture. If a child is reluctant, the teacher might approach the child, invite him to tell about the contents of the drawing, and then ask, "If you could write one thing about this story right down here (pointing to some white space at the bottom of the page), what would it be?" Then the teacher will encourage the child to put down letters for his words on the page. If the child knows some letters and seems able to think about sounds in words, the teacher can take the child through the steps of sounding out and recording some of the sounds in his words. This is sophisticated stuff for kindergarten, though. Many children will be making random marks and pseudo-writing, at least until the latter part of the kindergarten year.

Let us hasten to add that even with young children, writing workshop is about a lot more than spelling. The activity of thinking up messages, inscribing them in some form on paper, and sharing them later with interested classmates is the essence of authorship that is valuable in its own right.

Shared Reading

Shared Reading (Holdaway, 1979) is a flexible means of working through a text with a student or students, calling the students' attention to the important features of texts, and inviting children's engagement and response. The technique is adaptable because it is based on the needs of the students and on the possibilities presented by the text.

Scaffolding and Shared Reading.   The teacher's strategies during a Shared Reading session are summed up by the term *scaffolding* (Collins, Brown, & Newman, 1986). That is, the teacher offers the students just as much help as they need, with the goal that they should function as independently as possible as soon as possible. The teacher withdraws support as soon as it is no longer necessary.

Modeling.   In modeling (Roehler & Duffy, 1991), the teacher behaves like a skilled reader who describes her own thinking and perceptual processes as they are practiced. The teacher voices her own questions and lays out her own plans for inquiry. The teacher says what she wonders about and, as naturally as possible, draws out the students' own questions and suppositions: "You know, this title, *Nobody's Mother Is in Second Grade,* makes me think some child's mother is going to come to school, and the child will be embarrassed about it. Think that's what will happen?"

Challenging.   Here, the teacher gently challenges the students to practice specific comprehension strategies, especially ones that he has modeled: "I just told you my prediction of what will happen in this story, based on the title. What does the title make you think will happen?"

Praise.   The teacher congratulates the student for practicing a specific skill. The praise is highly specific: "Good for you! You got to the end of the sentence, realized that the word you read earlier didn't make sense, and went back and corrected yourself once you knew what the whole sentence was. That's a great strategy!"

Preparing for Shared Reading.   The teacher prepares for a Shared Reading session by considering the needs of the student or students who will be participating and the kinds of challenges that the text presents. The teacher needs to make several decisions about ways in which the text will challenge the students, and also help the students grow, in each of the following areas:

1. **Print Orientation.** Do these students need to be reminded that the print "talks," not the picture? Do they need to see the directional layout of print?
2. **Word Recognition.** What word patterns are presented that the children may be working on?
3. **Vocabulary.** What terms will the children need to know in advance, and what terms are they likely to learn from reading the text?

4. **Background Knowledge.** What knowledge will the children need in advance, and what are they likely to learn?
5. **Literary Genre.** Do the children have experience reading text of this type? What can be done to help them follow it successfully?
6. **Comprehension Strategies.** Which of the following comprehension strategies are the students already able to use? Which ones should be demonstrated and practiced in this lesson? *Summoning up background knowledge, setting purposes for reading and asking questions of the text, making predictions, making inferences, monitoring comprehension, visualizing, finding main ideas, summarizing.*

Conducting a Shared Reading Lesson. Shared Reading is best done with a big book (a 2- to 3-foot high version of a children's trade book) with multiple copies of regular-sized versions. It can be done with a whole class or with a smaller group. The teacher should make sure the students are seated comfortably where they can see the book the teacher is holding.

A Shared Reading lesson has a beginning, middle, and end. Teachers have different names for these three phases. Some call them *into, through,* and *beyond.* Others call them *introducing the book, reading and responding to the book,* and *extending the book.* Because we use similar phases with students in higher grades, too, we will use the same three terms for these phases at all levels: *anticipation, building knowledge,* and *consolidation.*

Anticipation is the phase in which the students first approach the text, find out what it is about, consider what they know about the topic, ask questions, and set purposes for reading.

Building knowledge is the phase in which students thoughtfully listen to or read the text, with their purposes and questions in mind, inquiring and seeking answers to their questions and to satisfy our purposes, and also raising new questions as the text suggests them and pursuing new purposes for their listening and reading.

Consolidation is the phase in which students do something with the new information they have gained: respond to it, question it, debate it, apply it, adjust their knowledge of the world in light of it—and decide where their inquiry should take them next.

In the Anticipation Stage. In this phase, the teacher attempts to arouse the students' interest in the text and get them ready to read meaningfully. The teacher works the following steps into this phase:

1. The teacher encourages the students to inspect what is to be listened to or read, look at the cover, consider the title, peruse a few pictures inside the book, and perhaps listen to or read a few lines. Their purpose is to determine what topic the book is about and also what form or genre of writing it is (story, informational book, poem, etc.). For younger children, rather than to speak of genre, the teacher can point out who the author is and recall other books by that author that the students have enjoyed. Then the teacher can gently direct their expectations by venturing a

question such as, "Do you think George is going to do something goofy, as he did in the other George and Martha books?"

2. The students should be reminded of other books of the genre that they already know, being as specific as they are able to. If it is a biography, they should think of other biographies they have read and what kinds of things they found out. If it is a work of fiction, they might want to decide whether the book appears to be fantasy, realistic, or folk literature because answers to these questions shape the expectations they should have for what might happen in the book.

3. If it is an informational book or a work of realistic fiction, the teacher should ask the questions that lead the students to reflect on what they already know about that topic. They should be aware of areas they don't know about or are unsure about that might be informed by this book. Then they should formulate questions about the topic that they hope to have answered by the text.

4. If it is a work of fiction, students should be asked to make predictions about what is likely to happen in the book, given the title, the illustrations, and the notes on the jacket.

5. The teacher should look through the book ahead of time to identify up to four words that the students might not be familiar with. These can be introduced into a discussion of what the book is about and defined in the course of that discussion.

In the Building Knowledge Phase.   After the teacher has introduced the text, aroused the students' interest and curiosity about it, and led them to set purposes for their reading, the teacher is ready to lead them into the text. We call this the *Building Knowledge phase* of reading. The teacher can take different approaches here, depending on the students' needs. The teacher might focus on *print orientation,* on *word recognition,* on *language expansion,* or on *comprehension.* The teacher will always focus on enjoyment: keeping the exercise moving ahead at a good pace and showing enthusiasm all the while.

To Stress Print Orientation.   If the teacher wishes to stress print orientation and word recognition, a big book should be used. The teacher reads a page of the book, reading very expressively (see the section entitled "Ten Pointers for Reading Aloud," Box 6.1, for read-aloud suggestions). Using a pointer or a finger, the teacher points to each word as it is read, makes the return sweep to the left, and drops down to the next line. If some of the students need extra help with print orientation, the teacher says aloud what he is doing: "Look, I'm going to begin reading up here in this corner. I'm going to read each word across, and then go down to the next word. See?" The teacher is careful not to belabor the talking about the print; it is important that the reading go along quickly so that students not lose the meaning.

To Stress Word Recognition.   The teacher is reading a page of text aloud. She comes to a key word in the text and covers the word with her hand:

Ahmed walked along, and walked along, until he came to a _____ (This word is covered and the teacher skips it) in the road.
   "Which way do I go?" he said.

Then the teacher asks the students what the word is. After they make several guesses, the teacher uncovers the first letter: f: _____ and again asks students what they think the word is now. If need be, the teacher keeps uncovering letters until they correctly guess the word *fork*.

To Stress Comprehension.   To develop comprehension, the teacher can model questions and comments and offer probes that encourage the students to listen or read to find out. As the teacher or the students read the text, the students are reminded to keep their questions and purposes in mind and to be alert to what they are learning (and not learning). The teacher also encourages the students to visualize what they are reading and to be alert to new directions and new questions that arise from the text.

Working almost conversationally, giving cues to the students, and taking cues from them, the teacher works the following steps into the students' activity in this phase:

1. Having begun the lesson by asking the students to venture predictions and raise questions, the teacher encourages the students to read with their predictions and questions in mind.
2. The teacher stops the reading periodically (usually four or five times per session) and asks the students whether their questions have been answered and whether their predictions were correct. The teacher also encourages the students to be alert for other details they have noticed that lead to new predictions and new questions.
3. The teacher reminds students of places where inferences should be made and helps them to make those inferences.
4. The teacher encourages the students to visualize settings or actions that have been described. The children might do this through spontaneous drama, even by reading aloud expressively: "Janet, say those words to George the way you hear Martha really saying them. Bill, show us what George is going to look like while Martha says those things to him."
5. The teacher makes sure the students are aware when they are understanding what the text is meaning: "Jeannie, can you say what the author just said, but put it in your own words?"

In the Consolidation Phase.   After the students have read the book or have otherwise reached a stopping point, the teacher takes steps to get them to talk about the work and to respond to it in other ways. These steps include the following:

1. The teacher might ask for a retelling of the work. The purpose of the retelling is to invite the students to summarize the work.
2. The teacher might ask the students to reflect back on the questions and predictions they posed at the outset and how the material they found in the text answered the questions and fulfilled the predictions. If some questions were not answered, the students can discuss where they can now turn for answers. If the predictions strayed significantly from what happened in the text, they can discuss what led them astray or what surprises occurred in the text.

3. The teacher might ask the students to say what was the most important idea the author told us in this work. The purpose of this is to lead students to think about main ideas.

4. The teacher will certainly ask the students for their personal responses to the work, especially if it is a work of fiction or poetry. The teacher uses open-ended questions such as "What is in your mind about this book (or chapter, or passage or reading) right now?" or "What are you feeling right now when you think of this book? Why? What makes you feel that way?" or "What does this book make you think of?" or "What was your favorite part? Why?"

5. The teacher might follow the students' personal responses to the work with two or three interpretive questions. Interpretive questions are open-ended: They invite different answers, yet they are still close to the text. After reading *Where the Wild Things Are,* for instance, the teacher could ask, "Why do you think the supper was still hot?"

6. To help students visualize the work, the teacher might ask students to draw or act out their favorite part or the most important or exciting part.

Guided Reading

Guided reading (Fountas & Pinnell, 1996) is done with a small group of between two and eight children to develop their reading, including word recognition, fluency, and comprehension. It is best done with moderately challenging texts—those written at the children's instructional level. The difficulty level of the texts rises along with the young readers' ability.

Penny Freppon (1997) provides an example of how to conduct a guided reading lesson:

> Each child has a copy of the story or informational text that is "leveled"—written in ways appropriate to the children's reading development. This text is at the children's instructional level and might be a basal excerpt or a little book. In ways similar to Shared Reading you introduce the book and in doing so build on the children's prior knowledge. "Hum. . ." you might say, "This looks like a story that could be about a friendship, see it says (pointing to the text) *Lost and Found* by Oliver Jeffers (2005) and if we look at the picture the boy and the penguin are hugging. What do you think it's about?"
>
> After children have the opportunity to talk with you and one another you may then shift to looking at some key vocabulary words that you have prepared in advance. These are words you have taken from the text and put on word cards. Remember too many words can overwhelm children, so just do a few, perhaps only two. As you show the words pronounce them and discuss their meanings. This is an opportunity for word study to begin but don't focus yet. Rather the next step is to read the story.
>
> Since this text is written at their instructional level, you guide children to **whisper read**—read in a low voice to themselves—the first few pages. As this

happens you listen carefully so you can intervene and help as needed. Next, you encourage them to take turns and read out-loud in their "quiet voices" in pairs with your support. Then you might invite volunteers to read on their own while others run their fingers under the text watching the words carefully. Take time to enjoy reading and discuss what has happened so far, continue to build understanding.

Although the main focus of guided reading is on reading fluency and comprehension, it also affords a fine opportunity to draw attention to key vocabulary words in the text. Again, you should prompt the children's thinking and engagement by saying, "Nice reading. I heard you work! You self-corrected and tried to read fluently with expression. Let's look at these pages now, do you see any key vocabulary words we have here (refer to the word cards)?" As children chime in finding text words and key vocabulary matches, draw their attention to word recognition skills, such as letter-to-sound correspondences. Then move onto more reading and thinking. This process of reading and thinking and then attending to some key vocabulary words may continue to the end of the story.

After they have finished reading, guide the children to closure by discussing the text they've read and making connections to what they know. Following this attention to words, you may include a review of the key vocabulary words, and give the children copies of the word cards for later practice at their tables or desks when they can re-read the book. A short writing and drawing activity may also be included. Children thrive on writing about their favorite part, and writing supports word learning.

Early Intervention Programs

Some research shows that nine out of ten children who are not reading at the end of first grade still lag far behind their classmates four years later (Juel, 1988). Special help might push them ahead by inches, but their classmates are sprinting ahead by miles.

Recently, a chorus of critics have pointed out shortcomings in our ways of helping slower readers and are proposing bold new solutions. The chief criticisms of remedial programs are the following:

1. **They Don't Work Well Enough.** While they might move poor readers ahead, they do not close the gap between poor readers and the rest of the class. Typically, remedial reading instruction has yielded about seven months' gain in a nine-month school year (Allington & McGill-Franzen, 1987).

2. **They Make Children Miss Other Subjects.** Remedial instruction has usually required that children be taken out of their other school subjects to get special reading skill instruction. Missing the information in these regular classes contributes to children's academic problems and even holds back their reading growth.

3. **They Are Not Intensive Enough.** Even teaching six children at a time, the smallest size of most remedial classes, can prevent a teacher from carrying out a careful diagnosis and giving each child fully responsive teaching and adequate amounts of real reading practice.

Reading Recovery

Perhaps the most promising solution proposed to date is early and intense literacy intervention. Reading Recovery™ (Clay, 1975), the most widely used program of this kind, targets the bottom 20 percent of the children in first grade and offers them one-on-one tutoring by an experienced and specially trained teacher. The tutoring lasts half an hour a day, five days a week, and continues until the children reach the medial level of reading ability in their classes—usually in 15 to 18 weeks. It is the hope of Reading Recovery advocates that the children will be able to advance with their classmates after the training is complete and will not need further remediation.

Reading Recovery instruction begins with a comprehensive assessment of a child's emergent literacy, followed by a period of informal teaching, called "roaming the known," intended to further explore the child's concepts about literacy. After the preliminary assessment period, instruction begins in earnest—though continuous assessment is built into every day's activities. Each day's lesson usually contains seven elements:

1. **Rereading of Two or More Familiar Books.** Reading Recovery tries to keep the child immersed to the greatest extent possible in real reading and writing tasks. Reading books on the child's level is done every day. (More on this later.)

2. **Independent Reading of the Preceding Lesson's New Book While the Teacher Takes a Running Record.** A running record is a diagnostic procedure developed by Clay (2000). A child reads aloud and the teacher makes detailed notes of the accuracy and fluency of the reading. (Strategies for making a running record are presented in Chapter 3.)

3. **Letter Identification Using Plastic Letters on a Magnetic Board** (only if necessary). Many educators have commented on the value of multisensory techniques in beginning literacy instruction. Plastic magnetic letters offer a concrete medium in which a child can call the letters by name as she arranges them to spell out words or to copy other words written out by the teacher.

4. **Writing a Story That the Child Has Composed, Including Hearing Sounds in Unfamiliar Printed Words via Sound Boxes.** Sound boxes are a phonological awareness training technique developed by Elkonin (1973). Writing with invented spelling, as we saw earlier in this chapter, has been shown to help children develop word and sound awareness, and awareness of phoneme-to-grapheme correspondences—in other words, to lay the foundation for learning to recognize words and to spell them. If a child cannot yet segment a word into its phonemes, the child's invented spelling will be very limited. Hence, the sound box may be used to develop phonemic segmentation ability.

5. **Reassembling a Cut-up Story.** A technique is included to help a child develop a concept of word and to practice word-to-word matching. A story that the child has dictated is cut into sentence strips, then these sentences are cut apart into words. The words are reassembled—first by matching them to another intact version and later by reading the words themselves.

6. **Introducing a New Book.** The teacher introduces a new book in each lesson, and the child will practice reading it several times on the day it is introduced and on subsequent days. Though the Reading Recovery program does not mandate any particular set of books, list of books graduated by difficulty level are circulated among teachers who are trained to use the program. One of the aims of the running record is to make sure that the child is reading with between 90 percent and 94 percent accuracy in word recognition. (Easier material won't teach the child new words; harder material will frustrate the child.)

7. **Practicing the New Book.** Practicing might be done by means of echo-reading (teacher reads a line, child follows) or choral-reading (they read simultaneously). The teacher aims to get the child to read the text over and over again (Iverson & Tunmer, 1993, after Clay, 1975).

Let us note that these lessons (1) base instruction on careful assessment and teach children what they need to know; (2) give practice that develops letter recognition, the concept of word, phonemic segmentation, and other concepts about print; (3) offer the child extensive daily practice reading real text on exactly the proper level for that child; (4) include writing as well as reading in a literacy lesson.

Questions about Early Intervention Programs

From its debut in the United States in the 1980s, Reading Recovery raised the hope that children who might otherwise fail to learn to read could be permanently "inoculated" against reading failure by intensive one-on-one tutoring in the first grade by specially trained teachers. The program is costly, but perhaps not more so than the traditional alternative, once we add up the costs—financial and motivational—of keeping struggling readers in special reading classes year after year. Besides, the traditional alternatives have not worked well.

A lengthy review of research by Shanahan and Barr (1995) has tempered some of our rosier hopes for Reading Recovery. The hope that children could be remediated once and for all in first grade has not been borne out. Shanahan and Barr found that children's future success after leaving Reading Recovery depended on the regular classroom instruction they received. If children are given little reading support at home, and—most especially—if they are not exposed to reading materials that continue to offer appropriate challenges at ascending levels of difficulty, it should not be surprising that some of their gains should be washed out. This is not an argument against Reading Recovery as much as an argument for constructive changes in regular classroom instruction.

Another question to be asked is whether the content of the Reading Recovery lesson might be improved upon. Most worthy of note, Reading Recovery lessons do not systematically teach phoneme-to-grapheme correspondences; rather, they leave it to the child to infer these correspondences indirectly. There is a raft of research, recently summarized in the National Research Council's *Preventing Reading Difficulties in Young Children* (Snow et al., 1998), that supports teaching children explicitly how the alphabetic writing system works.

Iverson and Tunmer (1993) compared the performance of 32 children who received Reading Recovery teaching plus these explicit procedures to teach phoneme-to-grapheme correspondences to another group of 32 who received standard Reading Recovery teaching and to still another group of 32 who received small-group instruction in a Chapter I classroom. (Note that the group who received explicit phoneme-to-grapheme correspondences was taught according to the "making and breaking words" procedure described earlier in this chapter.)

The results? Children who received small-group instruction in the Chapter I classroom gained very little in comparison to the two groups that used one-on-one teaching. Both of the Reading Recovery groups were successful in moving the children up to the median reading ability range of their first-grade classes and to sustain these gains at least through the end of the year. The group with the explicit phoneme-to-grapheme instruction, however, reached the desired level of reading performance in two-thirds the time it took the regular Reading Recovery group (in 42 lessons, on the average, instead of 57).

Given the expense of committing a teacher's time to providing one-to-one tutoring for a struggling child, speeding up the process will allow more children to be served, so the advantages of providing explicit instruction in phoneme-to-grapheme correspondences should be taken seriously.

Still another question is whether it is necessary to go to the expense of having a carefully trained teacher working one-on-one with the children. As for the importance of training, a research study by the core Reading Research advocates in the United States (Pinnell, 1994) found that reducing the training of Reading Recovery teachers markedly reduced their effectiveness. But efforts to construct a high-impact instructional program, according to current literacy principles, for small groups of Chapter I students (Hiebert, 1992) have shown impressive results that are comparable to those of Reading Recovery.

Early Intervention Programs Using Tutors

Finally, in an attempt to spread the benefits of tutoring to a larger audience than can be reached by professional teachers, several programs using volunteer tutors have come into being.

One of the best validated is Darrell Morris's Howard Street Tutoring Program (Morris, 1999), which begin in a storefront facility for inner-city Chicago children in the early 1980s. Morris's program is aimed at second and third graders, who are taught by volunteering college students and retired people, under the supervision of an experienced teacher. The teacher assesses each child upon entry to the program and prepares daily lesson plans and packets of materials to be used by the tutors, who work with the children twice a week for about 40 minutes. The lesson format is similar to that of Reading Recovery, except that the word study component explicitly and systematically teaches phoneme-to-grapheme correspondences.

Another successful program is Connie Juel and Marcia Invernizzi's Book Buddies Program. This program has involved college athletes in a tutorial program that has a lesson format very similar to that of Morris (Invernizzi & Juel, 1997).

Volunteer programs that recruit and field college students as literacy tutors recently got a boost from the federal government through the America Reads Program.

Summary

In this chapter, after situating the concept of emergent and beginning literacy among other kinds of understanding of early reading, we presented methods to structure your observation of children's *emergent literacy*, a term that applies to preliminary reading and writing, as well as their beginning literacy. The areas of literacy competence stressed in the chapter were *print orientation concepts, alphabet recognition, the concept of word, phonological awareness, phoneme-to-grapheme correspondences,* and *sight-word recognition.*

After a discussion of the importance of each aspect of literacy, we described at least one assessment procedure.

Storybook reading turns out to be a rich indicator of children's emerging concepts about literacy. The assessment of children's storybook reading can be done by having a child pretend read a favorite storybook and categorize the results according to Elizabeth Sulzby's scheme.

A child's ability to make the speech-to-print match in a memorized written sequence can be assessed by using the dictated experience story or some other easily memorized material. The voice-pointing procedure is used with either type of material to determine whether children can match spoken and written words in a familiar portion of text and whether a supported rereading activity helps them to recognize new words in print.

A phonemic segmentation task using invented spelling was described for the purpose of investigating children's ability to divide words up into their smallest sound units, a necessary part of word knowledge related to the application of phonics.

Print orientation concepts can be assessed by using the Concepts About Print Test or by adapting this procedure in minor ways, such as varying the questions asked and the text used. The Concepts About Print Test represents a real reading experience with prereaders. It helps a teacher to learn what a child knows about book orientation; directionality of print and pages; concepts of letters, words, spaces, and punctuation marks; and the communicative nature of print and pictures.

A student's comprehension can be assessed in several ways. The Informal Reading Inventory, featured in Chapter 3, is one elaborate way of doing so.

The acquisition of sight words can be assessed informally by using a sight-word inventory made up of words frequently occurring in beginning reading materials. Words are presented in isolation, but the presentation is untimed. A similar inventory can be used to examine the recognition of letters, uppercase and lowercase.

The chapter also shared several means of helping children's literacy to emerge. Big books, brought into popularity by New Zealander Don Holdaway, were suggested as an excellent aid for teaching print orientation concepts, since they enable children to read along with the teacher in a favorite story and notice features of the print as they do so.

Little books, short personalized texts to be taken home by children, are another useful sort of early reading material.

Techniques that were advanced for making children aware of the correspondences between letters and sounds were the word sort strategy and the strategy of making and breaking words.

Techniques for developing reading comprehension are the Directed Reading-Thinking Activity, Reciprocal Teaching, and Questioning the Author. All will be described in detail in Chapter 9. In the present chapter, we described a variation of Shared Reading, enhanced with special emphasis on developing comprehension. The chapter closed with a section of early intervention programs, including Reading Recovery.

MyLabSchool is a collection of online tools for your success in this course, your licensure exams, and your teaching career. Visit www.mylabschool.com to access the following:

- Online Study Guide
- Video cases from real classrooms
- Help with your research papers using Research Navigator
- Career Center with resources for:
  - Praxis exams and licensure preparation
  - Professional portfolio development
  - Job search and interview techniques
  - Lesson planning

References

Adams, M. J. (1998). The three cuing system. In J. Osborne & F. Lehr (Eds.), *Literacy for all: Issues in teaching and learning.* New York: Guilford Press.

Allard, H. (1977). *Miss Nelson is missing!* Illustrated by J. Marshall. Boston: Houghton Mifflin.

Allen, R. V. (1976). *Language experiences in communication.* Boston: Houghton Mifflin.

Allington, R., & McGill-Franzen, A. (1987). *A study for the whole school day experience of Chapter I and mainstreamed LD students* (Final Report of Grant #G008630480, Office of Special Education Programs). Washington, DC: U.S. Department of Education.

Bear, D., Invernizzi, M., Templeton, S., & Johnson, F. (1996). *Words their way: Word study for phonics, vocabulary, and spelling instruction.* Upper Saddle River, NJ: Merrill.

Beck, I., et al. (1997). *Questioning the author.* Newark, DE: International Reading Association.

Blachman, B. (1994). Early literacy acquisition: The role of phonological awareness. In G. P. Wallach & K.G. Butler (Eds.), *Language learning disabilities in school-aged children and adolescents.* Boston: Allyn & Bacon.

Blachman, B. (2000). *An overview of the STARS program.* Syracuse, NY: Syracuse University School of Education, Syracuse Reading Project.

Blachman, B., Tangel, D., Ball, E., Black, B., & McGraw, D. (1995). Developing phonological awareness and word recognition skills: A two-year intervention with low income, inner-city children. *Reading and Writing: An Interdisciplinary Journal, 11,* 273–293.

Bond, Guy L., & Dykstra, R. (1967). The cooperative research program in first grade reading instruction. *Reading Research Quarterly, 2,* 5–142.

Bradley, L., & Bryant, P. (1985). *Rhyme and reason in reading and spelling.* Ann Arbor: University of Michigan Press.

Bruner, J. *Child's talk: Learning to use language.* New York: Norton, 1985.

Chomsky, C. (1976, May). *Approaching reading through invented spelling.* Paper presented at the Conference on Theory and Practice of Beginning Reading Instruction, University of Pittsburgh, Learning Research and Development Center.

Chomsky, N. (1968). *Language and the mind.* New York: Harcourt, Brace, Jovanovich.

Clarke, L. (1988). Inventory versus traditional spelling in first graders' writings: Effects on learning to spell and read. *Research in the Teaching of English, 22*(3), 281–309.

Clay, M. (1975). *What did I write?* Portsmouth, NH: Heinemann Educational Books.

Clay, M. (1986). *The early detection of reading difficulties, with recovery procedures* (3rd ed.). Portsmouth, NH: Heinemann Educational Books.

Clay, M. (2000). *Record of oral language.* Portsmouth, NH: Heinemann.

Clay, M. (2000). *Running records for classroom teachers.* Portsmouth, NH: Heinemann.

Clay, M., Gill, M., Glynn, T., McNaughton, T., & Salmon, K. (1982). *The record of oral language and biks and gutches.* Portsmouth, NH: Heinemann Educational Books.

Collins, A., Brown, J. S., & Newman, S. (1986). *Cognitive apprenticeship: Teaching the craft of reading, writing, and mathematics* (Report No. 6459). Cambridge, MA: BNN Laboratories.

Dewey, J. (1910). *How we think.* New York: Macmillan.

Ehri, L. (1989, April). *Research on reading and spelling.* Paper presented at the George Graham Memorial Lectures, University of Virginia, Charlottesville.

Ehri, L. (1991). Development of the ability to read words. In R. Barr, M. Kamil, P. Mosenthal, & P. D. Pearson (Eds.), *Handbook of reading research: Vol. 2.* New York: Longman.

Elkonin, D. (1973). Reading in the USSR. In J. Downing (Ed.), *Comparative reading.* New York: Macmillan.

Ferreiro, E., & Teberosky, A. (1979). *Literacy before schooling.* Portsmouth, NH: Heinemann.

Fountas, I., & Pinnell, G. S. (1996). *Guided reading.* Portsmouth, NH: Heinemann.

Frith, U. (1985). Beneath the surface of developmental dyslexia. In K. E. Patterson, J. C. Marshall, & M. Coltheart (Eds.), *Surface dyslexia* (pp. 301–330). London: Erlbaum.

Gardner, H. (1991). *The unschooled mind.* Garden City, NY: Basic Books.

Gessell, A., & Ilg, F. (1949). *Child development: An introduction to human growth.* New York: Harper.

Goodman, K. S. (1967). Reading: A psycholinguistic guessing game. *Journal of the Reading Specialist 6,* 126–135.

Goodman, K. S. (1976). Reading: A psycholinguistic guessing game. In H. Singer & R. Ruddell (Eds.), *Theoretical models and processes of reading* (2nd ed.). Newark, DE: International Reading Association.

Goodman, Y. (1981). Test review: Concepts about print test. *The Reading Teacher, 34,* 445–448.

Goswami, U. (2000). Phonological and lexical processes. In M. L. Kamil, P. B. Mosenthal, P. D. Pearson, & R. Barr (Eds.), *Handbook of reading research: Vol. 3.* Mahwah, NJ: Erlbaum.

Graves, M., Juel, C., & Graves, B. (1998). *Teaching reading in the 21st century.* Boston: Allyn & Bacon.

Hall, S. L., & Moats, L. C. (1999). *Straight talk about reading.* Lincolnwood, IL: Contemporary Books.

Harste, J., Woodward, V., & Burke, C. (1984). *Language stories and literacy lessons.* Portsmouth, NH: Heinemann Educational Books.

Harste, J., Woodward, V., & Burke, C. (1985). *Language stories and literacy lessons.* Portsmouth, NH: Heinemann.

Hiebert, E. (1992). Reading and writing of first grade students in a restructured Chapter I program. *American Education Research Journal, 29*(3), 545–572.

Holdaway, D. (1979). *Foundations of literacy.* Portsmouth, NH: Heinemann Educational Books.

Invernizzi, M., & Juel, C. (1997). A community volunteer tutoring program that works. *The Reading Teacher, 50*(4), 304–311.

Iverson, S., & Tunmer, W. (1993). Phonological processing skills and the Reading Recovery programme. *Journal of Educational Psychology, 85*(1), 112–126.

Johnston, F., Invernizzi, M., & Juel, C. (1998). *Book buddies.* New York: Guilford Press.

Juel, C. (1988). Learning to read and write: A longitudinal study of 54 children from first through fourth grades. *Journal of Educational Psychology, 80*(4), 427–447.

Loban, W. (1963). *The language of elementary school children.* Urbana, IL: National Council of Teachers of English.

Mann, V., Tobin, P., & Wilson, R. (1988). Measuring phonological awareness through invented spelling. In Keith Stanovich (Ed.), *Children's reading and the development of phonological awareness.* Detroit: Wayne State University Press.

McConkie, G. W., & Hogaboam, T. W. (1985, April). *Eye position and word identification during reading* (Technical Report No. 333). Urbana: University of Illinois, Center for the Study of Reading.

McCormick, C., & Mason, J. (1989). Fostering reading for Head Start children with Little books. In J. Allen & J. Mason, *Risk makers, risk takers, risk breakers.* Portsmouth, NH: Heinemann Educational Books.

McCracken, R., & McCracken, M. (1987). *Reading is only the tiger's tail.* Winnepeg: Peguis.

Morris, D. (1981). Concept of word and phoneme awareness in the beginning reader. *Research in the Teaching of English, 17,* 359–373.

Morris, D. (1982). "Word sort": A categorization strategy for improving word recognition ability. *Reading Psychology, 3*(3), 247–259.

Morris, D. (1990). *Case studies in beginning reading: The Howard Street tutoring manual.* Boone, NC: Fieldstream.

Morris, D. (1993). The relationship between children's concept of word in text and phonemic awareness in learning to read: A longitudinal study. *Research in the Teaching of English, 27,* 133–154.

Morris, R. D. (1998). *Case studies in beginning reading.* New York: Guilford Press.

Morris, R. D. (1999). *The Howard Street tutoring manual.* New York: Guilford Press.

National Reading Panel. (2000). *Teaching children to read: An evidence-based assessment of the scientific research literature on reading and its implications for reading instruction.* Washington, DC: National Institute for Literacy.

Palincsar, A. M., & Brown, A. (1984). Reciprocal teaching of comprehension-fostering and comprehension-monitoring activities. *Cognition and Instruction, 1,* 117–175.

Palincsar, A. M., & Brown, A. (1986). Reciprocal teaching of comprehension-fostering and comprehension-monitoring activities. *Cognition and Instruction, 1*(2), 117–175.

Perfetti, C. (1985). *Reading ability.* New York: Oxford University Press.

Piaget, J. (1926). *The language and thought of the child.* New York: Harcourt, Brace, & World.

Pinnell, G. S. (1994). Comparing instructional models for the literacy education of high risk first graders. *Reading Research Quarterly, 29*(1), 8–39.

Raphael, T. (1982). Question answering strategies for children. *The Reading Teacher, 36,* 186–190.

Roehler, L. R., & Duffy, G. G. (1991). Teachers' instructional actions. In R. Barr, M. Kamil, P. Mosenthal, & P. D. Pearson (Eds.), *Handbook of reading research: Vol. 2.* New York: Longman.

Shanahan, T., & Barr, R. (1995). Reading Recovery: An independent evaluation of the effects of an early instructional intervention for at-risk learners. *Reading Research Quarterly, 30*(4), 958–996.

Slobin, D., & Welsh, C. (1971). Elicited imitation as a research tool in developmental psycholinguistics. In C. Lavatelli (Ed.), *Language training in early childhood education.* Urbana: University of Illinois Press.

Snow, C., Burns, S., & Griffin, P. (Eds.). (1998). *Preventing reading difficulties in young children.* Washington, DC: National Academy Press.

Spear-Swerling, L., & Sternberg, R. J. (1997). *Off track: When poor readers become "learning disabled" (renewing American schools).* Boulder, CO: Westview Press.

Stanovich, K. E. (2000). Toward an interactive-compensatory model of individual differences in the development of reading fluency. In *Progress in Understanding Reading.* New York: Guilford Press.

Stauffer, R. (1970). *The language experience approach to the teaching of reading.* New York: Harper & Row.

Stauffer, R. (1980). *The language experience approach to the teaching of reading* (2nd ed.). New York: Harper & Row.

Stern, D. (1982). *The first relationship.* Cambridge, MA: Harvard University Press.

Sulzby, E. (1985). Children's emergent reading of favorite storybooks: A developmental study. *Reading Research Quarterly, 20,* 458–481.

Temple, C., & Gillet, J. (1978). Developing word knowledge: A cognitive view. *Reading World, 18*(2), 132–140.

Trachtenburg, P. (1990). Using children's literature to enhance phonics instruction. *The Reading Teacher, 43*(9), 653–654.

Trelease, J. (1989). *The new read-aloud handbook.* New York: Penguin.

Trieman, R. (1993). *Beginning to spell: A study of first grade children.* New York: Oxford.

Trieman, R. (1998). Onsets and rimes as units of spoken syllables: Evidence from children. *Journal of Experimental Child Psychology, 39,* 161–181.

Vellutino, F. (1977). Alternative conceptualizations of dyslexia: Evidence in support of a verbal deficit hypothesis. *Harvard Educational Review, 47,* 334–354.

Vellutino, F. (1979). *Dyslexia: Theory and research.* Cambridge, MA: MIT Press.

Walsh, D., Price, G., & Gillingham, M. (1988). The critical but transitory importance of letter naming. *Reading Research Quarterly, 23,* 108–122.

Weaver, C., Gillmeister-Krause, L., & Vento-Zogby, G. (1996). *Creating support for effective literacy education.* Portsmouth, NH: Heinemann.

Yopp, H. K. (1988). The validity and reliability of phonemic awareness tests. *Reading Research Quarterly, 23,* 159–177.

Teaching Developing Readers

Chapter Outline

*C*arl Hardy's friends kid him that his third-grade classroom looks like one of those corner grocery stores way up on Broadway in New York City where he teaches. Every possible inch is crammed with something. The walls are hung with columns of words written on tagboard. There is a reading corner near the bookshelf with the classroom library. There is a listening center hung with sets of headphones. There is even a puppet theater for acting out stories. A colorful chart of the reptile family hangs on the wall opposite a large map of the world, with flags taped to the countries where his students came from. The students' own map of the neighborhood has push pins marking the places where students live. Prints of works by this month's artist, Pablo Picasso, hang from wires stretched below the ceiling. His desk is pushed to the side of the classroom to make room for the carpeted circle area where classroom community meetings and large- and small-group lessons are conducted. On his desk is a thick American Heritage Dictionary—Carl Hardy loves words.

In a file cabinet is a folder for each student in the class. It holds the students' work samples, Carl's observational notes of their reading and learning, and results for several kinds of reading assessment. The Informal Reading Inventory scores gave him an initial idea of what level of book in which to place the students, and also the strengths of different aspects of reading: word recognition, fluency, and comprehension. There are also more frequently administered monitoring assessments to keep track of the students' reading success.

The students' reading ability spreads across four grade levels, and that means that not only will the books be on different levels, but the strategies for word study will differ as well.

In this chapter we look at developing readers, those children who are reading more and more text and more rapidly learning sight words. In the stage-bound parlance of Chapter 1, we would say that these children should be passing into and through the stages of *building fluency* and *reading to learn and for pleasure*. Normally, such readers are found from late second grade through fourth grade, after which they could be entering a phase of *mature reading*. However, when children experience difficulty, this period of developing reading may begin later and last longer. As part of the public awareness campaign surrounding the No Child Left Behind Education Act, the U.S. Department of Education adopted from the National Reading Panel (2000) five essential components for reading instruction: *phonemic awareness, phonics, vocabulary, fluency,* and *comprehension* processes (see Figure 7.1).

Five Essential Components of Reading

The National Reading Panel (2000) identified five essential components of reading that children must be taught in order to learn to read. Adults can help children learn to be good readers by systematically practicing these five components:

1. *Recognizing and using individual sounds to create words, or phonemic awareness. Children need to be taught to hear sounds in words and that words are made up of the smallest parts of sound, or phonemes.*

2. *Understanding the relationships between written letters and spoken sounds, or phonics. Children need to be taught the sounds individual printed letters and groups of letters make. Knowing the relationships between letters and sounds helps children to recognize familiar words accurately and automatically and "decode" new words.*

3. *Developing the ability to read a text accurately and quickly, or reading fluency. Children must learn to read words rapidly and accurately in order to understand what is read. When fluent readers read silently, they recognize words automatically. When fluent readers read aloud, they read effortlessly and with expression. Readers who are weak in fluency read slowly, word by word, focusing on decoding words instead of comprehending meaning.*

4. *Learning the meaning and pronunciation of words, or vocabulary development. Children need to actively build and expand their knowledge of written and spoken words, what they mean, and how they are used.*

5. *Acquiring strategies to understand, remember and communicate what is read, or reading comprehension strategies. Children need to be taught comprehension strategies, or the steps good readers use to make sure they understand text. Students who are in control of their own reading comprehension become purposeful, active readers.*

FIGURE 7.1 *Five Essential Components of Reading*

In the first chapters of this book, we described a range of strategies and instruments for assessing the reading of developing readers. Some devices like the Informal Reading Inventory are used periodically to assess many aspects of a child's reading ability, including word recognition (in isolation and in context), reading fluency, and comprehension (both while reading and while listening). More frequently administered assessments such as the running record and observational procedures can be used to monitor children's progress in learning to read, particularly their word recognition and fluency, but also their comprehension and even their interest in reading.

Now we will focus on what to do with all of this information. How do we teach children so as to help them develop the aspects of reading ability that need strengthening?

Phonics and Word Knowledge for Developing Readers

In Chapter 6, we treated phonemic awareness in some detail. In this chapter we focus on phonics, vocabulary development, fluency, and comprehension.

Word Knowledge at Different Levels

In popular parlance, phonics is sometimes described as the cure-all for literacy problems. Understanding the ways letters and print relate to each other is surely important in learning to read. But to be useful, phonics instruction should be tailored to what the child already knows about words. What children know about words is different at different stages of development.

When we are observing children's attempts to read words that are just beyond their reach, we see different children using different strategies. One child will look at the first letter and say nearly any word that comes to mind that begins the same way. Another child will sound out every letter in the word, as if that letter announced an individual sound that had nothing to do with the sound that came before or after it. Another child will pronounce the first part of the syllable and then the latter part, as if they were two parts of the whole, and then say the whole word. Still another child will explain, if asked, that she sees a word she knows as part of the longer words. How would you teach "phonics" to all of these children? Differently, of course!

The German researcher Uta Frith (1985) observed that children pass through four stages as they learn to recognize words. Her stages are summarized in *The Handbook of Reading Research,* Volume III, by Usha Goswami (2000). Frith's stages are called *logographic, transitional alphabetic, alphabetic,* and *orthographic.* To these we have added one more stage: *derivational reading.*

Logographic Reading.   Preschool and kindergarten children who are just beginning to see familiar words around them tend to recognize words as whole displays. Children recognize McDonald's restaurants by their golden arches. They may recognize the word *look* by associating the two O's with eyes. Children in this stage may call the same word with different but related names, calling a Crest toothpaste label at one time "Crest" and at another time "toothpaste" (Harste, Woodward, & Burke, 1985). They are not yet focusing on the parts of the words, but are trying to find any identifiable feature that will help them remember them. This isn't a very powerful strategy, and logographic readers often give no response at all when faced with a word they do not know because they do not yet have strategy for sounding out words.

Because children would look at a word and call it by the few names of words they knew, Marsh et al. (1981) called this stage of word recognition "glance and guess." We shouldn't belittle this stage, though. Many teachers advocate encouraging children to learn to recognize several dozen words as wholes before they begin to call their attention to the parts of the words.

Transitional Alphabetic Reading.   Once they have sufficient practice with words as wholes more advanced children—usually in early first grade—begin to focus on the letters in words and use their knowledge of the letters' sounds to read them. At first, they may pay attention to the first and last consonant, and later pay attention to the vowel that comes in the middle. Some teachers advocate having children read *decodable texts*—texts that contain words composed of the most reliable spelling patterns—at this level.

The trade-off is that we want children to expect texts to mean something. Some excellent versions of decodable texts exist, though. Nancy Shaw's *Sheep* books are good examples.

Alphabetic Reading. By the middle of first grade and into early second grade, most children begin to read more and more letters in words. When they attempt to read a word, rather than calling out the name of another word that begins the same way, a child might sound out every letter, even if it means pronouncing something that doesn't make sense. A child might say, "We went to the fire sta-t-yon" instead of "fire station." With practice, students produce fewer nonsense word readings and read words more accurately.

Children are acquiring a growing body of sight words—words that they can read accurately and quickly without having to decode them. This rapid word identification occurs after a period of sounding out the words, or *phonological recoding*, as linguists call it. Ehri (1991) suggests that the earlier practice of reading words alphabetically—figuring them out letter by letter—lays down pathways to the memory that makes it easier for children to recognize the words when they see the words later. Ehri writes:

> When readers practice reading specific words by phonologically recoding the words, they form access routes for those words into memory. The access routes are built using knowledge of grapheme-phoneme correspondences that connect letters in spellings to phonemes in the pronunciation of words. The letters are processed as visual symbols for the phonemes, and the sequence of letters is retained as an alphabetic, phonological representation of the word. The first time an unfamiliar word is seen, it is read by phonological recoding. This initiates an access route into memory. Subsequent readings of the word strengthen the access route until the connections between letters and phonemes are fully formed and the spelling is represented in memory. (p. 402)

Orthographic Reading. By late first grade to the middle of second grade, most children are looking at words in terms of spelling patterns—not just one letter to one sound, but also familiar patterns such as *ake, ight,* and later *tion*. Children who can separate words into *onsets and rimes* and who are taught by means of *word sorts* (Gillet & Temple, 1979; Bear, Invernizzi, Templeton, & Johnston, 2004) can read by *analogy;* that is, if they can read *bake* and *take,* they can also read *rake* and *stake.* As they move further into the orthographic phase, children read not just by phonogram patterns, or onsets and rimes, as Trieman (1985) calls them, but increasingly by *root words* and even *historical morphemes.*

Derivational Reading. From about fourth or fifth grade and up, normally advancing readers enter a phase of word recognition that we call *derivational reading.* Readers from late first grade and second grade recognize that words like *firehouse* and *groundskeeper* contain within them other words they know. From fourth grade and later, more proficient readers recognize that words like *telegraph, telephone, biology,* and *biography* also contain word parts that they recognize: *graph,* from a Greek word meaning "to write";

tele from another Greek word meaning "at a distance." They recognize that *sanity* is related to *sane* and that *sign* is related to *signal.* Derivational reading thus combines something of word recognition and vocabulary.

Having laid out these stages that children are thought to pass through as they learn to recognize words, it is clear that children will need different instruction at the different stages.

Teaching the "P" Word: Phonics

Phonics is an important part of instruction for emergent and beginning readers, and in a previous chapter we laid out steps for teaching children to pay attention to words, the sounds in words, and the relations between letters and sounds. Readers are referred to Chapter 6 for a complete discussion of teaching phonics to emergent and beginning readers. Here we offer a set of principles for such teaching.

Steven Stahl (1992) suggested ten components of effective phonics teaching. According to Stahl, exemplary phonics instruction:

1. **Builds on What Children Already Know.** It builds on what reading is about, how print functions, what stories are and how they are worded, and what reading is for. This knowledge is gained by being read to, by shared reading of predictable books (see Chapter 6), by experience with dictated stories, and by authentic reading and writing tasks before reading begins. These are components of both whole language and traditional instruction in preschool, kindergarten, and primary grades.

2. **Builds on a Foundation of Phonemic Awareness.** It builds on a child's ability to perceive and manipulate sounds in spoken words. Phonemic awareness includes being able to think of words that rhyme; perceiving that some words have the same or very similar sounds at the beginning, middle, and end; and being able to segment and blend sounds in spoken words. A further explanation of phonemic awareness follows in a subsequent discussion.

3. **Is Clear and Direct.** Good teachers explain exactly what they mean, while some phonics programs appear confusing and ambiguous. Some years ago, debate raged about whether a phoneme, or letter-sound, had any existence outside of the spoken word. Teachers and programs who were influenced by this argument hesitated to pronounce any sounds in isolation—for example, never explaining that *b* produced the /b/ sound at the beginning of words such as *box, bear,* or *bed.* Of course, we want to avoid inaccurate pronunciations such as "buh-eh-duh" for *b-e-d,* but more harm is done when we beat around the bush and never directly show at least the common and predictable consonant sounds.

4. **Is Integrated into a Total Reading Program.** Phonics instruction should not dominate, but instead should complement, the reading instruction children receive. The majority of time should be spent in reading real texts, discussing them, acting them out, writing about them, and interpreting them. Phonics instruction should spring from

the words that children need to read in real texts, not from a preset hierarchy of skills or a scope-and-sequence chart. Stahl (1992) suggests that a maximum of 25 percent of instructional time be spent on phonics. On many days, even this will be excessive. In addition, the phonics skills that are taught should be directly applicable in the text being read at that time. A criticism of many basal phonics strands is that the skill being presented has only limited application in the accompanying story. Trachtenburg (1990) suggests using high-quality children's literature that features a particular phonic pattern to illustrate and practice the pattern, for example using *The Cat in the Hat* and *Angus and the Cat* to illustrate the short-*a* pattern. A fuller description of children's literature/phonics connections follows in a subsequent section.

5. **Focuses on Reading Words, Not Learning Rules.** Effective readers use patterns and words they already know that are similar, rather than phonics rules, when they decode. Most teachers already know that rules have so many exceptions that they are rarely useful, yet many phonics programs continue to stress them as though they were "golden rules." If a child can't decode *rake,* it is more helpful to point out that it has the same pattern as *make* and *take* than to cite the "silent *e* makes the vowel long" rule. Many poor readers can recite phonics rules fluently but cannot apply them in reading.

6. **May Include Onsets and Rimes.** Onsets, or beginning sounds, and rimes, or the part of the word or syllable from the vowel onward, have long been taught under the more common name of "word families." Teaching children to compare words using onsets and rimes helps them to internalize patterns and use known words, such as *make* and *take* in the previous example, to decode the unfamiliar *rake.* It is certainly more productive than having children sound out letters in isolation.

7. **May Include Invented Spelling Practice.** It has been widely recognized that when children are encouraged to invent spellings for unfamiliar words that they write, using the sounds in the words as they are pronounced, they practice decoding strategies within the context of real language use. Encouraging invented spelling has become a widely used and welcome aspect of primary literacy instruction.

8. **May Include Categorization Practice Such as Word Sorting.** The practice of word sorting is a series of exercises in which children group together words with common phonic features, such as beginning consonants, phonogram patterns, and other spelling dynamics. Word sorting encourages students to study the words they know and abstract features from them that they can then use to read and spell words that they do not know. Word sorting was reviewed extensively in Chapter 6 and is given book-length treatment in a book by Bear et al. (2004) and Gaushe (2006).

9. **Focuses Attention on the Internal Structure of Words.** Good phonics instruction helps children to see and use patterns in words. Whether they use individual letter sounds, similar words with the same rime, or invented spelling, children are encouraged to look closely at the patterns in words. We learn to read and spell not word by word, but pattern by pattern.

10. **Develops Automaticity in Word Recognition.** The purpose of all phonics instruction is not to be able to sound out words or "bark at print", but to be able to quickly and accurately "unlock" unfamiliar words so that the reader's attention may be reserved for understanding and enjoying what is read. Strict decoding emphasis programs of the past, such as DISTAR, encouraged children to learn to decode at the expense of comprehension; they failed because they created "word-callers" rather than effective readers. Effective phonics instruction today encourages automaticity (LaBerge & Samuels, 1974) in word recognition so that the mind may be freed for comprehension (Perfetti & Zhang, 1996).

Word Study at More Advanced Levels

Beyond the early stages of beginning to read, the kind of knowledge required to read words accurately changes in complex ways. Now it is more proper to speak not of phonics alone but also of children's word knowledge. The word *phonics* refers to the relationships between letters and sounds, but the word knowledge required for developing readers to recognize and understand words deals with several additional matters. In the case of developing readers, children's learning about words encompasses knowledge of

- Phonogram patterns.
- Grammatical affixes.
- Derivational affixes.
- Compound words.
- Homophones and homographs.
- Etymologies.

Phonogram Patterns.   *Phonogram patterns* are the rhyming parts of words like *bake* and *cake, dance* and *prance.* They are clusters of vowels or of vowels and consonants that are found in many words. Linguists (after Trieman, 1985) call phonogram patterns *rimes,* as in *onsets* (the consonant or group of consonants that comes at the beginning of a syllable) and *rimes* (the phonogram pattern or rhyming part that follows). Groups of words that share the same phonogram pattern are called *word families.* The words *light, tight, might,* and *right* belong to the same family. So do *bump, lump, grump,* and *stump.* Some years ago Wylie and Durrell (1970) identified 37 common spelling patterns that form the basis of word families in English. Those patterns account for more than 500 common words. They are:

ack	all	ap	aw	est	ight	ing	ock	ot	unk
ain	ame	ash	ay	ice	ill	ink	oke	uck	
ake	an	at	eat	ick	in	ip	op	ug	
ale	ank	ate	ell	ide	ine	it	ore	ump	

But Wylie and Durrell's list is not exhaustive. For example, *alk, ish, eed, eel, oak, old, ow,* and *y* are phonogram patterns whose word families have many members.

Words with Grammatical Affixes. An *affix* is a part of a word that usually cannot stand alone and is added to a base word to change or modify its meaning. English words add grammatical affixes to show the grammatical function of the word. The most common grammatical affixes are listed below.

- The affix *-s* can mark the plural form of a noun or the third-person singular present tense form of a verb. Note that the ending *-s* has two different pronunciations: /s/, as in *rocks*, /z/, as in *trees*. With words that end in *-es* it may have a third pronunciation of /iz/, as in *wishes.*
- The affix *-ed* marks the past tense of verbs and also regular past participles (verb forms that function as adjectives), as in "She wanted to go home" and "She had dyed hair."
- The affix *-ing* marks the present progressive form of verbs or present participles, as in "He was running" and "The stream was full of running water."
- The affixes *-er* and *-est* are the comparative (meaning "more") and superlative (meaning "most") forms of adjectives, as in "Akeesha was a fast*er* runner than Juan, but Maya was the fast*est* in the class."

Words with Derivational Affixes. Another class of affixes that change a word from one part of speech or function to another are *derivational affixes.* We call them derivational because they serve to derive one word from another. Recognizing derivational affixes and base words can give children a clue to both the reading of a word and its meaning. Once the child recognizes *-or* and *-er* as markers meaning "one who _____s," they may more easily read a word like *actor* by reading the word in parts: *act + or.*

Derivational markers that young readers encounter are *-er* and *-or* (*sleeper, teacher, creeper, actor*), *-ful* (*careful, wonderful, frightful*), *-ly* (*slowly, loudly, awfully*), *un-* (*unkind, unlucky*), and *re-* (*rerun, recycle, rewrite*).

Some derivational markers that older readers encounter are *-ment* (*pavement, government, treatment*), *-ist* (*racist, aerialist, cyclist*), *-ism* (*racism, alcoholism, feminism*), *-ant* (*triumphant, compliant, defiant, militant*), and *inter-* (*international, interaction*).

Being aware of derivational affixes helps children read words and to understand their meanings.

Compound Words. English has three kinds of compound words. Some words have been used together so frequently that they are written together: *shotgun, nightgown, afternoon.* Some compound words are joined by hyphens, especially when they are used as adjectives: *pig-stealing great-grandfather, self-cleaning oven, mother-in-law.* Some pairs of words are considered as compounds but are written separately: *shoe shine, boa constrictor, mail carrier.* For readers, the compounds written together are challenging, and children can be helped if asked "to find two words in this word." For spellers, compound words present quite a different challenge. Children may be unsure which compound words to write together, which to join with hyphens, and which to write separately.

Homophones and Homographs.   Two or more words that are pronounced the same but spelled differently are called *homophones. Waste* and *waist; to, too,* and *two;* and *road* and *rode* are examples. Two or more words that are spelled the same but pronounced differently are called homographs. *Lead* (as in "to guide") and *lead* (the heavy metal) are examples. So are *read* (present tense) and *read* (past tense).

Readers need to learn to attach the correct meaning to a homophone. They also need to pronounce homographs correctly. In both cases, the context of the passage helps.

Etymologies.   Another aid in recognizing words—in pronouncing them and knowing their meanings—is to know their etymologies, or histories. Take, for example, the words *telescope* and *telephone.* By normal pronunciation patterns, *tele* should be pronounced like *teal.* But the word stem *tele,* which comes from an ancient Greek word, is always pronounced like "telly," and it has the meaning of "far" or "at a distance." Similarly, the word *photograph* contains the *ph* grapheme, which, in words from ancient Greek, is pronounced like /f/. In words from Old English, though, such as *shepherd,* the *ph* has a different pronunciation. *Graph* comes from a Greek word meaning "to write or draw," and *photo* comes from a Greek word meaning "light." A *photograph,* then, is "written with light" (which you will know is literally true if you have ever worked in a darkroom). Even knowing these few word stems would enable a reader to figure out the meanings of *telegraph* and *phonograph.*

Guiding Word Study

At the developing reader level, students' word knowledge can be nurtured by some of the means we saw in the previous chapter as well as by some new methods.

Teaching Words with Shared Phonogram Patterns

Words that share phonogram patterns, or word families, can be readily taught through the *word sort procedure* found in Chapter 6. In making a word sort, words from more than one word family are written on word cards, scrambled, and sorted into two or three columns on a desk, according to their families. It is best to make sure that the children know at least one and preferably two words from each family. Thus, if the first word in a column is the known word *bunk,* the child may place the unknown word *skunk* underneath it by making a visual match—and then, after reading *bunk,* the child can be encouraged to pronounce /sk/ and add the rest of the rime, *unk,* and finally read *skunk.* The teacher or tutor must demonstrate this strategy several times before most children get it, but once they do, children can do word sorting in small groups, in pairs, or alone.

Word Hunts.   These present another way to work with word families. Especially after you have introduced the word family through a word sort procedure, children can be sent to look for other words from the same family in an old newspaper or magazine, cut them out, and paste them onto a page.

Word Family Walls.   These are adapted from Patricia Cunningham's *Word Walls* (1999). After a word family has been introduced and worked with, make a poster for the word family, beginning with three or four examples. Then, as children come across other members of that family in their reading, add those words to the Word Family Wall, with ceremony and flourish!

Word Family Dictionaries.   Children can make personal dictionaries of the words they find for each family. Have each child bring a small (3 inch by 5 inch) spiral notebook—bound note cards are preferable because they are more durable. Label the top of each page with a guide word for each word family. You may begin with three or four families and add more families over time. As children do word sort activities and word hunts, have them write new words on the page for each family.

Spelling.   Put at least two words from each word family on a spelling list for children to study. Test them on the words each week.

Word Games.   Since so many games work with groups of items, word families lend themselves to games like Go Fish! Once children have learned at least six word families, make a card deck with four word cards from each family. Deal out two-thirds of the cards to the players and put the other third in the Go Fish! pile. The players group the cards in their hand according to a word family. Then one at a time they say to one player, "Give me all your cards that rhyme with _____." If the other player has the card, she hands it over. If not, she says "Go Fish!" and that player draws a card from the pile.

Teaching Words with Grammatical Affixes and Derivational Affixes

Words with grammatical and derivational affixes, as well as compound words and even words with ancient roots such as we saw in the section on etymologies, can all be studied by means of word building exercises.

Word Building.   Word building can be done to help children work with grammatical affixes. For each child in a small group, prepare a set of cards with word stems such as *truck, cat, dog, bark, purr,* and *shout* on them, and another set with grammatical affixes such as *-ed,* and *-s* on them. Tell the children to join a word stem and an affix to put together words for:

More than one furry animal that purrs
Made that sound yesterday
More than one eighteen-wheeler
Spoke loudly yesterday
More than one animal that barks

Word building can also help children work with derivational affixes. For each child in a small group, prepare a set of cards with word stems such as *write, play, true, glad, thank, train,* and *quick* on them, and another set with grammatical affixes such as *-er, re-, un-,* and *-ly* on them. Tell the children to join a word stem and an affix to make a word for:

Someone who helps athletes get ready
Another word for an athlete
What you shouldn't believe
To do something, feeling happy about it
To make marks on paper for the second time
To do something without wasting time

Teaching compound words with the word building activity proceeds the same way. Prepare cards with single parts of the compound words on them, and prepare hints to guide students to construct the target words.

Teaching Homophones and Homographs

Read Fred Gwynne's *The King Who Rained* (1988) to introduce the children to the idea of homophones: words that have the same sounds but different meanings and different spellings. Prepare cards with pairs of homophones, one set for each student in the group. Call out a definition and ask the children to hold up the correct card. Some useful homophones are:

rain, rein, reign
two, to, too
road, rode
waste, waist
eight, ate
tacks, tax
die, dye

Have the children prepare homophone pages in their word study notebooks. To teach homographs, prepare ahead of time a list of words that are homographs and write them on the chalkboard. For example:

read
lead
produce
conduct
produce

Prepare clues to the pronunciation of different versions of the words. For example, "Yesterday I opened my book and I _____." The children raise their hands and provide the correct pronunciation as you point to the word.

Developing Sight Vocabulary

Individual words become *sight words* (recognized immediately without analysis) when they are seen repeatedly in meaningful context. Many youngsters acquire some sight words before school entry, and without direct teaching or drill, by looking at the same favorite storybooks many times over. First they learn what words are on the page as they hear the same story read to them again and again. Soon they can recite the words along with the reader; soon after that, they can recite independently, role-playing reading as they turn the pages.

If at this point the reader casually points to the words as they are read, the child begins to associate the word spoken with its printed counterpart. This speech-to-print matching is an important foundation for learning to recognize words in print.

It is essential for readers to have a large sight vocabulary so that they can move through print quickly and efficiently. Youngsters who have only a small store of sight words are forced to read very slowly with frequent stops to figure out words, stops that interrupt their comprehension and interfere with their getting meaning. Many youngsters read poorly for this reason. Increasing their sight vocabularies is mandatory for their reading improvement. This can be accomplished by a number of means.

Dictated Stories and Language Experience

Dictated stories are a part of the language experience approach to beginning reading (Allen, 1976; Hall, 1981; Nessel & Jones, 1981; Stauffer, 1980). The method of using dictated stories to teach reading has been used for many years. In fact, a variation of it was apparently used by John Amos Comenius in the 1600s! The method works as follows. An individual or small group dictates an account to someone who writes down the account verbatim. The account is reread chorally until the students can recite it accurately and point to the individual words while reciting. Then parts, or the entire account, are read individually, and words that can be immediately recognized first in context, then in isolation, are identified. These new sight words go into the student's word banks, collections of sight words on cards or in a notebook.

It was long held that the value of dictated stories lay in the preservation of children's natural language, which might differ considerably from "book language." This is important, but a greater usefulness of dictated words for developing sight vocabulary lies in the repeated rereading of the material. Students might reread dictated stories more willingly than other material because the stories concern experiences the students have had themselves. Rereading the stories chorally and independently, regardless of the topic or syntax used, reinforces the recognition of the words in other contexts.

As the students' sight vocabularies grow, and their word banks come to contain about 100 or more words, this is a sign that the student will have an adequate sight vocabulary to read other kinds of texts. Now the dictated stories are usually phased out, and other material is introduced. Dictation works best as an initial means of establishing and fostering sight vocabulary and also as a confidence-building transition into reading. When dictated stories are mentioned, some teachers of older poor readers associate the practice with very young children. They might immediately presume that older poor readers will be put off by what they assume is a juvenile practice. Although language experience is common in primary classrooms, it need not be reserved for little children. In fact, with many older and adult poor readers, what they dictate might be about the only print they can read successfully.

With young children, you need a concrete stimulus, or experience, to talk about: an object, picture, storybook, or immediate event. With older students, past or future experiences, hopes, fears, reminiscences, content-area subjects, and abstract concepts can serve as topics. Older students can usually move through steps more quickly than younger ones and can usually skip the voice-pointing step entirely. Older students often work best with this procedure individually or in pairs or threes rather than large groups. A word notebook might replace the word bank card collection. And if the teacher presents the activity with a businesslike air and explains why it is being done, the experience need not feel like a juvenile one.

Figure 7.2 lists the steps in using dictated stories with younger and older students, in groups or individually.

Support Reading: Echo Reading and Choral Reading

Support reading means helping readers get through text that is too difficult for them to read independently. Although students should never have to read material at their frustration levels without support, sometimes it is necessary for them to get through some difficult material. This is most often the case with older poor readers who are expected to get information from a content-area textbook that is beyond their instructional level. If appropriate material at their instructional level is not available, you can help them through difficult text using support-reading methods.

In *echo reading,* the teacher reads a sentence or two aloud, and the student immediately repeats what the teacher read while looking at and, if necessary, pointing to the words. Only one or two sentences, or even one long phrase, are read at a time to allow students to use short-term memory as they "echo." Older students might use specially prepared tapes, with pauses for repetition, to practice echo reading independently. Echo reading is an intensive support measure that is best used with short selections and material that is quite difficult or unfamiliar. Sometimes, it might be sufficient to echo-read only the beginning of a longer passage to get students started. One important characteristic of echo reading is that it allows the teacher to model fluent reading and the students to practice it.

Choral reading means reading aloud in unison. It is somewhat harder to choral-read than to echo-read, so this procedure is best for material that is easier or for text that has been silently previewed or echo-read first. Choral reading, with the teacher's voice leading and providing the model, is an excellent way of practicing oral reading without the anxiety of a solo performance. Complicated or unfamiliar text should be read aloud to the students first and may be echo-read initially as well. Again, tapes can be used effectively for independent practice.

WITH YOUNGER PUPILS:

1. Present a concrete stimulus—an object or event—to discuss.

2. Encourage describing and narrating so that the students will have plenty to say about it.

3. Tell students you will help them write the story using a chart tablet, transparency, or the board.

4. Ask for volunteers to contribute sentences for the story.

5. Print the account verbatim, allowing students to make changes or additions. Read aloud what you have written, including amended portions.

6. Read the completed account to the group.

7. Lead the group in choral recitation, pointing quickly to the words as you read. Repeat until the whole account can be recited fluently.

8. Ask for volunteers to read one or more sentences alone, pointing to the words as in step 7.

9. Ask for volunteers to point out and identify words they know. Keep a list of these for review.

10. Provide individual copies of the story for rereading and sight word identification.

11. Any words that a child can identify out of the story context can go into the child's word bank, to be used for sorting and other word study activities.

WITH OLDER PUPILS:

1. Work with groups of three or fewer.

2. Suggest, or allow students to suggest, a topic.

3. Lead discussion of the topic, encouraging as rich language use as possible.

4. Take the dictation as above, making minor word changes or additions as necessary to keep the story fluent. Cursive writing may be used instead of printing. Use a regular size sheet of paper if you wish.

5. Lead the choral rereading as above. Students might prefer to do more individual than group reading.

6. Provide an individual copy for each student, typed if possible, for practice rereading and word identification. Encourage rereading to a partner or someone else.

7. As individuals read to you and identify newly acquired sight words, have them enter the words in a sight word notebook. Older students might prefer a notebook to a traditional word bank.

FIGURE 7.2 *Steps in Using Dictated Stories*

1. Introduce the material by briefly discussing the topic with students.

2. Read the material aloud expressively.

3. Read the material a second time while children follow along in a large copy of the material (chart tablet sheet, transparency, or Big Book).

4. Choral-read the material several times until it is very familiar.

5. Begin adding pauses, sound effects, movement, tonal variety, or other expressive aspects to the reading.

6. Practice often so that all children feel very comfortable with it.

7. Ask children to suggest ways in which they can share their choral-readings with others, and follow up on their ideas.

FIGURE 7.3   *Choral-Reading Poetry or Predictable Books*

Source: Joyce K. McCauley and Daniel S. McCauley. "Using Choral-Reading to Promote Language Learning for ESL Students." *The Reading Teacher* 45, no. 7(March 1992): 526–533.

Choral reading is a superb way to enjoy poetry. Poetry deserves to be read aloud; many poems that are read silently are only pale shadows of what they are when rendered aloud. Add a little movement, a sound effect or two, and a bit of variety with voices (high/low, loud/soft, fast/slow) and you have more than a poetry reading—you have a performing art! Choral-reading of poetry and prose is a low-anxiety experience; children's individual mispronunciations or lapses disappear into the sound of the collective voices, while everyone gets to experience fluent reading. It encourages the rereading of text, which contributes to fluency and sight-word acquisition, while students barely recognize that they have read the same text many times over. Choral reading has been shown to particularly help children who are nonfluent English speakers (McCauley & McCauley, 1992). Figure 7.3 shows procedures for choral reading of poetry or other predictable text.

Developing Word Analysis Strategies

Immediate, accurate recognition of more than 90 percent of the words in running text is necessary for effective instructional-level reading. As students read more widely and sample various kinds of text, they will necessarily encounter words that they do not recognize on sight. The role of teaching word analysis is to help students acquire efficient strategies for figuring out unrecognized words.

Using Context

In addition to rapid, accurate decoding, good readers use the context of an unfamiliar word to help figure it out. Most words have meaning in isolation, but some have no real meaning, only a function in sentences; who can define *the,* for example? Many other words, including some of the most frequently occurring words, have many meanings, and only sentence context helps us to choose the right one; for example, there are at least six different meanings for *run:* a rapid gait, a tear in a stocking, a jogger's exercise routine, a small creek, a sequence of events, and a computer operation. Sentences have more meaning than the sum of meanings of their component words. For example, even if you know what *time, a, saves, stitch, in,* and *nine* mean, it is only when they are combined in a sentence, *A stitch in time saves nine,* that comprehension can occur. Sentences have meanings beyond the meanings of individual words; paragraphs and larger units of text have meanings beyond that of individual sentences. In language, the whole is indeed more than the sum of its parts.

Using these larger meanings to help make "educated guesses" about what an unfamiliar word might be involves using context as a word recognition strategy. It requires a reader to ask the mental question "What would make sense here?" Several strategies may be taught to help students use context effectively.

Cloze procedures were described in Chapter 3 as a means of identifying students' reading levels in relation to a particular text. They are also helpful teaching tools for helping students to use context. To complete a cloze passage, students must think along with the author, so to speak, using prior information, the meaning suggested by the entire passage, and grammatical and meaning clues provided by the words preceding and following the omitted words. Systematic practice with cloze procedures helps readers to become sensitive to "context clues" and use them when reading.

For teaching, it is not necessary to delete every fifth word as you do when making a cloze passage for assessment. It might be better to delete fewer words and leave more of the text intact. Particular types of words, such as pronouns or verbs, could be deleted to highlight their function. Allow students to insert their best guesses, then discuss their choices. Discussion should guide students to consider how several alternatives might make good sense in one instance, while only one possible choice would make sense in another instance, and how different choices can lead to subtle but important changes in meaning. Cloze passages should be accompanied by discussion; their effectiveness is reduced if they are used as worksheets to be completed individually. Older students or more fluent readers may use text they have not read before, then compare their efforts to the original text. Younger students or less fluent readers might be more comfortable, and more successful, with text that they have read or heard before, such as dictated stories, predictable books, and familiar rhymes.

Confirming from text involves covering part of the text as it is read, predicting what might come next, then uncovering the hidden portions and proceeding. Whole words, parts of words following an initial letter, word groups, or phrases may be covered, depending on what cues you want your students to use as they read the passage. Big books and stories that are put on transparencies or chart tablets work best for this activity.

If you are using a transparency, use a paper or tagboard strip to cover part of the text, have students read up to the covered part (and even a bit beyond it, in some cases), and ask them to predict what might come next. If you have covered a whole word, you might now uncover the initial letter or letters and have them predict again. Then slide the strip back and continue reading. At the end of the sentence, have students tell what clues they used to help them guess. If you are using a big book or chart tablet, words can be covered with small notepapers with a sticky strip on the reverse, and phrases or lines with a tagboard strip can be held in place with paper clips. Keep the activity moving so that students don't get bogged down, and don't cover so many words so that context is lost. It is better to do a little of this activity fairly often than to do it infrequently and drag it out too long.

Approaching Word Attack Strategically

Students read many words every day that they must come to either recognize immediately or figure out through some kind of analysis. One team of researchers put the number of different words students will encounter by the ninth grade in their school reading at 88,500 (Nagy & Anderson, 1984). Since more and more of those words are encountered when students are reading independently, the average students must identify more than a dozen new words every day. Students need to become strategic in their word recognition, which means both that they must be disposed to solve the problem of unlocking words and that they must possess the strategies for doing so.

J. David Cooper (1993) arrived at a set of six strategies that can be taught to students explicitly. The number of the strategies can be reduced and their working simplified when they are used at lower grade levels.

1. When you come to a word you do not know, read to the end of the sentence or paragraph and decide whether the word is important to your understanding. If it is unimportant, read on.
2. If the word is important, reread the sentence or paragraph containing the word. Try context to infer the meaning.
3. If context doesn't help, look for base words, prefixes, or suffixes that you recognize.
4. Use what you know about phonics to try to pronounce the word. Is it a word you have heard?
5. If you still don't know the word, use the dictionary or ask someone for help.
6. Once you think you know the meaning, reread the text to be sure it makes sense. (p. 202)

Figure 7.4 shows a simplified version of these strategies for primary-grade students.

Assessing Reading Fluency

The National Reading Panel defined reading fluency this way:

> Fluency is the ability to read a text accurately and quickly. When fluent readers read silently, they recognize words automatically. They group words quickly in ways that help them gain meaning from what they read. Fluent readers read aloud ef-

FIGURE 7.4   *Strategy Poster for Inferring Word Meanings*

fortlessly and with expression. Their reading sounds natural, as if they are speaking. (National Reading Panel, 2000, p. 22)

Reading fluency has moved from being a neglected skill (Allington, 1984) to an area of intense interest. In *Put Reading First*, Armbruster, Lehr, & Osborn (2001) define reading fluency this way:

Fluency is the ability to read a text accurately and quickly. When fluent readers read silently, they recognize words automatically. They group words quickly in ways that help them gain meaning from what they read. Fluent readers read aloud effortlessly and with expression. Their reading sounds natural, as if they are speaking. (p. 22)

Reading fluency is most simply measured by counting the number of words children read per minute, minus the errors. A more complete measure of reading fluency takes into account a reader's expressiveness and phrasing. This yields a measure called Words Correctly Read per Minute, which is calculated using this formula:

$$\frac{(\textbf{Total words read, minus words read incorrectly}) \times 60}{\textbf{Reading time in seconds}} = \textbf{WCPM}$$

Thus, for example, if a third grade student reads 125 words in one minute, but makes five reading errors, we would calculate her fluency rate of Words Correctly Read per Minute:

$$\frac{(125 - 5) \times 60}{60} = \frac{120 \times \cancel{60}}{\cancel{60}} = 120 \text{ WCPM.}$$

According to the data in Figure 7.5, this would be an acceptable reading rate for a mid-year third grader.

The following oral reading fluency norms were developed by Hasbrouck and Tindal (1992).

Grade	Percentile	Fall WCPM	Winter WCPM	Spring WCPM
2	75	82	106	124
	50	53	78	94
	25	23	46	65
3	75	107	123	142
	50	79	93	114
	25	65	70	87
4	75	125	133	143
	50	99	112	118
	25	72	89	92
5	75	126	143	151
	50	105	118	128
	25	77	93	100

(50th percentile for upper grades: 125-150 WCPM)

FIGURE 7.5   *Oral Fluency Norms*

Source: From *Curriculum-Based Oral Reading Fluency Norms for Students in Grades 2 Through 5,* by J. Hasbrouck and G. Tindal, 1992, *Teaching Exceptional Children, 24,* p. 42. Copyright 1992 by The Council for Exceptional Children. Reprinted with permission.

Reading fluency consists not only of speed and correctness, however, but of reading with expression and with proper phrasing. Zutell and Rasinski developed the Multidimensional Fluency Scale (see Figure 7.6) to help teachers observe several dimensions of fluency at once.

Those factors were expression and volume, phrasing, smoothness, and pace. The scale is a rubric to guide teachers' judgment. In order to carry out the procedure, the teacher selects a passage of at least 100 words that should be written at the student's instructional level and listens and marks the rubric as the child reads. It certainly helps to tape record the child's reading, so you can go through and mark one feature at a time.

	1	*2*	*3*	*4*
Expression and Volume	Reads in a quiet voice as if to get the words out. The reading does not sound natural like talking to a friend.	Reads in a quiet voice. The reading sounds natural in part of the text, but the reader does not always sound like they are talking to a friend.	Reads with volume and expression. However, sometimes the reader slips into expressionless reading and does not sound like they are talking to a friend.	Reads with varied volume and expression. The reader sounds like they are talking to a friend with their voice matching the interpretation of the passage.
Phrasing	Reads word by words in a monotone voice.	Reads in two- and three-word phrases, not adhering to punctuation, stress, and intonation.	Reads with a mixture of run-ons, mid-sentence pauses for breath, and some choppiness. There is reasonable stress and intonation.	Reads with good phrasing, adhering to punctuation, stress, and intonation.
Smoothness	Frequently hesitates while reading, sounds out words, and repeats words or phrases. The reader makes multiple attempts to read the same passage.	Reads with extended pauses or hesitations. The reader has many "rough spots."	Reads with occasional breaks in rhythm. The reader has difficulty with specific words and/or sentence structures.	Reads smoothly with some breaks, but self-corrects with difficult words and/or sentence structures.
Pace	Reads slowly and laboriously.	Reads moderately slowly.	Reads fast and slow throughout reading.	Reads at a conversational pace throughout the reading.

FIGURE 7.6 *Multidimensional Fluency Scale*

Source: J. Zutell and T. Rasinski, 1991.

Developing Reading Fluency

Tim Rasinski suggests that teaching reading fluency should include these four emphases:

1. Model good oral reading.
2. Provide oral support for readers.
3. Offer plenty of practice opportunities
4. Encourage fluency through phrasing. (Rasinki, 2003)

Modeling Fluent Oral Reading

Teachers should be careful to provide models of fluent reading for their students. We mean this in two senses. First, teachers should actually demonstrate the concept of fluent versus disfluent reading. Second, teachers should frequently read aloud to students and entice them with examples of rich language read well.

To introduce the very concept of fluent reading, begin by reading a passage to the students two ways. First read it haltingly and uncertainly, in a voice that suggests you are concerned with slashing your way through the words and getting a disagreeable experience over with: In other words, read disfluently. Then read it again, but this time with your voice full of expression and interest, with pauses and emphases. Show that you are enjoying the message of the text and not simply struggling to pronounce the words: That is to say, read fluently. Then ask the students which reading they preferred and why. In the discussion that follows, call attention to the qualities of fluent reading:

- The reader is thinking about the message and not just about pronouncing the words.
- The reader varies her voice between loud and soft, and between faster and slower.
- The reader groups words meaningfully.
- The reader may show emotion—enjoyment, surprise, and excitement—as she reads.

Later, read aloud to the students again, reading as fluently as you can, and "thinking aloud" as you read, that is, pausing to explain to the students of a decision you just made—such as where to pause, what words to group together, or how to read a character's voice—in order to read fluently. When you read a text aloud to your students you should take steps to call attention to your fluent reading. Make sure to point out to students how you

- Match the emotional qualities of the passages—serious, humorous, exciting, urgent—with your tone of voice.
- Stress the important words in the passages.
- Honor the punctuation—pausing at commas, stopping at periods, and raising your voice at the ends of sentences with question marks.

Read the dialogues as if people were actually talking.

Providing Oral Support for Reading

Providing oral support for students' reading means having them read a text aloud at the same time they hear others reading it fluently. This may be accomplished several ways.

Choral Reading. Choral reading happens when groups of students read the same text aloud. It can happen with poetry, or with speeches or other texts. When they are choral reading poetry, readers should practice over and over again to get the sounds right. Texts may be broken up for reading, with lines, phrases, or individual words read

- By the whole chorus, by individuals, by pairs, or by two alternating sections
- In loud or soft voices
- Rapidly or slowly
- Melodiously, angrily, giggling, or seriously.

You should prepare the children to choral read a text by discussing the circumstances or the context in which it might be said, so the text is read meaningfully. For example, the following poem, "The Grand Old Duke of York," has a martial rhythm. Invite the children to imagine they are a platoon of soldiers marching along a road. From a single vantage point, they are very quiet when they are heard from a distance, then louder as they approach, then very loud when they are right in front of the person, then quieter until they are very quiet. Have them practice reading the poem in unison, going from very quiet to VERY LOUD to very quiet again.

THE GRAND OLD DUKE OF YORK (Traditional)

The Grand Old Duke of York
He had ten thousand men.
He always marched them up the hill
Then he marched them down again.
And when they were up they were up.
And when they were down they were down.
And when they were only halfway up
They were neither up nor down.

Paired Reading. Students can practice reading a text in pairs, too. It is good practice to pair students with different reading abilities—but not too different. For example, if you group your students, groups 2 and 4 pair up. They take turns reading the same text aloud, alternating sentences or paragraphs.

Recorded Texts. Individual students can read along with recorded text, wearing headphones so as not to disturb others. Remind them to read in quiet voices. Recorded versions of children's books are available from www.Audible.com and other sources. More elaborate computer-based programs are also available—at proportionately higher costs—with texts read at varying rates, and with provisions for students' own reading to be recorded and timed, via speech recognition software. Insights Reading Fluency software (www.charlesbridge.com) and other programs have these features.

Providing Practice in Oral Reading

Rereading is the strategy of reading the same material more than once. Rereading helps students to gain fluency, bolsters students' self-confidence as readers, helps students to recognize familiar words at sight, and helps students use phrasing to support the meaning of what they read. It need not mean drudgery for students, however. There are a number of ways in which we can integrate rereading into our teaching. Some are as follows:

1. Have students read material silently before oral reading or discussion. If you will use predictive questions in your discussion, have them read silently up to a stopping point.
2. Encourage oral rereading for real purposes: to prove a point in a discussion, to role-play a dialogue, or to savor an effective descriptive passage, among other purposes.
3. Encourage the rereading of familiar or completed stories as seatwork or independent work or during free reading of sustained silent reading periods.
4. Use buddy reading: Select or have students choose reading partners or buddies, then reread completed stories or books aloud to their partners. (Buddy reading is discussed further below.)
5. Encourage children to take home familiar books to reread at home to family members. Since rereading is usually more fluent than the initial reading, children can show off their fluent reading at home this way.
6. Encourage rereading of favorite stories by revisiting old favorites when you read aloud to the class.
7. Have students listen to taped material, either professionally recorded or done by you or other volunteers. After listening and silently following along, have students imitate the reader as they listen, then eventually read the material alone. Tape-record their readings for self-critique.
8. Act out favorite stories using the technique of reader's theater, in which scripts are always read instead of memorized and recited.
9. Use choral reading frequently and perform for others.

Repeated Reading for Fluency

Repeated reading refers to a systematic practice of using timed oral rereadings to develop reading fluency. Described by Samuels (1979), the method involves helping the student select an instructional level passage and a reading rate goal, timing the first unrehearsed oral reading of the passage and successive readings after practice, and keeping a simple chart of the student's rate after successive timings. When the student is able to read the passage at or beyond the goal rate, a new passage of equal (but not greater) difficulty is begun.

This method of repeated reading is not intended to directly aid comprehension, but rather to help students acquire sight words and practice reading fluently and confidently. As they practice rereading their passages for timing, their reading rate for that passage climbs dramatically; keeping a chart that shows these increases is highly motivating, especially for older poor readers.

Of course, we are not surprised that their rates climb as they practice reading the same passage. What is surprising, and what is the real benefit of this practice, is that their reading rates also increase on each successive unrehearsed oral reading. The reason that this happens is that all that rereading has helped them to acquire more sight words and has helped them learn to read aloud fluently and confidently.

Figure 7.7 shows the steps in using the timed repeated reading method, and Figure 7.8 shows a partially completed chart.

Of course, it matters a great deal what students have to read. Expecting students to read frequently, copiously, and repeatedly in material that is at their level of competence assumes that plenty of lively and interesting reading material will be available at many different levels of difficulty. Fortunately, this is true. That is the topic of the next section.

---

1. Choose, or help each student to choose, a fairly comfortable, interesting selection to practice reading. It should be too long to memorize: 100 or so words for younger children, 200 or more words for older ones. Trade books and previously read basal stories are good.

2. Make up a duplicated chart for each pupil (see Figure 7.8). Omit the accuracy axis if you want to simplify the task.

3. Time each reader's first, unrehearsed oral reading of the passage. Mark the chart for Timed Reading 1.

4. Instruct the readers to practice the passage aloud as many times as possible for the next day or two. Let them practice in pairs, independently, and at home.

5. Time the reading again and mark the chart for Timed Reading 2. Show the students how to mark their own charts.

6. Continue timing at intervals of several days. As the rate increases for the first passage, help each child to set a new rate goal.

7. When the reader reaches the goal set, begin a new passage of equal (not greater) difficulty. Successive portions of a long story are perfect. Repeat steps 3 through 6.

FIGURE 7.7 *Steps in Using Repeated Reading*

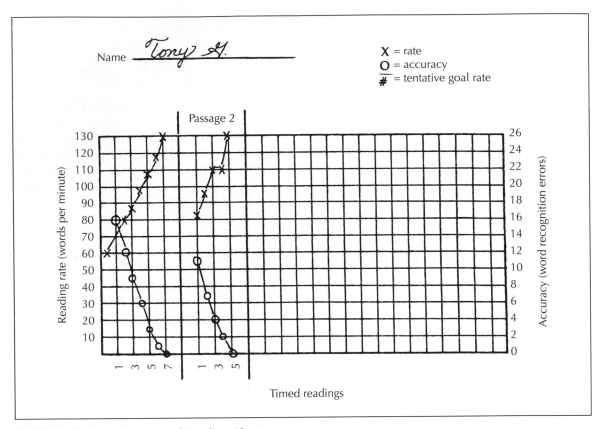

FIGURE 7.8 *Sample Repeated Reading Chart*

Predictable Books, "Easy Readers," and Other Easy Reading Fare

If we acknowledge that "children learn to read by reading" (as reading guru Frank Smith put it), then children need material that they can and will read. Such material must be available at all reading levels, and it should appeal to a range of interests. Some of it should appeal to more mature interests, even though its difficulty level is low.

It used to be that there were relatively few such books available. Primer-level basals were written in straight narrative style, and for that reason, dictated accounts and simple poems were often used in their place. Today, however, as the field of children's trade books has exploded to meet the demands of families and classrooms, more attention is being paid to the needs of developing readers. There are many wonderful predictable books for young readers, many of them available in big book format for group instruction. Some publishers, such as The Wright Group (www.wrightgroup.com) and Rigby books (www.harcourtachieve.com), have built their product lines around the use of predictable books in both big book and individual book formats. Many of the large commercial publishing houses, too, have special lines of books for young developing readers. In addition, a number of smaller education-oriented publishers publish collections of books that were written especially to appeal for students in the elementary grades and beyond who need special motivation and easier fare. Three varieties of such books that are discussed here are *predictable books, easy readers,* and *high-interest/low-reading-level books.*

Predictable Books. Predictable books have a rhyming or repetitious element that make them easy to read, even for students who recognize few words at sight. The pattern of repeated words or phrases or the rhyme scheme helps readers remember and predict what words are coming next.

Some predictable books repeat the same sentences or phrases. Eric Carle's *Have You Seen My Cat?* (Franklin Watts, 1973) is an example of such a pattern. On alternate pages, the sentences "Have you seen my cat?" and "This is not my cat!" repeat, as a small boy asks a variety of people from many cultures and finds a lion, a panther, and a cheetah, among other cats. On the last page, which reads "This is my cat!," he finds his own cat with a litter of newborn kittens. The inside back cover shows all the varieties of cats, labeled. Even the least-experienced prereader can recite this book and point to the words after only a few pages. Repetition makes it predictable. Bill Martin, Jr.'s *Brown Bear, Brown Bear, What Do You See?* (Holt, 1983) is another example familiar to many teachers. Each left-hand page identifies a color and an animal and asks, "What do you see?" On the right-hand page, the animal answers, "I see a _____ looking at me," and identifies the next color and animal: a yellow duck, a blue horse, a green frog, and so forth. Again, the last page lists all the animals cumulatively with small copies of the larger illustrations. Like many others, these books are available in big book, standard trade book, and miniature versions. Eric Carle's *The Very Hungry Caterpillar* (Philomel Books, 1969), *The Grouchy Ladybug* (Harper & Row, 1977), and *The Very Busy Spider* (Philomel Books, 1984) are other examples.

Some predictable books rely on rhyme rather than repetition. Nancy Shaw's *Sheep in a Jeep* (Houghton Mifflin, 1986) is an example. Although it has few words, the hilarious antics of the sheep that go for an ill-fated joyride make it appropriate for a wide range of ages. It sounds like this: "Uh-oh! the jeep won't go. Sheep leap to push the jeep. Sheep shove, sheep grunt. Sheep don't think to look up front." It is a great source of rhyming words, those that share the same spelling pattern (*sheep/jeep*) as well as those that don't (*grunt/front*), and colorful sound words (*splash! thud!*). The rhyming adventures of the sheep continue in *Sheep on a Ship* (Houghton Mifflin, 1989) and *Sheep in a Shop* (Houghton Mifflin, 1991).

Predictable books also serve as jumping-off places for students to create their own original books. Changing the topic and illustrations, while retaining the original pattern, can result in wonderful original versions that children enjoy reading as much as, or more than, the original version. For example, after mastering *Brown Bear, Brown Bear, What Do You See?,* a group of first graders created *The Vegetable Book:* "Green pepper, green pepper, what do you see? I see a red tomato looking at me." and so forth. With the basic pattern written on chart paper and blanks for the color words and nouns, the group chose the vegetable theme and volunteered the word pairs to fill the blanks: *brown potato, orange carrot, purple eggplant,* for example. Each couplet was then printed on a separate sheet, and pairs of students were assigned to illustrate each page. The resulting big book was stapled together and reread numerous times. Meanwhile, the text was typed on individual pages with space for illustration, duplicated, and stapled into individual copies. Each student then illustrated his or her own copy to keep. (During this time, the class brought in samples of the various vegetables for exploring and tasting.) Another group followed the same procedure with *Have You Seen My Cat?*, creating their original *Have You Seen My Dog?* and illustrating it with different breeds and colors of dogs. (This effort involved looking at numerous books about dogs to learn about different breeds.) These books remained very popular all year long for independent reading.

Both commercial and student-written predictable books are extremely useful for independent reading and as springboards for creative writing. They help students to acquire and reinforce sight words while providing successful reading practice for even the least fluent reader.

Easy Readers.   Children's books have been available in the United States for more than 200 years, but it was only in the past two decades that quality works that children could read themselves have become regularly available. Traditional picture books were written to be read to children by adults and only rarely by children (Temple et al., 2003), so there has long been a need for accessibly written works that appealed to children's desire for interesting fare. Now many of the major trade publishers put out lines of easy readers. The Putnam and Grosset Group publishes the *All Aboard* reading series. Dial Press has the *Easy-to-Read* series. The series from Random House is called *Step into Reading,* and HarperCollins publishes *I Can Read.* In conjunction with Bank Street College, Bantam publishes the *Bank Street Ready-to-Read* series. Although Macmillan has no particular name for its easy reader offerings, it has published more than a dozen easy readers about *Henry and Mudge* by Cynthia Rylant.

Easy readers have been produced by some of the best children's authors and illustrators we have. Cynthia Rylant has won Newbery and Caldecott Awards. Other award-winning children's authors such as Dr. Seuss, James Marshall, Tomie dePaola, Arnold Lobel, Lee Bennett Hopkins, and Joanna Cole have also written easy readers. An excellent source of reviews of easy readers is the *Adventuring with Books* series, published approximately every four years by the National Council of Teachers of English and containing nearly 2,000 annotated listings of books by topic and by difficulty level for students in grades pre-K through 6.

High-Interest/Low-Reading-Level Books and Magazines.   Since the 1960s, several educational publishers have produced works specifically for reluctant readers. The early efforts were not of particularly high quality (Ryder, Graves, & Graves, 1989), but the books have improved since. The books' strengths are also their weaknesses, note Ryder et al. To be "relevant" to reluctant readers, earlier versions of hi-lo books often highlighted the experiences of boys in the inner city who (if they come from minority groups) were African American or Hispanic. Other students felt as distant from the characters in these books as they did from white youths in gated suburbs. Also, to be more readable, the books have limited their vocabulary and sentence length, sometimes at the expense of comprehensible text.

Contemporary high-interest/low-reading-level materials are diverse and interesting. Some even come in computer-based formats. Susan Jones's Resource Room online is a good guide to hi-lo materials for readers at the sixth-grade level and above (http://www.resourceroom.net/comprehension/hilow.asp).

Developing Readers' Vocabulary

Every word we have in our vocabulary is a flashlight that illuminates a corner of our experience. Indeed, a famous research study showed that we most readily know—and most readily notice—what we can name (Brown, 1958). But the benefits of vocabulary are distributed unevenly among schoolchildren. Children from the lower socioeconomic groups enter school with half the vocabulary of children from the upper ones. By twelfth grade, students with larger vocabularies know four times as many words as their least proficient classmates, the size of whose vocabularies is even exceeded by many third graders (Beck, McKeown, & Kucan, 2002). It is not surprising, then, that the National Reading Panel (2000) made the teaching of vocabulary a top priority for literacy educators.

Vocabulary is important in reading. As Carl Smith puts it, "Most people feel that there is a common sense relationship between vocabulary and comprehension—messages are composed of ideas, and ideas are expressed in words" (1997, p. 1). But the relationship between children's vocabulary and their reading comprehension points in more than one direction, and the means of helping develop vocabulary have been subject to dispute, even while the teaching of vocabulary has not commanded much attention from elementary teachers (Beck et al., 2002). Before going on, then, we must pause to discuss vocabulary instruction and reading.

Vocabulary development interacts with word recognition, as children try to recognize in print words they already know—or partially know—in speech. But although younger children have most of the words in their spoken vocabulary that they are likely to encounter in print, there are still many words that occur in young children's picture books that children don't hear in the spoken language around them (Stanovich, 1992). If you need convincing on this point, read William Steig's *Sylvester and the Magic Pebble* (1987). By fourth grade, the vocabulary found in books is considerably richer than the words children use in speech.

Certainly, children can grow larger vocabularies from doing wide reading (Stanovich, 1992). As Nagy et al. (1985) point out, however, readers who encounter 100 unknown words will learn perhaps 5 of them. Children must do a great deal of reading, in at least moderately challenging texts, to learn large vocabularies from reading. But there are huge disparities in the amount of reading children do. As we saw in Chapter 1, in one study (Wilson, 1992), the top 20 percent of a fifth-grade class read twenty times as much as the bottom 20 percent. The bottom 20 percent read very little. If we count on children to learn vocabulary from reading, we will surely continue to see the huge disparities in vocabulary size described above.

One way to help children learn vocabulary is to show them how to learn more words from context (Szymborski, 1995). Another way we can help their vocabularies grow is to give them systematic vocabulary instruction (McKeown & Beck, 1988). We will look at both approaches below.

Levels of Vocabulary Knowledge

What do we mean by *knowing* vocabulary? Beck et al. (2002) suggest a continuum of word knowledge that looks like this:

- No knowledge.
- General sense, such as knowing *mendacious* has a negative connotation.
- Narrow, context-bound knowledge, such as knowing that a *radiant bride* is a beautifully smiling happy one, but being unable to describe an individual in a different context as *radiant.*
- Having knowledge of a word but not being able to recall it readily enough to use it in appropriate situations.
- Rich, decontextualized knowledge of a word's meaning, its relationship to other words, and its extension to metaphorical uses, such as understanding what someone is doing when she is *devouring* a book. (p. 10)

Knowing vocabulary well means not just understanding what words in a book mean, then, but knowing words in a range of contexts, in associations with other words, and in connection with our own experience—to have words as one's own.

Dissecting Children's Vocabulary

The job of teaching vocabulary seems truly immense. Nagy et al. estimate that by ninth grade, students are having to cope with a written vocabulary of 88,500 words (Nagy & Anderson, 1984). Were we to try to teach all those words, the prospect of teaching children nearly 10,000 words a year would be daunting indeed. But Beck et al. (2002) have found a useful way to break down those numbers.

Tier One Words.   There are many thousand words already in children's spoken vocabulary that we won't usually have to teach. These words Beck et al. call Tier One words, and they include examples like *mother, clock,* and *jump.*

Tier Three Words.   Then there are many more thousands of words that are so highly specialized that they are almost never used outside of the disciplines where they are encountered. These Tier Three words—like *monozygotic, tetrahedron,* and *bicameral*—are best learned in the science, social studies, and other classes where they are tied to the content under study. In Chapter 8 of this book, we will describe ways of teaching subject-specific vocabulary in the content areas.

Tier Two Words. That leaves the Tier Two words, the words with wide utility that most children don't have in their spoken vocabularies—words like *dismayed, paradoxical, absurd,* and *wary.* Beck et al. (2002) estimate that there may be about 7,000 Tier Two words, and even if we teach children half of them—or about 400 words a year—we will have gone a long way toward growing children's vocabularies and equalizing children's access to learning.

Approaches to Teaching Vocabulary

There is a wide consensus among researchers that vocabulary is best learned in the context of ideas under consideration, that learners should be actively involved in making meaning with new vocabulary, and that vocabulary be related to other words and new words tied to the learners' own experience (Smith, 1997).

Word Conversations. When young readers (kindergarten and first grade) are learning new words, Beck et al. (2002) suggest that teachers conduct a rich discussion of words, which includes these six steps:

1. Contextualize words, one at a time, within a story. For example, with kindergartners, the authors use Don Freeman's perennially popular *Corduroy* as a pretext for introducing the words *insistent, reluctant,* and *drowsy.* The teacher says, "In the story, Lisa was *reluctant* to leave the laundromat without Corduroy (her new teddy bear)."
2. Ask the children to repeat the word, so as to make a phonological representation of it.
3. Then explain the meaning of the word in a child-friendly way: "*Reluctant* means you are not sure you want to do something."
4. Now provide examples of the word in other contexts. "I am *reluctant* to go swimming in the early summer when the water is cold."
5. Next, ask children to provide their own examples: "What is something you would be *reluctant* to do?"
6. Now, ask the children to repeat the word they have been talking about, so as to reinforce its phonological representation.

Word conversations work best when they are prepared in advance. The teacher may choose the book to provide a meaningful context for introducing the vocabulary. Or, if the book is rich in many vocabulary words, the teacher locates the Tier Two words in advance and decides which ones will be most useful. The teacher thinks carefully how to explain the meaning of each word in a child-friendly way. She carefully plans questions to relate the words to the children's experience. And she is careful to remind the children of the words they are studying, giving them several opportunities to pronounce them (see Beck et al., 2002, for further discussion of this approach).

Exercises for Second Grade and Up

Activities to teach vocabulary should relate words to a meaningful context, to other words, and to the students' own experience. The following exercises satisfy these requirements.

Semantic Webs.   There are several ways to use *semantic webs*. The most open-ended way is to draw a circle on a page and write a topic-word in it. Then, together with the students, you think of aspects of the topic and come up with examples or aspects of that subtopic (see example for *dolphins* in Figure 7.9).

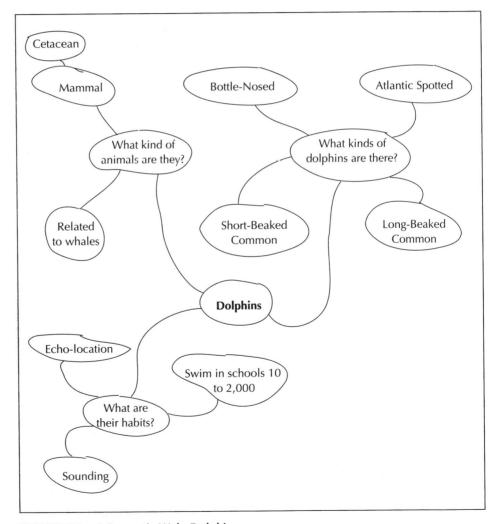

FIGURE 7.9 *A Semantic Web: Dolphins*

A particular approach to semantic webs is the *character web.* The name of a character is written in the circle in the middle of the display. Words that describe the character are written as satellites around the character's name, then examples that illustrate each attribute are written as satellites around the descriptive words.

Webbed Questions.   Schwartz and Raphael (1985) suggest guiding the students' responses to a semantic web, asking them to offer answers to three questions asked about the target word (see Figure 7.10, where this technique is applied to the dolphin example of Figure 7.9):

> What is it?
> What is it like?
> What are some examples of it?

Concept Ladder.   A more elaborate set of questions than the webbed questions above is found in the *concept ladder* (Temple & Gillet, 1984). The concept ladder is used with terms for concepts. The students are led to answer a structured set of questions about the concept (see Figure 7.11).

Semantic Feature Analysis.   *Semantic feature analysis* enables students to compare several terms at once and make judgments about the terms. The terms are placed in a grid like the one shown in Figure 7.12, and students are asked to write in a + sign if the answer to the question is positive and a – sign if the answer is negative.

M-Charts. A word has a *denotation,* which is its literal meaning, and a *connotation,* which is comprised of the attitudes it conveys or evokes. According to their connotations, words can have a positive or a negative "ring." To call attention to the connotations of words, you can use an M chart (see Figure 7.13). Put a target word in the

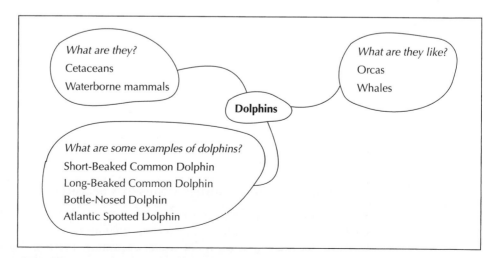

FIGURE 7.10   *Webbed Questions: Dolphin*

What kind of thing is this?	What is it a part of?	What causes it?
What are the kinds of it?	What are its parts?	What does it cause?

FIGURE 7.11 *A Concept Ladder*

	Bear live young	Have gills	Cold-blooded	Have milk
SHARKS				
DOLPHINS				

FIGURE 7.12 *Semantic Feature Analysis*

Positive	Neutral	Negative
CAUTIOUS	Reluctant to act	TIMID
PRUDENT		COWARDLY

FIGURE 7.13 *An M-Chart for Connotations*

middle and ask the students to provide terms that convey both positive and negative connotations. Write those terms in the left- and the right-hand columns. To personalize these words, ask the students to think of times when people might have thought they or someone else was *timid* when they were really being *cautious*.

Teaching the Use of Context Clues to Vocabulary

As we said above, learning words from context is usually inefficient. We can boost students' success in learning words from context by making them aware of the recurring kinds of clues to the meanings of words in context. There are four kinds of context clues:

1. **Definitions and Explanations.** Writers who are aware of their readers' needs for information often explain the meaning of a word or phrase right after the word is introduced. For example:

> Dolphins use *echo-location,* <u>which is the use of sound to locate objects</u>, as they hunt schools of herring on which to feed.

2. **Restating the Term in Other Words.** An uncommon word may be restated or followed up by words that gives clues to its meaning. For example:

> Because they are *herbivores,* elephants <u>eat only leaves and branches of trees</u>.

The phrase <u>eat only leaves and branches of trees</u> suggests that *herbivores* are creatures who eat such things.

3. **Providing Contrasting Words or Antonyms.** An unknown word may be followed by its opposite, its *antonym.* If the student knows the meaning of the antonym, he may find a clue to the meaning of the unknown word by reversing the meaning of the antonym. For example:

> Shirley was a <u>prompt worker</u>, not a *procrastinator.*

The phrase <u>prompt worker</u> is offered as the opposite of the term *procrastinator.* Therefore, *procrastinator* might mean someone who does not get her work done promptly.

4. **Providing Examples.** If an unknown word is the name of a category, followed by a list of examples, some of which are known, the examples provide a clue to the meaning of the unknown word. If the name of the category is known, it may also give a clue to the meaning of unknown examples. For instance:

> There was nothing on the table but *hors d'oeuvres* such as <u>crackers and cheese, pickled cauliflower</u>, and <u>deviled eggs</u>.

The items, <u>crackers and cheese, pickled cauliflower</u>, and <u>deviled eggs</u>, give a clue to the meaning of *hors d'oeuvres.*

Teachers can find passages in books to read aloud to students to practice using context clues such as these to approach the meanings of unknown words. They can be asked to be on the lookout for context clues in their own reading.

Developing Reading Comprehension

Throughout this book, we have noted that comprehension is an active process of making meaning. Good comprehenders summon up their prior knowledge about the topic of reading, they ask questions about the topic before and during the reading, they make appropriate inferences when ideas are not explicitly stated, they find main ideas, they summarize, and they make mental images from the words in the text.

Comprehension, in this view, requires an active reader, one who is confident and curious enough to bring her own ideas to the reading and to question the ideas in the text. However, in a decade-long study of what happens when elementary-grade students read textbooks, Beck and McKeown (1994) did not find many such readers. Traditional teaching required students to read and later answer factual questions about what they had read—questions that are more often intended to prove that they had understood the reading than to draw out their thinking about the subject matter. Too many students approached comprehension passively, as if comprehension worked by passively ingesting ideas from the text.

Since, as Isabel Beck's work suggests, the teacher's approach influences what students do when they attempt to comprehend, it is critically important that the instruction teachers provide students guides them into cognitive activities that bear fruit. In this section, we describe several strategies for instruction that have been tested by research and practice.

As we did in Chapter 6, we divide our treatment of comprehension into three phases, related to what should be done before, during, and after a reading. We call these the phases of *anticipation, building knowledge,* and *consolidation,* respectively.

For the Phase of Anticipation

Anticipation, it will be remembered, is the phase in which students inspect a text, remind themselves what they already know about it, raise questions or make predictions about what they will find out from reading it, and set purposes for their reading.

Developing Prior Knowledge.   Prior knowledge is what we already know or have experienced, directly or vicariously, that we bring to the act of reading. When we can somehow relate what we read to our prior knowledge, we understand and remember more clearly. When we lack prior knowledge to relate to what we read, chances are that we will become confused, misunderstand, and forget what we read. In this situation, we might also become disinterested in what we are reading, calling it boring or dull. And if our need is great to remember it, as in preparation for a test, we might resort to inefficient strategies such as memorizing. Helping students to develop, organize, and become aware of their prior knowledge is critical to improving their reading comprehension.

But two problems are associated with prior knowledge. One is that we might lack sufficient prior knowledge about a topic, not having heard or read of it before. A second problem is that much of our prior knowledge about a given topic might not be readily accessible; it has been buried, so to speak, under other information, and we can't summon it up and think about it readily. Because we can't bring it to mind immediately, we think we've forgotten it or never had it. Activities that develop prior knowledge center on helping students to establish some basis for new information and helping them to remember and organize prior knowledge that is not readily accessible.

Webbing.   A simple way to help students begin to recall prior knowledge and form relationships is to use *webbing,* an exercise in which the teacher writes a topic or term on the board, students offer terms or phrases that might be related, and the teacher draws lines connecting associated terms with each other. In the following reading, terms and relationships are noted, and the web may be revised to reflect new information re-quired. The webbing exercise serves to help students remember old information related to the reading and to form expectations about what they will be reading.

For example, let's say that Ms. Brown, a fourth-grade teacher, plans to have her students read a nonfiction basal selection about how museums are organized and the jobs museum workers perform. She suspects that some of the students have never vis-ited a museum and that the topic is relatively unfamiliar to many of them. She begins, then, with a web to explore with them what they already know.

First, she writes *museum* on the board and begins a brainstorming session, in which every student in turn offers a word or phrase related in some way to *museum.* Because some students look apprehensive, she suggests some questions to help get them started:

> What is a museum for?
> What are the names of some museums?
> What might be in them?
> What work do people do in museums?

As each student responds, Ms. Brown writes the response on the board around the key word. Because this is brainstorming, all responses are accepted without comment or evaluation. She notices that the first few responses appear to remind others of things they might have forgotten and that many appear excited as their turn nears. After every-one has responded once, volunteers might offer other suggestions until their informa-tion begins to wane. Then she reads over all the suggestions from the board.

The next step is to help students organize this seemingly random collection of terms into categories. One way Ms. Brown could do this is to use different colors of chalk to draw connecting lines, but because there are a lot of items on the board, this might not help to clarify. So she selects one term, writes it below the web, and says, "What other words go with this one?" Items are checked off and listed in categories, with students explaining why these items go together. These categories resulted:

paintings
scientists
mummies
statues
suits of armor
rockets
airplanes
old cars
Indian stuff
animals and birds
furniture
old cars
dinosaur bones

scientists
guards
guides

set up exhibits
clean up
take tickets
tours

Smithsonian
Museum of
Natural History

Students then suggest names for these categories: *things in museums, museum workers, jobs in museums,* and *names of museums.* Ms. Brown then says, "We're going to read an article about how museums are organized and what kinds of work must be done. As you read, watch for mention of the names of famous museums, their collections, and museum workers' jobs. Let's see which of the things we mentioned are in the article."

After the reading is completed, Ms. Brown leads her students in reinspecting the web, adding to the appropriate categories from the article that the students had not mentioned and marking those not appearing in the article to look up in another source.

A webbing activity like this is effective for several reasons. One is that it encourages all students to draw on whatever prior knowledge they have, no matter how extensive or limited, and apply it to the reading task. Another is that hearing others' ideas often triggers a forgotten bit of information in another's mind, so all benefit from sharing of information. A third is that seemingly unrelated information is directly organized so that relationships are sought and explored. A fourth is that prereading participation fosters curiosity and gives readers something to watch for as they read, and a purpose for reading. A fifth is that the exercise helps the teacher to realize what prior knowledge, if any, students have on the topic before they begin reading.

Previewing.   Another way to help students organize their prior knowledge and develop expectations about what they are going to read is to let them quickly *preview* a reading selection and predict what kinds of information they might find in it.

When students preview a reading selection, they do not begin to read it; rather, they scan each page, looking at illustrations and text features such as boldface print and headings. The time that is allowed for this is very short so that they can get an overall general idea of the content, just enough to begin to predict about specifics. Depending on the length of the selection, two minutes or less are usually sufficient. Previewing is effective with both fiction and nonfiction, as we will see in these examples.

Mr. Talbott works with a group of fifth graders reading at a third-grade instructional level. He has selected a basal story for them to read and discuss that deals with events surrounding the celebration of the Chinese New Year. Because this holiday and Chinese American customs in general are unfamiliar to his students, he uses previewing to help them form a basis for their reading. He tells the group to find the first and last pages of the story and then to look at the title and the pictures, but not to begin reading yet. He gives them 30 seconds to do so, telling the group when to begin and stop. Then he asks them to close their books and tell him what they saw in the pictures. He lists all the responses on the board:

Chinese people
a parade
fireworks
people in costumes
people wearing masks
some kind of big snake or dragon
people inside a dragon suit

some children looking scared
people eating
a building with a funny roof

Then he asks, "What do you think is going on in this story? What could be happening?" Again he lists responses:

party
celebration
parade
holiday

Then he introduces some terms from the story and encourages predictions about what they might mean and how they might be related to the story: *festival, calendar, temple, parade,* and *feast.* The students' predictions begin to form around the idea that a Chinese holiday celebration is occurring in which people prepare special foods, observe religious customs, wear ceremonial clothing, and participate in a street procession with costumes and fireworks. From this basis of information, Mr. Talbott guides his students to reexamine the illustrations and predict what might happen in the story—for example, who might the children be who are pictured several times? Why might they be frightened in this picture? What might happen at the end?

At this point, the students have developed a good basis of information and expectation and are ready to begin reading. Their previewing has helped them to develop a context for the story's events, introduced some of the story's key vocabulary, and helped them to set purposes for their reading.

Ms. Niles works with older poor readers from several grades. Seven of her students must read an earth science selection on glacier formation, but prereading discussion reveals that both prior information and interest in the topic are lacking. She uses previewing to help overcome both problems.

First, she asks the group to tell what they already know about glaciers. Other than that they are made of ice, her question is met with shrugs and blank looks. "All right," she says, "you have exactly two minutes to look over these pages and find out as much as you can, and we'll see who is able to gather the most information. Sally and Becky, you look at headings and boldface print. Maurice and John, you look at maps. Sam and Daniel, you look for topic sentences at the beginnings of each major section. Jessica, you look at photographs and their captions. All set? Begin!"

Ms. Niles has adapted the previewing task to fit the special informational demands of this selection and has given each student a specific task. She has also used a team approach and introduced an element of competition to arouse the students' interest in the task. After two minutes of silent study, she asks each student or pair to report on the specified area and begins listing terms, topics, and descriptions on the board under general headings. She compliments each responder on the amount of information gathered, without designating any "winner." After a quick review of the lists on the board, the students begin to read the selection, armed with an array of facts, terms, and concepts they had not possessed before, as well as with some confidence that they can read the chapter successfully.

Previewing is an effective means of helping students to acquire some prereading information about topics of which they know little beforehand and set some expectations about the text that they can compare to what the selection conveys. The previewing time should be kept short, and the discussion period should be conducted in an accepting, encouraging manner. Reading should begin when interest is aroused and some basis for reading has been established.

Developing Predictions.   Closely related to the topic of prior knowledge is the process of *prediction,* in which students compare what they already know or remember to what they think they are going to read. Prediction requires that students relate their prior knowledge to the reading task at hand and form expectations that they will apply to the reading. Thus, prediction forms the connection between prior knowledge and the new information coming in.

For the Phase of Building Knowledge

Building knowledge is the phase of reading and finding out.

DRTA: Active Reading of Fiction.   The directed reading-thinking activity (DRTA) is a guided group discussion activity that focuses on the formation and testing of prereading predictions. In essence, it is a set of procedures for guiding prereading predictions. In a DRTA, children develop critical reading and thinking by predicting possible story events and outcomes, then reading to confirm or disprove their hypotheses. As described by Stauffer (1975), in a DRTA, the students form a set of purposes for reading, processing ideas, and testing answers by taking part in a predict-read-prove cycle. The teacher *activates thought* by asking, "What do you think?"; *agitates thought* by asking, "Why do you think so?"; and *requires evidence* by asking, "How can you prove it?" (Stauffer, 1975, p. 37). The DRTA format helps students to read more critically and with improved comprehension because it engages them in this process of fluent reading in a structured fashion, slowing down and making concrete the phases of the prediction process.

Students might be asked to form tentative hypotheses about a story from the title, cover art, or first illustration. They might be asked to look at other illustrations or to read the first sentence, paragraph, or page. They are asked to predict what might happen in the story and how it might end up and to justify their predictions on the basis of what they have seen, read, and already know or believe. At preselected points in the story, they are asked to stop reading, review predictions and change them if necessary, form new predictions about upcoming material, and continue reading. Predictions might be recorded on the board to aid in recalling them later. Predictions that are disproved by later story events or that students no longer think are likely may be erased or crossed out. Students are continually asked to justify their positions on the basis of what they have already read. They may reread orally to back up their points. The predict-read-prove cycle continues through the story; as students get closer to the end, their predictions become more convergent as more and more of the story is revealed. At the story's end, predictions and clues may be reviewed or other kinds of follow-up questions may be asked.

K-W-L: *Active Reading of Nonfiction.* K-W-L stands for the three questions readers should ask themselves as they read a nonfiction selection: "What do I *know?* What do I *want* to learn? What did I *learn* from this?" The first two questions are asked before reading; the third is asked after the reading. They correspond to the mental operations of accessing prior information, determining reading purposes, and recalling information (Ogle, 1986). The procedure has three steps:

1. **Step K:** Before reading, the teacher guides students in brainstorming what they already know about the topic of the reading. The teacher records this information on the board or on a transparency. After the brainstorming, students are asked to use their prior information to predict what general types or categories of information they might expect to encounter when they read the passage. For example, if the topic is Columbus's voyage to the New World and students have recalled prior information about three ships, cramped quarters, and inadequate food, the teacher might lead them to identify categories of information such as "how they got there," "what the ships were like," and "what they ate and drank on the voyage." Since students often find this step difficult, the teacher needs to model and demonstrate this step numerous times until students begin to be able to perceive categories themselves.

2. **Step W:** As students complete the first step, disagreements and uncertainties will arise. These form the basis of the "What do I want to learn?" step. The teacher's role here is to highlight disagreements and gaps in prior information, raising questions that will help students to focus on the new information they will encounter. Students should write down the specific questions they want to have answered, thus making a personal commitment to the information. Students might be given a K-W-L worksheet to use for note taking, with the three questions as headings. An example of a completed worksheet is shown in Figure 7.14.

3. **Step L:** After completing the reading, whether they read the whole article or a portion of it, students should write down the information they recall from the passage. They should check their written questions to see whether they found answers to them; some questions might require further reading or checking other sources. The teacher guides a discussion of the questions generated and the answers students found, including areas of disagreement; students refer to the passage to resolve disputes. Carr and Ogle (1987) developed K-W-L Plus, an enhanced K-W-L with two additional steps for secondary students. After the reading and the use of the three steps, students engage in concept mapping and summarizing. A *concept map* is a graphic organizer that allows students to group pieces of information gleaned from the text, helping students to see associations and relationships among various pieces of information. This process is considered important because many students, particularly poor readers, acquire information from text only as isolated facts, failing to organize them into any coherent units of meaning. Practice in organizing information into main ideas or topics and supporting details improves

Topic: _Crocodiles_

K	W	L
What We Know	What We Want to Find Out	What We Learned

K — What We Know

eats people
eats meat
reptile
lays eggs
about 6 feet long
leaves its babies
solitary
vicious
has about 6 babies

W — What We Want to Find Out

do they eat people?
What do they eat?
How do they get their food?
How big are they?
How does it have its babies?
How many babies at one time?

L — What We Learned

Do eat people
also eat bugs, fish, ducks, birds, antelope
Actively hunt with others
Herds fish with tail
Shares its food
Live in groups
6-15 feet long
most common 6-8 feet
female digs a nest
use same nest year after year
guards the nest
helps babies dig out
helps babies break shell
father crocodile helps
can help break eggs
protects babies for 12 weeks

Categories of Information:

Diet   Getting Food
Size   Reproduction
              Family Life

FIGURE 7.14   *K-W-L Worksheet*

overall comprehension. An example of a concept map is shown in Figure 7.15. The concept map is then used as the organizer for a written summary, which requires students to reflect on information gleaned and express it in their own words in a logical and readable form. Practice in summarizing helps students to organize and include all

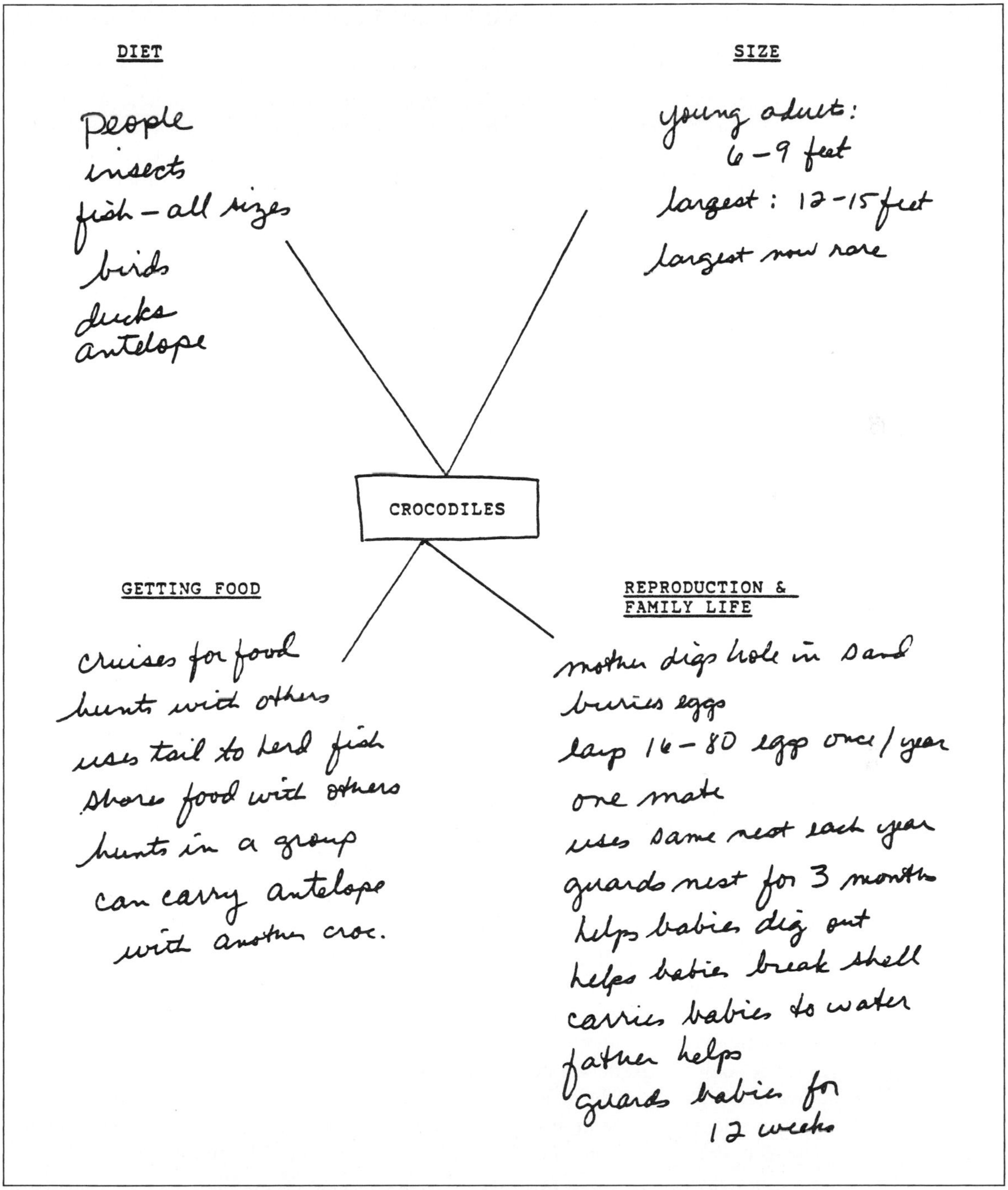

DIET

People
insects
fish – all sizes
birds
ducks
antelope

SIZE

young adult:
    6 – 9 feet
largest : 12 – 15 feet
largest now rare

CROCODILES

GETTING FOOD

cruises for food
hunts with others
uses tail to herd fish
shares food with others
hunts in a group
can carry antelope
    with another croc.

REPRODUCTION &
FAMILY LIFE

mother digs hole in sand
buries eggs
lays 16 – 80 eggs once / year
one mate
uses same nest each year
guards nest for 3 months
helps babies dig out
helps babies break shell
carries babies to water
father helps
guards babies for
    12 weeks

FIGURE 7.15 *K-W-L Plus Concept Map*

important information from a text, not just that information they found most memorable or interesting.

Questioning the Author: Close Reading for Comprehension.   Students also viewed the text as infallible, even when the text did not state ideas clearly or when it asked for prior knowledge that the students were not likely to have. Summing up their findings, McKeown, Beck, and Sandora (1996) concluded that "textbooks . . . are not serving students well [and] students often react to inadequate text presentations by developing a view of themselves as inadequate readers" (p. 97).

Beck, McKeown, and Kucan (1997) saw breakdowns at each point in the process of comprehension: The students often did not have sufficient prior knowledge, did not make necessary inferences, did not come away with important ideas.

Beck et al. (1997) developed a comprehensive teaching strategy that would, first, reorient the students' thinking about texts and, second, lead them into using the kinds of thinking processes needed to understand the texts. They call their strategy *questioning the author,* or QtA (Beck et al., 1997).

Preparing for a QtA Lesson.   The teacher prepares for a QtA lesson by deciding on a portion of text that can support intense questioning for a reasonable period of time, perhaps 20 to 30 minutes. Then the teacher follows three steps:

1. Reading through the text in advance and identifying the major understandings that the students should engage in this text.
2. Planning stopping points in the text that occur often enough to give adequate attention to the important ideas and inferences in the passage.
3. Planning the queries (probing questions) to be asked at each stopping point. (These are tentative plans only. The teacher will take his cue for the actual queries from the students' own comments and questions.)

Conducting a QtA Lesson.   The lesson proceeds in two stages:

1. *Prepare the Students' Attitudes.* The teacher begins the lesson by discussing the idea of authorship and explaining that texts are written by human beings who are not perfect people and their texts are not perfect works. Things might be unclear. Ideas might have been left out. Things might be hinted at but not stated. It is the readers' job to question the author. It might help to remind the students of what happens in a writing workshop (Calkins, 1986; Graves, 1982; Temple, Nathan, Temple, & Burris, 1992). When we listen to a classmate sharing her writing in a writing workshop, we know that sometimes she will mention something without telling us enough about it or even describe some things inaccurately. In a writing workshop, we question the author so that we can understand the writing better and also to help the author make the writing clearer. In a QtA session, students also question the author—but since the author isn't present in the classroom, the class will have to answer for the author.

2. **Raise Queries about the Text.** Next, the teacher has the students read a small portion of the text. When they stop, the teacher poses a query about what they have read. The kinds of queries the teacher might use are shown in Figure 7.16.

The Role of the Teacher in QtA. The earlier research by Beck, McKeown, and their colleagues suggested that the kinds of tasks teachers set and the kinds of questions they ask have a strong influence on how students approach the cognitive activity of comprehension. This influence can lead students in productive directions, or it can lead them toward passive and inefficient practices.

In QtA, the teacher is knowledgeable about what comprehension is and how it should be approached. The teacher understands that comprehension requires activity on the part of the students, so conducts discussions that require students to think and construct meaning. The teacher understands the difference between important ideas and details, so, in the words of McKeown and Beck (1997),

> he asks questions that focus . . . on meaning rather than on locating text information; for example, asking, "What did Tony mean when he said that to his brother?" rather than simply "What did Tony say to his brother?" (p. 114)

INITIATING QUERIES

What is the author trying to say here?

What do you think the author wants us to know?

What is the author talking about?

FOLLOW-UP QUERIES

So what does the author mean right here?

That's what the author said, but what did the author mean?

Does that make sense with what the author told us before?

How does that fit in with what the author has told us?

But does the author tell us why?

Why do you think the author tells us that now?

NARRATIVE QUERIES

How do you think things look for the character now?

How does the author let you know that something has changed?

How has the author worked that out for us?

Given what the author has already told us about this character, what do you think he's up to?

How is the author making you feel right now about these characters?

What is the author telling us with this conversation?

FIGURE 7.16 *Sample Queries for Questioning the Author*

Source: From *Improving Comprehension with Questioning the Author: A Fresh and Expanded View of a Powerful Approach* by Isabel L. Beck and Margaret G. McKeown. Copyright © 2006 by Isabel L. Beck and Margaret McKeown. Reprinted by permission.

An Example of a QtA Discussion.   Here a class is discussing a single sentence from *Ben and Me* (Lawson, 1988). The sentence, which is narrated by a fictitious mouse named Amos, reads, "This question of the nature of lightning so preyed upon his mind that he was finally driven to an act of deceit that caused the first and only rift in our long friendship."

Teacher: What's the author trying to say about Ben and Amos?
Temika: That their friendship was breaking up.
Teacher: Their friendship was breaking up? OK, let's hang on to that. What do you think, April?
April: I agree with the part that their friendship did break up, but, um, I think that they got back together because when you are reading um, further, it said that he was enjoying the mouse.
Alvis: I think that um, Amos is just, Amos is just lying because in the story it said if they weren't good friends, why would um, um, Ben build a um, kite for, build a kite for him so he could have fun?
Teacher: OK, so Alvis is telling us that, why would Ben go to all that trouble and build that beautiful kite if they weren't friends? A lot of people agreed that their friendship is broken up. Alvis doesn't think their friendship is broken up. Can somebody help me out? What's the author want us to figure out here? (Beck, McKeown, & Kucan, 1997, p. 110)

Reciprocal Teaching.   Reciprocal teaching (Brown, Palincsar, & Armbruster, 1984) is a method for demonstrating and developing reading comprehension in a group setting. The teacher models a systematic way of approaching a passage by using a sequence of comprehension processes: *summarizing, questioning, clarifying,* and *predicting.* After the teacher models these processes in four steps, students take turns following the same steps and leading the others in discussing the passage read. This procedure is useful with any kind of text; it is particularly useful with nonfiction, which often contains a great many facts and pieces of new information. Here are the steps in using reciprocal teaching:

1. The teacher divides the passage to be read into fairly short sections; depending on the total length of the selection, one or two paragraphs at a time might be sufficient. For long selections such as whole chapters, long chapter sections, and longer stories, several pages might be better. Or the teacher might wish to start the procedure with short sections, then make them longer as the reading progresses.

2. The teacher asks everyone to read the passage silently. To avoid having some students waiting for slow readers, the teacher should assign the reading before the activity begins. In this case, all students should quickly reexamine and review the passage before the discussion begins.

3. After the reading is completed, the teacher models the comprehension process by following these four steps:

   a. Summarize the section in one or a few sentences.
   b. Ask the group one or two good questions, avoiding picky details.

    c. Identify a difficult part of the passage and clarify it by explaining, giving examples, drawing analogies, or making other clarifying statements.

    d. Predict what the next section might be about or what might be learned from it.

4. The teacher should repeat steps 1 through 3 until the pattern is familiar to all students. Afterward, she can take turns leading the discussion steps previously mentioned: teacher-student-teacher-student or teacher-student-student. The teacher modeling and continued teacher involvement is critical to the students' success with the procedure.

Here is an example of how a teacher might use reciprocal teaching with a nonfiction passage: Ms. Brown has chosen an article about penguins from a nature magazine to supplement a science lesson with her fifth graders. The article is three pages long, with lavish illustrations, so she divides the reading into passages of several paragraphs each. First, she distributes copies of the article with the stopping points marked on them. (If she were using a textbook, she would have each student locate the stopping point and mark it with a strip of paper across the page.) She directs students to read the first three paragraphs, which contain general information about the penguins' habitat, habits, and diet. Then she models the use of the comprehension steps in this way:

> First, I'll summarize this passage. In these paragraphs, we read that penguins are large birds that are unusual because they do not fly, but they are excellent swimmers. Their wings are specially shaped like flippers to help them swim very fast and over long distances. They live in icy frozen areas of the world where there is little or no plant life. They live on a diet of fish.
>
>   I would ask these questions about these paragraphs:
>
> - In what ways do we know penguins are different from other birds? (Students answer that they do not fly, they swim very skillfully, they live in icy places where there are no plants.)
> - In what ways do you think penguins are like other birds? (Students answer that they have wings, other kinds of birds also eat fish, they lay eggs.)
> - In what ways might their environment affect how they survive? (Students discuss the lack of plant life for making nests, the dangers of cold.)
>
>   I thought that the paragraph telling about their environment was a little difficult. The passage used some difficult words like *barren, Antarctic,* and *ice floes,* which might need discussion. Let's write these on the board and discuss what each one means. (Discussion follows about the meaning of these terms; one student gets a dictionary, and they refer to it.)
>
>   In the paragraphs to follow, I predict that we will find out more about how penguins adapt to extreme cold temperatures and find out how they raise their young in this environment.

Ms. Brown then directs students to read to the end of the next section, and she again models these four steps. After the class reads the third section, she calls on a volunteer to follow the same steps: summarize, ask a couple of good questions, clarify a part or term, and predict what might be upcoming. When the article is finished, students briefly discuss the main points of the article and evaluate how well they answered questions and followed the steps in the comprehension process.

Reciprocal teaching helps students learn how effective readers approach challenging texts and helps them to develop systematic ways of dealing with the information in them. After a number of repetitions, students might begin to internalize the comprehension steps and apply them independently to other text material.

Reciprocal Question-Answer Relationships.   Successful readers use a variety of strategies to maximize their comprehension of text: They monitor their own comprehension, they self-question, they mentally summarize, and they seek relationships among ideas and facts presented in what they read. Unsuccessful readers often do not do these things; they tend to focus more on pronouncing the words and answering the teacher's questions, but they have few strategies for predicting what questions might be asked or for finding answers. Helfeldt and Henk (1990) propose an instructional strategy that helps at-risk readers use self-questioning to improve their comprehension. They call it *reciprocal question-answer relationships* (ReQAR). The procedure consists of four general steps: explaining what the students will do, reciprocal questioning (wherein students and teacher take turns asking each other questions about a passage that was just read and answering each other's questions), categorizing questions and their answers according to where the information is found ("in the book" or "in my head"), and finally combining steps 2 and 3 by combining reciprocal questioning and categorizing the answers. In this step, students ask the teacher a question about the material, and the teacher answers it and categorizes the answer as "in the book" or "in my head"; then roles are reversed, with the teacher asking and the student or students answering and categorizing.

For the Phase of Consolidation

Consolidation is the phase of looking back on the meaning, questioning it, interpreting it, applying, or reexamining one's ideas about the topic in light of it.

Story Mapping.   A good way to have students reflect on and consolidate their understanding of a story they have read is to have them construct a *story map.* A story map is a graphic representation of the parts of a story that shows how the story parts are related. Story maps "provide a practical means of helping children organize story content into coherent wholes" (Davis & McPherson, 1989, p. 232). "Story mapping," wrote Boyle and Peregoy (1990), "helps children use story grammar for comprehension and composing" (p. 198). Story maps can be used to help readers perceive and understand plot structure and a variety of text structures such as literal and implied information, cause and effect, sequential ordering, and comparison and contrast (see Figure 7.17). They are similar to other graphic organizers such as structured overviews, story diagrams, and webs.

Figure 7.18 shows a sample story map for the Aesop's fable "The Crow and the Water Jug." This story map emphasizes the essential story structures described in the previous section: setting, initiating event or "problem," internal response or "goal,"

Story maps can take many forms. At their simplest, story maps can ask children to reflect on and record what happened at different points of a story. More complex story maps lead children to think about story elements.

Introduce story maps by talking through a simple story with the children, such as the Aesop fable, "The Crow and the Water Jug." Involve the students in answering the questions as you write up their answers for all to see. Once they understand how to complete the story map, they can write them individually. It helps if you prepare and duplicate a form for them to complete, such as one of the following.

A Simple Story Map

What happened at the beginning?	What happened in the middle?	What was the climax?	What was the conclusion?
_____	_____	_____	_____
_____	_____	_____	_____
_____	_____	_____	_____
_____	_____	_____	_____

A More Complex Story Map

Your Name: _____ Story Name: _____

Describe the setting and the characters.

What is the main problem at the beginning of the story?

What goal do the characters set?

What *attempts* are made to reach the goal? What are the *outcomes*?

Describe the conclusion. What is the *resolution* of the problem?

FIGURE 7.17 *Story Maps*

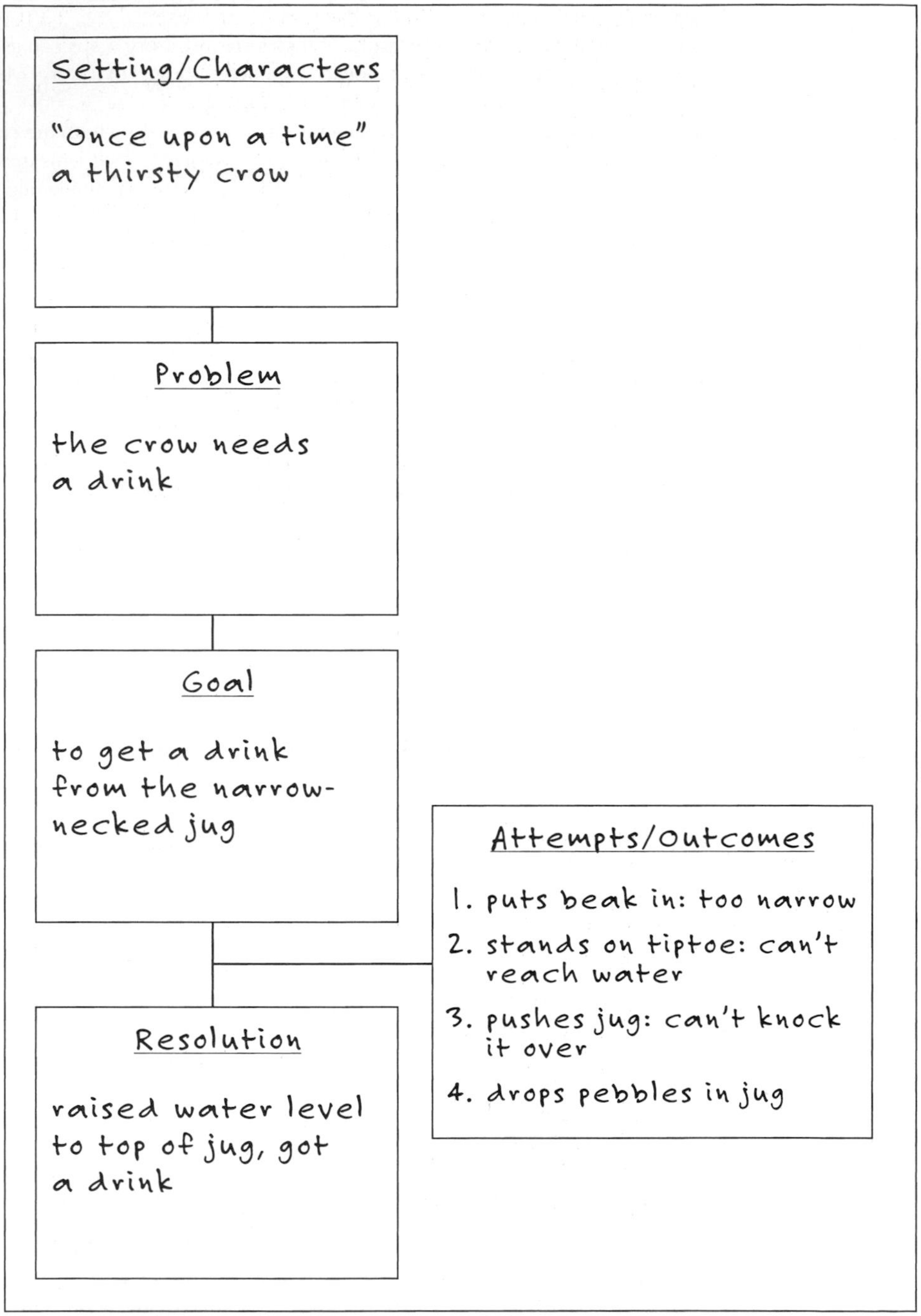

Setting/Characters

"Once upon a time"
a thirsty crow

Problem

the crow needs
a drink

Goal

to get a drink
from the narrow-
necked jug

Attempts/Outcomes

1. puts beak in: too narrow
2. stands on tiptoe: can't
   reach water
3. pushes jug: can't knock
   it over
4. drops pebbles in jug

Resolution

raised water level
to top of jug, got
a drink

FIGURE 7.18 *Story Map for "The Crow and the Water Jug"*

Source: Reprinted from Scholastic Reading Counts website. Reprinted by permission of Scholastic, Inc.

attempts and outcomes, and consequence or "resolution." Figure 7.19 shows another kind of story map, devised by Boyle and Peregoy (1990). In this model, the essential story grammar is boiled down to SOMEONE . . . WANTS . . . BUT . . . SO. Under each of these headings, the teacher or students list the character or characters and their problems, the goals, and means of achieving them. Other story maps might compare the advantages and disadvantages of some story action, the causes and effects of certain story events, or aspects of the various characters in a story.

To construct a story map, first think about the kinds of information or story structures you want to emphasize in your lesson. Make some notes about how this information might be arrayed. For example, comparison and contrast may be illustrated by listing items in two vertical columns; sequential order of story events might lend itself to a linear or timeline arrangement; details of characterization might be illustrated by a web-style arrangement of circles connected to a central circle with short lines; or the comparison of two stories or characters might be shown by two intersecting circles, sometimes called a *Venn diagram.* Examine your story map to make sure it emphasizes the logical flow of information. Don't make it too technical or detailed; emphasize just one pattern of organization at a time.

To teach with a story map, it is best to start with a straightforward, literal map of story events. Introduce it after the story has been read to help students recall and

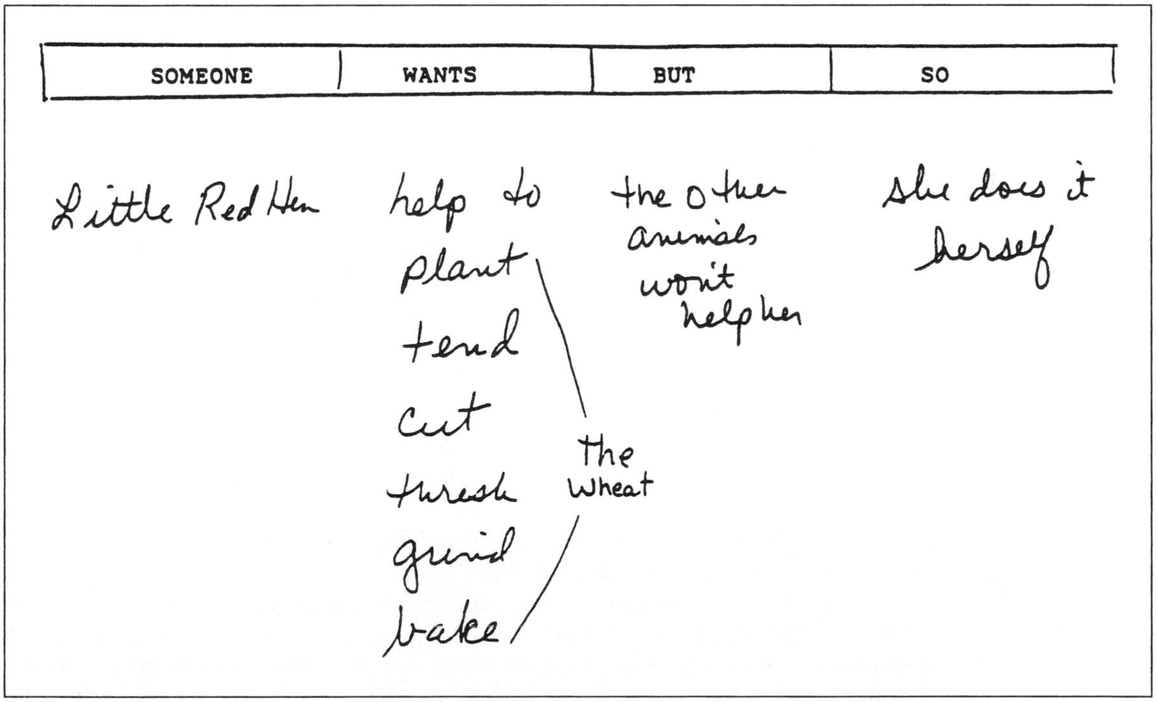

FIGURE 7.19 *Story Map for "The Little Red Hen"*

reconstruct what happened. When students are somewhat familiar with the story map and its use as a postreading activity, you might begin using story maps as a prereading organizer. Students might be given some minimal information and asked to predict story events or might be shown a partially completed story map and asked to predict what else might occur. Such prereading prediction has a positive effect on later recall and comprehension, just as it does with directed reading-thinking activities, K-W-L, and other related prediction strategies. After reading a portion of the story, the story map can be modified, and students can continue reading and changing the map until the story is completed. Story maps may also be used as a postreading activity, with students reconstructing a map individually or in cooperative learning groups; they may also complete partially completed maps, which Davis and McPherson (1989) call "macro cloze story maps."

Retelling.   We know that retelling stories helps children to understand and remember stories and develop a sense of story. Retelling requires readers or listeners to organize information and make inferences about it based on text information and their own prior information by constructing a personal rendition of the text. Thus, retelling focuses children's attention on relevant text information, sequences, and causes and effects. It requires that they organize that information into a coherent structure for retelling to another. Studies have shown that young children's story sense and story comprehension are significantly improved by practice in retelling stories they have heard (Morrow, 1984, 1985, 1986; Pellegrini & Galda, 1982). Similarly, retelling has been shown to improve reading comprehension (Gambrell, Koskinen, & Kapinus, 1985; Rose, Cundick, & Higbee, 1984). You can use retelling strategies in your classroom to help all readers to improve their story comprehension.

According to Koskinen et al. (1988), in its simplest form, a retelling activity involves two students working together during direct instruction time or independent work time; one reads or listens to a portion of a text or a whole story and then teams up with a partner to retell the story. Since the listener's role is an important one and good listening is active, rather than passive, the listener is asked to provide helpful questions or comments to the teller and may be asked to complete a retelling reaction sheet. Before students begin this activity, you need to model it so that students will have a clear understanding of what they are to do and why they are doing it. First, explain simply and clearly why retelling is a useful activity. Depending on the age of your students, you might say something like, "Retelling a story you have read or listened to helps you remember stories and helps you check to see if you understand what you have read or heard. It also helps you to learn to be a good storyteller. I will show you what to do to practice retelling stories and how to be a helpful listening partner. Then you will have time to practice retelling with a partner."

Model retelling by announcing to students what you are going to do: "I'm going to read a short passage from this story. Then I'm going to retell it to you without looking at the story. I'm going to try to include all the important areas and information. As I read it, listen for the important ideas."

Next, read aloud a fairly short passage from a story or nonfiction text or a short, complete story. Afterward, retell the story or passage in a few sentences, including the most important information, sequences, and the like. Then ask students for feedback on the retelling by asking them whether you included all the important ideas, accepting their contributions or suggestions. Immediately after the modeling, students can read a short passage from a basal reader, textbook, or other material that they all have. Guide them in group retelling by having volunteers retell to the group, using question prompts that are appropriate for the type of text with which they are dealing (see Figure 7.20).

When children seem to have the idea of retelling, which might be after more than one model and group practice, create opportunities for students to practice retelling to a partner. In this practice, one student silently reads a passage or text for retelling, then retells it to a partner. Both students need not have read the same material; if the partner has not read the story and has trouble understanding it from the retelling, this is a good indication to the student that more practice retelling is needed. This is an excellent opportunity for students to read and share trade books they are reading in class, and it provides another important way for you to work trade books into your reading instruction. Students might practice reading and retelling during independent work time or free reading time. They should do this regularly, several times a week.

Retelling is more effective for both students involved if the listener has an active role. Good listening is active and responsive, not passive. The student who is the listening partner should have something to do besides just listen. With guided practice, the

---

Narrative Text

Who are the main characters?

When did the story take place?

Where did the story take place?

What important events happened in the story?

How did the story end?

Expository text

What is the topic of the selection?

What are the important ideas in the selection?

FIGURE 7.20 *Prompts for Encouraging Retelling*

Source: Figure from Koskinen, P. S., Gambrell, L. B., Kapinus, B. A., & Heathington, B. S. (1988, May). "Retelling: A Strategy for Enhancing Students' Reading Comprehension," *The Reading Teacher 41*(9), 892–896. Reprinted with permission of The International Reading Association.

Name _____ Date _____

I listened to _____

I chose one thing my partner did well. _____

He or she told about the characters. _____

He or she told about the setting. _____

He or she told about the events in the story. _____

His or her story had a beginning. _____

His or her story had an ending. _____

I told my partner one thing that was good about his or her story. _____

FIGURE 7.21 *Example of a Retelling Reaction Sheet*

Source: Figure from Koskinen, P. S., Gambrell, L. B., Kapinus, B. A., & Heathington, B. S. (1988, May). "Retelling: A Strategy for Enhancing Students' Reading Comprehension," *The Reading Teacher 41*(9), 892–896. Reprinted with permission of The International Reading Association.

listening partner can learn how to ask helpful questions by using the prompts referred to in Figure 7.20 or by suggesting other important information that the teller omitted, if any. Students can also complete a retelling reaction guide, such as the one in Figure 7.21.

This procedure focuses on positive responses rather than criticism, which is very important. Providing this task for listeners helps them to set a purpose for listening and helps keep them focused on the task. Giving students systematic, structured opportunities to talk about what they have read helps develop comprehension and oral expression skills and provides teachers yet another way to incorporate fiction and nonfiction trade books in their regular instruction program.

Developing Listening Comprehension

Listening comprehension is related to reading ability in that students who are not yet fluent, mature readers can usually listen to and comprehend text that is read to them that they cannot yet read for themselves. The most common example of this is with emergent and beginning readers, who can listen to and understand a wide variety of materials but might not yet be able to read anything for themselves.

As students' reading abilities develop and their instructional levels go up, the gap between the instructional reading level and listening level might begin to close, and by the time they have become fluent, mature readers, there might be no difference between that they can listen to and what they can read successfully. For much of the time before a student has reached this zenith in reading development, however, there will be a gap between these two levels.

Experience is an important factor in listening comprehension. Even if all other things are equal, a student who has been read to and whose school and home environments are rich in oral language (regardless of dialect or language origins) has an advantage over the student who has not had this experience. In the same way, students who can read fairly effectively have a greater store of information, concepts, and vocabulary than illiterate students or very poor readers, and the first group's listening comprehension levels are more likely to be higher.

A student's listening comprehension level is important because it shows us how closely his or her ability to understand written text approaches the demands of the student's grade level and gives us an indication of how much potential for reading improvement the student has at this point in time. We must remember that unlike IQ or other intelligence measures, the listening level is not fixed; as the student's reading ability improves and he or she reads more, the listening level also rises. Thus, progress today paves the way for more progress tomorrow.

There are several typical patterns in listening comprehension and reading. One is that a student might have a below-grade-level listening level and an instructional reading level that matches it. Take, for example, Sam, a fourth grader whose listening and instruction reading levels are both at second grade. This means that Sam is currently reading about as well as he is able to and that he lacks the verbal concepts and vocabulary to understand third- or fourth-grade text either by reading or by listening. Attempting to raise Sam's reading level without also developing his listening comprehension will likely result only in frustration, for he will be asked to do what is beyond his present capability. In Sam's case, listening comprehension must be fostered so that his reading ability can grow.

Another common pattern is exemplified by Elaine, also a fourth grader. Elaine's instructional reading level is also second grade, but her listening comprehension level is fourth grade and even includes some fifth-grade text when the topic is something she knows about. Elaine is a poor reader in fourth grade, but she already has verbal concepts and vocabulary appropriate to other fourth graders and text typical of that grade. Elaine needs to develop her reading ability so that it more closely approaches her present listening level, which indicates that she has the present potential to improve her reading significantly.

Other patterns that occur less often are equally important. One is exemplified by Sarah, a fifth grader. Sarah's instructional level is only about third grade, but her listening level is at seventh. Sarah is a poor reader in fifth grade, but she has the verbal capacity to understand much more difficult text. In Sarah's case, this capacity far outstrips present performance, and she can benefit from intensive remediation. Her problems might lie in motivation, inappropriate instruction, or other factors that must be overcome. But she has the measured potential for at least grade-level reading achievement.

Consider, in contrast, the case of James, a ninth grader in a remedial program. James is functionally nearly illiterate, with only a second-grade instructional level. His listening level is fourth grade. James might be classifiable as a slow learner; he is certainly verbally impoverished, and his illiteracy has kept his listening comprehension from developing. Still, because there is a gap between the two levels, he can improve his reading somewhat. And if he does, his listening comprehension is likely to increase also, which in turn will make possible further reading progress if James is motivated toward such improvement. In his case, both reading remediation and listening comprehension development are needed.

The key to developing students' listening comprehension lies in immersion in a rich language environment and stimulation of their language. First and foremost, such students must be read to, regardless of their age. Reading to James in ninth grade is every bit as important to his literacy as reading to a primary grader, for it is by listening that all readers develop their first concepts about stories, a sense of how written language differs from talk, and a store of information to bring to reading. Students whose listening comprehension levels are below grade level should be read to daily from a wide variety of kinds of materials. Good literature that is appropriate for their age and written at a level they can understand should be a mainstay and should include nonfiction and poetry as well as fiction. Older students should also be read to from newspapers and magazines since we want to encourage them to use these sources as well as books. Tapes can be used, but they are not as effective as live readers because tapes cannot monitor listeners' interest, stop to answer questions, or reread a part for emphasis. Taped readings should never be used as a substitute for live reading but are useful for additional practice.

A directed listening-thinking activity (DLTA) is a good alternative to straight reading aloud. A DLTA is similar to the DRTA discussed previously in this chapter, wherein students make predictions about upcoming story events or, in the case of nonfiction, assert what they already know about a topic before reading and compare their predictions and assertions to what the text says. The only difference between a DRTA and a DLTA is that in the latter, the material is read aloud to students. DLTAs are an effective means of monitoring listening comprehension and fostering interest in listening.

Immersion in a rich language environment also means that students should be actively engaged in oral discussions and conversations. They must be guided to do more than just answer questions, the most common form of classroom talk. They should also describe, summarize, persuade and argue, using as specific, vivid, and precise vocabulary as possible. Many of the typical composition activities that are suggested in reading and English books, such as making up stories, recounting real events and reminiscences, describing objects, persuading others to some action or belief, arguing for or against some course of action, and composing directions, are just as useful for oral language and listening development. Speaking and listening cannot be separated; they will develop together. Students with underdeveloped listening comprehension need daily experience with both.

Oral reading by students for other students can be useful, too, but must be used with care. All oral reading should be rehearsed and prepared by the reader beforehand. No one is served by listening to someone stumble through text. Material for oral reading should be read silently several times, then read aloud for practice before the final reading. Also, oral reading should be done for some purpose, not as an end in itself. Some material deserves to be read aloud, and enjoyment of it is enhanced by being effectively read: poetry, vivid descriptions, and good dialogue are examples. The purpose of oral reading should be to share and enhance such material, not just to practice reading aloud.

Again, we return to the point of teacher modeling. The teacher sets the tone and provides the model by which students judge what is useful and important. Without dominating activities, teachers must show students by their modeling what they want them to be able to do. As teachers, we should prepare what we read aloud to the class so that our reading will be fluent and expressive. We should share portions of material we find appealing or especially effective with them and work to make our descriptions and summaries colorful and precise. We should exhibit interest in and curiosity about words and expressions and share with students interesting and unusual language in what we read. We should respond to students' efforts to use language more effectively with sincere interest, attention, and positive reinforcement. We should listen more to what they say than to how they say it, and we should respond first to their message.

The more direct experience with language students have, the more their language use will expand. The more it grows, the more their listening comprehension will improve. The more listening comprehension develops, the more they will be able to bring to reading, and thus their reading will improve. The roots of reading ability are buried deep in oral language, and we cannot overlook this foundation if we wish to help our students read better.

Time Spent Reading

So far in this chapter, we have concentrated on methods and issues that are related to reading instruction: helping students to develop sight recognition of words, use word analysis strategies fluently and effectively, organize and apply prior knowledge to new information acquired from reading, and use a variety of reading processes and skills to become more fluent and comprehend better. It might be thought that effective reading lies in instruction, and indeed, good instruction is an absolute requirement in helping children grow as readers. In spite of all the instructional techniques we apply, however, there is another factor that is critical: To become a good reader, a child must spend a lot of time reading.

This point seems self-evident. But how much time do children actually spend reading? A number of research studies have been conducted in attempts to determine this, and the results of these studies are disturbing. Walberg and Tsai (1984) studied the out-of-school reading behavior of 2,890 U.S. 13-year-olds. They found that the median child in their sample read 7.2 minutes per day and that the median child reported reading on about one day out of five. Forty-four percent of the subjects in the study reported spending no time reading for enjoyment, while only 5 percent reported spending three hours or more. Not surprisingly, these researchers found that frequency and amount of reading were related to reading achievement. Anderson, Wilson, and Fielding (1988) found that the average fifth grader read about five minutes outside of school.

For comparison, consider the amount of media (television, DVDs, video games) that the average young person aged 8 to 18 uses. One study put the figure at four hours.

These findings reveal, in Paul Wilson's words, "a bleak picture" of most children's voluntary reading habits (Wilson, Anderson, & Fielding, 1986, p. 76). We already know that in spite of our instruction, children generally do not do very much reading of connected text in school; of the hours they spend in school, only a few minutes a day are usually spent actually reading text. Much of the reading time is spent instead listening to the teacher and others, waiting, filling in blanks, or reading single sentences on worksheets and other exercises. According to Allington and McGill-Franzen (1987) and Gaskins (1988), in a major study of poor readers' time on task in reading, poor readers spent "an alarming amount of time in unproductive ways" (Gaskins, 1988, p. 751).

Now for some good news. If the amount of reading students do is so small, it should not be too hard to increase it significantly.

If teachers and librarians can persuade all parents of the importance of reading with their children, or of making sure that their children have books and space and 20 minutes a day in which to read them, we will have doubled the average child's time spent reading, according to the numbers from the Anderson et al. (1988) study. In school, if we have children drop everything and read for an extra 20 minutes every school day, that also will double their average reading time. But we can do more.

Classes that read books and also engage in peer discussions and teacher-student conferences about the books have better attitudes toward reading and produce greater gains in reading achievement than do those that practice only sustained silent reading practices, according to one study (Manning & Manning, 1984). These results suggest that students should not just drop everything and read, but also share their thoughts about what they read. The importance of following up the reading with discussion has been reemphasized recently by the National Reading Panel (Snow, Burns, & Griffen, 1998).

Summary

Corrective teaching is directed toward supporting a student's strengths while teaching and practicing skills and strategies the student needs. From diagnostic data, strengths and needs are identified and priorities are established. Instructional time is planned to fulfill priorities and provide instructional balance.

Readers can develop *sight vocabulary* when they see the same words repeatedly in meaningful contexts. *Dictated stories* feature rereading until students achieve fluency and can identify individual words in and out of context. *Support reading* helps students to get through difficult text and reinforces word recognition. Support reading includes *echo reading* and *choral reading*. *Predictable books* are useful because the same words appear repeatedly and help to build readers' confidence.

Fluency contributes to comprehension and is developed when students reread material.

Word analysis strategies are needed when students do not recognize a word at sight. Although debate still rages over the role of phonics instruction in learning to read, a growing body of evidence suggests that good readers are able to use decoding strategies automatically and accurately during reading, thus freeing the mind for comprehension. It also suggests that all students learn letter-sound relationships as part of learning to read. Exemplary phonics instruction builds on what students already know about letters, sounds, and words; emphasizes phonemic awareness; is clear and direct; is integrated into a total reading program; focuses on reading words rather than learning rules; includes the use of onset and rimes; focuses on the internal structure of words; and develops automaticity in word recognition. *Phonemic awareness* is the ability to manipulate speech sounds in words; it contributes to the ability to rhyme and use phonics. Phonics instruction may be integrated with literature by using trade books that feature particular phonic patterns. Decoding ability may be assessed using the *Names Test.* Using *context* is also an important word analysis strategy. *Cloze procedures* and *confirming* help students to develop facility with context. *Word sorting* helps students to apply phonic regularities by categorizing words sharing a similar word feature.

We divided our treatment of reading comprehension into three phases: *anticipation, building knowledge,* and *consolidation.* In the *anticipation phase,* we presented teaching strategies focusing on readers' use of *prior knowledge, prediction, webbing,* and *previewing.* For the *building knowledge phase,* we presented the strategies of the *directed reading-thinking activities, K-W-L* and *K-W-L Plus,* and also *reciprocal teaching, reciprocal question-answer relationships,* and *questioning the author.* *Story mapping* and *retelling* were presented as activities for the consolidation phase. (Many more strategies for this phase will be found in Chapter 8.)

Listening comprehension supports and promotes reading comprehension. The *listening level* provides an estimate of the reader's present potential for reading improvement. Means of developing students' listening comprehension include *reading to students, directed listening-thinking activities,* and *teacher modeling.*

A host of studies have shown that most students do little, if any, reading outside of school. Yet they also show a significant relationship between *time spent reading* and reading achievement. All students, especially poor readers, must increase their time spent reading; ways of doing so are discussed in this chapter.

---

mylabschool
Where the classroom comes to life!

MyLabSchool is a collection of online tools for your success in this course, your licensure exams, and your teaching career. Visit www.mylabschool.com to access the following:

- Online Study Guide
- Video cases from real classrooms
- Help with your research papers using Research Navigator
- Career Center with resources for:
  - Praxis exams and licensure preparation
  - Professional portfolio development
  - Job search and interview techniques
  - Lesson planning

References

Adams, M. J. (1990). *Beginning to read: Thinking and learning about print.* Cambridge: MIT Press.

Allington, R. L. (1983). Fluency: The Neglected Reading Goal. *The Reading Teacher, 36*(6), 556–561.

Allington, R. L. (1991). Beginning to Read: A Critique by Literacy Professionals and a Response by Marilyn Jager Adams. *The Reading Teacher, 44*(6), 373.

Allington, R., & McGill-Franzen, A. (1987). *A study of the whole-school day experience of Chapter I and mainstreamed LD students* (Final Report of Grant #G008630480, Office of Special Education Programs). Washington, DC: U.S. Department of Education.

Anderson, R. C., Wilson, P. T., & Fielding, L. G. (1988). Growth in reading and how children spend their time outside of school. *Reading Research Quarterly, 23*(3), 285–303.

Armbruster, B., Lehr, F., & Osborne, J. (2001). *Focus on fluency.* Washington, D.C. US Department of Education, National Institute for Literacy. http://www.nifl.gov/partnershipforreading/publications/reading_first1.html

Barr, R., & Drebeen, R. (1983). *How schools work.* Chicago: The University of Chicago Press.

Bear, D., Invernizzi, M., Templeton, S., & Johnston, F. (1996). *Words their way: Word study for phonics, vocabulary, and spelling.* Upper Saddle River, NJ: Merrill.

Beck, I., McKeown, M., & Kucan, L. (1997). *Questioning the author: An approach for enhancing student engagement with text.* Newark, DE: International Reading Association.

Beck, I., McKeown, M., & Kucan, L. (2002). *Bringing words to life.* New York: Guilford Press.

Boyle, O., & Peregoy, S. E. (1990). Literacy scaffolds: Strategies for first and second language readers and writers. *The Reading Teacher, 44*(3), 194–200.

Brown, A. L., Palincsar, A. S., & Armbruster, B. B. (1984). Instructing comprehension—Fostering activities in interactive learning situations. In H. Mandl, N. L. Stein, & T. Trabasso (Eds.), *Learning and comprehension of text.* Hillsdale, NJ: Erlbaum.

Brown, R. (1958). *Words and things.* Garden City, NY: Basic Books.

Calkins, L. (1986). *The art of teaching writing.* Portsmouth, NH: Heinemann.

Carr, E., & Ogle, D. M. (1987). K-W-L Plus: A strategy for comprehension and summarization. *Journal of Reading, 30*(7), 626–631.

Chaney, J. H. (1991). Beginning to read: A critique by literacy professionals and a response by Marilyn Jager Adams. *The Reading Teacher, 44*(6), 374.

Collins, C. (1980). Sustained silent reading periods: Effect on teachers' behaviors and students' achievement. *Elementary School Journal, 81*(2), 108–114.

Cooper, J. D. (1993). *Literacy: Helping children construct meaning.* Boston: Houghton Mifflin.

Cunningham, P. (1990). The names test: A quick assessment of decoding ability. *The Reading Teacher, 44*(2), 124–129.

Cunningham, P. (2004). *Phonics they use: Words for reading and writing* (4th ed.). New York: Addison Wesley Longman.

Davis, Z. T., & McPherson, M. D. (1989). Story map instruction: A road map for reading comprehension. *The Reading Teacher, 43*(3), 232–240.

Ehri, L. C. (1991). Development of the ability to read words. In R. Barr, M. L. Kamil, P. B. Mosenthal, & P. D. Pearson (Eds.), *Handbook of Reading Research: Vol. 2* (pp. 383–417). White Plains, NY: Longman.

Fountas, I., & Pinnell, G. S. (1996). *Guided reading.* Portsmouth: Heinemann.

Gambrell, L. B., Koskinen, P. S., & Kapinus, B. A. (1985, December). *A comparison of retelling and questioning as reading comprehension strategies.* Paper presented at the National Reading Conference, San Diego.

Gaskins, R. W. (1988). The missing ingredients: Time on task, direct instruction, and writing. *The Reading Teacher, 4*(8), 750–755.

Graves, D. (1982). *Writing: Teachers and children at work.* Portsmouth, NH: Heinemann.

Hall, M. A. (1981). *Teaching reading as a language experience* (3rd ed.). Columbus, OH: Merrill.

Hasbrouch, J., &. Tindal. G. (1992). Curriculum-based oral reading fluency norms for students in grades 2 through 5. *Teaching Exceptional Children, 24,* 42.

Helfeldt, J. P., & Henk, W. A. (1990). Reciprocal question-answer relationships: An instructional techniques for at-risk readers. *Journal of Reading, 33*(7), 509–514.

Kapinus, B. A. (1991). Beginning to read: A critique by literacy professionals and a response by Marilyn Jager Adams. *The Reading Teacher, 44*(6), 379.

Kirsch, I. S., Jungeblut, A., Jenkins, L., & Kolstad, A. (1993). *Adult literacy in America: A first look at the findings of the National Adult Literacy Survey.* Washington: National Center for Education Statistics.

Koskinen, P. S., Gambrell, L. B., Kapinus, B. A., & Heathington, B. S. (1988). Retelling: A strategy for enhancing students' reading comprehension. *The Reading Teacher, 41*(9), 892–896.

LaBerge, D., & Samuels, S. (1974). Toward a theory of automatic information processing in reading. *Cognitive Psychology, 6,* 293–332.

Manning, G. L., & Manning, M. (1984). What models of recreational reading make a difference? *Reading World, 23*(4), 375–380.

McCauley, J. K., & McCauley, D. S. (1992). Using choral reading to promote language learning for ESL students. *The Reading Teacher, 45*(7), 526–533.

McKeown, M., Beck, I., & Sandora, C. (1996). Questioning the author: An approach to developing meaningful classroom discourse. In M. Graves, P. Van den Broek, & B. Taylor (Eds.), *The First R: Every Child's Right to Read.* New York: Teachers College Press.

McKeown, M. G., & Beck, I. L. (1988). Learning vocabulary: Different ways for different goals. *Remedial and Special Education (RASE), 9,* 142–146.

Morrow, L. M. (1978). Retelling stories: A strategy for improving young children's comprehension, concept of story structure, and oral language complexity. *Elementary School Journal, 85,* 647–661.

Morrow, L. M. (1984). Effects of story retelling on young children's comprehension and sense of story structure. In J. A. Niles & L. A. Harris (Eds.), *Changing Perspectives on Research in Reading/Language Processing and Instruction, Thirty-third Yearbook of the National Reading Conference* (pp. 95–100). Rochester, NY: National Reading Conference.

Morrow, L. M. (1986). Effects of story retelling on children's dictation of original stories. *Journal of Reading Behavior, 18,* 135–152.

Nagy, W. (1988). *Teaching vocabulary to improve reading comprehension.* Urbana, IL: National Council of Teachers of English; Newark, DE: International Reading Association.

Nagy, W., & Anderson, R. (1984). How many words are there in printed school English? *Reading Research Quarterly, 19,* 304–330.

Nagy, W. E., et al. (1985, December). *Learning word meanings from context: How broadly generalizable?* (Technical Report No. 347). Urbana, IL: Center for the Study of Reading.

National Reading Panel. (2000). *Teaching children to read: An evidence-based assessment of the scientific literature on reading and its implications for reading instruction.* Washington: National Institute for Literacy.

Nessel, D. D., & Jones, M. B. (1981). *The language-experience approach to reading.* New York: Teachers College Press.

Ogle, D. M. (1986). K-W-L: A teaching model that develops active reading of expository text. *The Reading Teacher, 38*(6), 564–570.

Osborn, J., Lehr, F., & Hiebert, E. H. (2003). *A focus on fluency.* Honolulu: Pacific Regional Educational Laboratory. Retrieved February 23, 2007, from http://www.prel.org/products/re_/fluency-1.htm

Palincsar, A. M., & Brown, A. L. (1984). Reciprocal teaching of comprehension—fostering and comprehension-monitoring activities. *Cognition and Instruction, 1,* 117–175.

Pellegrini, A. D., & Galda, L. (1982, Fall). The effects of thematic-fantasy play training on the development of children's story comprehension. *American Educational Research Journal, 19,* 443–454.

Perfetti, C., & Zhang, S. (1996). What it means to learn to read. In M. Graves, P. Van den Broek, & B. Taylor (Eds.), *The first R: Every child's right to read.* New York: Teachers College Press.

Rasinski, T. V. (2003). *The fluent reader: Oral reading strategies for building word recognition, fluency, and comprehension.* New York: Scholastic.

Roberts, D. F., Foehr, U. G., & Rideout, V. (2005, March) "Generation M: Media in the lives of 8-18 year-olds." Kaiser Family Foundation.

Rose, M. C., Cundick, B. P., & Higbee, K. L. (1984). Verbal rehearsal and visual imagery: Mnemonic aids for learning disabled children. *Journal of Learning Disabilities, 16,* 353–354.

Rosenshine, B., & Stevens, R. (1984). Classroom instruction in reading. In P. D. Pearson (Ed.), *Handbook of Reading Research.* New York: Longman.

Ryder, R., Graves, B., & Graves, M. (1989). *Easy reading: Book series and periodicals for less able readers.* Newark, DE: International Reading Association.

Samuels, S. J. (1979). The method of repeated reading. *The Reading Teacher, 32*(4), 403–408.

Schwartz, R. M., & Raphael, T. (1985). Concept of definition: A key to improving students' vocabulary. *The Reading Teacher, 39,* 198–205.

Smith, C. (1997). *Vocabulary instruction and reading comprehension.* Bloomington, IN: ERIC Clearinghouse on Reading, English, and Communication.

Snow, C., & Burns, S. (Eds.). (1998). *Preventing reading difficulty in young children.* Washington, DC: National Academy Press.

Stahl, S. A. (1992). Saying the "P" word: Nine guidelines for exemplary phonics instruction. *The Reading Teacher, 45*(8), 618–625.

Stanovich, K. E. (1980). Toward an interactive-compensatory model of individual differences in the development of reading fluency. *Reading Research Quarterly, 16*(1), 3–71.

Stanovich, K. E. (1991). Word recognition: Changing perspectives. In R. Barr, M. L. Kamil, P. B. Mosenthal, & P. D. Pearson (Eds.), *Handbook of Reading Research: Vol. 2* (pp. 418–452). White Plains, NY: Longman.

Stanovich, K. E. (1992). Are we overselling literacy? In C. Temple & P. Collins (Eds.), *Stories and Readers.* Norwood, MA: Christopher-Gordon.

Stauffer, R. G. (1975). *Directing the reading-thinking process.* New York: Harper & Row.

Stauffer, R. G. (1980). *The language experience approach to the teaching of reading* (rev. ed.). New York: Harper & Row.

Szymborski, J. A. (1995). *Vocabulary development: Context clues versus word definitions.* M.A. Project, Kean College of New Jersey.

Temple, C., Martinez, M., Yokota, J., & Naylor, A. (1998). *Children's books in children's hands: An introduction to their literature.* Boston: Allyn & Bacon.

Temple, C., Nathan, R., Temple, F., & Burris, N. (1992). *The Beginnings of writing* (3rd ed.). Boston: Allyn & Bacon.

Torgeson, J., Rashotte, C., Greenstein, J., Houck, G., & Portes, P. (1987). Academic difficulties of learning disabled children who perform poorly on memory span tests. *Memory and Learning Disabilities, 27,* 276–286.

Trachtenburg, P. (1990). Using children's literature to enhance phonics instruction. *The Reading Teacher, 43*(9), 648–654.

Trieman, R. (1985). Onsets and rimes as units of spoken syllables: Evidence from children. *Journal of Experimental Child Psychology, 39,* 161–181.

Walberg, H. J., & Tsai, S. (1984). Reading achievement and diminishing returns to time. *Journal of Educational Psychology, 76*(3), 442–451.

Wilson, P. T., Anderson, R. C., & Fielding, L. G. (1986). Children's book-reading habits: A new criterion for literacy. *Book Research Quarterly, 2*(3), 72–84.

Wylie, R. E., & Durrell, D. D. (1970). Teaching vowels through phonograms. *Elementary English, 47,* 787–791.

Zutell, J., & Rasinski, T. (1991). Training teachers to attend to their students' oral reading fluency. *Theory Into Practice, 30,* 3, 211–217.

Assessing and Teaching Older Readers

Teaching Students Beyond the Primary Grades*

Chapter Outline

*With Samuel Mathews II and Josephine Peyton Young

Fermina Sanchez is principal of an urban middle school, where the students run the gamut from recent immigrants from Central America to middle-to lower-middle-class families, to working-class families and families on public assistance who have been hit hard by the loss of industrial jobs in the community. There is increased pressure from new state reading tests at the middle school level, and over half of the students are not meeting grade-level standards for reading. The teachers in her school are committed to their students, and they are looking for the best ways they can help them. They are grateful to Fermina for campaigning to the district for more funds for their school. In the past decade, the district had made a large push to help younger students get off to a good start in reading, and the larger share of the district's funding for reading programs had gone into that effort. The effort had done some good—more of the students coming into the middle school are better prepared in reading. But the majority of them still don't read well enough, and the teachers have the feeling that time may be running out for those whose needs are most severe.

Fermina is working with a committee of her teachers on a bold plan that will make all of the faculty teachers of reading. Those students who need greater levels of help in reading will get it, with some of them having frequent classes intended to teach them what they need to know to become successful readers. This will be an ambitious undertaking since attention must be paid to assessing the students at many points, providing materials at different reading levels, arranging and scheduling small and intense reading classes, training the faculty, and keeping everyone on the same page.

The Reading Issues of Older Students

If you have been teaching in a middle or secondary school in recent years, you may have been wondering why so much of the emphasis on reading has been shifting away from your level and onto children in the early primary grades. There are reasons, of course. First, there is evidence that intensive reading instruction in the early grades may go a long way toward heading off later reading failure. Second, there are early intervention programs like Reading Recovery and Book Buddies that are showing success in helping young at-risk children get off to a better start in reading. And third, the widespread testing required by the No Child Left Behind Act began at third grade and worked upwards, so a great many school districts put their resources where needs were so publicly exposed. But none of this means that students in U.S. middle and secondary schools don't need help in reading. On the contrary: The reading levels of our post-primary students are, if anything, cause for alarm.

Seventy percent of students in grades 4 through 12 do not read proficiently (U.S. Department of Education, 2005). That's 8.7 million students. A fourth of the students in that age group—more than 3 million—lack basic reading skills. Taken separately, nearly half of the African American and Hispanic students lack basic reading ability. The reading problems of students above the primary grades in some ways may be more serious than those of younger students. Younger students outscored most industrialized countries in the world on tests of reading ability, but older students lagged behind most countries in their comparison group (PISA). Moreover, while the reading problems of younger students are centered on word recognition and phonics, problems with word recognition affect only one older student in ten. Older students' problems lie in two other, thornier areas:

- **Older students don't read enough.** A famous study of the amount of reading done by fifth graders (Wilson, Anderson, & Fielding, 1988) showed them reading an average of under 10 minutes per day. The more avid readers managed about an hour, while many students devoted a minute or less to reading. Given that the average child averages more than 2 hours of television watching per day, the scant time spent reading cannot be blamed on a lack of leisure (see Figure 8.1).

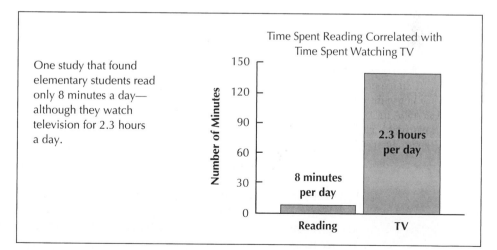

One study that found elementary students read only 8 minutes a day—although they watch television for 2.3 hours a day.

FIGURE 8.1 *Time Spent Reading*

Source: Smith, C., Tracy, E., & Weber, L. (1998). Motivating independent reading: The route to a lifetime of education. Master's Action Research Project, 40–143.

- **Older students don't understand what they read.** The main problem older students have is not understanding what they read. This matters more for older readers than for younger ones because beyond fourth grade so much of what students must learn comes to them through reading. Older students must read many different kinds of text, most of it informational.

Why Should We Be Concerned about Older Students' Reading Ability?

Teachers who worry about older students' reading ability may find themselves in a lonely spot because many, perhaps most, of the students who need help learning to read don't readily admit or even realize that they need help. For example, a very large national survey of adult literacy found that most of the poorest readers nevertheless claimed that they could read adequately. Few of even the poorest readers said they ever asked others to help them read important documents. In the case of older students in school, so many of their peers read poorly it should not be surprising that they won't see reading as cause for concern.

But it should be. Low reading ability not only affects grades in language arts, it limits what students can learn in other school subjects. As soon as students leave school it predisposes them to a host of unpleasant outcomes. Poor readers are far more likely than other teens to become involved with the penal system. Among adults, as we saw in Chapter 1, there is a strong association between reading ability and the likelihood of employment, the kind of job a person gets, a person's income, and a person's participation in civil society (U.S. Department of Education, 1992).

Responding to the Needs of Readers Beyond the Primary Grades

In a recent report for the Carnegie Corporation entitled "Reading Next," Snow and Biancarosa (2004) recommend several strategies to improve adolescent literacy. Those that were directed to the classroom include these:

1. **Direct, explicit comprehension instruction,** which is instruction in the strategies and processes that proficient readers use to understand what they read, including summarizing, keeping track of one's own understanding, and a host of other practices
2. **Effective instructional principles embedded in content,** including language arts teachers using content-area texts and content-area teachers providing instruction and practice in reading and writing skills specific to their subject area

3. **Motivation and self-directed learning,** which includes building motivation to read and learn and providing students with the instruction and supports needed for independent learning tasks they will face after graduation
4. **Text-based collaborative learning,** which involves students interacting with one another around a variety of texts
5. **Strategic tutoring,** which provides students with intense individualized reading, writing, and content instruction as needed
6. **Diverse texts,** which are texts at a variety of difficulty levels and on a variety of topics
7. **Intensive writing,** including instruction connected to the kinds of writing tasks students will have to perform well in high school and beyond
8. **A technology component,** which includes technology as a tool for and a topic of literacy instruction
9. **Ongoing formative assessment of students,** which is informal, often daily assessment of how students are progressing under current instructional practices
10. **Extended time for literacy,** which includes approximately two to four hours of literacy instruction and practice that takes place in language arts and content-area classes (Snow & Biancarosa, 2004)

But which students need what kind of help? Linda Diamond (2006), writing for the American Association of School Administrators, suggests that we think of these older readers in four different categories, for the sake of giving them appropriate help:

- *Advanced learners* are those who are reading at or above grade-level standards (which puts them ahead of most of their peers, you will remember). They may already know much of the content of their courses and often appear bored in classes. The challenge for teachers of these students will be to provide them with enrichment opportunities within the regular curriculum or to organize advanced classes for them where possible.
- *Benchmark learners* are average learners who can meet learning standards, especially if they are given encouragement and suggestions for organizing themselves for learning. They should have their learning progress assessed at least three times per year, and they should have frequent instruction in strategy instruction and vocabulary. They should also be encouraged to write.
- *Strategic learners* are those who fall below the norm, testing between the 30th and 49th percentile. These students are taught in regular classes, but they do not perform well without regular help. They have difficulty learning from their textbooks, so there are significant gaps in their knowledge that may impair further learning. For example, because they may not know which countries are in Europe, or when the Civil War and the World Wars occurred or who the combatants were, they may have trouble following class discussions or reading assignments in social studies. These students may be pulled out into a resource room or special reading class for part of the year and given intensive instruction in reading comprehension and

vocabulary. Their learning should be assessed monthly to make sure that the reading interventions are yielding progress.

- *Intensive intervention* students are those who need intensive intervention and typically test below the 30th percentile on reading measures, show low performance in their courses, regularly fail to turn in homework, and may miss a fair amount of school. They might best be served in special reading classes instead of their English classes. Like special intervention classes for younger students, such as Reading Recovery, these reading classes should be considered short-term fixes: not warehouses for failed students, but intensive experiences and tailored support to equip them to cope with the reading demands of the regular curriculum.

A Range of Responses to Older Students' Reading Needs

Most troubled readers beyond the primary years need to improve their comprehension and vocabulary (Snow & Biancarosa, 2004), and these abilities can be developed and supported in the subject areas (particularly English language arts, social studies, science, and health). The students who have greater reading needs, though, will need more focused help to develop skills of comprehension and vocabulary, and even word recognition. In the following sections, we will begin with a section that suggests strategies that nearly all teachers can use to support older students' reading. Then will come a section of more focused strategies that teachers can use with those students who need intensive reading support.

Reading Strategies for Use across the Curriculum

Instruction that supports students' understanding is instruction that (a) connects with students' prior knowledge and encourages them to ask questions and set purposes for learning, (b) guides their inquiry and helps them make sense of the materials under study, and (c) helps them reflect on what they have learned and consider its implications, interpret it, debate it, apply it, and extend it. These three phases of learning were called the ABC model in Chapter 7. *ABC* stands for *anticipation, building knowledge,* and *consolidation* (Crawford, Saul, Mathews, & MaKinster, 2005).

Anticipation

Learning begins when students get curious about a topic, when they activate their prior knowledge of the topic and prepare to make sense of the contents of the lesson. Thus in the first "anticipation" phase of a lesson, teachers give enticing previews of a topic, ask students what they already know about the topic, and encourage them to raise questions about the topic and set purposes for reading. They may preview the important vocabulary items in the text that students might not know. They hope that by awakening the students' curiosity, their thoughts, and their questions, the students will be prepared to enter the next stage, *building knowledge*, with alert and active minds.

Building Knowledge

Once their curiosity is tweaked, their questions have been raised, and their purposes are set, students select from a number of ways to explore the topic—or, in psychological terms, to assimilate the new information to their old knowledge structures. These many ways of making meaning include the comprehension strategies of visualizing, detecting the structure of the text and using following it to guide understanding, finding main ideas, understanding the meanings of words from the context of the passage, making inferences, and predicting what will come next.

Consolidation

In the *consolidation phase*, students look back over what they have made sense of, consider what they knew about the topic at the outset and what they know now, think about the implications of what they have found out, and reassess their assumptions about the topic in light of what they have just learned. Again, in psychological terms, students are now asked to go back and reassess or update their knowledge structures (ideas, beliefs, and attitudes) to accommodate their old ways of thinking to the new insights they have gained. In the consolidation phase of learning, students use strategies of making interpretations, responding to literature, applying ideas from the text to new situations, and debating what has been presented.

Teachers of all subjects can support students' reading with understanding if they will approach reading, and especially reading comprehension, using strategies drawn from each of the phases of the ABC model.

Strategies for the Anticipation Phase

Activities in the anticipation phase of a lesson are meant to summon up the students' prior knowledge about a topic, arouse their curiosity, and lead them to set purposes for their further studies. Strategies to accomplish these purposes are *advance organizers*, *anticipation guides*, *brainstorming*, *terms in advance*, *think/pair/share*, *free writing*, and *semantic maps*. In addition, the *know/want to know/learn* strategy begins in this phase.

The amount of emphasis given to the anticipation phase can vary according to the students' needs. For example, if the lesson treats an area in which the students are likely to have many misconceptions, the teacher may invest more time in the anticipation portion of the lesson to tease out those misconceptions so that students can correct them.

Advance Organizers

The educational psychologist David Ausubel (1970, 1978) developed the idea of the *advance organizer*, with the thought that beginning a lesson with a brief explanation of a topic to give students "the lay of the land" could help them make better sense of the information that was coming. So, for example, before having students read a passage about Marco Polo, the teacher talks briefly about the geography of Europe and Asia and the state of transportation in the late Middle Ages. The talk would give some context for the students' understanding of the passage on Marco Polo.

The Anticipation Guide

An *anticipation guide* (Vacca & Vacca, 1989) is another activity that activates students' prior knowledge and stimulates predictions about the text. An anticipation guide is a set of statements about the text that students respond to and discuss before the reading of the text. The teacher's role is to create the anticipation guide, accept a broad range of student responses, and facilitate discussion before reading. After reading the text, the teacher should lead students to contrast their own predictions with the author's stated meaning. Vacca and Vacca (1989, p. 145) provide guidelines for constructing and using anticipation guides:

1. Analyze the material to be read. Determine the major ideas—implicit and explicit—with which students will interact.
2. Write those ideas in short, clear, declarative statements. These statements should in some way reflect the world that the students live in or know about. Therefore, avoid abstractions whenever possible.
3. Put these statements into a format that will elicit anticipation and prediction making.
4. Discuss readers' predictions and anticipations before reading the text selection.
5. Assign the text selection. Have students evaluate the statements in light of the author's intent and purpose.
6. Contrast readers' predictions with author's intended meaning. A sample anticipation guide appears in Figure 8.2.

Once they have read the text, students return to their anticipation guides and compare what they know now with what they originally thought.

Group Brainstorming

The teacher sets out a topic and asks the class to *brainstorm*, that is, to think of everything that comes to mind about a topic in a fixed period of time—say, 5 minutes. The teacher lists these ideas on the board. The teacher might help the students to arrange their ideas into categories to elicit better coverage of the topic. In the case of Marco Polo, for example, the categories might be "Who?" (Who was Marco Polo? Who else is involved in his story?), "What?" (What did he do?), "Why?" (Why did he do what he

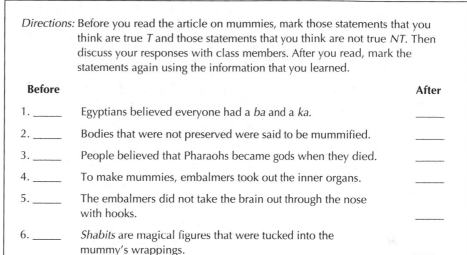

Directions: Before you read the article on mummies, mark those statements that you think are true *T* and those statements that you think are not true *NT*. Then discuss your responses with class members. After you read, mark the statements again using the information that you learned.

Before   **After**

1. _____   Egyptians believed everyone had a *ba* and a *ka*.   _____

2. _____   Bodies that were not preserved were said to be mummified.   _____

3. _____   People believed that Pharaohs became gods when they died.   _____

4. _____   To make mummies, embalmers took out the inner organs.   _____

5. _____   The embalmers did not take the brain out through the nose
           with hooks.   _____

6. _____   *Shabits* are magical figures that were tucked into the
           mummy's wrappings.   _____

7. _____   Everyone who died in ancient Egypt became mummies.   _____

FIGURE 8.2   *Anticipation Guide: Mummies in Egypt*

did?), and "So what?" (What was important about his accomplishments? Why is he remembered?).

Then the teacher has the students read a text (or listen to a lecture or watch a video) and see which of their ideas were borne out by the material they encountered.

Paired Brainstorming

This activity is similar to the one above, except that pairs of students list on a sheet of paper the facts and ideas that they know or think they know about a topic. They may also set questions to be answered in a reading. Teachers set a time limit for this activity—usually 5 minutes or less. Again, it might help if the teacher has them arrange their ideas into categories.

Terms in Advance

In advance of a lesson, the teacher might choose four or five key terms from a text and write them on the board. Pairs of students are given 5 minutes to brainstorm how those terms might be related, how they will be related—in a historical chronology, in the explanation of a scientific process, or in a work of fiction—in the text they are about to read. Once the pairs have agreed on a set of relationships among the terms, the teacher asks them to consider the text carefully to see how those same terms played out in the text. After they have read the text, the teacher will ask them to review their original answers and ask how similar they were to what the text actually said.

Think/Pair/Share

Think/Pair/Share (Slavin, 1996) is an engaging strategy that can be used at any point in a lesson in which we want students to think about issues. To use a Think/Pair/Share in the anticipation phase of a lesson, the teacher thinks of a discussion question that bears on the topic and that can be talked about briefly. The question might take the form of asking students to list what they know about a topic, recount a personal experience that has bearing on a topic, or reflect on a philosophical issue that has bearing on a topic.

During a period of 4 or 5 minutes, the teacher puts that question to the class and asks each student to prepare an answer. Then the student shares that answer with a partner and listens carefully to the partner's answer. Then the two of them may next prepare a joint answer. The teacher calls on three or four pairs to give a 30-second summary of their discussions.

The Think/Pair/Share strategy can be used at any point in a lesson, of course, and not only during the anticipation phase.

Free Writing

We can invite students to write down in 5 minutes, without stopping, everything that comes to mind when they think about a topic about which they are about to read (Elbow, 1989). When the 5 minutes are up (and it's advisable to call time after 5 minutes and give the students one more minute to finish up, as good ideas often come out under pressure), we might ask the students to read their papers aloud to partners.

At this point, many options are available. We can invite pairs to share ideas with the whole group, as in the group brainstorming, or we might ask the students to underline the ideas in their paper that they are least sure about and pay close attention to the reading to learn whether it sheds light on their areas of uncertainty.

Free writing also can be used at any point in a lesson and not only during the anticipation phase. It makes a useful activity in the middle of a lesson to summarize responses to what has been learned so far and to predict what might come ahead. It can also be used at the end of a lesson as a way of reflecting back on what was learned.

Semantic Map

Semantic maps or *clusters* are ways of previewing ideas that students already hold about a topic, so that they can identify gaps in their knowledge and identify questions they want to have answered through the reading. Semantic maps can also be used to introduce new vocabulary that students will need to understand the reading.

As was shown in Chapter 7, the teacher guides the students in making a semantic map by writing the name of the topic in the center of the chalkboard and then inviting students to say what they know about the topic. As the students suggest ideas, the teacher adds them to the chart by making satellites around the original topic. The teacher can organize the students' ideas into logical categories and then ask the students what other information they can offer to fill out a category. See Figure 7.9 on page 248 for an example.

Know/Want to Know/Learn

The *K-W-L strategy* (Ogle, 1986) asks students *what they already know* about a topic and what they *want to know*. Then the students read a text or otherwise investigate the topic, and later report on *what they learned*. As you can see, the first two parts of the K-W-L strategy take place in the anticipation phase of a lesson. The K-W-L strategy can be combined with other strategies described in this chapter. For example, students might first brainstorm ideas about a topic and share their ideas with a partner or create a semantic map of their prior knowledge, before offering their ideas to be added in a K-W-L activity. See Chapter 7 for more information about the K-W-L strategy.

Strategies for the Building Knowledge Phase

Once students have summoned up their prior knowledge, examined what they were sure of and not so sure of, raised questions, and set purposes for learning, they are ready for the building knowledge phase of learning. Depending on the students' needs and the purposes of the lesson, more or less time may be devoted to the building knowledge phase of a lesson. If the reading material is especially dense or if the students will be expected to understand the material to the point of mastery, more time may be devoted to this phase of a lesson.

The I.N.S.E.R.T. Model

I.N.S.E.R.T. (Vaughn & Estes, 1986) stands for *Instructional Note-taking System for Enhanced Reading and Thinking*. The device is used in two parts. Only the first is relevant to the building knowledge phase of a lesson. Here, students are given a system for marking the text as they pursue different kinds of information in it:

- ✓ A check mark (✓) indicates a statement that confirms an idea they already knew.
- – A minus sign (–) marks a passage that contradicts something they thought they knew.
- + A plus sign (+) marks a passage of interesting information that they had not anticipated.
- ? A question mark (?) goes next to a passage that they would like to know more about.

As students read the assigned text, they place the appropriate mark in the margin next to relevant passages.

Since the categories of information that students will be marking in the text relate back to what they knew or thought they knew about the topic of the text, the I.N.S.E.R.T. system works best when preceded by an anticipation activity that asks students to summon up their prior knowledge about the topic. Brainstorming or paired brainstorming works well for this purpose.

Text Coding

There are other ways to mark particular elements in texts in addition to the I.N.S.E.R.T. method. The teacher can ask the students to read to find a set of aspects of the text that will guide their comprehension. For example, if the text explains a procedure, ask them to write lightly with a pencil a "P" beside the procedure being described, and number 1, 2, 3, and so on for the steps of the procedure. They can mark with a "C" any cautions that are given.

If they are reading a text that contains

- *a sequence of events,* they can identify and number the events.
- *a persuasive argument,* they can mark the claim, the reasons that support the claim, and the evidence that supports each reason.
- *a descriptive paragraph,* they can mark the details that appeal to each of the senses.
- *a story,* they can make a mark next to the characters, the setting, the problem, the attempts at a solution, and the conclusion.
- *a poem,* they can make a mark next to the images, the metaphors and similes, the symbols, the repetitions, and the examples of onomatopoeia.

Study Guides

Study guides help to guide students' processes of inquiry even when the teacher is not present, as when students are reading an assigned reading independently. The students are expected to think about the study guide questions as they read the whole piece and write down their answers either as they read or after they read. Later, their answers to the questions can frame a whole-class or small-group discussion about the topic of the text.

For the purposes of promoting critical thinking, study guides work best when they do the following:

1. Help students to follow intricate patterns of thought or subtle ideas that they probably would not have reached on their own, but do not serve as a substitute for a careful reading of the text.
2. Invite critical or higher order thinking at every step.
3. Are used as a springboard to discussion or writing, and not as an end in themselves.

1. In what ways have humans adapted corn to our own uses?

2. How long have humans been manipulating corn plants for their own purposes?

3. Some people claim that it is unnatural, and therefore wrong, for people to "tinker" with nature. Using what you know about corn, construct an argument that agrees or disagrees with that position.

FIGURE 8.3   *Three-Level Study Guide: "Corn: What Good Is It?"*

Figure 8.3 shows an example of a three-level study guide. To guide their investigation, students are given this guide to consider before reading a lengthy passage about corn. Answers to the first two questions are woven through many parts of the assigned text. The third question asks readers to engage in higher-order thinking about the insights they were guided to assemble in the first two questions.

The questions that are asked on a three-level study guide such as the one in Figure 8.3 ask questions of this form (Vaughn & Estes, 1986):

1. What did the author say?
2. What did the author mean?
3. What can we do with the meaning?

In preparing a study guide, the teacher often proceeds in reverse order. That is, we decide what the most important use of the meaning in the reading is, and we formulate a question or questions about it. Then we decide which concepts or insights a student would have to have reached to get the main benefit from the article. Then we decide what facts the students would have to have noticed to derive those concepts or insights. Then we present the questions the right way around.

Study guides may take other forms, too. Pattern guides are specially constructed to call students' attention to the ways different genres of text organize information. An example of a chronological pattern guide is given in Figure 8.4. Other pattern guides will be considered later in this chapter when we discuss patterns of text organization.

Dual-Entry Diaries

Dual-entry diaries (Berthoff, 1981) are ways for readers to closely link material in the text to their own curiosity and their own experiences. They are especially useful when students are reading longer assignments, out of class.

To make a dual-entry diary, the students should draw a vertical line down the middle of a blank sheet of paper. On the left-hand side, they should note a part of the text that struck them strongly. Perhaps it reminded them of something from their own

A. Fill in the blanks with an event or events that happened in Burton in each time period:

Before A.D. 800	After A.D. 870	Tenth Century	Eleventh Century	Seventeenth Century
_____	_____	_____	_____	_____
_____	_____	_____	_____	_____
_____	_____	_____	_____	_____

B. Fill in the blanks with a brief description of what the town of Burton might have looked like in each period.

Before A.D. 800	After A.D. 870	Tenth Century	Eleventh Century	Seventeenth Century
_____	_____	_____	_____	_____
_____	_____	_____	_____	_____
_____	_____	_____	_____	_____

FIGURE 8.4   *A Chronological Pattern Guide for "Burton"*

experience. Perhaps it puzzled them. Or perhaps they disagreed with it. On the right-hand side of the page, they should write a comment about it: What was it about the quote that made them write it down? What did it make them think of? What question did they have about it? As they read the text, they should pause and make entries in their dual-entry diaries. Some teachers assign a minimum number of dual-entry diary entries: so many entries for every ten pages read, for example.

As we shall see, reviewing the students' entries to their dual-entry diaries later in class can structure a whole-class discussion.

Cooperative Learning: Jigsaw II

Jigsaw II is a popular cooperative learning technique developed by Robert Slavin et al. (1992).

The teacher should go through the text in advance and prepare four different expert sheets, which are sets of questions that relate to the most important points in the reading passage that will be assigned. (One suggestion for an expert sheet would be a study guide, such as the one discussed above.)

The lesson should proceed as follows:

1. **Set the Stage**. Explain that the class will be doing a cooperative learning activity called Jigsaw II. Announce the topic of the lesson and explain that everyone will be responsible for learning all parts of the text, but each person will become an expert on one part of the text and will teach others about it.

2. **Assign Students to Home Groups**. Assign students to home groups of four or five members.

3. **Read the Text**. Distribute copies of the text to all students. Also distribute to each student in a home group a different expert sheet. If there are more than four people in a home group, distribute copies of more expert sheets, so that not more than two people have the same expert sheet.

The expert sheet has questions to guide that person's reading of the text. The expert sheets differ because later, each person will be responsible for helping the others in the home group to learn about the aspects of the reading covered by his expert sheet.

Allow an adequate amount of time for everyone to read the passage. Everyone should read the whole text but should pay special attention to the material that answers the questions on his expert sheet. If people finish early, they should take notes on portions of the text that pertain to the questions on their expert sheet.

4. **Study the Text in Expert Groups**. Set up four tables or clusters of chairs to seat four expert groups. If there should be more than six students in any one expert group, divide that group into two groups. Appoint a discussion leader for each expert group. Spend a few minutes going over the rules of participation:

   a. "Everybody participates. Nobody dominates."
   b. "The group agrees on what the question means, or what the task is, before answering."
   c. "When you are not clear about something that is said, restate it in your own words."
   d. "Everybody sticks to the task at hand."

Explain that the expert groups will have 20 minutes to discuss their questions and answers to them. They should already have located answers to the questions in the text, and they should take notes on answers their group offers to the questions. Also, they should decide how they are going to teach their material to their home groups. The teacher should circulate among the expert groups to help them stay on task.

5. **"Experts" Teach the Text to Home Groups**. When the study period is up, have the students leave the study groups and return to their home groups. Now each student should take about 5 minutes to present to the home group what she learned in the expert group. The "expert's" task is not just to report, however, but to ask and entertain questions from the group, to make sure everyone learned her piece of the text.

6. **Evaluate the Process**. Ask each person to write about what he contributed to the discussion and what could make the activity go better.

Strategies for the Consolidation Phase

Many of the strategies that are followed during the anticipation and building knowledge phases are designed to culminate during the consolidation phase. Here are several that do.

The Discussion Web

An active discussion can cover a lot of ground, and it's not unusual for students to remember only the last things said or the ideas that were put forth most forcefully. Graphic organizers might help with this problem. *Graphic organizers*, written aids to capture and display the results of students' thinking, are useful at all stages of a discussion. They can help to frame a question, record and keep preliminary thoughts available for review, and communicate the group's findings to others.

One particularly useful graphic organizer, the *discussion web*, was published by Donna Alvermann (1991). The discussion web is used to organize a five-step lesson, arranged around any text or topic that invites controversy (the taking of two different points of view):

1. The teacher prepares the students to read the selection by setting up the appropriate exploratory activity, that is, by giving them whatever background knowledge, vocabulary, or predictive questions they are likely to need.

2. After the students have read the selection and perhaps have had an opportunity to share their personal responses to it with a partner or in a small group, the teacher assigns the students to pairs and asks each pair to prepare a discussion web like the one shown in Figure 8.5. The teacher should point out that the students will be asked to take sides on a question that is specific to the text. After reading the first half of Phyllis Reynolds Naylor's *Shiloh*, for instance, students might be asked, "Should Marty have lied to his family to save Shiloh?"

The discussion web has two columns, marked "Yes" and "No," and the pairs are asked to think of as many good reasons pro and con as they can—reasons why Marty was justified in lying and reasons why he was not. The students should try to list an equal number of reasons in each column.

3. After a few minutes, each pair is asked to join another pair and pool their reasons, pro and con. After they have considered all of the reasons, the foursomes are asked to reach a consensus agreement on an answer. They should write that answer at the bottom of the web in the space marked "Conclusion," and also write the best supporting arguments. The teacher should remind them that individuals may dissent from the consensus, but they should try to keep an open mind.

4. When each foursome has arrived at a consensus, the teacher gives each of them 3 minutes to share their conclusion with the class and to discuss which of their reasons best supports their finding.

"Should Marty have lied to his family to save Shiloh?"

                                         YES   NO

_____   _____

_____   _____

_____   _____

_____   _____

            Conclusion:

                    _____

                    _____

                    _____

FIGURE 8.5   *Discussion Web for Shiloh*

5. The teacher concludes the activity by asking students to write their own answers to the question, taking into account the other arguments they have heard. The teacher posts these answers on a bulletin board so that students can read what others have written.

The discussion web may stand on its own. It may also be used as a springboard for writing (have the students write a short essay in which they take and defend a side of the argument) or as the warm-up to a debate (have the class divide between those who are pro and con, with "undecideds" in the middle). In both these cases, it is preferable to stop the discussion web activity before step 3—that it, leave it to the individuals to reach their conclusions either in writing or by means of the debate.

Academic Controversy

Academic controversy (Kagan, 1992) is another cooperative learning activity that follows a pattern similar to that of the discussion web. But unlike the discussion web, students are responsible for finding reasons to support only one side of an argument at a time. This is easier for some students, in our experience, than listing arguments for both sides during the same step. Also, the procedure includes an explicit invitation for students to step out of their roles and argue what they really believe—an opportunity that most students enjoy. The activity proceeds as follows:

1. The teacher assigns a reading, preferably one that raises an issue that invites diverse responses.

2. The teacher prepares at least one issue for discussion, stated in a form that is likely to elicit at least two justifiable positions from students (for example, "Was Jack justified in stealing from the giant?").

3. Students are assigned to groups of four.

4. Within the groups, pairs of students are assigned a position on the issue that they must defend.

5. The pairs list reasons that support their position.

6. The pairs temporarily split up and form new pairs with classmates who are defending the same positions. They share the reasons each of the original pairs listed in support of the position.

7. Students return to their original partners and set out a position statement followed by supporting reasons: "We want to argue for _____ because of X, Y, and Z."

8. Each pair presents its argument to the other pair within their group while the latter pair listens and takes notes.

9. The two pairs then debate.

10. Optionally, the pairs within each group may now be told to switch positions and repeat steps 4 through 8.

11. Finally, the students stop defending any point of view and construct the position on which they can find consensus, supported by the best reasons that came to light in the previous discussion.

Helping Older Students Write

Comprehending and composing are reciprocal activities: two sides of the same coin. As students write—as they practice formulating main ideas and setting them forth on paper with the support of details, in a structure that includes an introduction, a body, and a conclusion—they are working with just those aspects of a text that are used in understanding a text when it is read. Moreover, writing enables students to capture their ideas on paper so they can return to them, reflect on them, and pursue their insights to more depth. In these and other ways, writing develops students' ability to understand written language.

Ten-Minute Essays and Other Free Writes

Following a reading or a class discussion, students can be helped to collected their thoughts if they are asked to write a ten-minute essay, using the *free write technique*. To set up a *ten-minute essay*, the teacher asks students to write without stopping on the topic of the reading and discussion.

Some writing teachers insist that the act of writing itself can open up wells of creativity in the mind that are unlike the more deliberate sort of thinking that we do when we plan what we are going to write (Elbow, 1989). Thus, in producing a free write, students write continuously without stopping. If they can't think of anything to write, they write, "I can't think of anything to write." The point is to keep the writing coming out without going back over it, examining it, or being critical of it.

Many teachers occasionally follow free writes with the invitation to go back through the free write, choose the most promising ideas, and craft a new essay, using these insights as the core of the paper—and eliminating all of the other chaff that usually comes out in a free write.

The Five-Minute Essay

The *five-minute essay* is used at the end of class to help students to get closure on their thoughts about the topic of study and to give teachers a better connection to the intellectual happenings of the class. The five-minute essay asks students to do two things: Write one thing you have learned about the topic, and write one question you still have about the topic.

The teacher collects these essays as soon as they are written and might use them to plan the next day's lesson.

Three-Part Diaries

Students need to interact with the material, and interact with the teacher regarding the material, if their inquiry is to be powered by personal curiosity, yet also have the benefits of a wise guide. For that reason, teachers use the *three-part diary*.

The diary is used throughout a whole course, and it is useful for shaping and recording a student's inquiry from day to day, as an aid to study, as a means of linking the student's learning in the course to her life outside of class, and as a means to frame longer written compositions. The three sections of the diary have different functions. The first section is used for the student to write her responses to the readings and discussions. A dual-entry diary format (see the discussion earlier in the chapter) is often used for this section; the student divides each page down the middle with a vertical line and writes notations on one side and comments on the other.

The second section is left for the student's own thoughts and associations about the topic. The student is encouraged to record thoughts that occur to him and notes from informal readings and other conversations—in short, any information and insights that further the student's understanding and appreciation of the topic of study. The material in this section will be used to inspire the writing of formal papers later on, but it will take some work by the teacher to make this happen. The teacher keeps her own three-part diary and, from time to time, reads to the class from the notes entered in this middle section. "Thinking aloud," the teacher demonstrates how she finds recurring patterns of interest or ideas strong enough to inspire further inquiry. The teacher then encourages students to do the same with this section of their diaries, meeting individually with students when there is time and encouraging students to interview each other about their entries in this section. The goal, again, is to find the thread of an inquiry, a recurring pattern of curiosity, an insight that is trying to be born.

The third part of the diary is reserved for letters to the teacher. Every month, at least, the students are asked to write the teacher a letter in which they comment on the class and their work in it, raise questions they have had, express hopes for their learning, and describe their own experience of learning in that course: What were their thoughts in the beginning? What goals do they have for themselves? How have they experienced growth in learning? What impediments are they facing? What would help?

The teacher collects the diaries (on a staggered schedule) every month and responds in writing to each student's letters.

The I-Search Paper

One popular kind of research project that highlights the process of research and stresses students' personal connection to the topic is the *I-Search paper*, developed by Ken Maccrorie (1988). The I-Search paper is developed in six stages:

1. *The students formulate questions about a topic.* After they have been immersed in a topic, the students are helped to search their knowledge and curiosity and formulate a researchable question.
2. *The students make a research plan.* The plan might incorporate several kinds of sources, including not only books and magazines, but also interviews, surveys, and Internet-based searches.

    The plan might include a graphic organizer such as the one shown in Figure 8.6.
3. *The students gather and record information.* Students should be given instruction in all of the ways they may do the research: ways of finding resources in the library, procedures for arranging and conducting interviews, and standards for discriminating between different sources on the Internet. They should also be taught note taking and outlining skills, as necessary. They may be taught to use graphic organizers as a way of visualizing their information before writing it up.
4. *The students write their papers.* Papers should be formatted according to the outline given below.

	Source #1	Source #2	Source #3	Source #4
Question #1				
Question #2				
Question #3				
Question #4				

FIGURE 8.6 *A Graphic Organizer for Sources of Information*

5. *The students present their papers.* The students submit the written papers and may also give oral presentations or poster sessions on the papers.
6. *Papers are evaluated.* Paper evaluations are conducted according to criteria that are tied to the process and form of the papers, and that are communicated to the students in advance—usually by means of a rubric.

The I-Search paper is organized in five sections: *questions*, the *search process*, *what was learned*, *lessons for the writer*, and *references*.

Questions.   In this section, students describe what they already knew about this question when they began their search, what associations they had for the topic, in what context the topic arose, and why they cared about their question.

The Search Process.   In this section, students describe the sequence of steps in the search for answers to their question. For example, students describe what sources they began with and how these led to further sources. They can recount problems they encountered and breakthroughs in their search. They can describe their personal experience and say when they became more interested in the topic, when they were disappointed, and what made them decide to focus the inquiry in a particular way. They can tell how their questions changed or expanded as a result of the search process. They should also acknowledge any help they received from others as they pursued answers to their questions.

What Was Learned.   Here students present on the main findings of their research. They should support the findings with examples, stories, tables of data, or arguments that will help the reader understand how they arrived at those conclusions. They should include any analyses they carried out that led to their conclusions: For example, they can list effects and their causes, arguments for and against a proposition, comparisons of phenomena, or sequences of steps. They should connect their findings with their original questions. They might also suggest questions they may want to explore in the future.

Lessons for the Writer.   This section gives students a chance to describe how they have developed as researchers. They should answer the question, "What do you now know about searching for information that you didn't know before?" To answer this question, students should describe those findings that meant the most to them. They might also discuss how their newly found knowledge will affect the way they act or think in the future. Finally, they might want to talk about the skills they have developed as researchers and writers.

References.   This section contains all of their references, following whatever format (APA, MLA, or Chicago) was assigned in advance.

The I-Search procedure can be done by small teams of two or three students or by individuals. The topic can vary between those that require students to go to written sources (such as the Kosovo War) and those that require them to do more direct observation and interviewing (such as what advice people over 70 have for young people's character development). Either way, the format and procedures of I-Search make it an engaging and enjoyable exercise for writers—and also a natural impediment to plagiarizing. Because the papers are highly personal, it won't work for students simply to download material from the Internet and pass it off as their own.

Providing Close Support for Students' Reading Development

Earlier in this chapter we suggested that as teachers decide how to provide help to older readers, they divide the student population into *advanced readers*, *benchmark readers*, *strategic readers*, and *readers needing intensive support*. In the case of the first two groups of reading, instruction that will help them grow as readers can be provided in the context of the regular subjects—not just English language arts, but also social studies, science, health, and so on. It is the last two groups of readers—strategic readers and those needing intensive support—who concern us here. Both groups need focused instruction in reading and writing. The difference is that strategic readers can make do with a couple of periods of instruction each week for short durations—perhaps a semester each year—whereas learners needing intensive instruction may require daily focused instruction on reading and writing, normally for most of the school year or for several years.

Organizing Focused Strategic and Intensive Instruction

The principle behind *focused instruction* is that it be just that: intensive and focused teaching that gives students what they need to be able to read successfully and to cope with the academic demands of the school curriculum. Such instruction should incorporate the following features. The plan of instruction should

- Be based on detailed information about the student's reading ability.
- Provide help to the student in demonstrated areas of need.
- Work in materials at each student's instructional and independent reading levels.
- Follow a consistent plan of activities over which the student can gain some control.
- Provide a variety of activities to maintain the student's interest.
- Provide emotional support and motivation for learning.
- Be supported by close and ongoing monitoring of the student's learning.

Assessing Readers for Focused Instruction

A *screening assessment* is normally done at the beginning of the school year or at the end of the previous one. Screening assessments for older students may be standardized tests, administered to many students at once. If a group-administered test is used, though, caution is advised in interpreting the results, as older low-performing readers are not reliable test takers. In any case, scores on screening tests are usually complemented by a teacher's recommendation, based on observation of the student's work in class.

Once a student has been identified for special help by the screening assessment, there is still a need for *diagnostic assessment* of the student's specific reading abilities. A diagnostic procedure such as an Informal Reading Inventory will be able to bring to light the student's

- Independent, instructional, and frustration reading levels.
- Strengths in word recognition.
- Reading fluency.
- Comprehension ability, including her relative strengths in getting main ideas, making inferences, and inferring vocabulary from context.
- Listening capacity, as compared to his reading comprehension.

All of this is information that a teacher will need to plan instruction for the student. However, even an Informal Reading Inventory, however well administered, is never a perfect predictor of how a particular student will respond to instruction, so during the first several lessons the teacher should be "roaming around the known," as Marie Clay (2000) puts it—that is, teaching experimentally and observing closely to see how the student responds to different kinds of reading tasks.

Once instruction has begun in earnest, the teacher will periodically perform *monitoring assessments* to see how the student is progressing and what instructional procedures seem to be working. In one sense, monitoring assessment occurs almost constantly, especially if a teacher keeps observational notes on how the lessons go and records the levels of texts the student is reading. Nonetheless, it is recommended that a more formal stock taking be done once each month, and more often for the more disabled readers. These monitoring assessments might consist of a careful reading of an extended passage of text written at a known reading level, in which the teacher

- Records the percentage of words read correctly (word recognition in context).
- Invites the student to retell the passage or asks comprehension questions to measure comprehension.
- Measures the student's fluency and reading rate.
- Asks the student what is working and what is not.

Planning Lessons for Disabled Readers

Students differ in the amount of time they are able to pay attention to learning tasks. It is a safe bet, however, that a disabled reader's attention span will be short rather than long. Besides, there is usually a menu of abilities these students will need to develop. So a teacher should plan a typical 50-minute lesson to include three to five different activities. The plan might proceed as follows:

1. **Focused lesson**. Here the teacher introduces a strategy that can be used to read better. Of course, there are many points that can be taught in a focused lesson, but some likely ones are these:

- *Previewing a text*: How to examine the title, any illustrations, headings, and the first paragraphs of a text to decide what it is about, to think about what we already know about it, and to raise questions and set purposes for reading
- *Searching for answers*: Once questions have been set, how to read and look for answers to them
- *Summarizing what has been said*: After a section has been read, saying in a few sentences the main ideas in what the text said
- *Perceiving and following patterns*: Perceiving the way the text is organized and predicting how the information will be presented based on that organization
- *Visualizing details*: As the text uses words to describe something, calling up in "the mind's eye" the images that the words evoke
- *Understanding vocabulary*: Using the context to approximate the meanings of unfamiliar words
- *Making predications*: Having read the first sections in the text, predicting what will come next
- *Noting important points for later studying*: Paying attention to main ideas, noting them down, and rehearsing them for later recall

A focused lesson may take no more than 10 to 15 minutes. The strategy used in the focused lesson can be *thinking aloud, visualizing, questioning the author,* or using a *graphic organizer,* all of which are explained elsewhere in this chapter. The teacher makes sure that the student is aware of the strategy and is able to articulate the steps in applying it.

2. **Guided practice.** Following the focused lesson, the student is asked to read a text and practice the strategy that was introduced in the focused lesson. The student may be asked to *think aloud,* or use the *ReQuest procedure,* or *reading and questioning,* or *reciprocal teaching,* or *repeated reading,* or *reader's theater* for fluency, all of which are described in Chapter 7 or later in this chapter. Guided practice may be done in moderately challenging reading material, text written at the student's instructional level.

3. **Independent reading.** The student should read some interesting text at his independent level. The reading may be supported by *audio books* and may be followed by a discussion. (Several discussion strategies were presented earlier in this chapter.)

4. **Vocabulary.** Poor readers typically have smaller vocabularies than proficient readers, and their limited vocabulary imposes limits on their comprehension—not only of written texts, but also of the information encountered in daily life. Vocabulary lessons should cultivate a respect for words, should share strategies for learning new words, and should teach the "Tier Two words" or "frontier vocabulary": high-utility words that students will frequently encounter.

5. **Writing.** Some writing should be included in nearly every lesson. Tasks for writing can include written responses to the reading, or a learning log in which the student

writes down the most important thing she learned from today's lesson, or one thing she wants to be sure to learn in future lessons. Or the writing task can follow the writing workshop format of *rehearsing, drafting, revising, editing,* and *sharing.*

Teaching Strategies to Build Reading Competence

A daily lesson such as the one outlined above may use activities drawn from those described below.

Thinking Aloud

Imagine learning to be a proficient skier if all you saw were people wiping out on the slopes, or becoming a proficient singer if all you heard were people who couldn't carry a tune or keep the beat. In most domains we seek out skilled models to imitate so that we can develop skills ourselves. That's true of reading, too. Imagine that you wanted to *show* students how to read well. You would demonstrate each step that good readers take as they work through a text. To think aloud, then, the teacher

- Surveys the topic, the title, and the genre and says what he expects to find in a text.
- Comments after reading the beginning of what the argument or the topic or the main problem of the text is.
- Makes predictions of what will come in the text.
- Visualizes what the text describes.
- Confirms or disconfirms the predictions after reading ahead in the text.
- Makes inferences where ideas are implied.
- Clarifies the meanings of rare words that can be explained from context.
- Summarizes from time to time what has been read.
- Suggests implications of what the text says.

The teacher asks the student or students to join in on these activities, following his model.

ReQuest Procedure

When students need support in reading text for information, one way to structure a reading so that they give each other that support is to use the *ReQuest procedure* (Manzo, 1970, 1991). In this procedure, two students read through a text, stop after each paragraph, and take turns asking each other questions about it.

For example, after reading the first paragraph (silently) in an informational text, the teacher asks Juana several good questions about that paragraph. She asks her questions about main ideas. She asks about nuances. She asks what importance some item in this paragraph might come to have later in the text. (She is trying not only to get Juana to think about the text, but also to model for Juana the kinds of questions she might ask when it comes to be her turn.) Juana has to answer those questions as well as she can. After Juana has finished answering the teacher's questions, it is her turn to ask the teacher questions about the same paragraph, and the teacher has to answer them. When Juana and the teacher have both brought to light the important information of that paragraph, they read the next one. After that paragraph is read, Juana now gets the first turn at asking the teacher all the good questions she can think of about that paragraph. When she is finished, the teacher gets to ask her questions. When both are finished, they read the next paragraph, and so on.

After the teacher has introduced the activity by being a questioning partner, the teacher sets up pairs of students to read and ask questions of each other.

Visualizing

Good readers form pictures in their "mind's eye" of what is described in the text. You can help students visualize settings and events in a text by first modeling visualizing by means of a think-aloud. Then you can guide students through the process by evoking images that appeal to each of their senses.

For example, the teacher reads aloud the following text:

> Along the north coast of Scotland, the winter wind howls through dark nights and gray days, and towering seas smash against black rocks. But in summer, the sea calms, and the days grow long, until the daylight lasts through 24 hours. Then the few fishermen who live on that remote coast row their nets out into the sea, to catch their livelihood. Even in summer, a sudden storm may overtake them; or a silent fog may creep upon them and make them lose their way. Then their loved ones go down to the shore and gaze for some sign at the mute waves, perhaps to see a seal stare back with big sad eyes. The people see the seals, and they wonder . . .

The teacher says, "The first words make me hear the wind howling and shrieking. It must really wear down the people to hear it all night and all day. I can picture the fisherman's door banging in the wind when he tries to close it behind him, and see his hand reaching out of the cottage to pull it shut. I see the fisherman's wife bent low in the fierce wind as she picks her way along the rocky ground toward the cottage. I imagine that she feels hard bits of cold rain hurled by the wind."

Then the teacher points out to the students how she has used the sense of hearing, sight, and feeling to evoke the scene in her mind's eye. Next the teacher instructs the students that she will read them another passage. The passage will be chosen from another text that is at or slightly above the students' reading level. Any vocabulary that is likely to be unfamiliar to the students should be explained to them.

The teacher tells the students to close their eyes and try to picture, hear, and feel what the words suggest to them. They should imagine a movie in their heads as the words are read to them.

Following the reading, the teacher asks individual students to say aloud what they visualized. The teacher specifically praises any visualizations that seem accurate and asks a student to rethink any that seem off the mark—rereading the relevant parts of the text to guide the student in adjusting the visualization.

Reading and Questioning

Reading and questioning (Temple, 2003) is a procedure that is aimed at helping students learn from an informative text. The procedure helps students read carefully and study materials with a partner (working together can be more motivating than working alone). The method is suitable for any content subject where the information from a text is to be understood and remembered. In terms of grouping, reading and questioning will work with an unlimited number of pairs. Each pair will need at least one text between them. The activity may take half an hour to complete. Often it is done by students independently, outside of class time.

Here is how it is done. The students take turns reading an assigned text in sections. The first student reads a section aloud, from one heading to the next heading. Then both students decide on key terms to write in the margin of the text. Both students make up several questions about the text, using the terms from the margins. The questions should resemble test questions the students think might appear on an examination covering the material. They write the questions on index cards or sticky notes. The students take turns answering each question. If both students agree with the answer, they write the answer to the question on the other side of the index card. They continue to trade roles until the assigned text is read.

In the days after the activity using the cards or slips of paper with the questions and answers on them, the students continue to quiz each other on the assigned material.

Reading and questioning can be done by the whole class, with students divided into pairs. If so, the first time you do the reading and questioning procedure, it is advisable to stop the class after the students have finished reading and questioning the first section of the text. Then review their terms, questions, and answers, and suggest corrections as necessary. Thereafter, you should circulate among the students and listen to their questions and answers. Also, before the students study from their questions and answers, it is a good idea for you to review the questions and answers to make sure they are adequate and accurate.

Reading and questioning can also be done with a tutor or can be recommended for students to use either by themselves or in pairs outside of class.

Audio Books

Many popular books for older children, young adults, and mature readers are available in audio book versions. Public libraries stock several, and, increasingly, school libraries do, too. Older students can listen to an audio book as they read the printed version. Hearing the book read aloud can open up for young readers the pleasures of literature, pleasures that have been denied to them since the earlier school years when teachers more commonly read aloud to students. Listening to books read aloud can also build vocabulary and familiarity with written language. After listening to an audio book, students can participate in many of the discussion activities described earlier in this chapter.

Introducing and Focusing Attention on New Vocabulary

Research suggests that students who are not proficient readers usually have smaller vocabularies than students who read: perhaps only half as many words on average. That matters because larger vocabularies make it easier to notice things and to learn about new things. The total number of words students encounter in their school books through ninth grade is enormous: 88,500 words, according to one careful estimate (Nagy & Anderson, 1984). That potentially works out to 10,000 words to be learned each year, or 50 words each school day, if the whole sum of words had to be taught from first grade through ninth. But Beck and her associates (2002) have reminded us that we don't have to teach all of these words in a reading class. She suggests we think of the total vocabulary in three tiers:

> *Tier I* words are the everyday words students already know that don't need to be taught: *mother, house, football,* etc.
>
> *Tier III* words are specialized terms that are learned in the context of science, math, and social studies classes: *bicameral, monozygotic, hypotenuse,* etc.
>
> *Tier II* words are those in between: They are useful words that are found in many contexts but that are probably not yet part of students' vocabularies. Tier II words—what some call "frontier vocabulary"—are the words we usually focus on in reading classes.

The following activities are useful for teaching vocabulary, particularly Tier II words.

Word Conversations

Research shows that the greater part of our vocabulary comes from written texts. Beck and colleagues (2002) developed the *word conversations* technique for teachers to use to help students learn new words from reading. The teacher conducts a rich discussion of words that follows six steps:

1. In a text that is to be read, locate up to 5 new words that are worth learning—"frontier vocabulary" (see above). Contextualize those words, one at a time, within a text that is being read. For example, from the poem "As Best She Could," one word is *furtive*. Teacher reads the word in its context: "Old widow crazed with hunger, you came in crippled / your back country eyes bright and *furtive*."

2. The teacher asks the student to repeat the word, both to call their attention to it and to create a memory trace, a phonological representation of it.
3. The teacher explains the meaning of the word in a student-friendly way: "*Furtive* means looking as if you don't trust anybody and don't want to call attention to yourself."
4. Now the teacher provides examples of the word in other contexts: "The thief gave a *furtive* glance at the rich lady's jewels," or, "Before they jumped the guard, the two prisoners gave each other a *furtive* signal."
5. Next the teacher asks the students to provide their own examples of uses of the words: "Tell me a time you have made a *furtive* look at someone or given a *furtive* sign."
6. Finally, the teacher asks the students to repeat the word they have been discussing to reinforce its phonological representation.

To use the word conversations technique effectively, teachers need to

- Choose texts that contain useful new words in meaningful contexts.
- Choose the words in advance of the lesson and think carefully about their meanings, about the different contexts in which they are used, and about a straightforward "student-friendly" way to define them.
- Plan questions to relate the words to the students' own experience.
- Make note of the words that they have introduced, so the students can be reminded to use them in their writing and will know their meanings when they encounter them in print.

The Frayer Model

The Frayer model is a graphic organizer for relating a word for a concept to other words (Buel, 2001). The Frayer model directs students to think of essential and nonessential characteristics of a concept, as well as examples and nonexamples of it. The model is best used to name a common concept that has many characteristics and examples. That way, students get to consider a larger number of words in context (see Figure 8.7).

Motivational and Emotional Issues of Adolescent Students with Reading Problems

By the time children reach adolescence, their teachers and peers expect them to be able to read and write independently. If adolescents lack the ability to read at grade level, they risk falling behind their literate peers academically. This often leads to other problems with social relationships and can ultimately result in severe behavior problems and finally school dropouts.

Working with adolescent students who are well behind their age group in reading, the tasks of the teacher often go well beyond instruction in comprehension, vocabulary,

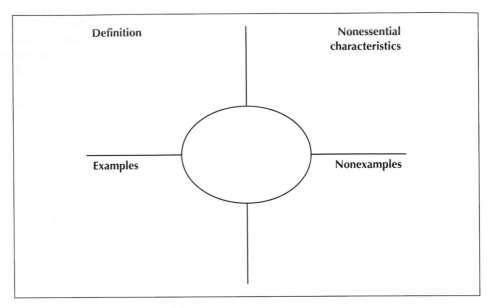

FIGURE 8.7 *The Frayer Model*

word attack, writing, and other skills associated with literacy. The first step is often simply rebuilding their trust in the educational system.

This section addresses ways of meeting the needs of adolescent students who have reading problems. In it we present the principles and theories that guide our decision making about assessment and instructional procedures.

Guiding Principles and Theories

Our approach is based on five principles:

1. Establishing trust
2. Providing literate role models
3. Reducing the feelings of learned helplessness or passive failure
4. Legitimizing personal knowledge and experiences
5. Developing a learning environment

Establishing Trust

The keystone for success with adolescent students with reading problems is the establishment of trust between the student and teacher. Without trust, students do not view the teacher, or anyone in authority, as a credible source of information. Erikson (1963) proposed that as early as infancy, individuals begin to develop trust or mistrust in others. This early trust is based on having general survival needs met.

The family is perhaps the earliest influence—positive or negative—on trust. The trust that is established during infancy can be enhanced or diminished as people grow and have experiences outside the family. Their initial experiences with schooling also can enhance or diminish trust.

Many adolescent students with reading problems have a basic mistrust of authority, whether from family or school experiences. Without this trust, the outlook for subsequent positive social and academic development is poor (Erikson, 1963). However, trust can be established between adolescents with reading problems and their teachers. With this trust, teachers have a solid base on which to address the problems of literacy for adolescents. Trust will foster risk taking in the adolescents' writing and reading efforts.

Providing Literate Role Models

One reason children fail to develop the ability or motivation to read by the time they reach adolescence is the lack of literate role models in their lives. When we think back over our own academic histories, we often find that there were very few occasions on which we observed teachers reading silently. If adolescents have no literate role models in their homes and have had few opportunities to observe teachers or peers reading silently, there is little reason to expect that reading will be a normal part of their lives.

To address the lack of role models for literacy, the classroom environment must be one in which reading and writing are pursued for pleasure as much as for formal school tasks. Children and adolescents model behavior they observe in trusted adults and peers (Bandura, 1986). This modeling extends beyond fashion and social behavior to the areas of reading and literacy in general.

Reducing the Feelings of Learned Helplessness or Passive Failure

Adolescents who meet with repeated failure due to the lack of literacy skills often resist the most well-intentioned attempts at assessment or instruction. At the extreme, this results in learned helplessness. *Learned helplessness* is a sense that no matter what one does, nothing will help. We see this in adolescents with reading problems when they honestly believe that no amount of effort will bring about escape from a cycle of failure. They see all their attempts at success as leading to failure. Harter (1992) proposed that children and adolescents who feel as though they have little or no control over their successes or failures in school often attempt to evade tasks that might result in failure. These young people tend to make excuses for their failures based on either an external or an internal failure. Some students will blame the test or the teacher for failure. This kind of helplessness provides some protection against an additional example of personal inadequacy and reflects the view that forces outside the students control their fates. Other students will sit quietly and whisper, "I knew I was going to fail, I'm just too dumb." This kind of helplessness represents a sense that internal forces are limiting the students' performances. Perhaps the most depressing combination of the reasoning behind success and failure in school is for students to attribute failure to the lack of ability (internal inadequacy) and success to the fact that the test was "so easy anyone could pass it" or "I was just lucky" (external control).

Johnston and Winograd (1985) used the phrase *passive failure* to describe the way in which students who have feelings of learned helplessness view the reading process. They suggest that readers who exhibit passive failure are not aware of the relationship between effort and success, attribute success in reading tasks to luck or simplicity of task, attribute failure to the lack of ability, and generally fail to persist in difficult tasks. Adolescents who are experiencing passive failure are not moved by simple cheerleader-type statements, such as "You can do it, all you have to do is try." They have heard that statement, they have tried, and they have failed.

One way in which learned helplessness and passive failure can be overcome is through modeling. Over time, modeling by a trusted and respected individual can be a strong motivation. If adolescents observe a trusted individual (e.g., a peer, a volunteer, or a teacher) modeling literate behavior and successfully reading a book or tackling a difficult writing assignment, they are more likely to attempt tasks involving literacy. When these attempts are used as building blocks instead of measuring sticks, the adolescents begin to overcome passive failure and learned helplessness. Some of the building blocks include

- Being able to read a printed version of a short dictated story.
- Coming to class.
- Opening a book or magazine.
- Asking for help reading a personal letter.
- Listening to a story that is read to the class and asking questions.
- Attempting to write.

Some of these might appear insignificant. However, the goal is to recapture the adolescent as a learner and overcome passive failure.

Legitimizing Personal Knowledge and Experiences

Classrooms today are much more culturally diverse than those of a decade ago. This trend will increase in the future as more students come to school with greater cultural and social differences. These differences are also seen between students and their teachers. This diversity can lead to the selection of inappropriate materials, inappropriate topics, and the misinterpretation of word meanings.

Adolescents with reading problems reflect this broad diversity of cultural and personal experiences and knowledge. Reading and writing instruction are particularly suited to the use of students' cultural and personal experiences to enhance instruction. A teacher can create opportunities for students to use their personal knowledge and experiences through self-selection of topics for writing, reading, and class discussion, thus legitimizing personal knowledge and experiences.

In summary, adolescents with reading problems learn best in an instructional environment in which

- A trusting relationship exists between the teacher and students.
- Literacy is modeled.
- Learned helplessness and the experience of passive failure are replaced by a willingness to try and opportunities for success.
- Personal knowledge and experiences are valued and used.

These guiding principles lead us to an environment in which a variety of print material is available. It is structured to allow teachers and other literate participants to model reading and writing. When possible, students select their own writing topics, reading materials, and classroom talks. Within these tasks, there are ample opportunities for legitimate successes in which efforts are related to outcomes. Finally, the students and teacher develop a trusting relationship through a freedom to express feelings, ideas, and opinions in a nonevaluative atmosphere.

Developing a Learning Environment

Davidson and Koppenhaver (1988) suggest that programs that have been successful in fostering literacy among adolescents

1. Spend a high proportion of time on reading and writing.
2. Teach skills in context.
3. Stress silent reading.
4. Teach strategies for reading comprehension.
5. Build on background information and experience.
6. Integrate speaking and listening with reading and writing.
7. Focus on writing.
8. Use modeling as a teaching technique.
9. Use involvement or experience-based curriculum approaches that foster conceptual development.
10. Facilitate discussions rather than lead them.
11. Give students access to a wide variety of materials.
12. Use varied groupings and value collaborative learning. (pp. 184–189)

The methods by which each characteristic is realized and the specific strategies that are taught should be based on students' needs, interests, and abilities. Teachers typically can seize the teachable moment and create instructional lessons that are based on legitimate tasks such as preparing for drivers' license examinations, writing birthday cards for friends, or completing job applications.

Discussions of topics that are currently on the minds of adolescents also provide the basis for many literacy lessons in these classrooms. For example, child abuse, drug addiction, and teen pregnancy can be key topics for many readings, class discussions, and written and dictated compositions. In this way, the classroom provides an opportunity not only for fostering literacy, but also for addressing pressing social issues in the lives of adolescents. Within such a classroom, a variety of approaches can be implemented to address the complex needs of adolescent students with reading problems.

Summary

Older readers—those beyond the primary grades—need our attention, too. Even though much of the current emphasis in reading improvement has been placed on early intervention to help young children avoid reading failure and learn along with their peers, there is plenty of evidence that older readers need attention, too. As many as 70 percent of them read below grade level, according to national studies. Indeed, as the testing mandated by the No Child Left Behind legislation works its way up through the grades, the reading problems of older students will surely become even more apparent.

In this chapter we distinguish between readers who are reading above and at or near grade-level expectations, and those who fall below those expectations. For all of them we recommend teaching procedures that can be imbedded in the teaching of all subjects. Several procedures for providing such instruction are shared in this chapter. But for the lower-achieving students, such instruction is helpful, but not sufficient. They need focused instruction in reading that will give them the skills they need to cope with academic challenges. This instruction should be based on careful assessment of the students' reading-related strengths and weaknesses. In this chapter, we argue that such instruction be focused and, to the extent possible, short term. Several teaching procedures, as well as a set of general principles for assessment and instruction, are shared in this chapter.

As children grow beyond the primary grades, those who experience difficulty learning to read almost invariably suffer the emotional consequences from not succeeding at a skill that is so centrally valued by schools. These consequences include embarrassment, anger, withdrawal, and what psychologists call *learned helplessness*. This chapter closes by exploring ways teachers can reach through students' emotional and motivational difficulties and help them learn to read.

(mylabschool *Where the classroom comes to life!*

MyLabSchool is a collection of online tools for your success in this course, your licensure exams, and your teaching career. Visit www.mylabschool.com to access the following:

- Online Study Guide
- Video cases from real classrooms
- Help with your research papers using Research Navigator
- Career Center with resources for:
  - Praxis exams and licensure preparation
  - Professional portfolio development
  - Job search and interview techniques
  - Lesson planning

References

Alvermann, D. (1991). The discussion web: A graphic organizer for learning across the curriculum. *The Reading Teacher, 45*(2), 92–99.

Ausubel, D. P. (1970, March). *The use of ideational organizers in science teaching* (Occasional Paper 3). Columbus, OH: ERIC Information Analysis Center for Science Education.

Ausubel, D. P. (1978). In defense of advance organizers: A reply to the critics. *Review of Educational Research, 48*(2), 251–257.

Bandura, A. (1986). *Social foundations of thought and action.* Englewood Cliffs, NJ: Prentice-Hall.

Beck, I., McKeown, M.,& Kucan, L. (2002). *Bringing words to life.* New York: Guilford.

Berthoff, A. (1981). *The making of meaning: Metaphors, models, and maxims for writing teachers.* Portsmouth, NH: Boynton/Cook.

Davidson, J., & Koppenhaver. D. (1988). *Adolescent literacy: What works and why.* New York: Garland.

Dillon, J. T. (1986). The remedial status of student questioning. *Journal of Curriculum Studies, 20*(3), 197–210.

Elbow, P. (1989). Toward a phenomenology of freewriting. *Journal of Basic Writing, 8*(2), 42–71.

Erikson, E. H. (1963). *Childhood and society.* New York: Norton.

Estes, T. H., & Shibilski, W. (1980). Comprehension: Of what the reader sees of what the author says. In M. Kamil & A. J. Moe (Eds.), *Perspectives on reading research and instruction.* Washington, DC: National Reading Conference.

Harter, S. (1992). The relationship between perceived competence, affect, and motivational orientation within the classroom: Process and patterns of change. In A. K. Boggiano & T. S. Pittman (Eds.), *Achievement and motivation: A social-developmental perspective.* New York: Cambridge University Press.

Kagan, S. (1992). *Cooperative learning.* San Juan Capistrano, CA: Kagan Cooperative Learning.

Manzo, A. V. (1970). Reading and questioning: The ReQuest procedure. *Reading Improvement, 7*(3), 80–83.

Manzo, A. V. (1991). Training teachers to use content area reading strategies: Description and appraisal of four options. *Reading Research and Instruction, 30*(4), 67–74.

Marshall, N., & Glock, M. (1978–1979). Comprehension of connected discourse: A study into the relationships between the structure of text and information recalled. *Reading Research Quarterly, 14,* 110–156.

National Center for Educational Statistics. (1992). *National Adult Literacy Survey.* Washington, D.C.: U.S. Department of Education.

Reutzel, D. R. (1985). Story maps improve comprehension. *The Reading Teacher, 38*(4), 400–404.

Slavin, R. (1996). Cooperative learning in middle and secondary schools. *Clearing House, 69*(4), 200–204.

Slavin, R., et al. (1992). Putting research to work: Cooperative learning. *Instructor, 102*(2), 46–47.

Steele, J., Meredith, K., & Temple, C. (1997). *A framework for critical thinking across the curriculum.* Washington, DC: The Reading & Writing for Critical Thinking Project.

Vacca, R., & Vacca, J. (1989). *Content area reading* (3rd ed.). Glenview, IL: Scott, Foresman.

Vaughn, J., & Estes, T. (1986). *Reading and reasoning beyond the primary grades.* Boston: Allyn & Bacon.

Wisconsin Department of Public Instruction. (1989). *Strategic learning in the content area.* Madison: Author.

Strategies for Teaching Reading and Writing to English Language Learners

Chapter Outline

*T*his chapter addresses the special needs and challenges of the significant number of children in our schools whose mother tongue or home language is not English. Their difficulties are most often not so much with reading and writing as with reading and writing in their second language: English. These children have been variously referred to as bilingual, migrant, immigrant, language minority, ESL, limited English-proficient, *and* non-English speaking students, *among many other terms. They are now referred to as* English language learners. *We tend to focus on the weaknesses of these students, rather than the many strengths they bring to reading and writing. As Miramontes (1990) points out, identifying, using, and valuing "the things students can do can help teachers purposefully engage students in bringing those abilities to bear on meaningful academic tasks." We are reminded by Goodman (1986) that bilingual children are not disadvantaged in some academic way. They are disadvantaged only if we do not appreciate their linguistic strengths and if our schools fail to build on their strengths.*

The audience for the chapter is composed of three groups: (1) bilingual teachers who teach reading and writing in a language other than English; (2) teachers of English language learners whose mother tongue instruction is conducted by paraprofessionals or other staff members under the teacher's supervision; and (3) all teachers of English language learners who teach English as a second language and/or reading in English.

Maricarmen Olivares is a sixth-grade bilingual teacher in a large urban school district. She is concerned about one of her students, 12-year-old Manuel Mora, who has been evaluated by a school psychologist. Maricarmen has administered an Informal Reading Inventory in English, but there is much about these assessments that puzzles Maricarmen. Manuel's WISC score indicates a markedly below-normal ability level. His accuracy scores on the IRI are very low, but his comprehension scores indicate that he is able to understand what he reads on the fifth-grade level in English. None the less, his instructional level is on the third-grade level because of his low accuracy scores. He mispronounces many words. He is on grade level in mathematics and excels in science, especially when he can participate in Spanish.

Maricarmen decides that Manuel's limited proficiency in English is hampering his progress in some areas of the curriculum. She asks the school psychologist to administer an intelligence test that isn't based on language. The school psychologist then administers the Leiter International Performance Scale-Revised, a non-verbal intelligence test. Manuel didn't have to understand English to perform on the test, and the school psychologist didn't have to use English or any other language to administer the test. The results indicate that Manuel's ability level is above average, as Maricarmen suspected.

She then administers another informal inventory, this one in Spanish. Manuel's instructional level on this one is seventh grade, his frustration level is eighth grade, and his independent level is fifth grade. Clearly, his ability to read in his mother tongue is excellent. The problem is with his English.

But Maricarmen wonders how Manuel's instructional level in English is so low when he seems to understand what he reads in English. She listens to her tape of his English oral reading accuracy once again and discovers that she had been penalizing him for mispronunciations in English because of his heavy Spanish accent. When she stops counting those mispronunciation errors, his instructional level in English increases to fifth-grade level.

Maricarmen then realizes that Manuel is a very capable student who brings many strengths in his cognitive abilities and his reading to the process of learning to read in his new second language. His oral reading mispronunciation errors aren't interfering at all with his English reading comprehension. She moves him to a more advanced group where he performs very well in English, but still with an accent.

The Context of Teaching English Language Learners to Read and Write

English Language Learners: Who Are They?

The 2000 U.S. Census reveals a significant and growing diversity in U.S. classrooms almost everywhere. One of the most striking aspects of this change is the number of children classified as *English language learners,* children who arrive in our classrooms with little or no English or insufficient English for learning to read and write in English. When we think of English language learners, we tend to think of Latino children, and indeed, they make up the largest category of English language learners. We usually think first of California, Texas, Florida, and New York as the states most impacted by the presence of Spanish-speaking English language learners. But schools in almost every region of the country are now experiencing major influxes of Spanish-speaking English language learners.

According to the 2000 Census, the Latino population of the United States has nearly doubled since the 1990 Census, rising from 9 to 12.5 percent of the total population (Campo-Flores, 2001; U.S. Bureau of the Census, 2000). Some of the largest percentage increases have occurred in surprising areas of the country, from 10.4 to 19.7 percent in Nevada, from 1.2 to 4.7 percent in North Carolina, from 1.2 to 2.8 percent in Iowa, and from 6.5 to 9.4 percent in Connecticut. The meatpacking and processing industry has attracted many Spanish-speaking workers and their families to such states as Alabama, Arkansas, the Carolinas, Georgia, Iowa, Kentucky, Minnesota, Nebraska, and Tennessee, accounting for major changes there.

The most dramatic trend in the growth of Latino populations in the 2000 Census, however, has been the rapid dissemination to smaller population centers and suburbs (Suro & Singer, 2002). Almost one-half of Latino population growth was in fast-growing Latino hubs and new Latino destinations; the other half was in established metropolitan areas.

The National Clearinghouse for English Language Acquisition and Language Instruction Educational Programs (NCELA, 2006) reports that there are almost 10 million children who don't speak English at home, and about half of those don't have sufficient English language proficiency to succeed in English in our schools.

The English language learners in our schools are not a monolithic population. Some are very proficient in speaking and understanding their mother tongue, and some are literate in that language. Some became literate in their home countries and others in programs of bilingual education here in the United States. As a result of living in refugee camps or in similar conditions, some upper elementary and adolescent children have arrived in this country with little or no school experience or literacy skills at all. Some English language learners are rural or migrant children without educational opportunities, and others are working and contributing to the family income. And some English language learners also have limited proficiency in their mother tongue, just as some children who speak only English are limited in their English proficiency. Some, like Manuel Mora in our opening vignette, are doing very well in English, but they need special attention in the assessment process. As we consider the situation of these many categories of English language learners, then, we must think in terms of many solutions.

What Do We Know about the Context of Learning and of Learning in a Second Language?

Several major principles guide our understanding of providing the best context for learning and for learning in a second language. Cummins (1986, 1989) contrasts two levels of language proficiency that underline the need for high-level proficiency in the second language before academic instruction is provided in the second language. *Basic interpersonal communication skills* (BICS) are those that permit English language learners to carry on a simple conversation in the new second language, and they appear to be proficient. But a higher level of proficiency, *cognitive-academic language proficiency* (CALP), is required for the student to learn to read in the second language or, for example, to learn the distributive principle of multiplication in mathematics. Cummins maintains that there is a threshold of language proficiency in the mother tongue that must be reached for the student to attain academic proficiency in the mother tongue and a second language.

Cummins's (1986, 1989) related linguistic interdependence principle indicates that what students learn in two languages is interdependent. It forms a *common underlying proficiency* (CUP) (Cummins, 1981) that provides the basis for positive transfer of skills. Children have knowledge and skills that they have learned in the mother tongue, and they can use them in the second language. They do not have to learn this knowledge or these skills again. In fact, it is axiomatic that children learn to read only once. They can transfer reading and writing skills to their new second language, just as we do as adults when we study a foreign language. Cummins indicates that CUP explains why children who have attended school in their country (and language) of origin tend to demonstrate higher achievement in English later than children who lack that experience.

Lambert (1975) contrasts *additive* and *subtractive bilingual education programs.* In the former, children add a new language and culture, with mother tongue and its accompanying culture, along with a positive self-image. In a subtractive program, English and its accompanying culture are substituted, often leading to low self-esteem, leaving school, low academic achievement, and other negative consequences.

These principles lead us to a counterintuitive but inescapable conclusion that success in English language proficiency is closely related to students' learning of reading, writing, and academic concepts in the mother tongue (Collier, 1989; J. Crawford, 1989; Cummins, 1989; Hudelson, 1987; Krashen, 1985; Krashen & Biber, 1988; Ramírez, 1991).

In their major meta-analysis of scientifically based research, *Preventing Reading Difficulties in Young Children,* Snow, Burns, and Griffin (1998) recognized the importance of teaching children to read in the mother tongue, wherever possible, before teaching them to read in English. They recommended, for children who arrived at school with no English but where a mother tongue literacy program could be provided, that "these children should be taught how to read in their native language while acquiring oral proficiency in English and subsequently taught to extend their skills to reading in English" (p. 325). When a program could not be offered in a language, the first instructional priority should be to develop children's oral proficiency in English, with English reading instruction delayed until a satisfactory level of English language oral proficiency was achieved.

Thomas and Collier (2002) conducted a major five-year developmental study that also provides strong evidence for this point of view. Many mother tongues were represented in their study of over 210,000 students in five school districts in Texas, Oregon, and Maine, but most subjects were Spanish-speaking. They concluded that enrichment one-way or dual language bilingual education programs that were 90–10 percent or 50–50 percent (the percentage of mother tongue instruction) were the only programs in which students reached the 50th percentile in both languages; they also had the fewest dropouts. Children whose parents rejected bilingual education programs, insisting instead on English only, had much lower achievement. The amount of formal mother tongue instruction was the strongest predictor of English language achievement in the study. They found that the highest achievement in bilingual education programs was associated with those that provided a natural learning environment in school, with rich oral and written language in both mother tongue and English, problem solving, group student activities, media-rich learning, challenging thematic units, and use of the students' bilingual-bicultural knowledge to access new knowledge.

The National Literacy Panel on Language-Minority Children and Youth (*Developing Literacy in Second-Language Learners,* 2006) published a major meta-analysis of studies about the language and literacy development of language-minority students in 2006. Its conclusions paralleled those of the National Reading Panel (2000). First, the panel concluded that phonemic awareness, phonics, fluency, vocabulary, and text comprehension instruction were major factors in the development of literacy. Second, it found that language-minority children were able to keep pace with their English-speaking classmates in the development of word recognition skills. They fell behind in comprehension and writing, however, which was attributed to the lower level of English language proficiency among these students. Third, the panel concluded that children's oral proficiency and reading ability in the mother tongue can be used to facilitate the development of literacy in English as a result of the positive transfer of skills, a finding similar to that of Snow et al. in *Preventing Reading Difficulties* (1998). Fourth, it concluded that there is a hierarchy of skills in English that must be attained before children can be successful in reading comprehension in English and that individual differences among children are a significant factor in this development. It further concluded that for language-minority children in special education programs, developing sight-word reading and holistic learning strategies might be more effective in teaching them to read and write. Finally, the panel concluded that most assessment tools used with language-minority children are not effective in measuring students' individual strengths and weaknesses. It also found little evidence of the effect of sociocultural variables on the development of literacy, except for the positive effect of home language experiences.

The Legal Status of Programs to Serve English Language Learners

The most sweeping policy change to affect the education of English language learners in recent years was the 1974 *Lau v. Nichols* decision of the U.S. Supreme Court, which ruled that equal education did not result from providing exactly the same education to all children (J. Crawford, 1989; *Lau v. Nichols,* 1974). The decision of the Court required that school districts take positive steps to overcome the educational barriers experienced by students who did not speak English. Soon after, the Elementary and Secondary Education Act (ESEA) was amended to include Title VII, which made limited English proficient students eligible for federal funds and permitted their enrollment in bilingual education programs.

A subsequent court decision (*Casteñeda v. Pickard,* 1981) established three criteria for determining how programs of bilingual education were to be held accountable for meeting requirements of the Equal Educational Opportunity Act of 1974:

- The program must be based on sound educational theory.
- The program must be effectively implemented with adequate resources for personnel, instructional materials, and space.
- After a trial period, the program must be shown to be effective in overcoming language handicaps.

The 1998 Unz English Initiative, Proposition 227 in California, and a similar measure in Arizona, now discourage most bilingual education in those states. Instead, both require a one-year period of immersion instruction in English as a second language, although the efficacy of this approach is not supported in the literature. In fact, there is substantial evidence that children need several years of instruction in English as a second language before they are ready to learn to read in English (Thomas & Collier, 2002). In an analysis of test scores from the 2002 California Stanford 9 test scores reported by the influential League of United Latin American Citizens (LULAC) (O'Leary, 2002), it was reported that English language learners in California were not developing English fluency and that many were falling further behind in academic subjects. O'Leary reported that, four years after the passage of Proposition 227, more than a million limited English immigrant students in grades 2 through 11 in California still had not been mainstreamed in English-only classes, indicating the failure of the policies implemented under the law.

Under provisions of the No Child Left Behind Act of 2002, ESEA Title VII, which formerly funded programs of instruction for bilingual children, was rescinded (García, 2005). The new law, Title III, continues to provide resources for English language learners. Annual assessments of English language proficiency are required, as are mandates that these children meet state academic content and student achievement standards in English (Office of English Language Acquisition, 2004). The term *bilingual* does not appear in the new law, which now stresses skills in English only. There is no federal interest in the development of academic bilingual education programs for these children.

Bilingual Education: One Solution

Although the *Lau v. Nichols* decision did not mandate bilingual education as a remedy, school districts soon found that it was one of the few ways to ensure that English language learners had equal access to education, that is, education in their mother tongue while they learned English. Most programs have taken the transitional form, in which children learn to read and write and also study the other subjects of the academic curriculum, mathematics, social science, science in the mother tongue. Simultaneously, the children study English as a second language, a process that typically takes two to five years or more. Through a transition process called *positive transfer of skills,* children can then do in English what they learned to do in the mother tongue. Even learning to read in English as a second language is a relatively smooth and effortless process—we learn to read only once. When children do not have the opportunity to learn academic subjects in the mother tongue, they fall behind in those subjects during the period of time they are learning English.

Children in transitional bilingual programs usually continue their academic studies only in English after the onset of transition to English, although they typically receive continuing support in the mother tongue, as needed. More infrequently, children are placed in maintenance bilingual education programs and continue to receive instruction in the mother tongue even after transition, the goal being to be a bilingual, biliterate, and bicultural individual at the end. Because of the lack of instructional materials in the mother tongue and often a lack of trained bilingual teachers in many languages, non-Spanish-language bilingual education programs are less common and usually limited in scope.

Language Policy Decisions about the Language of Instruction: The Transition Process

A fundamental precept of literacy for children from language-minority populations is that they will learn to read and write more rapidly and more effectively in their mother tongue than in a second language that they learn later. One of the first important and authoritative positions taken on this issue was that of a UNESCO conference (UNESCO, 1953), which concluded that children learn better to read in a new second language if they first learn to read in the mother tongue. This work was corroborated by many investigators in subsequent years.

Saville and Troike (1971) concluded that once a child has learned to read, transferring that ability to another language is not a difficult matter. In an important study, Modiano (1968) found that Mayan children in Mexico who were learning to read learned more rapidly in their mother tongue of Quiché than others who learned to read in their second language of Spanish. Later, they read better in Spanish than those who first learned to read in Spanish. Through succeeding years, the preponderance of evidence indicates that children learn to read most effectively in their second language by first learning to read in their primary language (Cummins, 1986, 1989; Krashen & Biber, 1988; UNESCO, 1953).

English-as-a-second-language instruction is the keystone of programs to meet the academic needs of English learners. It is especially important where only small numbers of children speak the same mother tongue or where a lack of trained personnel and appropriate materials prevents the implementation of programs of bilingual education. It is also the major element of those full bilingual education programs in which we use the mother tongue for academic instruction while children develop sufficient proficiency in the second language to benefit from academic instruction in that language.

The foundation for communicative approaches to second language acquisition is based on concepts, theories, and hypotheses that have converged around the interaction on constructivist notions about making meaning. Vygotsky (1978) described the *zone of proximal development* as the area between the actual developmental level as determined by independent problem solving and the level of potential development as determined through problem solving under adult guidance in collaboration with more capable peers. This key concept emphasizes the social dimension of learning that results from the support of mothers, teachers, older siblings, and other caregivers. The collective wisdom of the cooperative learning group has an obvious role here, as well. The convergence between communicative approaches to second language acquisition and literacy is particularly prominent in the constructivist paradigm.

Language policy is a factor of great importance in literacy for children. Clearly, children will learn to read and write most quickly and most effectively in the mother tongue. Many factors must be taken into consideration, however, before that decision is made (A. N. Crawford, 1995). For example, if children speak a minority language for which there is a well-developed written form, if skilled bilingual teachers are available, and if there are instructional materials in that language, then we can provide instruction in that mother tongue. If this is not the case, then we should consider using the language experience approach described in Chapter 6 and later in this chapter.

If children speak a minority language for which there is not a well-developed written form, such as Hmong, then we must teach the children to speak and understand English and then to read and write in English, probably using the language experience approach. If bilingual teachers are not available, then even the presence of instructional materials will not be sufficient to permit mother tongue instruction. A literate speaker of the minority language might be trained as a paraprofessional to work under the supervision of a fully trained teacher who is not proficient in the mother tongue of the children.

Finally, some families will insist that their children learn to read and write only in English, although they do not speak or understand that language. Some might even believe that using the minority language for literacy is a tool to maintain speakers of that minority language in an inferior social position. In this case, teachers need to demonstrate respect for the mother tongue, and they need to assure the children and their families that they will also have the opportunity to learn to speak, read, and write English. In addition, they need to reinforce the idea that children learn to read and write only once and that learning to read and write in another language that they learn later is a relatively simple transfer process. Finally, they need to reinforce the idea that reading is comprehension, not pronouncing or "reading" sounds. Nonetheless, some families will still insist on English only.

Second Language Acquisition

Whether or not children learn to read and write in their mother tongue, they must learn to speak and understand English. It is difficult to even address literacy for English language learners without considering the close links that must exist between the teaching of reading and writing and the teaching of English as a second language. Because of the nature of the most effective approaches to teaching both, those that are constructivist or whole-part-whole, we know that they complement each other very effectively. In addition, literacy in English is so closely related to learning to speak and understand English that they must be considered together.

At this point, we should also examine the dichotomy between constructivist and reductionist models of instruction. A *constructivist* view of instruction focuses on the construction of meaning, using what the child already knows and combining it with new ideas to be integrated. It is learner-based, an important factor in working with the students from diverse backgrounds who are often at risk in any case. The factor of background knowledge is well recognized as being a key to success in reading and writing, especially in reading comprehension. English learners have no lack of background knowledge, but there is often a discontinuity between the background knowledge they have and that assumed by the texts from which they will learn to read and read to learn. Within the constructivist view, language acquisition is embedded in function. Skills are taught in a meaningful context, not in a systematic, artificial, and fragmented way. *Reductionist* or *skills-based models* conversely focus on the disassembly or fragmentation of curricular elements so that isolated skills and concepts can be mastered within a linear paradigm.

Until recent years, most students have studied a second language, whether English or a foreign language, using such grammar-based approaches as the grammar translation and audiolingual methods. These are reductionist or skills-based approaches that move learners from part to whole.

The results of recent research have changed our conceptions of how a second language is acquired and how this acquisition is best promoted in elementary and secondary classrooms. There has been a major paradigm shift away from these grammar-based approaches to language learning and toward those we call *communicative,* which are also consistent with meaning-based or constructivist approaches to literacy (A. N. Crawford, 1994a).

Underlying Principles of Communicative-Based Approaches

Krashen's Hypotheses.   Krashen (1982a) has offered several important hypotheses that underlie current practice in most communicative approaches to second language acquisition. Among Krashen's most important contributions is his *input hypothesis.* He concludes that growth in language occurs when learners receive comprehensible input, or input that contains structure at a slightly higher level than what they already understand. The input hypothesis corresponds to Vygotsky's (1978) zone of proximal development. The context of the input provides clues to maintain the integrity of the message. According to the input hypothesis, a grammatical sequence is not needed. The structures are provided and practiced as a natural part of the comprehensible input that the child receives, much as it occurs with infants acquiring their mother tongue. Krashen (1981) relates the input hypothesis to the *silent period,* the interval before speech in either the mother tongue or a second language in which the child listens to and develops an understanding of the language before beginning to produce language.

In his *acquisition learning hypothesis,* Krashen illustrates the difference between the infant's subconscious acquisition of the mother tongue and the secondary school French student's conscious learning of a second language. We *acquire* language subconsciously, with a *feel* for correctness. *Learning* a language, on the other hand, is a conscious process that involves knowing grammatical rules. Of course, the infant is almost always successful in acquiring communicative competence, while the secondary school foreign language learner is usually not (A. N. Crawford, 1994a).

Gee (1992) has expanded Krashen's concept of acquisition to incorporate a social factor that reflects Vygotsky's zone of proximal development and also the concept of approximation:

Acquisition is a process of acquiring something subconsciously by exposure to models, a process of trial and error, and practice within social groups, without formal teaching. It happens in natural settings that are meaningful and functional in the sense that acquirers know that they need to acquire the thing they are exposed to in order to function and that they in fact want to so function. (p. 113)

According to Krashen's *natural order hypothesis,* grammatical structures are acquired in a predictable sequence, certain elements usually being acquired before others. He has concluded that the orders for first and second language acquisition are similar, but not identical. It is important to note, however, that Krashen does not conclude that sequencing the teaching of language according to this natural order is either necessary or desirable.

Krashen's related *monitor hypothesis* describes how the child's conscious monitor or editor functions to make corrections as language is produced in speaking or writing. Several conditions are necessary for the application of the monitor: (1) time to apply it, a situation that is not present in most ordinary oral discourse, especially in classroom settings; (2) a focus on the form or correctness of what is said, rather than on the content of the message; and (3) knowledge of the grammatical rule to be applied. These conditions serve to illustrate why so few children or adults learn to understand and speak a foreign language in a grammar translation or audiolingual secondary school or university foreign language course.

In his *affective filter hypothesis,* Krashen concludes that several affective variables are associated with success in second language acquisition. These include high motivation, self-confidence and a positive self-image, and, most important, low anxiety in the learning environment.

Other Basic Principles.   Results from recent research have led to other major changes in educators' conceptions of how a second language is acquired and how this acquisition is best facilitated in the elementary and secondary classroom, one of which is the obvious similarity between primary and second language acquisition. Both include the formation of an incomplete and incorrect interlanguage by both primary and second language learners (Selinker, Swain, & Dumas, 1975), with most children moving through similar stages of development in this incomplete language.

The role of *correction* is also similar in both primary and second language acquisition. *Approximation* is a related process in which children imitate language in all of its dimensions, oral and written, and test hypotheses about it. The process of approximation underlies oral and written language in that children are acquiring new skills and understandings within the context of authentic wholes. Children exhibit behaviors in which they approximate the language behavior of their models, growing closer and closer to their level of proficiency. In his view of successive approximation, Holdaway (1979) describes the process as one in which Vygotsky's (1978) adults and more capable peers use the output from children's responses to construct, adjust, and finally eliminate the scaffolding that facilitates progress in learning. According to Terrell (1982) and Krashen and Terrell (1983), we should therefore view correction as a negative reinforcer that will, at best, raise the affective filter and the level of anxiety in a language classroom, whether with children or adults. When there is no interference with comprehension, we should recognize that the correction of errors has no more place in the second language acquisition program than it does when infants acquire their mother tongue. Caregivers might expand incorrect or incomplete forms, such as *Kitty gots four feet,* and say *Yes, Kitty has four feet.* There is little evidence, however, that this expansion has any positive effect. Errors can be viewed as signs of immaturity, not incorrectness; they will disappear naturally as part of approximation in the development process of language acquisition.

Basic Instructional Strategies for Second Language Acquisition

The implications of Krashen's hypotheses and of related similarities between first and second language acquisition are that approaches to second language acquisition should provide comprehensible input, focus on relevant and interesting topics instead of grammatical sequences, and provide for a silent period without forcing early production. There are approaches to second language acquisition that meet these criteria. They are categorized as *communicative approaches;* the ones that are most appropriate for elementary and secondary classrooms include the *total physical response method* and the *natural approach.*

The Total Physical Response Method.   Asher's (1982) total physical response (TPR) method is an important communicative approach in the initial stages of second language acquisition. The TPR method provides for comprehensible input, a silent period, and a focus on relevant content, rather than on grammatical form. The focus of TPR is on physical responses to verbal commands, such as "Stand up" and "Put your book on the desk." Because little emphasis is given to production, the level of anxiety is low.

Lessons can be given to small groups or to an entire class. In the beginning, the teacher models one-word commands. This is done first with a few children, then with the entire group, then with a few children again, and finally with individual children. The teacher says, for example, "Sit," and then models by sitting down. Later, the teacher issues the command without modeling. As the children's levels of language increase, the teacher begins to use two- and three-word commands, such as "Stand up" and "Bring the book." The children demonstrate their understanding by physically carrying out the commands. The order of commands is varied so that the children cannot anticipate which is next. Old commands are combined with new ones to provide for review. Whenever the children do not appear to comprehend, the teacher returns to modeling. After a silent period of approximately 10 hours of listening to commands and physically responding to them, a child then typically reverses roles with the teacher and begins to give those same commands to other children. It is important for the teacher to maintain a playful mood during classroom activities.

The total physical response approach can be extended to higher levels of proficiency by using the technique of nesting commands. The teacher might say the following:

Jamal, take the book to Svetlana, or close the door.
Noriko, if Jamal took the book to Svetlana, raise your hand.
If he closed the door, stand up.

A high level of proficiency is necessary to carry out such commands, but no oral production is needed. Parents of young children will recognize that their infants can understand and carry out such commands long before they begin to speak themselves.

The Natural Approach. Terrell's (1977) original concept of the natural approach provided for three major characteristics: (a) Classroom activities were focused on acquisition, that is, communication with a content focus leading to an unconscious absorption of language with a feel for correctness, but not an explicit knowledge of grammar; (b) oral errors were not directly corrected; and (c) learners could respond in the target language, their mother tongue, or a mixture of the two.

Krashen and Terrell (1983) later added four principles that underlie the natural approach to language acquisition. The first is that comprehension precedes production, which leads to several teacher behaviors: The teacher always uses the target language, focuses on a topic of interest to the children, and helps the children to maintain comprehension. The second principle is that production emerges in stages ranging from nonverbal responses to complex discourse. Children can begin to speak when they are ready, and speech errors are not corrected unless they interfere with communication. The third principle is that the curriculum consists of communicative goals. Topics of interest make up the syllabus, not a grammatical sequence. Finally, activities must lead to low anxiety, a lowering of children's affective filter, which the teacher accomplishes by establishing and maintaining a good rapport.

Terrell's (1981) natural approach is based on three stages of language development: (1) preproduction (comprehension), (2) early production, and (3) emergence of speech.

The Preproduction Stage. Topical, interesting, and relevant comprehensible input is provided by the teacher in the first stage, which closely parallels Asher's (1982) TPR approach. The teacher speaks slowly, using gestures to maintain comprehension. Children may respond with physical behaviors, shaking or nodding their heads, pointing at pictures or objects, and saying "Yes" or "No." It is important that input is dynamic, lively, fun, and comprehensible. A. N. Crawford (1994a) provides an example in which the teacher uses a pet turtle and says:

> This is a turtle. It is four years old. Is it green? Who wants to hold it? [Hand to child.] Who has the turtle? Does Tran have the turtle? Yes, he does. Does Rosa have the turtle? No, she doesn't.

This basic input can be repeated with other objects in the classroom, such as large-format illustrations and posters (A. N. Crawford, 1994a). Crawford suggests that each child in the group be given a different illustration, and the teacher provides input:

> Who has a picture of an airplane? Yes, Olaf, you do. Is the airplane large? Olaf, give your picture to Zipour. Who has a picture of a boat? Yes, Nicole has a picture of a boat.

Classroom props allow for relevant expansion of this and subsequent stages of the natural approach (A. N. Crawford, 1994a). Any manipulative or concrete object is helpful, including flannel boards and puppets. Large, colorful illustrations, such as those in travel posters and big books, are also very helpful. Sources of free color illustrations include calendars, outdated or otherwise; large posters available from textbook and trade book publishers; and colorful illustrations in the annual reports of many large corporations, usually available on request through announcements in major business magazines.

The Early Production Stage.   In the stage of early production, the child begins to produce one-word utterances, lists, and finally two-word answers, such as "little dog" and "in house." Some of the latter, such as "me like" and "no want," are grammatically incorrect or incomplete. According to A. N. Crawford (1986), we should view these errors as immature, not incorrect. In the presence of good models, these errors will disappear in time, just as they do among infants developing their mother tongue.

Table 9.1 shows several types of questions can be used to elicit the one- and two-word responses within the reach of children as they transition into the early production stage.

As in the preproduction stage, these strategies should be integrated into activities that permit a variety of responses, ranging from physical responses from those who are not ready for production to brief oral responses from those who are. As the children begin production, conversations should increasingly require one-word responses. Within the same conversation, the teacher can address questions calling for longer responses to those children who are ready.

> Kjell, show us your picture. What is in Kjell's picture? [A sandwich.] Yes, it is a sandwich. What is on the sandwich? [Catsup.] Is there apple on the sandwich? [No. Laughter.] What else is on the sandwich? [Meat, mayonnaise.] How does it taste? [Good.] What do you like with a sandwich? [Chips. Soda.] I like milk with mine.

The Emergence of Speech Stage.   During the emergence of speech stage, children begin to produce structures that are longer, more complex, more rich in vocabulary, and more correct. This production proceeds from three-word phrases to sentences, dialogue, extended discourse, and narrative. At this stage, Terrell (1981) recommends such activities as preference ranking, games, group discussions, skits, art and music, radio, TV, film-strips, pictures, readings, and filling out forms. An example of a chart that incorporated preference ranking is provided by A. N. Crawford (2003) in Table 9.2.

TABLE 9.1   *Sample Questions*

Question Type	Question
Yes/no	*Are you hungry?*
	Do you like ice cream?
Here/there	*Where is the picture of the dog?*
Either/or	*Is this a pen or a key?*
One-word	*How many apples are there?*
Two-word	*What animals are in the picture?*

TABLE 9.2 *Preference Ranking*

Name	Favorite Pizzas					
	Cheese	Sausage	Pepperoni	Tomato	Anchovy	Mushroom
Margarita		X		X		X
Sofik		X				
Abdul						
Nguyen	X		X	X		
Petra		X		X		X

Does Sofik like pizza? [Yes.] What kind of meat does Sofik like? [Sausage.] How many like tomato on their pizza? [Three, Margarita, Nguyen, and Petra.] How does Abdul like pizza? [He doesn't like it.] Which children like the same kind of pizza? [Margarita and Petra.] Is there a topping that no one likes? What is it? [Anchovy.] How do we know? [Nobody wants anchovy.]

Not only is the chart a valuable source of comprehensible input, but the process of gathering the data for the chart is, as well. In addition, children begin to read each other's names and the words for popular foods.

The Curriculum of a Communicative Program. According to A. N. Crawford (2003), teachers who would advocate teaching the first-person present indicative tense to a 7-year-old English-speaking child in a primary school classroom would be incredulous at the suggestion that a parent teach the same concept to a 3-year-old at home. Of course, both children can use the tense correctly, neither as the result of instruction. This leads us to conclude, as do Krashen and Terrell (1983) and others, that the content of second language acquisition programs should be based primarily on content, not on grammatical sequence.

Under the assumption that needed language structures will emerge and be acquired naturally within the context of topical lessons, a communicative second language curriculum is usually organized around a set of topics to ensure the introduction of new vocabulary and concepts of interest and utility to the children. Grammatical sequences also appear as a subcategory of some communicative curricula.

Terrell (1981) suggested that the initial content should be limited to following commands for classroom management; names of articles in the classroom; colors and description words for articles in the classroom; words for people and family relationships; descriptions of children, clothing, school areas, and school activities; names of objects in the school that are not in the classroom; and foods, especially those eaten at school. Later, in the acquisition process, topics of interest to children would include the children's families, their homes and neighborhoods, their favorite activities, and pleasant experiences they have had. They also enjoy discussing their preferences about food, colors, television programs and films, and other aspects of their lives.

We begin to see the close link between literacy and the acquisition of second language when, as a part of the natural approach, Terrell (1981) recommended that key words be written on the chalkboard in the second language for older children who are literate in their mother tongue. This corresponds to the key vocabulary to reading approach (Veatch, 1996; Veatch et al., 1979) described later in the chapter. In the early production stage of Terrell's natural approach, children may express themselves quite appropriately in one- or two-word utterances as they begin to acquire a second language. A. N. Crawford (1994a) indicated that it is altogether proper that they also begin to read key vocabulary that they have expressed for their teacher to write for them.

Assessing English Language Proficiency

There are many commercial instruments for assessing English language proficiency. Most examine pronunciation, knowledge of syntax, vocabulary knowledge, and other discrete skills. To teach English learners to read in English, teachers need to know how well they comprehend English.

The use of the Informal Reading Inventory (IRI) as a test of listening comprehension, often termed *capacity level,* is not as common as its use to determine instructional, frustration, and independent levels (see Chapter 3), but teachers can use it very effectively for this purpose. A. N. Crawford (1982) suggested that the IRI, a set of graded reading passages ranging through the levels of primary school, shows promise as a measure of second language proficiency when used as a test of listening comprehension or reading capacity in English. The teacher can use the IRI to determine readiness for reading instruction in given materials by reading a selected passage aloud to the child. Crawford reported that children who read in the mother tongue and respond correctly to 75 percent of comprehension-level questions about the material in English usually have sufficient second language proficiency to begin learning to read in English at the highest level at which they are successful in meeting that criterion. For children who are learning to read in their mother tongue in a bilingual program, this is often at or near the grade level at which they are reading in that mother tongue.

Teaching English Language Learners to Read and Write in English

Let us now examine some approaches and strategies to reading and writing that promote second language acquisition within a constructivist perspective. Only a few years ago, it was commonly held that second language learners should not begin learning to read and write in the second language until they had reached an intermediate level of fluency. We now recognize that the processes of reading and writing in the second language can begin early in the acquisition process, especially for those children who have developed literacy skills in the mother tongue. In addition, literacy can play a major role in support of the acquisition of the second language. Krashen and Terrell (1983) describe reading in the second language as an important source of comprehensible input.

Early Literacy Experiences

According to A. N. Crawford (1993), most English language learners have had some emergent literacy experiences at home and in the community. They recognize food and soft drink labels, they know brands of automobiles, and many have watched a parent read, refer to a calendar, respond to a letter, or write a check. In many homes, parents and grandparents tell stories and read to their children. Except in the most rural and isolated areas, most children also have abundant print in their environment. In this way, many children have begun to understand the underlying concept of print representing spoken ideas, often even for a second language that they are only beginning to understand.

A classroom environment that is rich in print is an important step toward providing meaningful material to read (A. N. Crawford, 1994b). Children don't need to know letter names or sound-symbol correspondences to begin recognizing and discussing their own names, labels, and other forms of print to which they are exposed. Surrounding them with sources of print in the classroom will serve to extend their experiences with authentic text. When reading instruction is provided in the mother tongue, teachers will often label their classrooms in that mother tongue until the children are ready for labels in English, a relatively short time. Teachers should avoid labeling simultaneously in both languages so that children are not in the position of learning English in terms of the mother tongue. Children should learn English terms through direct experience with their classroom environment, not through translation from the mother tongue.

Most bilingual teachers who teach reading in the mother tongue recognize that children's motivation to begin reading and writing in a second language early is strong. Although we have already noted that it is most beneficial for children to learn to read and write first in the mother tongue, when possible, teachers can begin an early introduction to literacy in a second language to take advantage of that motivation. The key vocabulary and language experience approaches should be used with caution, however, to ensure that the second language acquisition program does not evolve into just a second language literacy program presented before the child is ready. Being able to read and write in the mother tongue is always the most desirable base from which to establish literacy in the second language later because of the positive transfer of literacy skills to that second language.

If children have an extremely limited background in the language of initial instruction, especially if it must be in English as a second language, then the key vocabulary approach (Veatch, 1996; Veatch et al., 1979) might serve well as a bridge to literacy from the mother tongue that children use to communicate orally. This approach is a major source of written language for providing authentic, meaningful, and early literacy experiences. During an individual meeting with the teacher, each child in the key vocabulary approach selects a word of personal importance, which the teacher writes on a card.

After the child traces the word with a finger, the teacher records it in a key word book or a sheet of paper and also records a sentence or phrase that is dictated by the child about the word. The child then reads the dictation back to the teacher and illustrates it. Finally, the child copies the word and the sentence.

Adapting the Language Experience Approach for English Language Learners

Moving from the dictation of key vocabulary to predictable language patterns in the *language experience approach* (LEA) is a natural step, and one that quickly leads to more traditional LEA strategies (Heald-Taylor, 1986). A dictation about story theme preferences might result in each of several children dictating an idea conforming to this predictable pattern (A. N. Crawford, 1994a):

> I like stories about animals.
> I like stories about airplanes.
> I like stories about children in other countries.

And so on.

Using the language experience approach in the second language is an excellent way to initiate children into print that is interesting and relevant to them (Dixon & Nessel, 1983; Moustafa & Penrose, 1985; Nessel & Jones, 1981). According to A. N. Crawford (1993), the language experience approach also provides a means through which children can experience literature, and the new culture that it represents, in their second language that is above their ability to read and comprehend. After a teacher tells or reads a story aloud, English language learners can then retell it for the teacher to record, though usually in a less complex version than the original. Peck (1989) found that listening to read-aloud stories in this way helps children to develop a sense of story structure, which should be reflected in the dictated version, and enhances their abilities to predict in this and other stories. The dictated text allows children to think, talk, read, and write about the piece of literature and to be exposed to its valuable cultural content. At the same time, they are actively interacting with it at a level of comprehension and of second language proficiency that is appropriate for their stage of development. They will be able to activate background knowledge from this experience that will transfer positively into the second language when they later read the literature for themselves in their new second language. This background knowledge also underlies their comprehension of what they read.

The language experience approach (Crawford, Allen, & Hall, 1995) for teaching reading and writing is an approach in which a small group of children or an individual child and a teacher talk about an idea or topic, such as a favorite story or another topic of interest. Children tell their own ideas to the teacher, who writes them down sentence by sentence to use as reading material. The children read the text many times with help from the teacher. After many exposures to the text, children begin to recognize words that are used over and over in the dictated material, and soon they are able to read other materials as well. Children also begin learning to write early in this approach.

The language experience approach is particularly useful for teachers who work with older English learners who are preliterate, an increasingly common phenomenon. Migrant children or the children of refugees might never have been in school, even when they are 10 or 12 years of age, or older. The language experience approach is also useful where books and other instructional materials might not be available to teachers at all in the children's mother tongue.

The language experience approach to reading works well because it is based on the children's oral language; children understand what they are reading because the ideas and language are their own. It is more interesting because they read about real ideas, not artificial syllables, leading English language learners to quick and early success in reading with this approach. One way to reinforce for English language learners this concept that we read for meaning, not for pronunciation, is to have them read aloud from LEA charts in different voices. Ask one child to read the chart in an angry voice, another in a happy voice, and another in a questioning voice.

As children dictate text for the teacher to record, some will use incorrect syntactical structures and inappropriate vocabulary. There is some controversy about whether teachers should record exactly what the children dictate. Children will most easily learn to read the type of oral language they use. When teachers correct the language of children as they dictate, if often signifies to the children that the teacher lacks respect for them. It is best to write exactly what the children say, especially at the beginning. But words that are not pronounced correctly should be spelled correctly.

The language experience approach is best captured in an old Chinese proverb, which can be paraphrased as follows:

- What I can think about, I can say.
- What I can say can be written by me or someone else.
- I can read what I can write.
- I can read what other people write for me to read. They can also read what I write.

One nonthreatening way to elicit text that reflects more mature syntax and vocabulary is an adaptation called the *collaborative chart story.* When children are dictating and beginning to read with confidence later in the process, the teacher can ask children to negotiate their suggested text with the group. The teacher can invite questions from other children about a suggested sentence, for example, by asking how they feel about the way it is stated and how effectively the vocabulary provided expresses what the group wants to say. When children who have dictated sentences with grammatical errors hear suggestions from other children about how it might be said in another way, they invariably agree to the change. The children do not view this collaboration as correction, but rather as reflecting the contributions they all make together in communicating with the audience that will read their text later. It is probably better to accept exactly what is dictated at the beginning of the LEA process so that children can see the direct links among what they say, what the teacher writes down, and what the group reads back later.

Text-Based Strategies

English language learners will indicate their readiness to move from the language experience approach to reading by expressing their interest in what they will call "real books." A valuable form of written text for second language learners early in the reading process is the big book, particularly big books with predictable or repetitive language patterns (A. N. Crawford, 1993).

Teachers read to children, who then read with them and finally back to them, although this reading might consist of telling about the story while looking at the illustrations (Trachtenburg & Ferruggia, 1989). Using big books provides an opportunity for the teacher to model so that children can clearly see what they will later do in their own independent reading. In addition, children begin to notice correspondences between letters in familiar texts and the sounds they represent (Holdaway, 1979). If parallel versions of a text are available and have been used in the mother tongue, then children will not only bring that background knowledge to bear in the English version, but also grow in English proficiency as a result of this early literacy experience.

According to Lynch (1986), the shared reading process begins with consideration of the book language that may already have been acquired by children whose parents or other family members read to them. For those who lack this experience, shared reading takes on increasing importance. English language learners will sometimes come from homes where printed material is scarce or where parents' own literacy skills may be limited. We cannot make assumptions about the conceptual knowledge of print that any English language learners brings to the classroom (A. N. Crawford, 2003).

With beginning readers, their first reading may take the form of group echo reading with a teacher or lead reader, usually following a read-aloud by the teacher (Peetoom, 1986). As the lead reader reads very expressively, the time gap between that person and the group of children will diminish. When an individual or a part of the group stumbles, the lead reader should take charge and read until the group is together again. This activity lowers anxiety about oral reading because children's approximations, a very natural aspect of early reading, are not noticeable and comprehension is maintained. Most important, everyone is reading.

Peetoom (1986) describes timed and repeated readings in which children read aloud passages of about 150 words from carefully selected literature. With practice, children read them more accurately and in less time. Dowhower (1987) has reported that such repeated and rehearsed readings can result in gains in the reading rate, accuracy, and comprehension of 7-year-old children, with some evidence of transfer to unpracticed passages, as well. As a part of her study, children read along with an audiotape until they could read easily, or they practiced reading a passage until they could read at a preestablished set rate. This can be an especially useful independent activity for dyads of children working together. Again, they will be reading instead of completing written drill and practice activities on skill development. Samuels (1979) associated repeated readings with the development of *automaticity,* the stage at which children read and recognize words unconsciously, permitting their full attention to focus instead on meaning. Automaticity in reading seems to parallel the process of oral production without employing the monitor in language acquisition. It also has much in common with Terrell's (1986) concept of *binding,* in which a linguistic form evokes meaning without any delay.

A. N. Crawford (1993) suggests that a bilingual teacher present a piece of literature from English in a read-aloud or storytelling format, but in the mother tongue. The children will interact with it by dictating and reading a retelling in their mother tongue, but they will be exposed to the cultural content and background knowledge that it contains. When they are later able to read it in their new second language, they will have background knowledge from the earlier experience that will transfer positively into English.

Many teachers are concerned about how children can begin to read a big book or predictable book before they have learned to read, that is, to decode or call the words. Smith (1988) describes the process as one of demonstration in which the teacher or parent reads the big book to the child, who in turn "reads" it back to the teacher or parent. As children gain confidence through this early successful experience with reading and through a process of approximation, they begin to read with increasing accuracy and faithfulness to the actual text. Predictable text is a characteristic of some children's literature that makes it especially well suited for the shared reading process. Predictable patterns are often repetitive, with small changes often signaled by accompanying illustrations. Sometimes, these patterns are cumulative, in that early repeated elements are added to new elements so that children must remember them in sequence.

Children soon begin to identify which parts of the text tell about corresponding parts of the story, and they also begin to recognize certain words of interest to them. These words are not necessarily easy words from an adult's point of view. In terms of the frequency of their appearance in primary texts or in the number of syllables they contain, they are instead easy from a child's point of view because of their interest and utility. Such words as *elephant* and *yellow* are more likely to be remembered and read correctly on second or third reading than more difficult words, such as *come* and *as.*

Lynch (1986) points out that repetition of familiar stories leads to increased success, not to boredom on the part of the children. Their abilities to predict will grow, and they will increase the kind and variety of cues they use to predict, moving from illustrations and background knowledge of a story to familiar words and other visual cues. The later use of graphophonic cues, the phonics and structural analysis skills that are of so much concern to some educational decision makers, emerges then as a result of this process, not as its cause (Smith, 1988).

Vocabulary Development

We have already considered Krashen's assertion that second language acquisition and literacy contribute mutually to each other's development, with reading providing much comprehensible input. Reading is also a major factor in the vocabulary development of English language learners.

In keeping with a meaning-based approach to teaching English language learners, Harmon (1998) provides an excellent contextualized strategy for vocabulary development that reflects the philosophy of the natural approach to second language acquisition. She describes how a teacher uses a new term and then elaborates and extends its meaning immediately:

> "Let's start recounting the events of the story. We will tell about the beginning, middle, and end."
>   "This is an excerpt—one tiny piece."

In another strategy described by Nagy et al. (1993), Spanish-speaking students can use cognates they recognize from Spanish and English to support their reading comprehension in English. Words such as *general* are the same in spelling and meaning in both languages, and many other cognates are the same in meaning and similar in spelling, such as an example provided by Nagy et al.: *transform* in English and *transformar* in Spanish. But looking beyond their study, children must also be taught to be wary of false cognates, such as *actual,* which means "*nowadays*" in Spanish, and *dime,* which means "*give me*" in Spanish.

Adapting Phonics and Decoding Strategies for English Language Learners

A constructivist view of learning tells us that children unify what they already know about the world with new information that they gain through authentic experiences. Even in the largely synthetic process of learning about the isolated letters and sounds of a language, we will find that English language learners have background knowledge about the sound system of their mother tongue, phonemic awareness, and usually some knowledge about the symbols that represent those sounds, as well. Phonics, then, is the process of unifying that knowledge of sounds and letters in an authentic experience that permits children to generate new knowledge—that is, how to pronounce the sound of a letter or combination of letters in an unknown word. When this is accomplished within the context of what children already know, then instruction in phonics is not inconsistent with the constructivist paradigm.

We have already recognized that English language learners bring to the classroom phonemic awareness of sounds in the mother tongue. They should then learn phonics in the mother tongue out of the context of words they already recognize on sight, probably learned from the print environment and from language experience charts and big books. Children who learn phonics in the mother tongue generally have a much easier time learning phonics in English than do children who must learn phonics first in English. Some languages, such as Spanish and Korean, are very regular in the phoneme-grapheme relationships; not only is phonics simpler to learn, but children have more confidence in it than do children learning to read in a language in which phoneme-grapheme relationships are not regular, such as English.

The real dilemma for English language learners is when they must learn phonics in English first. Although they might have learned to speak and understand English, they still lack the phonemic awareness skills in English of a native speaker. For example, a native Spanish-speaking child will speak the 43 sounds of English using the 25 sounds of Spanish. There are only 5 vowel sounds in Spanish, but 15 in English. This accounts for the difficulty that Spanish-speaking children have in pronouncing short vowels in English, especially the *schwa;* they have similar difficulty in "reading" (correctly pronouncing) these sounds in a phonetic approach to reading. Although there are variations in the differences between other languages and English, similar difficulties arise for children who speak most other languages. For those who learn phonics in their mother tongue, the process of learning English phonics is much easier because they have already figured out how the process works. It transfers from the mother tongue, even if many of the sounds do not.

The language experience approach and shared reading are holistic strategies for teaching reading. In these strategies, we do not begin with phonics. But learning about letters and sounds (phonics) is a part of learning to read in all methods, including these. In a constructivist approach to teaching about letters and sounds, children should learn about reading first. They should dictate many LEA charts and read them, learning to read some 100 to 200 words on sight. They should have many shared book reading experiences, and then they are ready to learn about letters and sounds using words they already know.

Writing and Spelling

A major principle of the constructivist view of literacy is the interdependence of listening, speaking, reading, and writing. Hudelson (1984) observed that second language learners address the four language processes as a totality, not as separate entities. According to Fitzgerald (1993), writing begins when children can draw, and there is no need to wait for reading. We can certainly extend these ideas to English language learners, who should be encouraged to write in the second language early, especially if they have writing skills in their mother tongue. The errors that they make should be viewed in the same way that we view errors in oral production, as a part of the natural processes of approximation and acquisition (A. N. Crawford, 1994a).

Ferreiro (1991) described the process of writing as one of making meaning through construction and reconstruction. Samway (1993) reinforced this idea in her study of how a sample of non-native-English-speaking primary schoolchildren from 7 to 11 years of age evaluated their own writing and that of others. Although these high-risk children were experiencing difficulties in school, they tended to focus on meaning in their evaluative comments. Most of their comments were categorized as *crafting,* how well a story had been developed, or *understanding,* making sense of the text.

Spelling is another area in which instructional strategies must be adapted for English learners. Consistent with the communicative approach principle of minimizing error correction and with the developmental nature of second language acquisition and literacy, teachers of English language learners, like teachers of English speakers, should accept the invented spellings of their children as a very natural aspect of their developmental growth in writing. There are differences, however, in how English language learners will progress through some of Gentry's stages of invented spellings (see Chapter 2).

In the semiphonetic stage, English learners begin to approximate an alphabetic orthography and to conceptualize the alphabetic principle. They begin to demonstrate the relationship between sound and letter, and they sometimes use letter names as words. They begin to understand the left-to-right convention of most Western languages, and they may begin to segment words. Differences in the nature of invented spelling between languages will appear. The use of consonants tends to predominate over the use of vowels when children write in English as a mother tongue, for example, but vowels predominate over consonants when children write in Spanish as a mother tongue (Ferreiro & Rodríguez, 1994).

In the correct stage, children have learned most basic rules of the orthographic system. They are aware of such word structures as prefixes, suffixes, contractions, compound words, and homonyms, and they continue to learn some less common spelling patterns and rules. It is at this stage that they begin to recognize when a word looks correct, a phenomenon that corresponds to the natural approach characteristic in which second language learners begin to recognize when something sounds right or feels right. They are able to spell a large number of words automatically.

English language learners who are literate in another language will tend to move much more rapidly through Gentry's stages in their new second language of English than in their primary language. Nathenson-Mejia (1989) found that in their English writing, Spanish-speaking children in the beginning stages of English spelling made extensive use of their Spanish pronunciation in their invented spellings in English. Edelsky (1982) made the same observation in a more generic sense. She took the positive point of view that children are applying some mother tongue writing skills to the second language, rather than the negative point of view that it reflects interference from the first language on the second.

Scaffolding Strategies for Improving Reading Comprehension

When reading instruction moves away from the controlled environment of the traditional basal reader or decodable text toward authentic children's literature, often in anthologies, including fiction and nonfiction trade books, children are exposed to oral and written ideas that demand higher levels of background knowledge, vocabulary, and language proficiency (A. N. Crawford, 1997). In their work with English language learners, teachers face great challenges in providing for the equitable access of all children to authentic literature in English while helping them make progress in reading and writing.

Whether or not English language learners read literature in the primary or the second language, we can organize a set of scaffolding strategies to support their reading comprehension into three categories: *prereading strategies, guided or directed reading strategies,* and *postreading strategies. Scaffolding* is the temporary support that teachers provide when children are engaged in a task within Vygotsky's zone of proximal development. Bruner (1978) has described scaffolding as a temporary launching platform designed to support and encourage children's language development to higher levels of complexity. Pearson (1985) later elaborated the temporary nature of scaffolding in describing it as the gradual release of responsibility. Good teachers intuitively use such scaffolding strategies as higher-order questioning, prompts, illustrations and other visual resources, demonstrations, dramatization, gestures, comprehension monitoring, graphic organizers, and rephrasing (A. N. Crawford, 1994b).

The recommended strategies that follow are those that will provide the underlying support or scaffolding needed for reading comprehension. It is the isolated skills that teachers should set aside. We should view skill development as an outcome of learning to read, not as its cause (Samuels, 1971; Smith, 1985). When a child's needs suggest that a directed skill lesson is needed, teachers should seek out an appropriate one in the teacher's editions and workbooks of traditional reading and language arts programs.

Prereading Strategies

There is increasing recognition of the importance of bringing background knowledge to bear on making sense of new information (Smith, 1988). The activation of this background knowledge, and often its development, constitute a vitally important prereading activity for the English language learner. The background knowledge that we have acquired about the world forms the structure through which we assess new information and incorporate it. We use this knowledge to make and verify predictions about the new information to which we are exposed. According to Krashen (1991), background knowledge also makes second language input more comprehensible and therefore facilitates second language acquisition. In addition, we can consider vocabulary itself as an important aspect of background knowledge to be activated or installed.

Background Knowledge.   All children have acquired background knowledge, but there is often a discontinuity between the background knowledge a child has, what Moll and González (1994) refer to as "funds of knowledge," and the assumptions that teachers, authors, and textbook publishers make about that knowledge. A. N. Crawford (1994a) indicates that this discontinuity must be assumed to be deeper when the child comes from a language or culture different from that of those for whom the materials are designed or intended, usually middle-class native English speakers.

Many prereading activities were introduced in earlier chapters. We will elaborate some of them here and add a few more that are of particular value to English language learners.

Group Discussion.   The activation or development of background knowledge in children without previous exposure can often be accomplished through a sharing of the group's knowledge. Although no individual child might know a great deal about a topic, several children in a group will each have some knowledge (María, 1989).

Semantic Mapping.   A useful strategy for providing structure to the development of background knowledge is semantic mapping (Heimlich & Pittelman, 1986). Knowledge is activated from long-term memory, shared with other children, and discussed in terms of needed vocabulary. It is then recorded in a graphic format that promotes organizing schemata so that relationships become more clear. The resulting semantic map might also serve as an advance organizer that will promote reading comprehension when the children later read the selection.

The teacher writes a word on a chart, chalkboard, or transparency and asks children to tell what they know about that concept. Although most children won't know much, a few will know something. The process of discussing and systematically recording their background knowledge on a semantic map permits them to share what they know while the teacher organizes it into logical categories. Semantic maps are widely used to develop vocabulary in the same way. In fact, a major difference between authentic literature and basal reader stories or so-called decodable text is the variety of vocabulary that the skilled author uses, selecting the precise word needed to best express an idea.

According to A. N. Crawford (1993), semantic mapping is not a strategy to use every day. The nature of the literature selection, the desirability of formally structuring the background knowledge into a semantic map, and the existing background knowledge of the children should all be factors in deciding when and if the gains from devoting a considerable amount of instructional time to the activity are warranted.

The cumulative semantic map acts as a graphic thesaurus (A. N. Crawford, 1994a). Ordinarily, a semantic map for activating background knowledge or vocabulary is developed and completed during one or two related lessons and is not referred to subsequently. However, teachers often find that they are dealing with some concepts on repeated occasions. It can be useful to return to a semantic map on such a topic, to add to it, and to consider new additions in contrast with earlier ones.

We can see in Figure 9.1, for example, a cumulative semantic map as it might appear after two months of school (A. N. Crawford, 1994a). A teacher might introduce the new word *furious* from a piece of literature and ask children where it should be added to an existing cumulative semantic map for words about feelings and emotions. At that point, the children can discuss how angry *furious* is in comparison to *miffed, enraged,* and *upset,* which had been added to the semantic map on earlier occasions. When written on removable self-stick notes, the various words can be arranged and rearranged in ascending order of increasing anger as children negotiate their meaning with each other. Moustafa (1996) suggests placing words on cards with cellophane tape across the top. Using the same tape over and over, the teacher can then stick these to a large wall chart made of plastic shower curtain material. Moustafa's strategy can be adapted to the cumulative semantic map, facilitating the moving of words from one place to another on the chart or in making room for a new word to be added. Many weeks later, the map has been elaborated, as seen in Figure 9.2, and, of course, this process continues through the school year.

In a later writing assignment, English language learners might again refer to the cumulative semantic map on the wall when they want to select just the right word to convey the degree of anger they have in mind (A. N. Crawford, 1994a). Discussing the choice of word with the teacher or with other children will be particularly helpful. When children are ready to add yet another synonym for *angry* a week or a month later, they will have the opportunity to review other words or expressions for the same feeling within a context of known or somewhat familiar vocabulary. We can view a well-

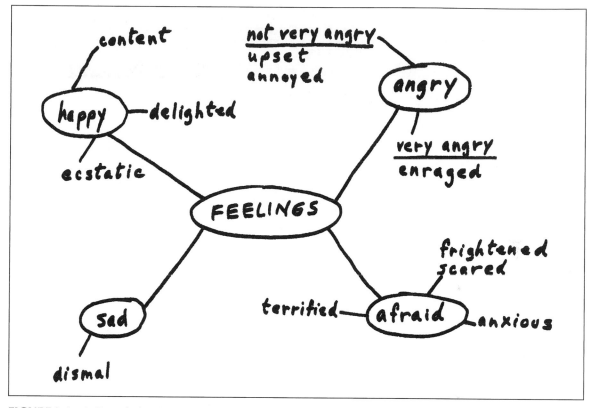

FIGURE 9.1   *A Cumulative Semantic Map*

developed cumulative semantic map as a graphic thesaurus. Other suitable topics for cumulative semantic maps might include seeing (*stare, peek, glare,* etc.), motion (*crawl, creep, dawdle, dash, poke along, lope,* etc.), and touching (*poke, tap, jab, stroke,* etc.). Only the topics come from the teacher; the source of vocabulary is the literature the children are reading.

Vocabulary Development.   When children read, their lack of vocabulary knowledge is often an obstacle to comprehension. Because they might have insufficient academically related background knowledge and vocabulary development in the mother tongue that would accompany it, this can be an even greater problem for children who must read in their second language. We can consider vocabulary as an aspect of background knowledge in prereading, but we will treat it separately here to examine several concepts that relate more specifically to vocabulary.

Let us consider two different aspects of the question of vocabulary development. One is the richness of language that surrounds children. It is well recognized that children become familiar with the meanings of words when those meanings are highly

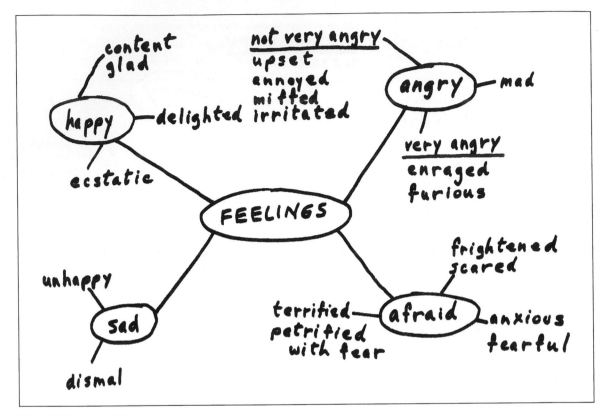

FIGURE 9.2   *An Elaborated Cumulative Semantic Map*

contextualized, not when they are studied in isolation as new vocabulary words. It follows, then, that a richer language environment should result in increased exposure to contextualized vocabulary and therefore to understanding of their meanings (A. N. Crawford, 1994b).

We often postpone or even eliminate instruction for at-risk children, however, in the very areas of the curriculum in which new vocabulary words will be offered in the most highly contextualized ways—in science, social studies, art, music, health, and other areas of the curriculum. This is even more common for children who are learning in their second language. According to A. N. Crawford (1993), we must ensure that these areas of the curriculum are provided for all children, including English language learners, and that they are presented so that contextualized exposure to a rich vocabulary is promoted.

Another aspect of vocabulary is the issue of direct instruction. Although many vocabulary words will be acquired incidentally, some literature or content selections will contain a few vocabulary words that must be clearly grasped if the text is to be understood. There will be other words not known to the children that need not be addressed through direct instruction because they are not critical to understanding the selection or because they can be quickly analyzed through the context in which they appear.

Many of the strategies that are recommended for the activation or development of background knowledge constitute direct approaches to vocabulary instruction. Semantic mapping is one of these strategies, but its application should be limited to those key and conceptually difficult vocabulary terms that are more in the realm of background knowledge. Otherwise, there will be little time left for reading after prereading activities are completed.

English language learners often benefit from read-aloud activities by the teacher, followed by discussion. A read-aloud is simply the process of having a teacher read a literature selection, or a part of one, aloud to the children before they read it themselves. Vocabulary will have been presented in context, and someone in the group will likely have some knowledge of most words. Other words might be analyzed by reviewing the illustrations in a story or an appropriate illustration, manipulative, or visual aid provided by the teacher. Because illustrations provide important visual information, paging through a selection and discussing them before reading provide an opportunity for presenting new vocabulary and also for making predictions about the text. A partial or complete read-aloud of a literature selection as a prereading activity may be called for in a particularly challenging piece.

Guided Reading Strategies

According to Smith (1985), we learn to read by reading. This fundamental and obvious idea should underlie our thinking as we consider how children's time is spent during reading instruction. Rather than having children study about reading by mastering skills, we must instead maximize the amount of reading that they do. Some obviously counterproductive strategies are pencil-and-paper exercises. Another is the still common practice of round-robin oral reading, in which each child takes a turn reading aloud to the group or class. This usually consists of having a child laboriously reading aloud a passage that she has never before read, even silently, while the rest of the children in the group pretend to listen or read along. The child who is reading focuses on pronunciation, not on understanding what is being read, and the other children are alternatively bored or preparing to read when their turn comes. This practice is especially deceiving with children who read in Spanish, for example. They can read orally with confidence in English, albeit with a Spanish accent and no comprehension. They are, in fact, pronouncing, and not reading.

Our own experiences in learning another language remind us of the importance of reading for comprehension, as opposed to word calling. Most of us had the experience of being asked to read aloud in a secondary school or university foreign language class. We read with great intensity, attempting to correctly soften the intervocalic *d* of Spanish or accurately pronounce the difficult initial *r* of French. When we finished, the teacher asked us to tell about the content of what we had read in our own words. Of course, we had little idea because we had been focusing on pronunciation. We must remember that communication and comprehension are the focus of reading and writing, just as they are in a communicative approach to oral language development. There are many guided reading strategies that will help us to ensure that children focus on comprehension instead of only on correct pronunciation.

As we noted above, when English language learners begin to read themselves, they may benefit from having their teacher read to them from the selection first. Occasionally, the teacher might find that presenting the entire selection as a read-aloud is helpful. When a parallel version of a text is available in the children's mother tongue, the teacher might read it aloud before the children read later in the second language. Children in school are not bored or disturbed by several exposures to the same literature selection, any more than a 3-year-old objects to hearing the same story before bed every night. The familiarity of a story that is an old friend becomes a real comfort. Familiarity with the background knowledge and structure of a story permits a child to read with good comprehension and with fewer time-consuming visual cues, especially for children's early literacy experiences in the second language. The teacher's read-aloud also provides the teacher with the opportunity to model predicting, thinking about context, and other strategies by talking through some of the metacognitive processes that are used during the teacher's oral reading.

Elementary schoolchildren should read silently on an extensive basis. It is through more rapid silent reading that children can read for the most practice and be exposed to the most background knowledge and contextualized vocabulary. It is more difficult for teachers to provide extra support to second language learners, however, because their need for it might be less obvious during the largely independent activity of reading silently. The need should be based on children's abilities to interact with the teacher and each other about what they have been reading—that is, their comprehension of what they have been reading.

One strategy for providing this support during the silent reading of literature selections is to direct or structure children's reading with questions. Some would decry this as an annoying and unnecessary strategy that is destined to destroy any enjoyment of the selection by the child. That might indeed be the case for some children. The reality is, however, that many English language learners struggle to read, and their many failure experiences can result in a lack of motivation and interest in reading. Their teachers often have difficulty reading themselves during silent sustained reading because of their need to supervise closely the reading of their sometimes reluctant students.

According to A. N. Crawford (1993), guiding children's reading with questions, a variation on directed reading-thinking activity, provides valuable support in maintaining comprehension. The teacher should precede the children's reading of a page or passage of a piece of literature by asking a higher-order question, that is, an open-ended question whose answer requires the child to use background knowledge and combine it with information that is in the selection to be read. An example of such a question is "Please read page 71 to find out why the main character is worried." Students will read page 71 to find the answer to the question; it focuses them on comprehension, not on production and accurate oral reading. This questioning strategy brings key story concepts to their attention as they read and, perhaps more important, provides moral support, interest, and motivation from someone who cares about them, the teacher. Children who cannot or will not read a lengthy selection alone might do so a page or two at a time within the security of a supportive teacher-directed group. Their reading can be structured by questions that elicit predictions, with timely resolution of those predictions through discussion and any needed mediation. Finally, these questions should be formulated to require higher-order thinking on the part of the children, demonstrating the teacher's high expectations for them. Peetoom (1986) suggests chunking stories by having children read them in manageable and comprehensible sections. Questions can be used very effectively and naturally to accomplish this chunking.

Although there is considerable debate about the value of teaching reading comprehension skills through direct instruction, there are sufficient other reasons to guide silent reading with questions. A teacher will take no longer to formulate and ask a higher-order comprehension question than a low-level recall question before asking children to read to find the answer. It is often said that teachers have low expectations for at-risk children and English language learners. Guided silent reading provides an opportunity for children to make inferences and predictions, identify cause-and-effect relationships, and apply other higher-order critical thinking skills when their comprehension is supported (A. N. Crawford, 1993).

Postreading Strategies

After children read, there are other opportunities to provide scaffolding. We have already considered the retelling of stories that are told or read to children as a means of producing text through LEA for them to read themselves. Retelling is also an excellent postreading strategy for English language learners. An oral retelling provides children with the opportunity to negotiate with each other about the meaning of the selection. It is often through this process that children can incorporate new information gained through reading into existing background knowledge. Koskinen et al. (1988) found that the verbal rehearsal that occurs in the retelling process also serves to improve the reading comprehension of less proficient readers. Some children may elect to retell in their mother tongue what they read or heard in their second language. Brown and Cambourne (1990) observe that retelling also promotes multiple readings of text as a part of the negotiation process.

Retelling also provides a means for integrating writing into the program. Either through a cooperative learning process or through individual or paired writing, children can prepare a written retelling (Strickland & Feeley, 1985). As a result of their earlier discussion, of the knowledge they gained through reading, and of such prereading activities as semantic mapping and the examination of story grammar, children are better prepared to write a well-structured retelling. Like the modeling that teachers provide during reading, teachers should also model retelling with an actual example.

The most obvious postreading activity should not be overlooked: more reading. If we are successful in providing high-quality literature that children will choose to read and also in supporting their comprehension, then we should expect gains in all areas of the language arts. Krashen (1985, 1993) has concluded that reading is more powerful than direct instruction in developing vocabulary, grammar, spelling, and reading comprehension, especially for English language learners. He advocates extensive free voluntary reading with messages that are understood in low-anxiety situations. Finally, he believes that good writing is promoted more by extensive reading than by writing.

Some Issues in Assessing the Reading and Writing of English Language Learners

Instruments and Procedures

Most assessment strategies used with English speakers will function well in other languages and also with English language learners in English. There are, however, some adaptations indicated. For example, one element of evaluating oral reading accuracy in the Informal Reading Inventory (see Chapter 3) is mispronunciation, each occurrence of which is counted as an oral reading error or miscue. When a mispronunciation error can be attributed to a conflict point with the mother tongue and when it does not interfere with comprehension, a short *i* pronounced as a long *e,* for example, then an error would not be counted.

In a personal communication with the author, Kenneth Johnson (1977) provided a test sentence to illustrate this principle for the African American child whose mother tongue is African American Vernacular English. The sentence often elicits a mispronunciation that has the potential to interfere with comprehension. The child is asked to read the following aloud:

As I passed the sign, I read it.

In conformance with Southern Regional dialect, the African American child sometimes pronounces *passed* as *pass,* dropping the *-ed* suffix that is also a past tense marker. If the child comprehends the marker, that is, if he understands that *passed* is in the past tense, even though pronounced as in the present tense, then the child will pronounce *read* in the past tense. If not, he will pronounce the identically spelled word in the present tense. According to Johnson, the child will invariably correctly pronounce *read* in the past tense. In a study of teachers who administered IRIs to Spanish-speaking children, Lamberg, Rodríguez, and Tomas (1978) concluded that, to avoid such problems, teachers need special training to use them with English language learners.

Grouping for Instruction

Using assessment data to group English language learners for reading instruction is always a challenge. When most or all children speak another language in common, such as Spanish, and when the teacher is bilingual, then a mother tongue reading program and a strong ESL program are in order. As children become ready to transition to English language reading instruction, the grouping structure becomes more complex, often resulting in instruction in two languages at several levels within each language. It is tempting to move children who speak English to another classroom at that point, but this practice leads to a phenomenon called *fossilization*, a danger that Selinker et al. (1975) point out as the isolation of English language learners from native speakers. It leads to a stopping-in-place of language development caused by a lack of comprehensible input from expert speakers of the new second language.

One school district developed a model that effectively alleviates this problem at the elementary level (Krashen & Biber, 1988). English language learners are organized for mother tongue instruction in reading and the language arts during the morning, along with a natural approach program of acquiring English. In the afternoon, English language learners are mainstreamed with English-speaking children in art, music, and physical education. As English language learners gain proficiency, they begin to receive sheltered instruction in that second language in the more concrete areas of the curriculum, such as mathematics and science. Social studies in English is introduced later.

Sheltered instruction is a context-embedded intermediate ESL methodology in which content is provided to English language learners in English, but with special support through strategies such as those developed by the Los Angeles Unified School District (1985). They recommend that teachers simplify input by speaking slowly and enunciating clearly, using a controlled vocabulary within simple language structures. When possible, they should use cognates and avoid the extensive use of idiomatic expressions. They suggest that teachers make frequent use of nonverbal language, including gestures, facial expressions, and dramatization. They also recommend the use of manipulatives and concrete materials, such as props, graphs, visuals, overhead transparencies, bulletin boards, maps, and realia. Comprehension should be maintained through extensive use of gestures, dramatization, illustrations, and manipulatives. Teachers should check frequently for understanding by asking for confirmation of comprehension; by asking students to clarify, repeat, and expand; and by using a variety of questioning formats. Schifini (1985) additionally recommends a focus on student-centered activities, especially at the secondary level, where lecturing and textbook use predominate.

Sheltered Instruction Observation Protocol (SIOP)

The Sheltered Instruction Observation Protocol (SIOP) (Echevarria, Vogt, & Short, 2004) is a carefully organized professional development model that incorporates strategies you have seen in this chapter and previous chapters:

- **Preparation:** lesson planning, content objectives, instructional materials
- **Building background:** integrating student background knowledge and developing academic vocabulary
- **Comprehensible input:** teacher speech presentation strategies and multimodal techniques

- **Strategies:** scaffolding instruction and promoting higher-order thinking skills
- **Interaction:** encourage elaborated student speech and group students appropriately
- **Practice/Application:** activities to extend student learning of language and content
- **Lesson delivery:** deliver lessons that meet teaching objectives
- **Review/Assessment:** teacher review of key language and content concepts, assessment of student learning, and feedback to students

A SIOP lesson plan incorporates all of these elements. This model is designed for English language learners, but you can see how it would be very effective with speakers of African American Vernacular English and with any student struggling with language and literacy. As a framework for planning and teaching effective lessons, it highlights best teaching practice for all children.

Selection of Literature and Other Instructional Materials

The principles of selecting literature for English language learners do not differ greatly from those for English-speaking students. Authentic children's literature in languages other than English is increasingly available, especially in Spanish. The interests, culture, and background knowledge of the students, of course, must be considered. Children are anxious to see themselves in the literature they read, whether in English or the mother tongue.

Most major publishers now provide anthologies of literature for children that are parallel in English and Spanish. The best ones are not translations from English to Spanish, but rather those that are parallel and similar in thematic content, with many stories overlapping in both languages. At least some of these stories have been translated from Spanish to English for exposing English-speaking children to literature from another culture.

The use of the programs provides many advantages. Children can begin learning to read in the mother tongue, moving into English two to three years later when they have learned enough English to reach the level of cognitive-academic language proficiency. When they later read many of the same selections in English, they have the advantage of prior experience with concepts and story grammars, providing a strong support to their comprehension as they move into their new second language.

Older Preliterate Children

Many teachers of older English language learners from other countries observe that some lack literacy skills entirely. Some have been in refugee camps without educational services, others have worked to contribute to family income, and still others are from very rural or isolated areas where attending school was not possible because of long distances and inadequate transportation. Indigenous children from Latin America frequently leave school because instruction is provided only in Spanish, which they may not speak or speak well. There are communities of speakers of Zapotec, Mixtec, Maya,

Quechua, and many other indigenous languages living in the United States. Even their Spanish may be very limited, and they speak little or no English.

Other English language learners have had very limited school experience and left school, either for the reasons cited above or occasionally because of the poor quality of education. According to Schifini (1996), many children have major gaps in instruction in the primary grades, and they struggle as nonreaders in the higher grades. He recommends several strategies for meeting the needs of these older preliterate English language learners:

- Develop a print-rich classroom environment that reflects student interests, including advertisements, brochures, bumper stickers, comics, drawings, magazines, messages, murals, newspapers, photos, postcards, posters, and recipes, including many examples of their own work.
- Include native language print in the classroom environment.
- Encourage students through reading and writing workshops and shared reading and literature studies.
- Provide read-aloud activities for access to the core curriculum not available through reading.
- Use writing activities such as quick-writes to connect students to their background knowledge.
- Provide shared book experiences with predictable and patterned books that are of standard textbook size and that have mature story lines.
- Use collaborative chart stories, language experience charts, and other forms of shared writing.

Freeman and Freeman (2002) offer four keys for closing the gap for these preliterate children:

- Provide a challenging, theme-based curriculum to develop academic concepts.
- Use the children's background, including their experiences, culture, and language.
- Provide collaborative activities and scaffold instruction to build their academic language proficiency in English.
- Help children become confident students who value school and themselves as learners.

Summary

In this chapter, we address the special needs and challenges of the significant number of children in our schools with apparent problems in reading and writing that we characterize as English language learners, those whose mother tongue or home language is not English. The difficulties they have are more often with second language issues than with reading and writing. We present interrelated strategies for teaching English as a second language and literacy—strategies that are based in meaning, rather than isolated skills development.

English language learners must first learn to speak and understand English, and communicative approaches—such as total physical response (TPR) and the natural approach—provide very effective strategies to meet this need. They parallel the development of the mother tongue, in which children are almost universally successful.

Evidence suggests that when English language learners can learn to read and write in their mother tongue, it benefits their long-range acquisition of English and their abilities to read and write in English. Strategies for teaching reading and writing to English language learners should be based on meaning, with the key vocabulary and language experience approaches serving well at the level of emergent literacy. As English language learners move into English text, they need extra support for comprehension. Their program should include prereading, guided reading, and postreading activities that provide scaffolding for comprehension in their new language.

(mylabschool™ *Where the classroom comes to life!*

MyLabSchool is a collection of online tools for your success in this course, your licensure exams, and your teaching career. Visit www.mylabschool.com to access the following:

- Online Study Guide
- Video cases from real classrooms
- Help with your research papers using Research Navigator
- Career Center with resources for:
  - Praxis exams and licensure preparation
  - Professional portfolio development
  - Job search and interview techniques
  - Lesson planning

References

Asher, J. J. (1982). The total physical response approach. In R. W. Blair (Ed.), *Innovative approaches to language teaching* (pp. 54–66). Rowley, MA: Newbury House.

August, D., & Shanahan, T. (Eds.). (2006). *Developing literacy in second-language learners: Report of the National Literacy Panel on Language-Minority Children and Youth.* Mahwah, NJ: Erlbaum.

Brown, H., & Cambourne, B. (1990). *Read and retell: A strategy for the whole-language/natural learning classroom.* Portsmouth, NH: Heinemann.

Bruner, J. (1978). The role of dialogue in language acquisition. In A. Sinclair, R. J. Jarvella, & W. M. Levelt (Eds.), *The child's conception of language* (pp. 241–256). New York: Springer-Verlag.

Campo-Flores, A. (2001, June 4). A town's two faces. *Newsweek,* 34–35.

Castañeda v. Pickard, 648 F.2d 989 (5th Cir. 1981).

Collier, V. P. (1989). How long? A synthesis of research on academic achievement in a second language. *TESOL Quarterly, 23,* 509–539.

Crawford, A. (2003). Communicative approaches to second language acquisition: The bridge to second language literacy. In G. García (Ed.), *English learners: Reaching the highest level of English literacy* (pp. 152–181). Newark, DE: International Reading Association.

Crawford, A. N. (1982). From Spanish reading to English reading: The transition process. In M. P. Douglass (Ed.), *Claremont reading conference year-*

book (pp. 159–165). Claremont, CA: Claremont Reading Conference.

Crawford, A. N. (1986). Communicative approaches to ESL: A bridge to reading comprehension. In M. P. Douglass (Ed.), *Claremont reading conference yearbook* (pp. 292–305). Claremont, CA: Claremont Reading Conference.

Crawford, A. N. (1993). Literature, integrated language arts, and the language minority child: A focus on meaning. In A. Carrasquillo and C. Hedley (Eds.), *Whole language and the bilingual learner* (pp. 61–75). Norwood, NJ: Ablex.

Crawford, A. N. (1994a). Communicative approaches to second language acquisition: From oral language development into the core curriculum and L_2 literacy. In C. F. Leyba (Ed.), *Schooling and language minority students: A theoretical framework* (2nd ed., pp. 79–131). Los Angeles: Evaluation, Dissemination and Assessment Center, California State University, Los Angeles.

Crawford, A. N. (1994b). Estrategias para promover la comprensión lectora en estudiantes de alto riesgo. *Lectura y Vida, 15,* 121–127.

Crawford, A. N. (1995). Language policy, second language learning, and literacy. In A. N. Crawford (Ed.), *A practical guidebook for adult literacy programmes in developing nations* (pp. 9–16). Paris: UNESCO.

Crawford, A. N. (1997). Estrategias para promover la comprensión lectora. In M. Lavadenz & C. Velasco (Eds.), *Hacia un futuro sin fronteras* (pp. 77–85). Santa Barbara, CA: University of California Linguistic Minority Research Institute.

Crawford, A. N., Allen, R. V., & Hall, M. (1995). The language experience approach. In A. N. Crawford (Ed.), *A practical guidebook for adult literacy programmes in developing nations* (pp. 17–46). Paris: UNESCO.

Crawford, J. (1989). *Bilingual education: History, politics, theory and practice.* Trenton, NJ: Crane.

Cummins, J. (1981). The role of primary language development in promoting education success for language minority students. In California State Department of Education (Ed.), *Schooling and language minority students: A theoretical framework* (pp. 3–49). Los Angeles: Evaluation, Dissemination and Assessment Center, California State University, Los Angeles.

Cummins, J. (1986). Empowering minority students: A framework for intervention. *Harvard Educational Review, 56,* 18–36.

Cummins, J. (1989). *Empowering minority students.* Sacramento: California Association for Bilingual Education.

Cummins, J. (1994). Primary language instruction and the education of language minority students. In C. F. Leyba (Ed.), *Schooling and language minority students: A theoretical framework* (2nd ed., pp. 3–46). Los Angeles: Evaluation, Dissemination and Assessment Center, California State University, Los Angeles.

Dixon, C. N., & Nessel, D. (1983). *Language experience approach to reading and writing: LEA for ESL.* Hayward, CA: Alemany Press.

Dowhower, S. L. (1987). Effects of repeated reading on second-grade transitional readers' fluency and comprehension. *Reading Research Quarterly, 22,* 389–406.

Echevarria, J., Vogt, M., & Short, D. J. (2004). *Making content comprehensible for English learners: The SIOP model.* Boston: Pearson.

Edelsky, C. (1982). Writing in a bilingual program: The relation of L_1 and L_2 texts. *TESOL Quarterly, 16,* 211–228.

Ferreiro, E. (1991). La construcción de la escritura en el niño. *Lectura y Vida, 12,* 5–14.

Ferreiro, E., & Rodríguez, B. (1994). *Las condiciones de alfabetización en medio rural.* México: CINVESTAV.

Fitzgerald, J. (1993). Literacy and sudents who are learning English as a second language. *The Reading Teacher, 46,* 638–647.

Freeman, Y. S., & Freeman, D. E. (2002). *Closing the achievement gap: How to reach limited-formal-schooling and long-term English learners.* Portsmouth, NH: Heinemann.

Gee, J. P. (1992). *The social mind: Ideology and social practice.* New York: Bergin & Garvey.

Goodman, K. (1986). *What's whole in whole language?* Portsmouth, NH: Heinemann.

Harmon, J. M. (1998). Vocabulary teaching and learning in a seventh-grade literature-based classroom. *Journal of Adolescent & Adult Literacy, 41,* 518–529.

Heald-Taylor, G. (1986). *Whole language strategies for ESL students.* San Diego: Dormac.

Heimlich, J. E., & Pittelman, S. D. (1986). *Semantic mapping: Classroom applications.* Newark, DE: International Reading Association.

Holdaway, D. (1979). *The foundations of literacy.* Sydney: Ashton Scholastic.

Hudelson, S. (1984). Kan Yu Ret an Rayt en Ingles: Children become literate in English as a second language. *TESOL Quarterly, 18,* 221–238.

Hudelson, S. (1987). The role of native language literacy in the education of language minority children. *Language Arts, 64,* 827–840.

Johnson, K. R. (1977). Personal communication.

Koskinen, P. S., Gambrell, L.B., Kapinus, B.A., & Heathington, B. S. (1988). Retelling: A strategy for enhancing students' reading comprehension. *The Reading Teacher, 41,* 892–896.

Krashen, S. D. (1981). Bilingual education and second language acquisition theory. In California State Department of Education (Ed.), *Schooling and language minority students: A theoretical framework* (pp. 51–79). Sacramento: Office of Bilingual Bicultural Education, California State Department of Education.

Krashen, S. D. (1982a). Theory versus practice in language training. In R. W. Blair (Ed.), *Innovative approaches to language teaching* (pp. 15–30). Rowley, MA: Newbury House.

Krashen, S. D. (1982b). *Principles and practice in second language acquisition.* New York: Pergamon Press.

Krashen, S. D. (1985). *Inquiries and insights: Second language teaching, immersion and bilingual education, literacy.* Hayward, CA: Alemany Press.

Krashen, S. D. (1991). *Bilingual education: A focus on current research.* Washington, DC: National Clearinghouse for Bilingual Education.

Krashen, S. D. (1993). *The power of reading.* Englewood, CO: Libraries Unlimited.

Krashen, S. D., & Biber, D. (1988). *On course: Bilingual education's success in California.* Sacramento: California Association for Bilingual Education.

Krashen, S. D., & Terrell, T. D. (1983). *The natural approach: Language acquisition in the classroom.* New York: Pergamon/Alemany.

Lamberg, W. J., Rodríguez, L., & Tomas, D. A. (1978). Training in identifying oral reading departures from text which can be explained as Spanish-English phonological differences. *The Bilingual Review/La Revista Bilingüe, 5,* 65–75.

Lambert, W. E. (1975). Culture and language as factors in learning and education. In A. Wolfgang (Ed.), *Education of immigrant students.* Toronto: O.I.S.E.

Lau v. Nichols, 414 U.S. 563 (1974).

Los Angeles Unified School District. (1985). *Strategies for sheltered English instruction.* Los Angeles: Author.

Lynch, P. (1986). *Using big books and predictable books.* New York: Scholastic.

María, K. (1989). Developing disadvantaged children's background knowledge interactively. *The Reading Teacher, 42,* 296–300.

Miramontes, O. B. (1990). A comparative study of English oral reading skills in differently schooled groups of Hispanic students. *Journal of Reading Behavior, 22,* 373–394.

Modiano, N. (1968). Bilingual education for children of linguistic minorities. *American Indígena, 28,* 405–414.

Moll, L. C., & González, N. (1994). Critical issues: Lessons from research with language-minority children. *Journal of Reading Behavior, 26,* 439–456.

Moustafa, M. (1995). Children's productive phonological recoding. *Reading Research Quarterly, 30*(3), 464–476.

Moustafa, M. (1997). *Beyond traditional phonics.* Portsmouth, NH: Heinemann.

Moustafa, M., & Penrose, J. (1985). Comprehensible input plus the language experience approach: Reading instruction for limited English speaking students. *The Reading Teacher, 38,* 640–647.

Nagy, W. W., García, G. E., Durgunoǧlu, A.Y., & Hancin-Bhatt, B. (1993). Spanish-English bilingual students' use of cognates in English reading. *Journal of Reading Behavior, 25,* 241–259.

Nathenson-Mejia, S. (1989). Writing in a second language: Negotiating meaning through invented spelling. *Language Arts, 66,* 516–526.

National Clearinghouse for English Language Acquisition and Language Instruction Educational Programs. U. S. Department of Education. (2006). *Introduction to language instruction educational programs.* Retrieved July 19, 2006, from http://www.ncela.gwu.edu/about/lieps/

Nessel, D. D., & Jones, M B. (1981). *The language-experience approach to reading.* New York: Teachers College Columbia University.

Office of English Language Acquisition (OELA). (2004). Retrieved July 19, 2006, from http://www.ed.gov/print/programs/sfgp/index.html

O'Leary, D. (2002). *Widening achievement gap.* Tucson: League of Latin American Citizens.

Pearson, P. D. (1985). Changing the face of reading comprehension instruction. *The Reading Teacher, 38,* 724–738.

Peck, J. (1989). Using storytelling to promote language and literacy development. *The Reading Teacher, 43,* 138–141.

Peetoom, A. (1986). *Shared reading: Safe risks with whole books.* Richmond Hill, Ontario, Canada: Scholastic.

Ramírez, J. D. (1991). *Final report: Longitudinal study of structured English immersion strategy, early-exit and late-exit bilingual education programs* (NTIS 300-87-0156). Washington, DC: U.S. Department of Education.

Samuels, S. J. (1971). Letter-name versus letter-sound knowledge in learning to read. *The Reading Teacher, 24,* 604–608.

Samuels, S. J. (1979). The method of repeated readings. *The Reading Teacher, 43,* 403–408.

Samway, K. D. (1993). This is hard, isn't it? Children evaluating writing. *TESOL Quarterly, 27,* 233–257.

Saville, M. R., & Troike, R. C. (1971). *A handbook of bilingual education.* Washington, DC: Teachers of English to Speakers of Other Languages.

Schifini, A. (1985). *A sheltered English: Content area instruction for limited English proficient students.* Los Angeles: Los Angeles County Office of Education.

Schifini, A. (1996). Reading instruction for the pre-literate and struggling older student. *NABE News, 20*(5–6), 20, 30.

Selinker, L., Swain, M., & Dumas, G. (1975). The interlanguage hypothesis extended to children. *Language Learning, 25,* 139–152.

Smith, F. (1985). *Reading without nonsense.* New York: Teachers College Press.

Smith, F. (1988). *Understanding reading.* Hillsdale, NJ: Erlbaum.

Snow, C. E., Burns, M. S., & Griffin, P. (Eds.). (1998). *Preventing reading difficulties in young children.* Committee on the Prevention of Reading Difficulties in Young Children. Commission on Behavioral and Social Sciences and Education, National Research Council. Washington, DC. National Academy Press.

Strickland, D. S., & Feeley, J. T. (1985). Using children's concept of story to improve reading and writing. In T. L. Harris & E. J. Cooper (Eds.), *Reading, thinking and concept development* (pp. 163–173). New York: College Entrance Examination Board.

Suro, R., & Singer, A. (2002). *Latino growth in metropolitan America: Changing patterns, new locations.* Washington, DC: Brookings.

Terrell, T. D. (1977). A natural approach to second language acquisition and learning. *Modern Language Journal, 6,* 325–337.

Terrell, T. D. (1981). The natural approach in bilingual education. In California State Department of Education (Ed.), *School and language minority students: A theoretical framework* (pp. 117–146). Los Angeles: Evaluation, Dissemination and Assessment Center, California State University, Los Angeles.

Terrell, T. D. (1982). The natural approach to language teaching: An update. *Modern Language Journal, 66,* 121–132.

Terrell, T. D. (1986). Acquisition in the natural approach: The binding/access framework. *Modern Language Journal, 70,* 213–227.

Thomas, W. P., & Collier, V. P. (2002). *A national study of school effectiveness for language minority students' long-term academic achievement final report: Project 1.1.* Santa Cruz, CA: Center for Research on Education, Diversity and Excellence.

Trachtenburg, P., & Furruggia, A. (1989). Big books from little voices: Reaching high risk beginning readers. *The Reading Teacher, 42,* 284–289.

UNESCO. (1953). *The use of vernacular languages in education.* Paris: Author.

U.S. Bureau of the Census. (2000). *Census 2000.* Washington, DC: Author.

Veatch, J. (1996). From the vantage of retirement. *The Reading Teacher, 49,* 510–516.

Veatch, J., Sawicki, F., Elliott, G., Flake, E., & Blakey, J. (1979). *Key words to reading: The language experience approach begins.* Columbus, OH: Merrill.

Vygotsky, L. S. (1978). *Mind in society.* Cambridge, MA: Harvard University Press.

Factors Related to Reading Problems

Chapter Outline

*I*n this chapter we discuss intellectual, physical, linguistic, and learning factors that can be secondary or contributing causes of reading problems. Although these factors are often considered peripheral to reading, they can affect
the entire enterprise of learning.

Most classroom teachers are more or less accustomed to assessing reading
within their classrooms. The assessment of intelligence, vision and hearing,
emotional and personality development, and special learning problems, however,
usually takes place outside the regular classroom. The school nurse may provide
vision and hearing screening, the school psychologist may administer intelligence tests, the guidance counselor may do personality and interest assessments,
the speech-language pathologist may administer speech and language tests, and
so forth.

Teachers might not be familiar with these special assessment devices and
their results, which are typically used to determine whether students qualify for
special programs and to plan instructional interventions. In the sections that
follow, we discuss legislation related to students with special educational needs,
the referral process, generic ways special learning problems are assessed, and
some classroom-based interventions for students with special needs.

Philosophical and Legal Issues Related to Special-Needs Students

In the past, children with special intellectual, physical, or emotional needs were largely
excluded from the regular curriculum. Changes in educational policy for special-needs
students are the result of growing public awareness and legislative action (Patton,
Kauffman, Blackburn, & Brown, 1991). Public schools are required by law to provide
"appropriate educational experiences" for all students, including those with emotional,
physical, intellectual, and/or cognitive processing problems. The key issue is what is
"appropriate" in each case.

Past Legislation Affecting Special-Needs Students

Initially, all students with handicapping conditions, including those with emotional,
physical, intellectual, and/or cognitive processing disabilities, were afforded the right to
free and appropriate public education in the least restrictive environment with the passage and signing of the Education for the Handicapped Act (EHA) in 1975 (P.L. 94-142).

Provision: Free public education will be provided for all handicapped persons between the ages of 3 and 21 years of age.

Implications: Schools must serve the needs of students who are both older and younger than those served in the past. The traditional concept of school-age children between ages 5 and 18 has been drastically modified. Since the law creates financial incentives for schools to identify disabled preschoolers and provide special services for them, kindergarten and primary-grade teachers are involved in early identification programs.

At the other end of the age scale, teachers are affected by the inclusion of older students with disabilities into regular education classes. This is particularly important in high school, where students up to age 21 may be included in regular classes.

The legislation was reauthorized in 1990 and renamed the Individuals with Disabilities Education Act (IDEA) (P.L. 101-76). IDEA continued the major provisions of P.L. 94-142 while extending these rights to younger children with disabilities and to students with disabilities 16 years of age and older. IDEA emphasized the transition from school to the workplace and included postsecondary education, vocational training, rehabilitation services, and referral to adult service agencies.

Provision: Students with disabilities will be placed in the least restrictive environment whenever and wherever possible.

Implications: In 1997 IDEA was reauthorized as the Individuals with Disabilities Education Act Amendments of 1997 (P.L. 105-17), extending some of the existing components of the two earlier versions of the legislation. Most importantly, P.L. 105-17 clarified the rights of disabled students to spend much or all of their instructional time in general education settings and have access to the general education curriculum. This means that special education is not a separate place or program, but rather is a network of support services enabling exceptional students to reach the outcomes identified for all students in general education. The law also stipulates that students with disabilities participate in the same assessments expected of all students; if they are unable to do so, alternative assessment procedures with individualized criteria must be developed and implemented to ensure student progress toward their program goals.

Provision: Every student with a disability receiving special education services will be provided with an individualized educational program, called an IEP, which spells out present abilities, short- and long-term goals, and the means by which goals will be achieved. Each student's IEP will be developed jointly by the special and general education teachers, the parents, and the student, where possible.

Implications: The inclusion of handicapped students in general education classrooms for part or all of the school day affects nearly every teacher. General education teachers are full members of the IEP team, along with the student's parents. All teachers working with disabled students have direct responsibility for the planning, implementation, and evaluation of instructional programs. This means that teachers must understand handicapping conditions and how they affect learning, management techniques, and teaching strategies. In developing and updating IEPs, teachers join forces with the parents of students with disabilities for greater parental involvement and teacher accountability. In many cases, the students themselves are also included in the development of their IEPs, to the extent that they are able to participate.

Provision: All tests and evaluative instruments used will be prepared and administered in order to eliminate racial and cultural discrimination.

Implications: Because of the disproportionate representation of minority children in special education, IDEA of 1997 reflects decisions handed down by the courts over the years (see *Diana v. Board of Education,* 1970; *Larry P. v. Riles,* 1979). Tests and assessment devices must be closely scrutinized to eliminate bias. No single test, measure, or score can be used to classify a student. When necessary, tests must be modified so that students with disabilities can respond to them in ways that are best for them—for example, in Braille, sign language, or the student's first language. These modifications entail widespread changes in test construction, administration, and interpretation.

This provision has also been interpreted to mean that schools must provide a multidisciplinary team as an integral part of the identification process.

The provisions of the Individuals with Disabilities Education Act also establish certain basic rights for students with handicapping conditions:

- The right to due process protects the individual from erroneous classification, capricious labeling, and denial of equal education.
- The right of protection against discriminatory testing ensures against possible bias in tests used with ethnic and minority children.
- The right to placement in the least restrictive educational environment protects the individual from possible detrimental effects of segregated education for the handicapped.
- The right to have individual program plans ensures accountability by those responsible for the education of the handicapped.

The law also stipulates that a student's status and the special services being provided must be reviewed at least once every three years. The purpose of this triennial review is to determine whether the child is still eligible for special services. The review must include a complete reassessment of learning aptitude, speech, hearing, school achievement, adaptive behavior, and so forth.

More recently, and as we will see in the section entitled "Identifying Special-Needs Students," the law provides for a variety of experts to "reason together" to determine a student's handicapping conditions and plan remediation. But parents may interpret their children's needs differently. In most cases, parents and educators in disagreement reach compromises, sometimes with the assistance of an appeal process. Sometimes, however, legal action is necessary. In some cases, parents have won the right to require that school districts pay for private schooling if the court is convinced that an "adequate" education is not possible within the local schools.

IDEA (2004) and NCLB

The revised Individuals with Disabilities Education Improvement Act of 2004 (IDEA-2004) provides several amendments to the earlier legislation. IDEA-2004 is carefully aligned with provisions of the No Child Left Behind (NCLB) initiative of the Department of Education (NEA, 2004). Special education teachers who teach a core subject, including English, reading, or language arts, are required to be "highly qualified," and students with disabilities are required to be assessed annually in NCLB-required assessments, with some reasonable accommodations, such as means of presentation and response, timing, and setting of the test. Alternative tests of grade-level knowledge are now allowed for as many as 2 percent of special-needs students in a district, and they may be applied to alternate achievement standards.

Students served under IDEA-2004 must meet the same state standards as all other students, including English language learners, with some exceptions for students with severe cognitive disabilities. Needless to say, these provisions in the law are the subject of much discussion in all school districts as they attempt to meet these new requirements.

In addition, the amendments are designed to reduce paperwork requirements for the IEP, even while ensuring that students continue to have access to a free, appropriate public education (FAPE).

Reading First is an area of NCLB that also applies here (Karger, 2005). Implications of Reading First for NCLB and IDEA include early identification of struggling readers so that they can be involved in the general curriculum. This is designed to occur as a result of effective instructional techniques in reading that assist students with disabilities.

Student Participation in General Education

The concept of inclusion, or including students with disabilities into general education classes, has long been a topic of controversy. The amended IDEA of 1997 is more deliberate than earlier laws about students with disabilities participating in general education. Although it still considers the least restrictive environment when placing children, it indicates that these students are to be placed in settings where they have access to the same curriculum as all other students and receive this instruction in the same settings as these students, whenever possible. It also suggests that the general education teachers who are expected to teach inclusion students with disabilities develop partnerships with special educators when planning and implementing educational programs (Villa & Thousand, 2000).

Better ways of meeting the needs of exceptional learners are being explored today. These include helping general education teachers to use methods that are effective with exceptional children, using special educators as co-teachers and consultants rather than providers of separate instruction, establishing teams to ensure that only those students who truly need special services are so identified, structuring classrooms to promote cooperative learning among students of various ability levels, and using materials and methods to improve students' attitudes toward handicapped and exceptional peers (Friend & Bursuck, 2002).

Another result of the inclusion movement is to provide special services to identified students on a "push-in" basis, in contrast to a "pull-out" program in which identified students leave their regular classroom for special, separate instruction. The pull-out model allows special-needs students privacy and limits distractions during their instruction, but it can also isolate them from peers, disrupt their daily schedule, and inhibit general and special education teachers' efforts to collaborate.

In the push-in model, the special educator or reading specialist works with identified students as a co-teacher in the regular classroom. Special-needs students do not miss important learning or regular classroom events while they receive the extra support and attention they need. In addition, special educators and classroom teachers can share their areas of expertise and support each other's efforts. However, push-in programs require teachers to utilize very different skills and include expectations for teachers to work closely together in the same workspace. Administrative support and encouragement are essential for this cooperative effort to be successful.

Since general education teachers will continue to have greater responsibility for teaching children identified as having special needs, informal diagnostic methods take on even greater importance and utility.

Identifying Special-Needs Students

Individual school divisions differ in minor ways in the procedures they follow regarding referral and classification, but a sequence of events such as this is typical:

1. A request is made by teachers or parents to have a student considered for screening or diagnostic testing. Since each school must have a standing committee to handle identification procedures, this committee or evaluation team receives such requests.

2. Parental permission for testing is sought by the principal, special education supervisor, or screening committee. If parents or legal guardians refuse to give permission, no further action can be taken. The student's progress can be monitored and further requests made, but without parental permission no examination can take place.

3. After parental permission is given, the committee usually meets to discuss the child's progress and difficulties, determine what measures have already been taken to help the child, and decide what further assessment may be called for. If further assessment is recommended, arrangements are made for these assessments to be done. The committee must be multidisciplinary and typically includes a special education representative, a school psychologist, the school principal or principal's designee, one or more classroom teachers, and one or more parents. Other committee members may be a reading specialist, a speech-language pathologist, a visiting teacher or home-school liaison, or other specialists.

4. After assessments are completed, the team reconvenes to discuss the results and make recommendations. The student's parent(s) or guardian(s) and classroom teacher are included in this meeting. Parents may choose to bring their own advocate to help them understand the results and recommendations. Teachers working with the student are invited to share informal assessment data, observations about the child's performance, behavior, and so forth that might assist the committee.

5. The committee makes a joint recommendation about the student's eligibility for special services, including types of services that can be offered and the most appropri-

ate placement for the student. Parental consent is needed for services to be provided. If parents do not give their permission, a mediator reviews the case and makes a determination that is binding on all parties.

6. After eligibility has been determined, an IEP must be developed. Included are the student's present achievement or performance levels, short-term and long-term goals, beginning and estimated termination dates for special services, evaluation procedures and criteria to determine if goals have been met, detailed descriptions of services to be provided, accommodations that the student will be permitted (e.g., taking tests orally or having an interpreter present), a statement of the student's involvement in general education classes, and how the student will be assessed. Again, parental agreement is required before an IEP can be implemented. If agreement cannot be reached with parents on aspects of the IEP, a hearing is held to ensure the family's right to due process.

7. Finally, the student is placed in the least restrictive educational environment and IEP implementation begins. All educators or agencies involved with the student's educational plan are required to make good faith efforts to help the student achieve the IEP goals. Parents can request program review and revision if they believe such good faith efforts have not been made. IEPs are reviewed and revised yearly to ensure that goals and procedures are appropriate. As mentioned previously, students are reassessed triennially to determine what changes have taken place and whether services are still required.

Assessment of Special Educational Needs

The IDEA requires that assessment for special services must include educational, psychological, medical, and sociological components. This ensures that the student's assessment is as comprehensive as possible. The use of a combination of standardized and informal assessments is common and in some states is required.

As you read in Chapter 5, formal assessment devices are usually standardized, norm-referenced tests. Administration, scoring, and interpretation procedures are clearly set forth. Formal tests yield many different types of scores and are given for many different purposes, but most compare a student's performance to others.

As discussed in Chapters 2 and 3, informal procedures yield results that are directly related to instruction. They often show what a student can do more directly and precisely than formal tests. Thus, both kinds of assessment provide useful information about students' abilities and achievement.

Screening assessments are mandated and reviewed by the school's identification or child study team, of which the general education classroom teacher and/or reading teacher are often a part. A team approach to assessment is a safeguard against potential bias. The IDEA contains two provisions to safeguard against test abuses:

1. Testing must be conducted in the language of the student, measures used must be nondiscriminatory and validated for the purpose for which they are used, and no single test score may be used as the sole basis for determining special education placement.

2. In determining mental or cognitive disability, concurrent deficits in both intelligence test performance and adaptive behavior must be demonstrated.

Assessment instruments have different purposes and assess different aspects of performance and potential. They fall into these general categories.

Tests of Learning Aptitude.   *Learning aptitude* refers to the student's capacity for altering behavior when presented with new information or experiences. These often include intelligence tests, which measure scholastic aptitude, not general aptitude or intelligence, and also indirectly assess achievement in areas such as vocabulary and math computation. Intelligence tests are the primary means used to assess learning aptitude. Learning aptitude is also sometimes referred to as *cognitive ability, learning potential, cognitive factors,* and similar terms. Some school achievement batteries contain sections that assess learning aptitude, comparing it to present achievement levels.

Tests of Achievement.   These are the primary means used to assess students' present levels of scholastic performance. These tests assess what has been learned, not what the child is capable of learning. Achievement test batteries include subtests dealing with reading, spelling, mathematics, written language, and the like. Tests that assess achievement in single areas only, such as separate reading, spelling, mathematics, and writing achievement tests, may be used instead of a battery.

Tests of Adaptive Behavior.   *Adaptive behavior* refers to how effectively an individual meets standards of personal independence and social responsibility normally expected of her age and cultural group. These measures are used when mental or cognitive disability is suspected.

Tests of Specific Learning Processes.   These test various discrete learning processes such as auditory discrimination, short-term memory, visual perception, motor abilities, and the like. Some tests assess only one process; others are batteries with subtests assessing different processes. Most intelligence tests also include measures of many of these abilities, such as short-term memory, visual perception, and visual-motor coordination.

Tests of Classroom Behavior and Adjustment.   These include evaluation scales and rating scales for behavior, self-concept scales, and interest inventories. These are most often used in the identification of emotionally disturbed students or those with behavior disorders, either as the primary or a secondary problem.

Intellectual Factors

When diagnosing a reading problem, one of the most frequently used instruments is an intelligence test. But research shows seemingly contradictory findings: that good readers tend to perform better on IQ tests than poor readers and that reading problems are not limited to lower-IQ students, but are found across the whole range of intellectual abilities.

General agreement has long existed that intelligence and reading achievement are fairly well correlated, particularly in the upper grades. What this means is that better performance on reading tests and intelligence tests tends to occur together; students generally do well on both or poorly on both. It does not imply causation; we cannot infer from positive correlations that one factor causes the other, only that they coincide.

It may be that above-average intelligence encourages above-average reading achievement. It may be equally true that good reading helps students do better on intelligence tests. Or it may be that both reading tests and IQ tests call upon the same kinds of abilities and knowledge. But poor readers may come from all ability levels.

What do IQ tests tell us? That depends very much on which test is used. Not all measure the same skills, and in order to evaluate results, we have to know something about their characteristics.

Tests of Intelligence and Learning Aptitude

Intelligence tests are essentially measures of verbal abilities and skills in dealing with abstract symbols. They are not intended to measure innate intelligence or potential but rather to predict future learning by sampling behavior already learned. The premise of these measures is that present performance is a predictor of future performance (McLaughlin & Lewis, 1990). They are appropriately viewed as predictors of academic success; misinterpretation of their purpose and results leads to misunderstanding and inaccurate judgments about children.

Group Intelligence Tests.   Some tests that yield an IQ or some kind of "ability quotient" are group tests. Group tests usually require students to read and mark answers; they consequently penalize poor readers, who generally score poorly on such measures, so they tend to underestimate poor readers' potential. Group intelligence tests or tests of learning aptitude are useful only as general screening devices, and results can be generalized only to large numbers of students, not to individuals.

Individual Intelligence Tests.   An individually administered test that does not require a student to read or write will give a better estimate of real academic potential than a group test.

The **Wechsler Intelligence Scale for Children-III (WISC-III)** is the individual test most often used to assess intellectual performance of children between the ages of $6\frac{1}{2}$ and 16. It is one of several related tests that span all age levels. The **Wechsler Preschool and Primary Scale of Intelligence-Revised (WPPSI-R)** is appropriate for children between 4 and $6\frac{1}{2}$ years of age. The **Wechsler Adult Intelligence Scale-Revised (WAIS-R)** is used for persons between 16 and 74 years of age. These tests may be administered only by someone specially trained and certified to do so. Modified instructions for administering the WISC-III to deaf children are available (Sattler, 1992).

The WISC-III assesses intellectual functioning by sampling performance on many different types of activities. The test attempts to assess verbal and nonverbal aspects of intelligence separately with 13 subtests—10 required and 3 optional or supplemental. The 13 subtests are organized into two scales, with those involving language operations directly in one, the Verbal Scale, and those involving the nonverbal or indirectly verbal operations in the other, the Performance Scale. Each scale yields a separate scale IQ, which can be compared to determine if both aspects of a child's intelligence seem to be equally well developed, and the scale IQs can be converted into a Full Scale IQ.

Raw scores from each subtest are converted to scaled scores, standard scores ranging from 1 to 19 with a mean of 10 and a standard deviation of 3. Transforming raw scores into standard units makes it possible to compare results of different subtests.

The Full Scale IQ represents a subject's overall intellectual functioning as measured by performance on the 10 subtests. The Verbal, Performance, and Full Scale IQs all have a mean of 100 and a standard deviation of 15. The test uses the following classification scheme for IQ scores:

130 and above	Very superior
120–129	Superior
110–119	High average
90–109	Average
80–89	Low average
70–79	Borderline
69 and below	Mentally deficient

To avoid overinterpreting IQ scores, keep in mind that they represent a sample of behavior taken at one point in time and consider IQ scores only in relation to the range in which they occur, rather than as single, fixed scores. The average standard error of measurement for the Full Scale IQ score is 3.2 IQ points. A Full Scale IQ could thus be expected to vary by three or four points in either direction. It is more accurate to speak of a student's IQ score as "within the high average range," for example, than to say that the student "has an IQ of 117."

Clinicians often look for differences between Verbal and Performance IQs and patterns of scores on individual subtests to recommend further psychological and academic testing (Sattler, 1992).

The **Kaufman Assessment Battery for Children (K-ABC)** is another widely used individual measure, appropriate for children between 2½ and 12½ years of age. The K-ABC battery contains mental processing and achievement subtests. A Mental Processing Composite, an index of intellectual functioning, is derived from the mental processing subtests. Two other global scores are derived from groups of subtests: Sequential Processing and Simultaneous Processing. Global scores have a mean of 100 and a standard deviation of 15.

A nonverbal scale is available that allows the examiner to conduct several of the subtests in mime with only motor response required. The scale is useful with hearing impaired, emotionally disturbed, speech or language impaired, and non-English-speaking students.

The **Stanford-Binet Intelligence Scale** has recently been radically changed from its old format. Earlier versions of the Stanford-Binet were developed on the premise that as a child grows older, he develops knowledge and skills in a fairly steady, sequential way, resulting in a measurable mental age. For example, if a 7-year-old could correctly respond to items typically correctly answered by 9-year-olds, the student's mental age would be 9 years and some months. IQ scores were converted from mental ages. However, the concept of mental age has been convincingly challenged over the years; the development of the Wechsler Scales was a successful attempt to measure intelligence based on a scale other than age.

Items on the Stanford-Binet are arranged in ascending order of difficulty into 15 subsets that attempt to assess abilities other than strictly verbal. Scaled subtest scores can be combined into several global scores in Verbal Reasoning, Abstract-Visual Reasoning, Quantitative Reasoning, and Short-Term Memory, with an overall score similar to a global IQ score. These changes make the new Stanford-Binet more like the Wechsler Scales.

The **Kaufman Brief Intelligence Test (K-BIT)** is a brief assessment of verbal and nonverbal intelligence of children and adults from the ages of 4 to 90. It was developed to be used as a screening device, not a substitute for more comprehensive individual IQ tests.

The K-BIT has two subtests: Vocabulary and Matrices. Designed to measure verbal and school-related skills, the Vocabulary subtest assesses a person's word knowledge and verbal concept formation. The Matrices subtests measure the ability to solve problems and other nonverbal skills.

The K-BIT yields age-based standard scores having the same mean and standard deviation as the Wechsler and Kaufman scales. Scores are generated for each subtest and for an overall K-BIT IQ Composite or IQ standard score (Kaufman & Kaufman, 1990).

These individual intelligence tests assess both verbal and nonverbal intellectual abilities. Academic skills such as reading and writing are deemphasized. Although these tests yield results that can be used to predict academic success, no single test, used exclusively, can predict or evaluate a child's academic achievement. There are many factors that influence test results. One of these factors is the role of experience.

The **Leiter International Performance Scale-Revised (Leiter-R)** is a completely nonverbal individually administered measure of intelligence and cognitive abilities. Test items are game-like, maintain the student's interest, and require no language from the examiner or the student being tested. It is designed for use with subjects from infancy through adult. It is especially appropriate for non-English-speaking students, attention-deficit, and autistic students. Psychometric studies of the Leiter-R have demonstrated its appropriateness for subjects from all ethnic groups and cultures.

The Role of Experience

Standardized assessments are only part of the overall assessment and evaluation process when determining the educational abilities and needs of children. We cannot underestimate the importance of developmental experiences, both real and vicarious, in shaping standardized test performance and apparent educational ability.

What kind of experience are we talking about? Essentially, we learn in two ways: directly, by having real, concrete experience with objects and events, and vicariously, by observing and remembering the experiences of others. Students with disabilities, or those from other cultural backgrounds, use oral and other nontraditional communication forms to "engage in sophisticated acts of literacy and communication"—in both the informal and formal settings of schools, home, and communities where students spend their time (McIntyre, Rosebery, & Gonzalez, 2001, p. 5).

Real experiences in the formative years contribute to what most of us think of as an enriched environment. Enrichment means having plentiful opportunities to manipulate things; experiment with causes, effects, and consequences; talk and be talked to; and be encouraged to extend cognitive horizons and try new things. Learning is a process that involves both social as well as cognitive developments, and the essential experience for individual learning and development to occur is founded in people's interactions with others (Vygotsky, 1978).

These characteristics of an intellectually enriching environment know no economic, ethnic, social, or linguistic boundaries. They flourish where adults respect and nurture children's attempts to become competent and where those adults give conscious thought to providing opportunities for children to become independent and capable.

Direct, concrete experience with things and events is one critical aspect; experience with language is another. Verbal intelligence flourishes in the home, and later the school, where children are talked to by adults, where adults really listen to their responses and encourage conversation, where events and behaviors are explained and verbal reasoning is demonstrated, and where adults model language use by expanding and elaborating on what children say.

In environments where children are rarely addressed except in commands, where their spontaneous utterances are rarely listened to or responded to, where their requests for explanations are routinely answered by "Because I said so, that's why!" and explanations are rarely given, verbal intelligence is stunted. These children enter the world of language poorly adapted to participate in it fully. Their learning opportunities are restricted by language, rather than expanded by it. Whatever their socioeconomic status, they are disadvantaged in school readiness.

The other important aspect of experience is vicarious experience. Fortunately for all of us, we can learn from observing others as well as by experiencing things ourselves. Learning from the experiences of others saves us from having to experience everything personally, and we can derive nearly as much from those experiences as from our own.

Perhaps the greatest benefit of literacy is that through reading we can vicariously experience events, emotions, and ideas completely outside our own environment. We can travel to places we will never go to, including places that exist only in the mind; visit the past and the future with as much ease as the present; meet the most famous people of history and share their innermost thoughts; and experience joy, rage, grief, amazement, and every other human emotion by reading. All this makes good reading a life-long joy and avocation.

Reading and books, however, are more than a source of pleasure. In spite of the inroads of TV, videos, and cyberspace, print is still the largest source of information for many people.

These issues also arise in concerns about the overrepresentation of children from linguistic and ethnic minorities in special education (Hill, Carjuzaa, Aramburo, & Baca, 1993). Historically, children were often assigned to special education classes on the basis of supposed language disorders and/or mental retardation that might be nothing more than limited English proficiency. Under provisions of *Diana v. State Board of Education* (1970) and subsequent special education legislation, such as P.L. 94-142, this is no longer permitted. Damico (1991) suggests that care be taken to ensure that referral to special education is not based on the following:

- Other factors that might explain the child's learning and language difficulties, including lack of opportunity to learn, cultural dissonance, and stressful life events, for example, among refugee children
- Language difficulties that the student has at school, but not at home or in the community
- Ordinary needs of children to acquire English as a second language or the Standard American English dialect
- Cross-cultural interference
- Bias in the assessment process, including data analysis that does not take into account the child's culture, language, and life experiences

There are many strategies that can be used very effectively in teaching children with these needs. According to Gersten and Baker (2000), teachers should do the following:

- Build children's vocabulary and use it as a curricular anchor.
- Use visual representations to reinforce major concepts and vocabulary.
- Use the children's mother tongue as a support system.
- Adapt cognitive and language demands of instruction to the children by using sheltered English strategies.

It is not only the physical needs of these students that should be addressed in inclusion efforts, but also the content of the curriculum. If students of color or girls need to see themselves in the literature they read, then so should students with disabilities. According to Landrum (2001), this benefits not only those students, but also students without disabilities, who need to learn about and accept differences. Landrum has developed a set of criteria for the evaluation of novels that feature characters with disabilities. Among her criteria are the following:

- *Plot:* Story events are realistic, not contrived; disabled characters are active participants.
- *Character development:* Disabled characters are presented as strong and independent, not passive and dependent; the focus is on what they can do, not on what they cannot do.
- *Tone:* The text avoids using such terms as *retarded, handicapped,* and *crippled.*

Physical Factors

Many physical conditions and processes can be related to reading problems. The factors most commonly considered are visual and auditory. Each of these areas has been extensively studied in relation to reading difficulties, but the various conditions and processes themselves are complex and sometimes confusing. In this section, we consider vision and hearing.

Vision and Visual Problems

Reading is a visual act (for sighted persons) because we cannot read in the dark. It is, of course, much more than just a visual act because more goes on behind the reader's eyes than in front of them, but some visual competence is needed to activate the cognitive processes involved in reading. To make sense of print, the reader must be able to gain information from print through vision. For this reason, poor readers are often subjected to vision screening in diagnosis.

Teachers are often the first line of defense against vision problems. They are usually in an ideal position to spot potential problems and refer children for appropriate screening because they, more than parents, observe children in close contact with reading and writing materials. Also, children with vision problems often don't realize that others see differently, and they don't call adult attention to their difficulty. Therefore, it is important for teachers to understand vision problems and their symptoms. Figure 10.1 summarizes the nature and symptoms of some common visual difficulties.

When symptoms of vision problems are displayed frequently, are not common to the rest of the class, and are evidenced even when performing easy tasks, they signal a need for a parent conference and referral to an eye specialist. Referrals should be made through the principal, school nurse, supervisor, or other designated personnel.

Hearing and Auditory Problems

The relationship between auditory problems and reading difficulties has long been established. Hearing and language are as intimately related as language and reading. As teachers observe the oral and written language of their students, they can become aware of possible hearing problems.

When children learn to read, they employ their whole experience with oral language. Hearing problems can interfere with, delay, or even prevent the development of oral language fluency, and it is in this respect that hearing problems can affect reading.

Another factor is the interference of hearing problems with normal phonemic awareness. Across the entire spectrum of approaches, some features of every beginning reading program are standard: learning letter names and sounds, use of simple phonic analysis strategies to decode words, and frequent oral reading. These activities put a premium on clarity of hearing, and the youngster with auditory problems is at a distinct disadvantage.

Technical Name	Common Name	Condition	Symptoms
Myopia	Nearsightedness	Clear vision at near point; blurring of distant images	Squinting at the board; holding print close to face; inattention to board work
Hyperopia	Farsightedness	Clear vision at far point; blurring of close objects	Holding print well away from face; disinterest in close work; eye fatigue during reading
Astigmatism		Distortion and/or blurring of part (or all) of visual field, far and near	Eye fatigue; headache; squinting; tilting or turning head; nausea during reading
Amblyopia	Lazy eye	Suppression of vision in one eye; dimming of vision without structural cause	Tilting or turning head to read; eye fatigue on one side; headache
Strabismus	Crossed eyes	Difficulty converging and focusing both eyes on the same object	Squinting; closing or covering one eye to focus; eyes misaligned
Phoria or fusion problems; binocular coordination		Imbalance of ocular muscles; difficulty converging and focusing both eyes equally	Squinting; closing or covering one eye
Aniseikonia		Differences in size or shape of image in each eye	Blurring

FIGURE 10.1 *Vision Problems*

Thus, hearing problems that occur any time in the first eight to ten years of life may affect a child's reading by interfering with language development in the preschool years or with the development of phonemic awareness and phonics in beginning reading.

Testing of auditory acuity (keenness) involves assessment of the ability to hear speech sounds, music, and noises. In reading, the speech sounds are critical.

Hearing losses can affect the perception of pitch or volume or both. If the child can hear some sound frequencies but not others, it can be devastating in learning to read because it means that the child can hear some speech sounds accurately but not others. Hearing loss involving the high-frequency sounds is more common than loss of low-frequency sounds. Children with high-frequency hearing loss can accurately hear vowel sounds and maybe some consonant sounds, but not all of them.

Those with high-tone losses may hear spoken words in a garbled, indistinct fashion, depending on how many consonant sounds are affected. If only vowels can be heard, words are almost totally meaningless because consonant sounds are what make spoken words intelligible. (Read a line of print aloud to someone, pronouncing only the vowel sounds; repeat the line pronouncing only the consonant sounds. Which version could the listener more easily understand?)

Hearing losses are not always as severe as the previous example. Often only a few consonant and blend sounds are affected, but phonics instruction is made very difficult by this loss, and the student may be very poor at word analysis and word recognition. Also, the words that are most often taught in beginning reading frequently vary only in their consonant sounds, as in the word families and rhyming word patterns (*cat–hat–pat–mat–sat*). Learning word families can be very difficult for the child with high-tone hearing loss.

A topic related to auditory acuity is auditory discrimination, the ability to distinguish between highly similar sounds and to detect whether two (or more) sounds are alike or different. Being able to detect subtle differences in speech sounds helps students to master phonics; those with poor auditory discrimination may have persistent trouble with phonic analysis and may also have speech impairments.

Auditory discrimination can be assessed formally or informally. The student is required to distinguish between pairs of words or syllables that differ minimally (*rat–rap, ome–ote*). Teachers frequently make up and give such exercises themselves. Formal auditory discrimination tests are also common, and some standardized readiness tests include such a subtest.

In beginning reading it is common to combine phonics instruction with auditory discrimination practice. Beginning readers or prereaders who at first seem to have difficulty with auditory discrimination often need only to learn what to listen for and how to respond. In other words, they have no auditory disability, but have to learn what the task is.

Auditory discrimination skill generally improves as children progress through the primary grades. It is as much a learned skill as an innate perceptual ability.

Language Factors

Print is a form of language, and to be a reader, one must be a language user. Serious language disorders can inhibit children's development as readers and writers. Those that occur in the early years, when language is being acquired, have the most serious effects on later literacy.

Language Acquisition and Difficulties in Infancy and Early Childhood

As discussed in Chapter 6, children begin to use language, first to understand speech and then to produce it, in the first two years of life. Most children show that they can understand simple speech before they can produce any intelligible words and begin using one-, two- and three-word utterances before age 3. First words are most often names of things (*ball, doggy, mama*) and social expressions (*bye-bye, no-no*) (Nelson, 1973). Words referring to animals and sounds, childhood games, and food and drink names occur very frequently among toddlers' first 50 words (Tomasello & Mervis, 1994).

Between 1½ and 2 years, babies begin putting words together. Using just two words, they can express an amazing number of ideas, relationships, and needs; comment about objects and events; announce their own or others' actions; and even confess their own transgressions. Two-word, or telegraphic, utterances like "Allgone milk," "Doggie bye-bye," "Baby poopie," "Coat on," and "No nap!" convey a wealth of information with an economy of expression; indeed, as Trawick-Smith put it, "Babies speak as though they were paying for every word!" (1997, p. 202).

Longer utterances quickly follow, gaining in complexity. Young children seem to intuit and apply simple rules of their native language to determine the order of words in their two-word and longer utterances; rarely do they make word order errors like "On coat" instead of "Coat on." When they are unsure of word order, toddlers often produce the utterance with a rising, or questioning, inflection, as if to say, "Is this right?"

Although children acquire their language at somewhat different times and rates, most children have begun to babble expressively by the end of the first year, speak individual words by about 1½, and combine words by 2½. When these language features are absent, parents and caregivers often suspect a problem that may be interfering with normal language acquisition.

Language Development and Difficulties in Preschool and Primary Grades

For most children, language acquisition and development proceed rapidly in the years between 2 and 6. In the early childhood years children learn to recognize and use the most common sentence forms, including statements, questions, commands and exclamations. They acquire a working vocabulary of 5,000 to 8,000 words and can understand several thousand more (Reich, 1986).

In the preschool years, children's language develops along four equally important fronts:

- Their speech becomes clearer, articulation improves, and fluency develops. These areas of speech production are referred to as *phonology*.
- Their vocabularies grow as they acquire many new words and expressions, while they learn to understand even more words than they produce; thus, both expressive and receptive language grow. The system of word meanings is referred to as *semantics*.
- As they learn more words, their sentences become both longer and more complex. They begin to use embedded clauses, past and future tenses, plural forms, and the common sentence forms adults use most often. These aspects of language are referred to as *syntactic*.

■ They develop greater skill in using language socially: to get things done, get their needs met, and direct the behavior of others in socially acceptable ways. The social uses of language are referred to as *pragmatics.*

Atypical phonology is fairly common in the preschool years, and most problems of pronunciation can be addressed with speech intervention. Many English phonemes, or phoneme clusters like *skw* or *sl*, are not typically mastered until 7 to 9 years of age. Children who make irregular or inconsistent sound substitutions such as saying *rabbit* as "babbit" one time and "dabbit" another time, are highly disfluent after most children have developed fluency, or who generally cannot be understood are at risk for significant language delays and need identification and intervention.

Bilingual children often use the phonemes of their first, or more dominant, language when speaking their other language. A child bilingual in German and English, for example, might pronounce English words like *will* as "vill" or *valley* as "falley." These are language differences, not difficulties; they are caused by trying to learn and coordinate two different phonological systems.

Atypical semantic development is seen in children who suffer general language delay, as well as in Down syndrome children and others with serious cognitive deficits. These children often understand and produce words at a level similar to normal children who are much younger.

Some children show a somewhat different difficulty: They appear to have difficulty retrieving words and may use a variety of compensatory strategies to "fill in the blanks" in their communication. Children with word retrieval difficulties may stutter or pause for long periods as they try to recall the name of an object or a particular describing word; they may use very general terms like *that, things,* or *stuff* instead of labels for common objects; or they may describe objects by their function rather than by their names, as in "what you put your cereal in" for bowl.

Speech-language pathologists often use tests of receptive and expressive vocabulary to determine if a child has a language retrieval disability or a general linguistic delay. Two commonly used diagnostic tests for children up to the age of 7 are the Receptive One Word Picture Vocabulary Test and the Expressive One Word Picture Vocabulary Test-Revised. In the former, the child points to the correct picture that goes with a word pronounced by the examiner; the child does not need to speak. In the latter test, the child names pictures of objects shown by the examiner. For subjects from age 7 through adulthood, the Peabody Picture Vocabulary Test-Revised is often used. This test of receptive vocabulary also requires subjects to point to the correct picture and does not require speech.

Atypical syntactic development is evidenced when children do not construct sentences in age-appropriate ways. In this case children may fail to acquire, or acquire much more slowly, the basic sentence forms, questions, negatives, and word parts like *-ed, -s,* and *-ing* that most children use by about the age of 5. Children with atypical syntax usually use shorter utterances and fewer words than their peers. Their utterances tend to be grammatically confusing, and others often have trouble understanding what they mean.

Atypical syntax can be caused by intellectual deficits or mental retardation, deafness, and general language delays. A subtest of the Clinical Evaluation of Language Function called "Producing Model Sentences" may be used as a diagnostic tool. This assessment requires children to repeat sentences of increasing grammatical complexity. Long-term language intervention is required for these children.

Finally, children with quite profound disabilities often have atypical pragmatics development. The ability to use language socially, to get along with others, influence others and get one's needs met typically develops in the preschool years, as children learn how to use words, tone of voice, and body language to affect others' behavior. Most children quickly learn how to use language to get other children to give them a toy, share materials with them, or allow them to join in play.

But children with disabilities such as cognitive deficits or mental retardation, emotional disturbance, autism, and deafness may have great difficulty learning how to use language effectively in social ways. Intervention for these children involves teaching them to speak so that the listener understands, take turns talking, show interest in others' talk, use appropriate position and body language, ask and answer questions, and so forth. When these children's social use of language becomes more effective, they are often better able to form relationships, become active members of a group, and experience enhanced feelings of self-worth.

Language Development and Difficulties in Later Childhood

Between the ages of about 5 and 12, children continue to develop as language users, primarily broadening their vocabularies and polishing their language use. They acquire the few sentence forms that are less common, including passive forms like "A passing grade was earned by only three students" and produce longer, more grammatically complex sentences with imbedded clauses. Their spoken vocabularies grow from around 5,000 to 20,000 or more words. By about 12, most children's language equals that of most adults.

The greatest part of language development, then, occurs in the early childhood years and around the age of school entry. The middle and later childhood years are periods when language does not change substantially, but becomes broader, richer, and more precise. The pragmatic system develops fully, and by middle childhood most children have a variety of types of language they use in different social settings and for different purposes: The language of school, for example, may be somewhat more formal and more precise than the language of the playground or basketball court, and most children speak differently to a grandparent or teacher than they do to their best friends. Children learn more effective turn-taking and in general use language in a variety of ways to influence others.

Language intervention for older children often takes the form of direct teaching of language pragmatics, vocabulary development, and effective use of statements, questions, and other sentence forms. Children with disabilities or language delays can progress in language development when given appropriate special instruction.

Special Learning Problems

Learning disabilities and *dyslexia* are terms used for special learning problems. The issues involved in defining the terms, identifying students with these problems, and discovering methods of remediation have aroused considerable controversy for the past several decades, but educators appear to be moving toward a greater understanding of them.

Learning Disabilities

A *learning disability* is a severe problem in learning that qualifies a child for special education services. In 1977 the federal government adopted the following definition of *specific learning disability,* based on a 1969 definition proposed by the National Advisory Committee on Handicapped Children. This definition reappeared in the 1990 version of the Individuals with Disabilities Education Act (IDEA), P.L. 101-476, and its 1997 reauthorization:

> *Specific learning disability* means a disorder in one or more of the basic psychological processes involved in understanding or in using language, spoken or written, which may manifest itself in an imperfect ability to listen, think, speak, read, write, spell, or to do mathematical calculations. The term includes such conditions as perceptual handicaps, brain injury, minimal brain dysfunction, dyslexia, and developmental aphasia. The term does not include . . . learning problems that are primarily the result of visual, hearing, or motor handicaps, or mental retardation, or emotional disturbance, or of environmental, cultural, or economic disadvantage. (*Federal Register,* December 29, 1977, p. 65083)

According to the National Joint Committee on Learning Disabilities (NJCLD), *learning disabilities* refers to a group of disorders that include significant difficulties in the acquisition and use of listening, speaking, reading, writing, reasoning, or mathematical abilities. These disorders are intrinsic to the individual and are presumed to be due to central nervous system dysfunction. Problems in self-regulation, social perception, and social interaction may exist with learning disabilities but by themselves do not constitute a learning disability. Although learning disabilities may occur with other handicapping conditions such as sensory impairment, mental retardation, serious emotional disturbance, or with extrinsic influences such as cultural differences or insufficient or inappropriate instruction, learning disabilities are not the result of those conditions or influences.

Definitions of learning disability share these characteristics:

- Learning disabilities are thought to be caused by central nervous system dysfunction.
- Some degree of information processing difficulty interferes with academic or learning tasks.
- Children with learning disabilities show marked discrepancy between their potential and actual achievement.
- Other causes for the difficulty are ruled out.

Students with learning disabilities constitute a very diverse group, similar only in their unrealized academic potential. Many, but not all, children with learning disabilities have reading problems (Helveston, 1987; Merrell, 1990; Stanovich, 1988).

Many such students have basic sight recognition and decoding problems. Poor sight recognition of words and inefficient or inaccurate decoding skills can lead to poor comprehension, avoidance of reading and writing, and deficits in general knowledge.

Thus, poor readers with learning disabilities tend to share many of the same problems as other poor readers. They tend to have problems reading right from the start, especially with word recognition strategies taught in primary grades. They may experience a lag in the development of phonological sensitivity, the awareness and perception of speech sounds in words (Ackerman, Anhalt, & Dykman, 1986).

Because these students may not intuit how letters represent speech sounds in words by wide exposure to print, as more able learners do, they may need more systematic exposure to letter-sound patterns in words and more practice with decoding than their peers and many of the remedial techniques we have discussed for helping poor readers develop sight recognition and word analysis skills are effective.

Although remedial instruction for these students often focuses on the teaching and practice of isolated reading skills, struggling readers with learning disabilities need the same emphasis on meaningful reading of connected text that other poor readers need. Practicing reading skills without using them in the context of real reading is ineffective for any student.

In the long run, LD teachers work with many youngsters who are poor readers, and both regular classroom teachers and reading specialists will find that some of their poor readers may have learning disabilities. Regardless of whether they have been so identified, poor readers *all* need help in consolidating skills they have mastered, acquiring strategies they do not yet have, and closing the gap between their potential as readers and their present performance. They require instruction that is tailored to their individual strengths, needs, ages, interests, and prior experiences. They need to be placed in appropriate materials at their instructional levels; provided instruction that achieves a balance in word identification, comprehension, listening, speaking, and writing; and taught at a pace that is appropriately challenging without frustration. No single instructional method has been shown to be more effective than others in remediation.

Dyslexia

Dyslexia is a medical term for a profound inability to read or to learn to read. Dyslexia is a condition that everyone seems to agree exists, but about which there is little agreement otherwise. No single set of symptoms, means of diagnosis or identification, or method of remediation have been identified.

One of the first definitions was proposed by Samuel Orton (1937), who described dyslexic children as delayed in reading compared to their peers, suffering from frequent letter and word reversals, and often being able to read only by holding the print up to a mirror. This led to widespread belief that dyslexia was primarily a neurological disorder involving visual perception and memory. Even today, many people believe that reading *was* as *saw* or writing letters backwards is a sure sign of a dyslexic child. In many school districts until fairly recently, well-meaning teachers were training young children to distinguish between nonsensical geometric shapes and pursuing other highly dubious instructional procedures that were intended to train children's visual perception.

By the 1970s, however, evidence was accumulating that suggested that dyslexia was a language processing problem rather than a problem of visual perception. Stanovich (1986) demonstrated that dyslexic readers made no more reversal errors than did normally developing readers *at their same level of reading development.* Liberman et al. (1974) found that dyslexics were far more likely to have trouble processing sounds in words—specifically in recognizing that spoken words could be broken down into smaller bits of sound called phonemes (see Chapter 7). A number of researchers, including Bradley and Bryant (1985) and Ball and Blachman (1991), found that teaching children before first grade to be aware of speech sounds in words significantly reduced later reading failure. Today the central importance of language problems as causal factors in dyslexia is well established. The two factors that turn up most often in severely disabled readers is difficulty in segmenting words into phonemes and also rapidly naming objects ("serial rapid naming"). Of the two, however, phonemic segmentation is far more amenable to instruction, so it gets the lion's share of attention.

Is dyslexia a disease—analogous to tuberculosis—or is it a condition that occupies one end of a continuum that goes from healthy to unhealthy—analogous to high blood pressure? There is a growing agreement that it is the latter (Snow et al., 1998). Stanovich has demonstrated that what we might call *dyslexia* can develop over time, beginning as a relatively mild lack of ability that snowballs into a complex problem of disability. In his famous "Matthew Effects" article, Stanovich (1986) demonstrated that a first grader who has more difficulty than his classmates will be slower to learn to recognize words. (In alphabetic languages such as English, word recognition, after all, requires that a reader be able to make associations between written letters and phonemes. A child who doesn't have ready access to phonemes in speech may find word recognition difficult.) Depressed word recognition impairs reading fluency, and if after a certain point a student doesn't find it reasonably easy to read with fluency, he is not likely to practice reading. And if he doesn't practice reading . . ., the sequence continues until we find a child by fourth or fifth grade who appears dyslexic.

How many children have dyslexia? Estimates of the numbers of dyslexics in the school population range as high as 20 percent. But when Frank Vellutino and his associates (1996) identified a large number of struggling first graders and tutored them intensively for a year using conventional best practices, only 3 percent of them continued to have difficulty learning to read, and only 1.5 percent had severe difficulties. Vellutino and associates concluded that the difficulties in learning to read may well be caused by deficits in certain of the cognitive abilities underlying the ability to learn to read, especially phonological abilities such as phoneme analysis, letter-to-sound decoding, name encoding and retrieval, and verbal memory. However, they found that "the number of children impaired by basic cognitive deficits represents a relatively small percentage of beginning readers compared with the substantially larger percentage of those children whose reading difficulties are caused by experiential and instructional deficits" (Vellutino & Scanlon, 2001, p. 317).

No single set of symptoms exists that would clearly distinguish the characteristics of children with dyslexia from those who have other learning disabilities. In general, however, many people who have been labeled dyslexic share some or most of these characteristics:

- Measured intelligence at least in the average range, but often significantly above average
- Profound difficulty with phonemic awareness, phonemic segmentation, and decoding operations
- Frequent reversals of letters and words in both reading and writing
- Poor spelling, particularly when attempting to use phonetic strategies to spell unfamiliar words
- Both reading and writing far below their intellectual potential
- Persistent reading and writing failure in spite of personal motivation and appropriate special instruction

Dyslexics do not read up to their expected potential, in spite of having normal intelligence and having experienced adequate instruction. That seems to be the most persistent symptom of dyslexia. As we noted above, however, Vellutino et al. (1996) found that providing intensive instruction to underperforming children, his team was able to get all but a small number of them to improve in reading. And Stanovich (1986) has shown that if even a single factor goes wrong in a child's reading development, that breakdown can lead to a lack of successful practice, which then affects the development of many other factors. It is no wonder that by fourth or fifth grade, seriously disabled readers show a variety of symptoms. If they have found reading aversive and have not practiced reading, many things will be wrong with their reading ability.

Some researchers have been working on other explanations for the variety of symptoms of dyslexics. Max Coltheart (2005) has developed a model of word recognition that shows two routes between letters on the page and words in the mind. One of the routes connects letters to sounds directly in the mind. The other route relates groups of letters to words that are stored in memory. A disability that interrupts either route will result in a different kind of dyslexia.

Some readers seem to have limited access to stored words in memory, and tend to depend heavily on letter-to-sound correspondences and pronounce words as they are spelled. This phenomenon is called *surface dyslexia.* Evidence of surface dyslexia, according to Coltheart (2005), is found when readers pronounce phonetically regular words correctly, but mispronounce irregularly spelled words. Thus they would read *howl, growl,* and *fowl* correctly, but read *bowl* so that it rhymes with the first two. *Pretty* will be read to rhyme with *Betty* and *petty.*

Other readers appear to have a breakdown in the letter-to-sound route, but still have access to the storage or words in memory. These readers, who are rare, and most of whom have had trauma to the brain according to the reports, would see the word *goose* and say "*duck*" or "*waterfowl.*" This condition is called *deep dyslexia.*

Still other researchers argue for the existence of a third kind of dyslexia in which the visual perceptual apparatus appears faulty. Readers with this condition are said to suffer from *visual dyslexia* (Smith, 1991).

There is room here for skepticism. Before we conclude that any reader who sees *goose* and says "duck" suffers from deep dyslexia, we should remember the normal readers who sometimes sample what a text is saying and pronounce the word they expect to be there without really looking at it. And before we conclude that a reader or writer who reverses letters suffers from visual dyslexia, we should compare that reader's tendency to reverse letters with other readers who function on that reader's same level.

Efforts to determine which remedial methods are most effective are similarly confusing. Those who have been referred to as dyslexic are, like everyone else, more different from each other than alike. Most methods proposed have been successful with at least some people thought to be dyslexic. But none are reliably effective with everyone.

Most often, remediation centers around efforts to help the person compensate for his difficulties by using recorded books and texts, teaching them to use special study skills and procedures to organize and learn aurally, and teaching them to use devices like digital dictionaries, spell-check, and grammar-check computer programs.

Some general approaches that have been somewhat successful for dyslexics are

- Teaching students how to break academic tasks into their component parts, adapt such tasks to their special academic needs, and tackle one part of a task at a time.
- Emphasizing whole-word or sight-word recognition and the use of context as a word recognition strategy, rather than overemphasizing phonic decoding. This is especially true if a reader tends to read by sounding out letters and produces nonsense words. (But we should remember the stages of word recognition we saw in Chapter 7. This could be an *alphabetic reader* who needs help to develop into an *orthographic reader,* to use Uta Frith's [1985] terminology.)
- Teaching phonics if a reader shows a lack of awareness of letter-to-sound correspondences. But the teacher should be mindful of the need to teach the child about whole words, too, and to develop fluency and comprehension at the same time phonics is stressed.
- Developing listening comprehension and general background knowledge by listening rather than relying on reading to convey information; using oral aids like taped texts and lectures, voice-activated microrecorders, and oral note taking.
- Teaching students how to break down writing assignments into manageable steps utilizing the steps in the writing process.
- Emphasizing specific thinking skills such as comparison-contrast and cause-effect using oral discourse, so that dyslexic students can comprehend what they see and hear and not have to read everything.

- Teaching students to compose written work orally first, such as dictating onto audiotape, then writing while listening to the tape; some students need to have their oral compositions typed for them.

Designing Individualized Interventions

The central purpose for creating curriculum or teaching accommodations is to provide equal access for students with disabilities. As mentioned earlier, since the legal provision is for students with disabilities to participate more fully in general education curriculum and environments, both general and special education teachers are searching for innovative ways for these students to successfully participate in the same ways as all students. Changes in the environment, delivery, curricular content, and/or assessments may be required to benefit these students based on decisions about their individualized learning needs. By assessing individual strengths and needs and using this information to develop strategies to meet individual learning requirements, teachers will, in fact, develop effective interventions where all students, not only those with disabilities, will benefit.

The key to success in planning accommodations or curricular modifications is to match the student with the goals of the lesson. Begin planning effective accommodations and/or modification by identifying the general education curricular goals. Starting with general education outcomes helps to clarify the fundamental decisions that will guide your teaching while allowing for all students' participation in learning the essential knowledge and skills. Once the outcome learning is clarified and the tasks that demonstrate mastery of the essential learning are specified, design the individualized adaptations for students. Keep in mind that although the essential learning may be the same for all students, the content knowledge and/or skills may be adjusted for individual students who require adaptations while still meeting the objectives set out in the essential learning.

The following considerations will be useful when planning adaptations for students with disabilities:

- Will the student participate in the same curriculum as other students? If so, what environmental, delivery, or assessment accommodations will be required for her successful participation?
- Will the student participate in the same curriculum with modified objectives such as some of the same spelling words along with others more suited to a student's individualized requirements? If so, what environmental, delivery, curricular content, or assessment accommodations and modifications will be required for his successful participation?
- Will the student have the same objectives, but use a parallel curriculum on a more appropriate level? If so, what environmental, delivery, curricular content, or

assessment accommodations and modifications will be required for her successful participation? As noted above, in this circumstance the student will still participate in the same essential learning objectives but will be using individualized content material that is matched to the student's individualized needs (adapted from Giangreco, Cloninger, & Iverson, 1993).

Interventions for Phonological Awareness

One of the most consistent indicators of a child's potential for reading success is acquisition of phonological awareness. Phonemic awareness is a child's recognition that words and syllables can be broken into smaller units, individual speech sounds called *phonemes.*

Emergent readers must grasp that the sounds of speech are represented by letters and that these speech sounds can be purposely manipulated (Adams, 1990). Common deficiencies include an inability to identify and separate internal word sounds; an inability to understand that these word sounds are sequential; and difficulty with beginning, middle, or ending sounds (Simmons, Gunn, Smith, & Kameenui, 1994).

Phonological awareness can be improved for children with reading difficulties through direct, systematic instruction. Although this instruction can be taught separately or embedded into the curriculum, depending on the instructional style of the teacher's program, it is important that it be delivered individually or in small groups and taught on a consistent basis. Brief periods of about 20 minutes each day of explicit instruction in phonological awareness will improve student performance significantly (Blachman, 1997). The following guidelines will assist you when designing intervention strategies:

1. Begin with the auditory features of words; rather than focusing on alphabetic symbols, ask students to blend and identify sounds in a word.
2. Teach natural sound segments in language before moving to more complex sounds within words. Start segmenting sounds in sentences and then move to words into syllables, then syllables into phonemes.
3. Ensure student success by introducing words with fewer phonemes and where consonant and vowel patterns can be easily distinguished (e.g., *v-c* or *c-v-c* words).
4. Model blending and segmenting for practice and to ensure retention.
5. Once students are skilled with the auditory tasks, move to sound-letter correspondence. (Simmons et al., 1994, cited in Mercer, 1997)

This framework will be helpful when developing intervention strategies that are used with skill-building activities such as memory, flash cards, and rhyming activities.

Multisensory Language Experience.   Integrating multisensory experiences with direct, systematic, and sequential instruction can be an effective means for students struggling to learn fundamental language skills. Multisensory Language Experience (MSLE) approaches expose learners through a variety of language concepts and associations while integrating vision, hearing, movement, and touch into the process (Birsch, 1999). In MSLE students trace letters with their fingers while seeing, saying, and hearing them; they can walk on letters written on the floor or touch textured letters and words to improve their understanding of how sounds are manipulated and sequenced in the written word. Writing using multiple crayons or markers; practicing using a paintbrush with watercolors or fingerpainting letters; writing with shaving cream; using raised or sunken letters, sandpaper letters, or sand trays for letters are all effective ways to increase sensory input into the language experience.

Whole-Word Recognition. Whole-word recognition strategies can be particularly effective with words that are not easily decoded using phonics. These strategies are also effective with older readers who can lose the literal comprehension of the text when struggling with decoding. Whole-word recognition is most successful when the student is exposed repeatedly to the words. The most effective way is to develop a running list of sight words and set aside time each day for students to practice the words with a partner. Write sentences or definitions on the back of the card. As the student learns words, these cards can be eliminated while new ones are added. The cards can be taken home for practice. Making up games similar to Concentration, matching words or words and their definitions, helps to motivate the student while using the flash cards. A variation that also helps build vocabulary skills along with word recognition is to pair the student with a partner. One student takes a turn writing the vocabulary word on the flash card while the partner must then write its definition on the back of the same card. Then, together, the students read each definition and then take turns identifying the word when its definition is read.

Another effective strategy for teaching whole-word recognition is variation on cloze procedures. Teachers can use a written selection with blanks that are to be filled in from a list of several choices for each omitted word, or from a word bank, to change traditional cloze activities to multiple-choice word recognition (Mercer, 1997).

Word Sounds and Word Categorization. One of the most helpful ways to teach students with reading difficulties to learn to organize words is by teaching word pattern similarities and highlighting the sound similarities in each word's phonemic components. Repetitive use of similar patterns in words that sound alike (*mat, bat, sat*) or similar sounds but different letter patterns (*site, right*) can assist children to see how the internal components of sounds are represented in written form. Using vocabulary or spelling words to demonstrate similar relationships can help students to reinforce these similarities. Teachers begin by associating spelling words with words the student already knows—the student's name, family or pet names, or other common words for children. Then, connect the spelling words with the familiar words to create simple sentences (Hammeken, 2000). For more advanced students, have students become word detectives—write the words on cards and do a code investigation, sorting them by sound or letter patterns.

Interventions for Improving Fluency

With students who are having trouble tracking the direction of the reading, use an index card with an arrow drawn on it pointing from left to right as a guide. Placing the card under the sentence while students are reading also helps to limit distractions or reduce instances of students' losing their place. Another strategy for students who tend to lose their place is to show them where to begin reading and then provide ongoing context clues to help them keep track of where they are when reading. A variation on this is to cut out a long rectangle in the card to place on the sentences and move along as the student reads.

Using highlighters to color-code reading selections can be very useful for students who respond well to visual organization during reading. Using different colors also assists students in picking out main ideas, recognizing important information they need to remember, and locating vocabulary or spelling words. When it isn't practical to highlight directly in the book, clear overlays can be taped into the book with the color-coded selections on them for easy removal later (Hammeken, 2000). Consider breaking a reading selection into more manageable segments or assigning only the essential portions of a chapter so students won't feel overwhelmed by too much reading. Smaller segments make it easier for a student to keep track of the content. These segments can be highlighted or bracketed prior to reading and previewed to ensure that students will be familiar with what to expect from the selection.

Audio cassettes are another effective way to facilitate fluency for all students, not just those with reading problems. Most textbooks and reading series are available on tape. Other resources to check for books on tape are the school librarian or the lending library for the visually impaired. Book talks or literature circles where readers read to each other aloud in pairs can be recorded for use at a later time or put into the library for future use. Some of the recordings can be used with below-level readers for them to read along with for repetitive practice. The recordings of these below-level readers could also be used with younger readers from another class.

A variation on reading along with the audio cassette is to have students read chorally while the teacher leads them. Choosing a text that provides repetitive response is the simplest way to begin, gradually progressing to assigning groups for different character and narrator responses. In choral reading each group is assigned a specific response selection, will read the responses of various characters, or will read a reading at the appropriate time.

Interventions for Improving Comprehension

Often students spend so much time and effort at reading a selection that they lose the meaning of the material they are reading. Comprehending what we read involves the complex process of matching information from our prior learning experiences with the content of the text. Below are several strategies that will assist students in understanding what they are reading if they are getting bogged down due to decoding or fluency problems or seem to be losing the meaning of the text due to language processing difficulties.

Previewing Texts.   Read the text aloud to class using a guided reading procedure. Provide a variety of cues as to where the teacher is with the reading and ask questions to probe for understanding. Sometimes it is more beneficial to divide the class into two or three groups when doing guided reading previews. A co-teacher or paraprofessional could take one of these groups, or students could be assigned independent work while the teacher works with the smaller group. Simple adjustments such as changing the pacing of the reading or dividing the text into more manageable segment sizes can go a long way in reducing the stress students feel.

Another way to preview a reading selection is to provide a student, in advance, an outline or brief overview of the upcoming material. Bold or color-code the important information and vocabulary in the overview for easy reference (Hammeken, 2000). Then have the student review the outline individually, with a partner, or with the paraprofessional prior to the guided reading. The overview enables students to link upcoming material with prior knowledge or experiences that activate her learning. Associating the new material with previous stories or with a personal experience or interest using questions at the end of the overview assists students to understand the relevance of the material.

Keep in mind that students will need to be taught how to preview upcoming reading selections. Have them read and discuss the title and hypothesize what the reading selection may be about. Next, review the table of contents, read the chapter titles, and see if they offer clues about what the selection is about. Finally, have students examine the illustrations or any maps, tables, or graphs to see if they offer clues about possible subject matter. Ask them to make predictions and then encourage the use of questions as reading progresses to make sure they are correct. Previewing is an ongoing process that requires teachers to continually backtrack and review along with a continual search for context clues.

Teaching Abstract Concepts.   Students with reading disabilities will often require concrete activities and examples for them to grasp abstract concepts—for example, story sequences and the significance of a series of events. Creating illustration or word cards with a story element or event on each card is a way to teach the sequence of the story as well as how events will lead up to a climax and resolution.

The use of graphic organizers is also an effective way for teachers to demonstrate abstract concepts and new information by making them concrete. Graphic organizers are effective because they provide students with a concrete reference point for material when these reference points may not be solidly established in memory. Graphic organizers are an organizing representation of the new or abstract material. They provide visual representations of ideas, concepts, information, or facts. They also allow for visual comparisons, showing relationships and extending learning to other areas. Story maps range from simple relationships to hierarchal pyramids. These can be pictures or symbols that stand for concepts or ideas of objects, or they can show levels of details in a pyramid that can be used to examine the structure of a paragraph or longer selection. They can also be used to assist students in organizing details and to show evidence that supports main ideas. Character maps, a variation of story maps, expect students to complete simple illustrations that show how the character thinks, feels, sees, hears, smells, does, goes, says, and so on, or develop more complex comparisons between characters.

Summary

This chapter deals with special factors associated with reading. Among these factors are those that qualify learners for special education services under the Individuals with Disabilities Education Act (IDEA) and related legislation. Within this legislation are provisions that mandate serving these learners with appropriate educational programs that use the least restrictive environment. The identification of these learners and subsequent placement in special education programs must be conducted with assessment instruments and methods that protect against discrimination, erroneous classification, and undue labeling.

Identification of the special-needs student typically is initiated by the classroom teacher. Before additional assessment and screening can occur, permission must be obtained from the parents or legal guardians of the child. Once permission is granted, *assessment* and *screening* can take place. This assessment typically includes one or more of the following areas: intellectual, physical, special learning, or affective factors.

Initial assessment of *intellectual factors* typically includes the use of an initial screening instrument such as the Kaufman Brief Intelligence Test (K-BIT). If the initial screening instrument indicates a potential problem, additional testing is conducted using a more comprehensive assessment of intellectual factors such as the Weschler Intelligence Scale for Children–III (WISC–III). These tests typically provide scores for subtests, Verbal, Performance, and Full Scale IQ scores. When selecting assessment instruments, care should be taken to select instruments that do not penalize a child with cultural differences. The Leiter International Performance Scale-Revised (Leiter-R) is a nonverbal measure that can be substituted for English language learners and others with language deficits.

Vision and *hearing problems* are also associated with reading difficulties. Again, a classroom teacher is often the first to notice potential problems during daily classroom activities. As with intellectual factors, the re-ferral for additional screening begins with parental or guardian permission. Screening in the areas of vision and hearing is typically conducted by professionals or paraprofessionals in the allied health fields.

Language disabilities most often occur in late infancy and the preschool years, when normally oral language appears and develops fully. Most children are fluent language users, with extensive *receptive* and *expressive vocabularies* and well-developed grammatical capabilities, by the age of 5 or 6. In the early years, *hearing impairment or deafness, Down syndrome*, and *general language delay* can impair or inhibit language acquisition. In the later preschool and school years, difficulty with speech sound production (*atypical phonology*), acquisition of vocabulary and word meanings (*atypical semantics*), acquisition of grammatical forms and rules (*atypical syntax*), and use of language for social purposes (*atypical pragmatics*) can inhibit language learning and impact literacy.

Special learning problems include *learning disabilities* and *dyslexia*. While universally accepted and detailed definitions of these terms have yet to be identified, professionals do agree that they include a wide range of problems related to the acquisition, comprehension, and production of written language. Children who manifest these problems typically possess average or above-average intelligence, but exhibit serious, long-standing learning difficulties.

Reading is a complex process affected by a student's level of intellectual functioning, experiences, motivation, and physical and emotional well-being. By assessing the impact of these special factors on a student's literacy, appropriate changes in instructional strategies, referrals, and placements are more likely to be made.

Individualized interventions are designed to accommodate the specific needs of the learner and are best achieved by matching goals for learning with learner abilities. Principles for selecting adaptations include whether the learner will be participating in the same curriculum with or without modifications or whether she will require individualized learning goals and participate in a parallel curriculum.

Teachers must first determine whether a student requires interventions for deficiencies in phonological awareness, fluency, or comprehension and then apply appropriate instructional strategies to meet these need areas. Recent studies indicate that interventions are effective when applied consistently during brief daily activities. Interventions such as *multisensory language experiences, whole-word recognition, choral reading,* and *previewing texts* are all effective ways to improve reading skills while engaging the learner.

MyLabSchool is a collection of online tools for your success in this course, your licensure exams, and your teaching career. Visit www.mylabschool.com to access the following:

- Online Study Guide
- Video cases from real classrooms
- Help with your research papers using Research Navigator
- Career Center with resources for:
  - Praxis exams and licensure preparation
  - Professional portfolio development
  - Job search and interview techniques
  - Lesson planning

References

Ackerman, P. T., Anhalt, J. M., & Dykman, R. A. (1986). Inferential word-decoding weakness in reading disabled children. *Learning Disability Quarterly, 9*(4), 315–324.

Adams, M. J. (1990). *Beginning to read: Thinking and learning about print.* Cambridge, MA: MIT Press.

Ball, E. W., & Blachman, B. A. (1991). Does phoneme awareness training in kindergarten make a difference in early word recognition and developmental spelling? *Reading Research Quarterly, 26,* 49–66.

Birsch, J. R. (Ed.). (1999). *Multisensory teaching of basic language skills.* Baltimore: Brookes.

Blackman, B. (Ed.). (1997). *Foundations of reading acquisition and dyslexia: Implications for early instruction.* Mahwah, NJ: Erlbaum.

Bryant, P., & Bradley, L. (1985). *Children's reading problems.* Oxford: Blackwell.

Coltheart, M. (2005). Modeling reading: The dual route approach. In C. Hulme & M. Snowling (Eds.), *Science of reading: A handbook.* London: Blackwell.

Damico, J. S. (1991). Descriptive assessment of communicative ability in limited English proficient students. In E. Hamayan & J. S. Damico (Eds.), *Limiting bias in the assessment of bilingual students* (pp. 157–218). Austin, TX: PRO-ED.

Diana v. State Board of Education, No.C-70-37 (N.D. Cal. 1970).

García, E. E. (2005). *Teaching and learning in two languages: Bilingualism and schooling in the United States.* New York: Teachers College Press.

Friend, M., & Bursuck, W. D. (2002). *Including students with special needs* (3rd ed.). Boston: Allyn & Bacon.

Frith, U. (1985). Beneath the surface of developmental dyslexia. In K. E. Patterson, J. C. Marshall, & M. Coltheart (Eds.), *Surface dyslexia* (pp. 301–330). London: Erlbaum.

Gersten, R., & Baker, S. (2000). What we know about effective instructional practices for English-language learners. *Exceptional Children, 66,* 454–470.

Giangreco, M., Cloninger, C., & Iverson, V. (1993). *Choosing options and accommodations for children (COACH): A guide to planning inclusive education.* Baltimore: Brookes.

Hammeken, P. A. (2000). *Inclusion: 450 strategies for success: A practical guide for all educators who teach students with disabilities.* Minnetonka, MN: Peytral.

Helveston, E. M. (1987). Volume III Module I: Management of dyslexia and related learning disabilities. *Journal of Learning Disabilities, 20*(7), 415–421.

Hill, R., Carjuzaa, J., Aramburo, D., & Baca, L. (1993). Culturally and linguistically diverse teachers in special education: Repairing or redesigning the leaky pipeline. *Teacher Education and Special Education, 16,* 258–269.

Karger, J. (2005). Access to the general curriculum for students with disabilities: A discussion of the interrelationship between IDEA '97 and NCLB. Wakefield, MA: National Center on Accessing the General Curriculum.

Kaufman, A. S., & Kaufman, N. L. (1990). *Kaufman brief intelligence test manual.* Circle Pines, MN: American Guidance Services.

Landrum, J. (2001). Selecting intermediate novels that feature characters with disabilities. *The Reading Teacher, 55,* 252–258.

Larry P. v. Riles, 343 F. Supp. 1306 (N.D. Cal. 1972), 502 F. 2d 963 (9th Cir. 1974), No. C-71-2270 RF (N.D. Cal., October 16, 1979), 793 F. 2d 969 (9th Cir. 1984).

Liberman, I. Y., Shankweiler, D., Fischer, F. W., & Carter, B. (1974). Explicit syllable and phoneme segmentation in the young child. *Journal of Experimental Child Psychology, 18,* 201–212.

McIntyre, E., Rosebery, A., & Gonzalez, N. (Eds.). (2001). *Classroom diversity: Connecting curriculum to students' lives.* Portsmouth, NH: Heinemann.

McLaughlin, J. A., & Lewis, R. B. (1990). *Assessing special students* (3rd ed.). Columbus, OH: Merrill.

Mercer, C. D. (1997). *Students with learning disabilities* (5th ed.). Upper Saddle River, NJ: Merrill.

Merrell, K. (1990). Differentiating low achievement students and students with learning disabilities: An examination of performances on the Woodcock-Johnson Psycho-Educational Battery. *Journal of Special Education, 24*(3), 296–305.

Moustafa, M. (1997). *Beyond traditional phonics: Research discoveries and reading instruction.* Portsmouth, NH: Heinemann.

National Education Association (NEA). (2004). *NCLB: The intersection of access and outcomes.* Washington, DC: National Education Association.

National Reading Panel. (2000, December). *Teaching children to read: An evidence-based assessment of the scientific research literature on reading and its implications for reading instruction.* (Reports of the Subgroups.) Washington, DC: National Institute of Child Health and Human Development, National Institutes of Health.

Nelson, K. (1973). *Structure and strategy in learning to talk.* Chicago: University of Chicago Press.

Orton, S. (1937). *Reading, writing, and speech problems in children.* New York: Norton.

Patton, J., Kauffman, J., Blackburn, J. M., & Brown, G. (1991). *Exceptional children in focus* (5th ed.). New York: Macmillan.

Reich, P. A. (1986). *Language development.* Upper Saddle River, NJ: Prentice-Hall.

Sattler, J. M. (1992). *Assessment of children* (3rd ed.). San Diego: Author.

Simmons, D. C., Gunn, B., Smith, S. B., & Kameenui, E. J. (1994). Phonological awareness: Applications of instructional design. *LD Forum, 19,* 27–10.

Smith, C. R. (1991).*Learning disabilities: The interaction of learner, task, and setting.* Boston: Allyn & Bacon.

Snow, C. E., Burns, M. S., & Griffin, P. (Eds.) (1998). *Preventing reading difficulties in young children.* Washington, DC: National Academy Press.

Stanovich, K. E. (1986). Matthew effects in reading: Some consequences of individual differences in the acquisition of literacy. *Reading Research Quarterly, 21,* 360–406.

Stanovich, K. E. (1988). Explaining the difference between the dyslexic and the garden-variety poor reader: The phonological-core-variable-difference model. *Journal of Learning Disabilities, 21*(10), 590–604, 612.

Tomasello, M., & Mervis, C. N. (1994). Commentary: The instrument is great, but measuring comprehension is still a problem. *Monographs of the Society for Research in Child Development, 59,* 242.

Trawick-Smith, J. (1997). *Early childhood development: A multicultural perspective.* Upper Saddle River, NJ: Merrill.

Vellutino, F. R. (1979). *Dyslexia: Theory and research.* Cambridge, MA: MIT Press.

Vellutino, F. R., & Denckla, M B. (1991). Cognitive and

neuropsychological foundations of word identification in poor and normally developing readers. In R. Barr, M. L. Kamil, P. Mosenthal, & P. D. Pearson (Eds.), *Handbook of reading research: Vol. 2.* White Plains, NY: Longman.

Vellutino, F. R., & Scanlon, D. M. (2001). Emergent literacy skills, early instruction, and individual differences as determinants of difficulties in learning to read: The case for early intervention. In S. Neuman & D. Dickson (Eds.), *Handbook for research on early literacy.* New York: Guilford Press.

Vellutino, F. R., Scanlon, D. M., Sipay, S., Small, G., Pratt, A., Chen, R., & Denckla, M. B. (1996). Cognitive profiles of difficult-to-remediate and readily remediated poor readers: Early intervention as a vehicle for distinguishing between cognitive and experiential deficits as a basic cause of specific reading disability. *Journal of Educational Psychology, 88,* 601–638.

Villa, R. A., & Thousand, J. S. (2000). *Restructuring for caring and effective education: Piecing the puzzle together* (2nd ed.). Baltimore: Brookes.

Vygotsky, L. S. (1978). *Mind in society: The development of higher psychological processes.* Cambridge, MA: Harvard University Press.

Author Index

A
Ackerman, P. T., 375
Adams, C., 78–79
Adams, M. J., 181, 380
Aesop, 264
Afflerbach, P., 13
Ahrens, M., 3, 5
Allen, R. V., 229, 332
Allington, R. L., 9, 26, 70, 209, 235, 274
Alvermann, D., 294
Anderson, R. C., 5, 6, 20, 234, 246, 274, 281, 306
Anhalt, J. M., 375
Anyon, J., 6
Applegate, A. J., 43
Applegate, M. D., 43
Aramburo, D., 367
Armbruster, B. B., 235, 262
Asher, J. J., 326–327
Ausubel, D. P., 286

B
Baca, L., 367
Baker, S., 367
Ball, E. W., 376
Bandura, A., 309
Barr, B., 80
Barr, R., 211
Bear, D. R., 126, 138, 195, 221, 223
Beaver, J., 48, 50
Beck, I. L., 4, 245, 246, 247, 252, 260, 261, 306
Beers, J. W., 126
Berthoff, A., 291
Betts, A. E., 54
Biber, D., 319, 322, 347
Birsch, J. R., 381

C
Caldwell, J., 13, 43
Calkin, L. M., 260
Cambourne, B., 345
Campo-Flores, A., 317
Carjuzaa, J., 367
Carle, E., 243
Carr, E., 257
Chall, J., 92, 181
Chase, C. L., 155–156
Clark, K. J., 43
Clarke, L., 174, 179
Clay, M. M., 13, 16, 17, 24, 54, 80, 124, 171, 173, 189, 210, 211, 301
Cloninger, C., 380

Blachman, B., 179, 192, 199, 376, 380
Blackburn, J. M., 356
Bleich, D., 19, 20
Bond, G. L., 181
Borich, G., 153, 161
Boyle, O., 264, 267
Bradley, L., 178, 376
Bridwell, N., 185
Brown, A. L., 262
Brown, G., 356
Brown, H., 345
Brown, J. S., 204
Brown, R., 5, 245
Bruner, J., 178, 338
Bryant, P., 178, 376
Burke, C. L., 64, 220
Burns, P. C., 43
Burns, S., 171, 274, 319
Burris, N., 260
Bursuck, W. D., 359

D
Dale, E., 92
Damico, J. S., 367
Davidson, J., 311
Davis, Z. T., 264, 268
dePaola, T., 244
Diamond, L., 282
Dickinson, D. K., 16
Dixon, C. N., 332
Dowhower, S. L., 334
Duffy, G. G., 204
Dumas, G., 325
Durrell, D. D., 224
Dykman, R. A., 375
Dykstra, R., 181

Cohen, L., 97, 101
Cole, J., 244
Collier, V. P., 319, 321
Collins, A., 204
Coltheart, M., 377
Comenius, J. A., 229
Cook, J., 32
Cooper, J. D., 234
Cooter, K., 43
Cooter, R. B., Jr., 43
Crawford, A., 37–38, 43, 98, 166, 322, 324, 327, 328–329, 330, 331, 332, 334, 335, 337, 338–339, 340, 342, 344, 345
Crawford, J., 319–320
Cummins, J., 318–319, 322
Cundick, B. P., 268
Cunningham, P., 9, 70, 71, 74, 227

E
Echevarria, J., 347
Edelsky, C., 338

Subject Index